S0-AHQ-028

RUSSIA'S COTTON WORKERS AND THE NEW ECONOMIC POLICY

Soviet and East European Studies: 69

Editorial Board

Ronald Hill (*General editor*)
Judy Batt, Michael Kaser, Anthony Kemp-Welch
Margot Light, Alastair McAuley
James Riordan, Stephen White

Soviet and East European Studies, under the auspices of Cambridge University Press and the British Association for Soviet, Slavonic and East European Studies (BASSEES), promotes the publication of works presenting substantial and original research on the economics, politics, sociology and modern history of the Soviet Union and Eastern Europe.

Soviet and East European Studies

Series list continues on p. 301

RUSSIA'S COTTON WORKERS AND THE NEW ECONOMIC POLICY

Shop-floor culture and state policy 1921–1929

CHRIS WARD

Department of Slavonic Studies
University of Cambridge

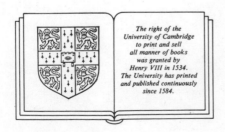

The right of the
University of Cambridge
to print and sell
all manner of books
was granted by
Henry VIII in 1534.
The University has printed
and published continuously
since 1584.

CAMBRIDGE UNIVERSITY PRESS

Cambridge
New York   Port Chester   Melbourne   Sydney

Published by the Press Syndicate of the University of Cambridge
The Pitt Building, Trumpington Street, Cambridge CB2 1RP
40 West 20th Street, New York, NY 10011, USA
10 Stamford Road, Oakleigh, Melbourne 3166, Australia

© Cambridge University Press 1990

First published 1990

Printed in Great Britain at the University Press, Cambridge

British Library cataloguing in publication data
Ward, Chris
Russia's cotton workers and the New Economic Policy:
shop-floor culture and state policy 1921–1929 –
(Soviet and Eastern European studies; 69)
1. Soviet Union. Cotton manufacturing industries.
Industrial relations, history
I. Title   II. Series
331′.0478721′0947

Library of Congress cataloguing in publication data
Ward, Chris.
Russia's cotton workers and the New Economic Policy:
shop-floor culture and state policy. 1921–1929/Chris Ward.
    p.   cm. – (Soviet and East European studies: 69)
Bibliography.
Includes index.
ISBN 0-521-34580-4
1. Cotton textile industry – Soviet Union –
Employees – History – 20th century.
2. Soviet Union – Economic policy – 1917–1928.
I. Title.   II. Series.
HD8039.T42S659 1989
331.7′67721′0947 – dc20   89-7287 CIP

ISBN 0 521 34580 4

For my parents

Contents

Plates

Tables

Our guide confessed in a depreciating tone that the machines were antiquated. I was no wiser for his frankness. Through room after room we paced, and save that the notices on the wall were in Russian we might have been in Bolton. Only when we stepped outside into the deep snow and felt the shrewd wind that blew its dry powder in our faces, was I forced to realize that we were in Moscow. From a distant weaving shed in the vast confusion of buildings, familiar in their busy ugliness, the workers were tramping to the dining room. The women with their shawls over their heads seemed no stranger than the machines they tended; the men, indeed, wore leather jackets or sheepskin coats, but under their fur caps, I guessed, the same pattern of cares and hopes, of resentments and ambitions must have been weaving itself in Moscow as in Bolton. Their feet fell softly; one missed the clatter of clogs, but here as in Lancashire the same pervasive hum of the same tyrannous machines dominated the scene and subdued the exotic glitter of the snow. Industry is everywhere a leveller.

Henry Noel Brailsford visiting the Trekhgornaia mill in 1927

Acknowledgements

Research is a lonely business, but no historian can work alone. My thanks therefore must go first of all to the ESRC for two years' funding, and to the British Council and its officers in Moscow for their forbearance in allowing me an extended period of study in the Soviet Union.

Dr Irina Nikolaevna Olegina of the Kafedra Istorii SSSR at Leningrad University was my adviser in Russia for nearly two and a half years. I am grateful to her for helping me to chart a course through the confusing shallows of the Soviet bureaucracy. The staff of the Biblioteka Akademii Nauk and Saltykov-Shchedrin Libraries in Leningrad, and of the Institut Nauchnoi Informatsii po Obshchestvennym Naukam (Akademii Nauk SSSR) and Lenin Library in Moscow, were always prompt in dealing with my requests for often obscure materials. Somewhat closer to home, Stuart Rees of Essex University Library and Jenny Brine of the Alexander Baykov Library at the Centre for Russian and East European Studies, University of Birmingham, were models of patience and professionalism; both put their time and expertise freely at my disposal. The librarians of the Royal Geographical Society were also helpful. Acknowledgements are due to the officers of the Russia Company for permission to use their records lodged in the Guildhall Library and to Anne Jones of the Greater Manchester Museum of Science and Industry for her help with the photographs. The Amalgamated Textile Workers' Union, the British Textile Employers' Association and the machine makers Platt Saco Lowell – all based in Lancashire – assisted in the initial stages of the research, as did the Soviet Textile, Clothing and Light Industry Workers' Union. A special thank you should be given to the spinners and power-loom weavers of Field Mill in Lancashire for allowing me to waste their time with idle questions, and to Mr Ashworth, the mill's manager, and Mr Oxton, the mule room overlooker.

This study grew out of my doctoral thesis undertaken at the University of Essex. Among the many academics who helped bring it to a conclusion I must thank Dr Jordon Goodman and Dr Harry Lubaz of Essex University; Aleksandr Turgaev of Leningrad University; Professor O. Ashmore, Professor D. Farnie and Professor A. Musson of Manchester University; Dr John Barber and Dr Cathy Merridale of King's College, Cambridge; Professor Cardwell of UMIST; Dr Vladimir Andrle of York University; Alf Edeen and Bengt and Marta of the Swedish Ministry of Foreign Affairs; Professor W. Fletcher of Kansas University; Professor R. Floud of Birkbeck College; Dr Stuart Thompstone of the University of Nottingham; Dr Judith Shapiro of Goldsmith's College; Professor Harold Perkin of North-Western University; John Crowfoot, Dr Julian Cooper, Professor Robert Davies and Dr Stephen Wheatcroft of CREES, and Dr Lizzie Waters, now at the Australian National University in Canberra.

The kindness and encouragement shown by Geoffrey Hosking, late of Essex University and now Professor at SSEES, has been out of all proportion to the short time he was associated with the research. Dr Mary McAuley and Alastair McAuley not only offered invaluable help, advice and criticism at many stages of the preparation and writing but also gave me a warm welcome into their family and home. My greatest debt is to Dr Stephen Smith of the Department of History at Essex, my doctoral supervisor for some five years. Only he and I know how much of what is good in the book is due to his constant help and encouragement: without him it would probably never have been written at all. My final thanks go to Gladis Garcia for patiently checking the typescript. The mistakes and misunderstandings are all my own.

Abbreviations

1923 census	*Trudy tsentral'nogo statisticheskogo upravleniia (1924)*
1926 census	*Vsesoiuznaia perepis' naseleniia 1926 goda (1929–30)*
1928 spravochnik	*Tarifno-spravochnik rabochikh khlopchato-bumazhnogo proizvodstva (1928)*
2-go plen TsK VPST 1925	*Postanovleniia 2-go plenuma TsK vsesoiuznogo soiuza tekstil'shchikov, 21–23 maia 1925g v Leningrade (1925)*
3-go plen TsK VPST 1923	*Rezoliutsii 3-go plenuma TsK soiuza tekstil'shchikov (12–15 aprelia 1923g) (1923)*
BI-VGSB	*Biulleten' ivanovo-voznesenskogo gubernskogo statisticheskogo biuro*
BI-VGTT	*Biulleten' ivanovo-voznesenskogo gosudarstvennogo tekstil'nogo tresta*
B TsK RKP (b) Zh	*Biulleten' otdela TsK RKP (b) po rabote sredi zhenshchin*
BVTS	*Biulleten' vserossiiskogo tekstil'nogo sindikata*
I. gub. ind. census 1918	*Spisok fabrik, zavodov i drugikh promyshlennykh predpriiatii ivanovo-voznesenskoi gubernii. Po dannym vserossiiskoi promyshlennoi i professional'noi perepis' 1918 goda (1919)*
ISNOT	*Initsiativnyi sovet po nauchnoi organizatsii truda pri tsentral'nom komitete soiuza tekstil'shchikov. Kratkii otchet (1924)*
IS TsK VPST	*Informatsionnaia svodka TsK vsesoiuznogo profsoiuza tekstil'shchikov*
ITPT	*Izvestiia tekstil'noi promyshlennosti i torgovli*
I-V gubotdel VPST 1923–24	*Otchet o rabote ivanovo-voznesenskogo gubernskogo otdela vserossiiskogo soiuza tekstil'shchikov za vremia s 1 iiunia 1923g po 1 apr. 1924g. XIII–XIV s"ezd (1924)*
I-V gubotdel VPST 1924–25	*Otchet gubernskogo otdela soiuza 15-mu gubernskomu s"ezdu tekstil'shchikov ivanovo-voznesenskoi gubernii (apr. 1924g–mart 1925g) (1925)*

I–V gubotdel VPST 1925–26	*Otchet o rabote ivanovo-voznesenskogo gubernskogo otdela vsesoiuznogo soiuza tekstil'shchikov za vremia s apr. 1925g–mart 1926g. 16-mu s"ezdu soiuza (1926)*
Lengubotdel VPST 1924–25	*Otchet leningradskogo gubernskogo otdela vsesoiuznogo professional'nogo soiuza tekstil'shchikov. Okt. 1924–1925gg (1926)*
Lentekstil' 1924–25	*Otchet za 1924–25g. Leningradskii gosudarstvennyi tekstil'nyi trest 'Leningradtekstil' (1925)*
Moskgubotdel VPST Aug-Oct 1923	*Otchet o rabote moskovskogo gubernskogo otdela vsesoiuznogo professional'nogo soiuza tekstil'shchikov avg.–okt. 1923g (1923)*
Moskgubotdel VPST 1923–24	*Otchet o rabote moskovskogo gubernskogo otdela vsesoiuznogo professional'nogo soiuza tekstil'shchikov mai 1923g–mart 1924g (1924)*
Moskgubotdel VPST Oct–Dec 1924	*Otchet o rabote moskovskogo gubernskogo otdela vsesoiuznogo professional'nogo soiuza tekstil'shchikov okt.–dek. 1924g (1925)*
Moskgubotdel VPST 1924–25	*Itogi roboty moskovskogo gubernskogo otdela profsoiuza tekstil'shchikov s 1 apr. 1924g po 1 okt. 1925g (1926)*
TNB 1925	*Rezoliutsiia 1-go vsesoiuznogo s"ezda otdelov truda i T.N.B. tekstil'noi promyshlennosti (20–26/IX–1925g) (1926)*
TsK VPST 1922–23	*Otchet TsK vserossiiskogo professional'nogo soiuza tekstil'shchikov sent. 1922g–sent. 1923g. K 4-i vseross. konferentsii soiuza 1923g (1923)*
TsK VPST 1922–24	*Otchet TsK vsesoiuznogo professional'nogo soiuza tekstil'shchikov k VI vsesoiuznomu s"ezdu tekstil'shchikov. Okt. 1922g–okt. 1924g (1924)*
TsK VPST 1924–26	*Otchet o rabote TsK vsesoiuznogo professional'n-ogo soiuza tekstil'shchikov k 7-mu vsesoiuznomu s"ezdu tekstil'shchikov. Iiul' 1924g–ianv. 1926g (1926)*
V-A Trust 1922–24	*Tri goda raboty vladimirsko-aleksandrovskogo tresta khlopchatobumazhnykh fabrik, 1922–24gg (1925)*
VI Congress VPST	*Rezoliutsii i postanovleniia 6-go s"ezda professional'nogo soiuza tekstil'shchikov (1924)*
Vladgubotdel VPST 1923–24	*Otchet o rabote vladimirskogo gubernskogo pravleniia professional'nogo soiuza tekstil'shchikov s sent. 1923g po sent. 1924g. K 7-mu gubernskomu s"ezdu soiuza (1923)*
Vladgubotdel VPST 1924–25	*Otchet o rabote vladimirskogo gubernskogo pravleniia professional'nogo soiuza tekstil'shchikov okt. 1924g–okt. 1925g. K 8-mu gubernskomu s"ezdu soiuza (1925)*

Map 1 Russia in 1927: the cotton industry provinces

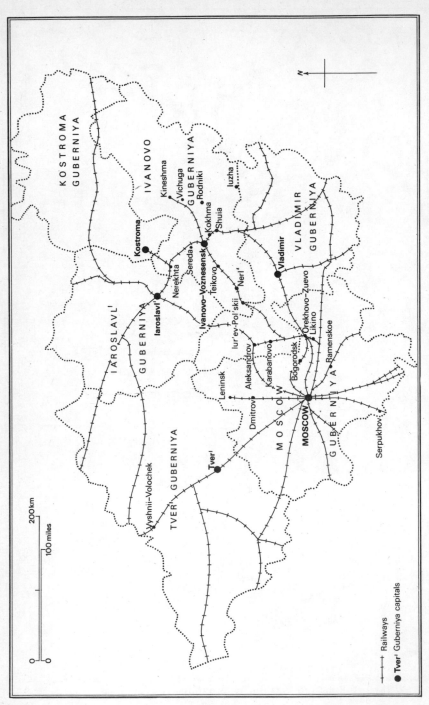

Map 2 The cotton districts of the Central Industrial Region

Introduction

Imagine yourself catching a train at the Iaroslavl' station on an April day in 1924. Soon the line would take you out of Moscow's noise and confusion and very shortly a new pattern of human activity would start to become familiar. Sometimes nearby, sometimes in the middle distance, small villages scarcely touched by the modern world would appear: clusters of squat cabins, the more substantial decorated with elaborate fretworks hanging from their eaves, tributes to the centuries-old skills of long-forgotten Chinese craftsmen. Peasants – the men bearded and dressed in high boots and belted cotton shirts, the women modestly hidden behind brightly coloured shawls contrasting vividly with the brown, green and white of the sodden land – would be attending to the season's work, repairing the ravages of the northern winter and marking out their little strips for the spring sowing amongst the last stubborn scallops of snow. Figures bent over the hoe, weathered faces to the barren soil, a physical attitude born of economic necessity unaltered throughout Russia's centuries: *krest'iane* – 'those who bear the cross'. Only rarely would someone be walking with a horse.

By midday, as the train left 'calico Moscow' far behind, cut through the low undulations of the Moscow heights, branched east at Aleksandrov and rattled on, first through Vladimir province and then into the recently created Ivanovo guberniya, another sight would become commonplace – vast cotton factories, their tall chimneys silhouetted against the skies of the Central Russian Plain, slowly disgorging black smoke into the clear air. Occasionally, as the tracks curved towards them – at Iur'ev–Pol'skii, Nerl' and Teikovo – sheer red-brick walls would flash by, not a stone's throw from the carriage window. More often than not they would remain on the horizon, huge and enigmatic, brooding over a sliver of water caught by the declining sun, invariably some tributary of the Volga.

The Baranovs, Konovalovs and Morozovs had vanished forever, but their mills, now renamed in the spirit of the times – Red Dawn, Red October, Freedom, Communist Vanguard; their arched entrances bedecked with red bunting or surmounted by a crude hammer and sickle – remained firmly in place, solid monuments to industrial capitalism. Cotton mills had always utilized free labour, long before Alexander II's reforms of the 1860s, and the industry's success had little to do with Witte's late nineteenth-century drive towards modernization and imperial greatness. Rather, the entrepreneurs who built their huge factories in St Petersburg and the Central Industrial Region (CIR) and drew in labour from the surrounding countryside – or, in the case of the Imperial capital, from distant provinces – owed their prosperity to mass demand, much like their west European counterparts. Thus whatever qualms there might be about the legitimacy of Lenin's revolution in terms of the level of capitalist development under tsarism, here was an industry which was clearly the product of private initiative and market forces patterned on the model of development familiar to Marx.[1] It is here, if nowhere else in Russia, that the forces of production created by international capitalism fell into the hands of men dedicated to socialist transformation. This was their inheritance; of all sectors of the young Soviet economy, it was one of the largest, oldest and most highly-mechanized branches of factory production.

But although built in the British manner, equipped with British machinery – and until recently managed by expatriates from Oldham, Bury and Manchester – the mills' uniform architecture concealed another, less tangible legacy: the social diversity of the workforce. By late afternoon the shifts would be changing all over Russia. In these rural districts it would be hard to tell the difference between departing workers and peasants in the fields. Many would be walking home, alone or with a relative or a friend, to silent hamlets and cottages five or six miles away where the rest of the family had spent the day busy on the farm. They would not be indoors until long after nightfall. Others would be chatting in small groups, delaying their return to noisy, over-crowded barracks. A few of the younger ones might be reading a newspaper. Up the line at Kostroma and Iaroslavl', south to Vladimir, or to the west in Smolensk and Tver', men and women would be spilling out of the big gates and thronging the muddy thoroughfares, their clothes and manners a mixture of the provincial dweller and the rural immigrant, peasant blouses mingling with shabby suits and leather caps. Most of the workers' districts would be

[1] See O. Crisp, *Studies in the Russian Economy before 1914* (1976), pp. 13, 44–5.

tumbles of wooden houses, nineteenth-century accretions on the body of these ancient towns. To the south-west, in Ramenskoe, Egor'evsk, Orekhovo-Zuevo, Shchelkovo, and north-east in Ivanovo-Voznesensk – the 'Russian Manchester' – the crowds would wear a different aspect, less varied. Here several generations had worked, lived and died amongst the monotonous squalor characteristic of purely industrial settlements. Only in the odd corner would you still find traces of the original Russian village. But in distant Leningrad, where mills were jumbled in with palaces or tucked behind broad, tree-lined avenues which once housed the flower of the old middle classes, or in the capital, where some were located no more than half an hour's walk from the Kremlin, chattering girls, gauche young lads, old men and middle-aged women would soon be indistinguishable from the heterogeneous metropolitan masses crammed into trams, shops, bars and cafes.

Just prior to our imaginary train journey Lenin had died. At the very last, before paralysis stilled his pen and stopped his tongue forever, he seems to have been at his wit's end. Advancing towards socialism turned out to be just as difficult for the new regime as maintaining absolutism had been for the old. Although the Revolution was now an accomplished fact, bureaucracy, the bane of successive reformers for more than a century, displayed an uncanny ability to transmogrify the most iconoclastic marxist into a boorish *chinovnik*, destroying all hopes of administrative efficiency, let alone Soviet democracy. As the country began to settle down, the dream of a principled leadership firmly linked to a conscious, disciplined, revolutionary working class dissolved into thin air. Lenin was obliged to admit that apart from the peasantry, no easily identifiable social group had survived the holocaust of revolution and civil war intact – and least of all Russia's tiny proletariat.[2] 'Where and how we must now reform ourselves, adapt ourselves, reorganize ourselves so that after the retreat we may begin a stubborn move forward', he said in his last sombre speech late in 1922, 'we still do not know'.[3] Some nine months earlier at the eleventh party congress delegates listened to his first announcement that the 'retreat' was at an end; the New Economic Policy (NEP) did not appear to be helping workers, yet the seemingly contradictory need to appease the countryside remained paramount. The message of conci-

---

[2] 'Permit me to congratulate you', jeered Shliapnikov in 1922, 'on being the vanguard of a non-existing class': cited I. Deutscher, *The Prophet Unarmed, Trotsky: 1921–1929* (1970), pp. 14–15.
[3] Cited E. H. Carr, *The Interregnum 1923–24* (1969), p. 13.

liation towards the peasantry was repeated at the fourth Comintern congress in November and reiterated in his last but one public utterance a week later.[4] Thereafter he had little to offer.

Nevertheless, Lenin is to be credited with having had the courage to give up his dreams and embrace the methods of *laissez-faire* economics in order to preserve the regime. Lenin's 'forced retreat' into NEP, announced at the tenth party congress in 1921, was above all a pragmatic measure. The successful conclusion of the civil war coincided with the threat of a third revolution, typified by the Tambov rising and the Kronstadt revolt. Years of disruption had reduced the economy to a state of primaeval barter, overlaid since 1918 by the tribute system of War Communism. Where there was nothing to buy and no stable currency, farmers had no reason to produce surpluses, so the state fed the army and what was left of the urban population by taking grain by force. After 1921 peasants were allowed to enjoy their property with relatively little central interference. Taxes in kind, later in money, replaced forced levies and farmers disposed of their surplus as they saw fit. Experiments in communal agriculture were all but forgotten and total collectivization receded to the status of a future hope to be realized at some indeterminate time when peasant wishes harmonized with regime aspirations. For industry – almost all of which remained nationalized, unlike the trade and retail sectors – the categorical imperative was the satisfaction of consumer demand, which in Russia meant peasant demand. This would simultaneously stimulate food production by making available commodities for the peasants to buy and bring about a revival of urban life by re-establishing the exchange of goods between town and countryside. Two words encapsulate the means and ends of NEP: *smychka*, the 'link' between the world of the town and that of the village, was to be effected by *khozraschet*, the application of commercial principles to industry in order to guarantee efficiency and sensitivity to the market.

Lenin's prognoses for NEP and those of his associates require no further elaboration here. It would be pointless to try to replicate the work done by many others on the intra-party struggle, and inappropriate in a study attempting to address quite different problems. It is enough to record that in one obvious way NEP worked. Most people are agreed that, on the whole, by 1926 Russia had regained the ground lost since 1913. More interestingly, the policy injected into Soviet life a dynamism which, until very recently, has never been allowed to

4 *Ibid.*, p. 12.

re-appear, and it raises the possibility that there may have been an alternative – some other variant of socialism – to the tragic course subsequently adopted.

In this brief interlude, lasting from 1921 until Stalin's collectivization drive of 1929, cotton was to play an important role. Economic commentators, trade union leaders and party and state officials were united in their recognition of the industry's importance. In the early months of NEP an authoritative publication from the Council for Labour and Defence (STO) stated quite plainly that 'the products of cotton mills are the basic means of exchange between town and countryside'.[5] M. O. Braginskii, a long-standing member of the central committee of the textileworkers' union and a prolific writer on textile affairs, made the same point in 1926; mills must increase output, improve quality and restructure their internal organization in order to satisfy the peasants.[6] Even in 1929 propagandists were still concentrating on the vital importance of cotton: 'Increases in output, improvements in quality, reductions in costs, these strengthen and unify the *smychka* between the working class and the poor and middle peasants ... Decreasing output, falling quality, rising costs, these weaken the *smychka* and have a detrimental effect on grain deliveries'.[7]

Because cotton was an important element in the *smychka*, operatives stood at the point of intersection between politics and economics. When the exchange of goods between town and countryside was disrupted and the stability of the regime threatened, pressure was brought to bear on the workforce, and this is what forms the subject of this book. It is the contention of this study that looking at the varieties of work and the diversity of workers' lives can help us to appreciate the extent to which operatives could deflect aspects of policy with which they disagreed, were obliged to accept and implement policy, or acted back on policy makers and made them think again. Thus we can not only explore the experience of NEP for workers and the ways in which power was handled by its recipients, we can also see whether power could actually be transmitted when the regime felt it should be. For these reasons, the ways in which policies were designed and the role played by managers, the party and intermediate strata in the textileworkers' union will receive far less attention than will the story of what happened when they reached the shop floor.

[5] *Na novykh putiakh. Itogi novoi ekonomicheskoi politiki, 1921–1922gg,* vyp. 3 (1923), p. 9.
[6] *Trudy pervogo vsesoiuznogo s"ezda po ratsionalizatsii v tekstil'noi promyshlennosti, 19–24 maia 1926 goda* (1926), p. 13.
[7] V. A. Buianov, *Tekstil'shchiku, o trudovoi distsipline* (1929), p. 6.

Part I

The New Economic Policy and cotton

When we talk about the *smychka* it is essential to think of it as a material thing. The *smychka* is the endless ribbon of cloth which stretches between the town and the countryside ... A *smychka* without cloth has no content. It is merely an empty word.

Trotsky, 1926

1 Industry

Our task is to give the peasant the cheapest possible product from our mills. He wants this from us, and we must strive towards it.

Kutuzov, president of the textileworkers' union, speaking in Leningrad at the 'Day of the Textile Worker' in September 1924

The development of the cotton industry

On the eve of war and revolution Nicholas' Empire was one of the great cotton-spinning centres of the world, fourth in the league table after Britain, the United States and Germany.[1] Although Russia's industrial achievement often seems sudden, in textiles factory production arose on the basis of a long tradition of peasant, artisanal and merchant endeavour. In the villages of Ivanovo and Voznesensk considerable numbers of people drew their main income from domestic textile working from as far back as the seventeenth century. The first manufactory was established there in 1742, and despite the vast distances separating them from the epicentre of the Industrial Revolution, local entrepreneurs were quick to take advantage of new technologies. Steam power was first applied to cloth printing in 1832, mechanized weaving started in the 1850s, and by the end of the decade there were seven steam engines working in the vicinity.[2] As industrialization accelerated the prime factors influencing location proved to be proximity to markets and the availability of cheap labour. Consequently growth was not confined to the Ivanovo-Voznesensk area but fanned out into the poor-soil regions of north-European Russia; by the end of the 1850s Vladimir guberniya had lost its lead to regions surrounding St Petersburg and Moscow. The next decade gave a boost to industrialization in general and promoted the spread of

[1] V. I. Feoktistov, *Ekskursiia na bumagopriadil' nuiu fabriku* (1924), p. 6.
[2] Iu. F. Glebov, T. N. Letukov, *Ivanovo* (1981), pp. 6–7, 10–12; *Ivanovo-Voznesenskaia guberniia za desiat' let oktiabr'skoi revoliutsii (1917–1927gg)* (1927), p. 37.

the factory system in textiles to other provinces,[3] but this was not matched by significant changes in the structure of ownership. Most of the cotton kings had established their position before the third quarter of the nineteenth century and they took the opportunities afforded by expansion to extend and consolidate their own holdings: by 1913, for instance, the Morozovs' four companies controlled mills in the Tver', Orekhovo-Zuevo and Bogorodsk districts with just under a quarter of a million spindles and 54,000 workers.[4] Concentration of ownership was matched by the concentration of production in large units. Their importance as a factor in Russia's gross national product became evident at the time of the 1897 census when slightly less than 1,000 cotton mills accounted for 15 per cent of the Empire's total industrial output by value.[5]

By then the inheritance that was to pass to socialism was taking final shape. Cotton manufacture relied heavily on mass demand, so growth and development was sensitive to fluctuations in the peasant economy; only in the last three full years of peace is there much evidence of market diversification – rising urban sales.[6] Over 90 per cent of all factory-based cotton machinery was then situated in the Central Industrial Region and western and north-western parts of the Empire, but post-emancipation developments had once again altered the balance between regions. As St Petersburg diversified into metals and engineering, cotton, although still expanding, declined in importance. Increasingly, the capital's mills worked up specialist lines and high-quality cloths. In Moscow guberniya large factories sprouted to the east and south-east of the city, particularly as domestic weaving gave way to the power loom. Ivanovo-Voznesensk grew up as a mono-industrial town. Of the district's 190 enterprises, 148 were textile mills, employing 145,000 out of 150,000 workers.[7]

[3] P. Mathias, M. Postan, eds., *The Cambridge Economic History of Europe*, vol. 7, part 2 (1978), p. 326; O. Crisp, *Studies in the Russian Economy before 1914* (1976), pp. 45–6; P. A. Khromov, *Ocherki ekonomiki tekstil'noi promyshlennosti SSSR* (1946), p. 49; K. A. Pazhitnov, *Ocherki istorii tekstil'noi promyshlennosti dorevoliutsionnoi Rossii: khlopchato-bumazhnaia, l'no-pen'kovaia i shelkovaia promyshlennost'* (1958), pp. 17–18, 132.

[4] W. L. Blackwell, ed., *Russian Economic Development from Peter the Great to Stalin* (1974), p. 169; H. J. Habakkuk, M. Postan, eds., *The Cambridge Economic History of Europe*, vol. 6, part 2 (1965), p. 854.

[5] Pazhitnov, *Ocherki istorii*, p. 141; V. Ia. Laverychev, 'Protsess monopolizatsii khlopchato-bumazhnoi promyshlennosti Rossii (1900–1914 gody)', *Voprosy istorii*, 2, February 1960, pp. 137–8.

[6] Crisp, *Studies*, p. 32; Glebov, Letukov, *Ivanovo*, pp. 7–8; *Istoriia rabochego klassa SSSR. Rabochii klass Rossii, 1907 – fevral' 1917g* (1982), p. 59; Blackwell, *Russian Economic Development*, pp. 164–5.

[7] M. Dobb, *Soviet Economic Development Since 1917* (1966), pp. 56–7; *Ivanovo-Voznesenskaia guberniia* (1927), p. 3; P. M. Ekzempliarskii, *Istoriia goroda Ivanova. Chast'*

Although the Russian Industrial Revolution swept away domestic and artisanal spinning there is evidence that small-scale manufacture, much of it cottage based, was still flourishing in the first years of the twentieth century.[8] Until the Emancipation most weavers worked on the putting-out system. Thereafter the balance shifted in favour of mechanized production: according to one source there were 167,000 power looms as against 50,200 handloom weavers in 1879.[9] In subsequent decades the Lancashire loom steadily encroached on this last stronghold of the artisan, but there is little doubt that handloom weaving continued to be important down to the Great War. Geographically, domestic weaving was centred on the Moscow/Ivanovo-Voznesensk axis, and village artisans around Bogorodsk were still working up cloth for Morozov in 1914.[10]

Decline and recovery

Cut off from fuel and raw materials and heavily reliant on long-distance transport, cotton mills quickly fell victim to the temporary agrarianization of the Russian economy after 1917. By June 1921 99 per cent of all spindles stood idle, and to all intents and purposes economic activity ceased entirely during the following four weeks.[11] Some mills were able to keep going a bit longer because they used local peat fields for fuel,[12] but all experienced the equality of poverty. The only difference amongst the mills was the timing of collapse: for the Moscow district the low point came in spring and early summer 1921, for Petrograd late 1919 to early 1920, and for Ivanovo and Vladimir summer 1920.[13]

There is no need to labour the point that, until the mid 1920s at least,

1. *Dooktiabr'skii period* (1958), pp. 272–4; *Trud* (Ivanovo-Voznesensk), 5, May 1923, p. 18; R. E. Johnson, *Peasant and Proletarian. The Working Class of Moscow in the Late Nineteenth Century* (1979), pp. 15, 18–19.

[8] A. Kaufman, *Small-scale Industry in the Soviet Union* (1962), tables 1, 2 pp. 19–20.

[9] Blackwell, *Russian Economic Development*, p. 175.

[10] There were around 213,000 power looms in the Empire in 1910: Khromov, *Ocherki ekonomiki*, pp. 45, 58, 173.

[11] *Tekstil'shchik, k stanku*, 10 September 1921; *Na novykh putiakh. Itogi novoi ekonomicheskoi politiki 1921–1922gg*, vyp. 3 (1923), p. 10.

[12] A. M. Zaikov, *Na khlopchatobumazhnoi fabrike* (1926/27), p. 6.

[13] I. M. Aleshchenko, 'Iz istorii rabochego klassa Moskvy v vosstanovlennyi period (1921–1925gg)', *Istoriia SSSR*, 1, January–February 1959, p. 109; Iu. F. Iakovlev, *Vladimirskie rabochie v bor'be i ukreplenie soiuza s krest'ianstvom v 1921–1925 godakh* (1963), p. 5; *Biulleten' ivanovo-voznesenskogo gubernskogo statisticheskogo biuro*, 1, October 1922, p. 15 (hereafter *BI-VGSB*); O. I. Shkaratan, 'Izmeneniia v sotsial'nom sostave fabrichno-zavodskikh rabochikh Leningrada 1917–1928gg', *Istoriia SSSR*, 5, 1959, p. 26.

NEP favoured light at the expense of heavy industry, but the achievement for cotton is all the more remarkable in view of the industry's absolute collapse. The nadir for all large-scale industry in the Russian and White Russian Republics came in summer 1921 when just over half of all mines, factories and other enterprises were shut.[14] And yet cotton, starting from a much lower base, had 90 per cent of all equipment on stream by 1926/27, exceeding within another year the output levels of 1913. While easy to comprehend at the national level, recovery in the localities was a complicated, syncopated process, much influenced by successive crises. Some mills which closed during War Communism never re-opened until the late 1920s or were stripped of their machinery and absorbed into neighbouring enterprises.[15] Others, like the Leningrad factories formerly belonging to the Anglo-Russian Cotton Company, approached pre-war output levels well before 1925.[16] Nevertheless, the plethora of factors influencing the timing of closure and re-opening had no effect at all on the industry's structure and location. No new mills were built before 1927, and the first one was simply an addition to the Ivanovo-Voznesensk agglomeration.[17] Throughout NEP the Bolsheviks administered their inheritance wherever they happened to find it, but the disproportionate rate of recovery of cotton meant that wherever there were cotton mills, their significance increased in comparison with pre-war times.

Leningrad provides the best illustration of this trend. The relative decline of textiles there after 1850 has already been noted. In 1912 textile output by value was about half that of metals and the number of metalworkers three times greater than the number of mill hands. Sixteen years later textiles accounted for over one quarter of all output and was the biggest single industry. Metals now took second place, contributing 18 per cent or so by value to the city's economy. In terms of employment the trend is more striking still. In 1921 the number of metalworkers stood at 26.6 per cent of the 1913 figure, while for textiles the proportion was 8.8 per cent. Four years later metal enterprises employed 60.3 per cent of their pre-war numbers and

---

[14] A. A. Matiugin, *Rabochii klass SSSR v gody vosstanovleniia narodnogo khoziaistva (1921–1925gg)* (1962), pp. 198–9.

[15] *Tekstil'nye fabriki SSSR* (1927), lists many mills still in mothballs and many others which existed only in name, all their equipment having been relocated.

[16] Anglo-Russian Cotton Factories Ltd., *Report of Proceedings of Annual General Meeting of Shareholders at Company Offices*, London, 16 June 1926, GL L69.55 MS11–760, p. 2.

[17] Details of planned expansion are given in *Tekstil'nye novosti*, 10–11, October–November 1927, p. 366.

textiles employed 98.9 per cent.[18] For the CIR the picture is much more straightforward. Vladimir and Ivanovo guberniyas' heavy reliance on textiles meant that virtually all recovery evident by mid-decade was based on cotton. By 1927/28 both had surpassed pre-war output levels,[19] but they were overshadowed by the Moscow region, the most important textile district. Moscow guberniya alone accounted for 40 per cent of the entire Soviet output of cotton by value in 1926/27; within the province cotton took 47 per cent of all industrial output by value in 1923/24, rising to 50 per cent during the following economic year. Textiles were not the primary industry in the city itself, where large numbers were employed in chemicals, metals, printing, clothing and transport, but in the suburbs, and particularly in the rural hinterland, cotton mills dominated the industrial landscape.[20]

As not much will be said about it later on, this brief survey would not be complete without a glance at domestic industry in the 1920s and its relationship to cotton. It has already been suggested that handloom weaving played a subsidiary but by no means insignificant role during the first years of the twentieth century, and the weight of evidence suggests that domestic industry in general experienced a renaissance under NEP. The disasters attendant on war and revolution continued for so long that the social and economic ingredients likely to generate economic recovery in a new guise had time to ferment. To change the metaphor, there is evidence of something like an industrial take-off fueled by domestic workers, even if it never reached the stage of self-sustained growth. Disorganized communications, worthless money and the withering away of the national market put a premium on unambitious enterprise proximate to a particular locality. The flight to the countryside obliged industrial workers of all kinds, many of whom were only first-generation immigrants to towns or industrial settlements, to adapt their skills to new conditions and become petty producers in the village.[21] What is particularly interesting is the strength of the artisanal sector even at the very end of NEP: in 1928

---

[18] L. I. Derevnina, *Rabochie Leningrada v period vosstanovleniia narodnogo khoziaistva: chislennost', sostav i material'noe polozhenie* (1981), table 5 pp. 60–1; *Planovoe khoziaistvo*, 4, April 1928, p. 295; *Vosstanovlenie promyshlennosti Leningrada (1921–1924gg)* (1963), p. 124.

[19] *BI-VGSB*, 1, October 1922, pp. 34–5, 46; 8, 1923, p. 3; 9, 1925, p. 2; 20, 1929, table 1 p. 36, table 2 p. 46, table 3 pp. 50–7.

[20] *Fabrichno-zavodskaia promyshlennost' g.Moskvy i moskovskoi gubernii 1917–1927gg* (1928), table 1 p. 8; *Rabota moskovskogo gubernskogo soveta profsoiuzov s oktiabria 1924g po ianvar' 1926g* (1926), p. 77; L. I. Vas'kina, *Rabochii klass SSSR nakanune sotsialisticheskoi industrializatsii. (Chislennost', sostav, razmeshchenie)* (1981), pp. 131, 136.

[21] Kaufman, *Small-scale Industry* pp. 1–2, 30–2; A. Dunaev, Iu. Goriachev, *Iartsevskii khlopchato-bumazhnyi kombinat. (Kratkii istoricheskii ocherk)* (1963), p. 52.

there were somewhere around three to four million domestic workers in the Soviet Union, compared to three to five million in 1913.[22]

Notwithstanding Lenin's death-bed conversion to co-operation and Bukharin's lively notion of 'growing into' socialism through the more or less autonomous activity of millions of small producers, many Bolsheviks were far from happy with this phenomenon, rightly or wrongly seeing it as a threat, a vigorous if still nascent movement which, at worst, might well open the flood-gates of capitalism, and at best seemed to have nothing to do with some vaguely imagined statist view of the future. Nevertheless, whatever their misgivings, NEP could only work if élites were willing to compromise with Russian society as it actually existed, and this entailed due recognition of domestic industry's economic virility – hence the de-nationalization decrees of 1921. Tax revenues from private traders and small enterprises of all kinds rose from 91 million to 192 million roubles between 1925/26 and 1926/27,[23] so it is perhaps reasonable to assume that the sector – if left alone – still had the capacity to exceed pre-war performance.

Domestic workers were massed in the poor-soil regions of the Russian countryside and concentrated around industrial centres. These 'nests' were sometimes integrated into the production chain of a particular industry and additionally provided a reserve of skilled or semi-skilled labour in times of expansion.[24] This was clearly so in the cotton industry. Trusts in Ivanovo and Moscow guberniyas recognized a duty to spin thread suitable for handloom weavers; the fact that in 1926 over 38,000 handlooms in the Moscow district were idle because large mills could not or would not produce the right yarns, and that workers were thus occasionally supplied with imported thread, is a further indication of the strength of handloom weaving.[25]

Organization

The organizational antecedents of the pattern of management and control established in the industry after 1921 are to be found in the strategies adopted by the Bolsheviks' political opponents. In December 1917 *Tsentrotkan'*, a committee set up by the owners and the

[22] Matiugin, *Rabochii klass*, p. 229.
[23] M. Gordon, *Workers Before and After Lenin* (1941), pp. 373, 392.
[24] *Ibid.*, pp. 355–6; Kaufman, *Small-scale Industry*, pp. 31–2.
[25] *Izvestiia tekstil'noi promyshlennosti i torgovli*, 6, 15 February 1926, p. 1.

Provisional Government to try to impose order on a chaotic supply situation, was taken over by the Moscow Soviet and used as a registration body for nationalization. Renamed *Tsentrotekstil'* the following March, membership was expanded to include representatives of workers, engineers and other interested groups. As economic collapse accelerated *Tsentrotekstil'* assumed sole responsibility for all textile production and in December 1918 created *Natsional'tkan'* a sub-department, to deal with its original business, the administration of nationalized enterprises. By the end of 1919 almost all mills had been taken into public ownership, but so vast was the industry that a single chief administration answerable to the Supreme Economic Council (Vesenkha) never emerged. Instead the industry was divided into forty 'unions' with a short-lived central body, *Glavtekstil'*, acting less as a directing agency and more like a co-ordinating committee between the unions and Vesenkha.[26] By 1920 there was precious little actual production for these bureaucracies to administer, consequently, as the sinews of the national economy atrophied, authority shifted to the localities. Regional or mill-based shock committees, proletarian and communist in composition, arose to pick over the carcass of what was left of the industry. In an attempt to keep some kind of production going warehouses and fuel dumps were scavenged and output concentrated in a few selected mills. Twenty-two such committees were busy in the Ivanovo-Voznesensk region at various times between September 1920 and March 1922.[27]

As far as personnel changes in management in the cotton industry were concerned, the upheavals of the immediate post-revolutionary and early NEP years provided ample opportunity for upward social mobility for those committed to the new order and the chance of re-employment for others left over from the *ancien régime*.[28] In London, for instance, anxious shareholders of the Anglo-Russian Cotton Company learned to their dismay that the only company representative present in Petrograd in 1921 had, by the following year,

26 E. H. Carr, *The Bolshevik Revolution 1917–23*, vol. 2 (1966), pp. 85–6, 178–9, 182; Dobb, *Soviet Economic Development*, pp. 86–7.
27 *Iz istorii rabochego klassa SSSR* (1967), pp. 86–7; *Trud* (Ivanovo-Voznesensk), 5, May 1923, p. 19; *Rabochii krai*, 24 November 1920; 22 February 1921; 17 March 1921; 26 March 1922.
28 On this issue see Carr, *Bolshevik Revolution*, 2, p. 188; W. J. Conyngham, *Industrial Management in the Soviet Union: the Role of the CPSU in Industrial Decision-making 1917–1970* (1973), p. 22; J. B. Sorenson, *The Life and Death of Soviet Trade Unionism 1917–28* (1969), pp. 91–105; *Stenograficheskii otchet 1–go vserossiiskogo s"ezda rabotnikov tekstil'noi promyshlennosti v Moskve, 12–16 okt. 1922g* (1923), preface; *Tekstil'shchik, k stanku*, 20 July 1920.

become one of the directors of the city's textile trust.[29] The chairmen of shock committees, workers with long service in the party, old specialists, engineers and managers – in brief, these were the people who were to become mill directors or departmental heads in the industry's local and central directing agencies.

The principles underlying the organizational forms which emerged after the tenth party congress were those considered expedient for effecting the *smychka* and enforcing commercial practice in industry, but in spite of Lenin's well-known strictures[30] managerial discretion at plant level was circumscribed. Mill directors were responsible for matters of internal production but power was shared with factory committees and the enterprise's party secretary. A 1924 statute made it plain that directors should look to the trust and not the consumer, and that their functions were administrative rather than entrepreneurial; wage regulation, for example, was increasingly a matter decided between trades unions and various state agencies. But disagreements over the relationship between trust and director continued and prefigured a further order of 1927 stressing the authority of the director in the factory and his responsibility to the trust. In February 1928 Vesenkha insisted once more that directors were autonomous within the four walls of their enterprise, but that they were to confine their responsibilities to production matters.[31]

Trustification, the regional grouping of factories in one industry, was given legal expression in two decrees issued by Vesenkha and STO in August 1921, but some sectors of the economy anticipated these decisions by several months.[32] Whatever their original intent, and like NEP itself, these orders turned out to be the beginning of a process; provisional statements subject to continuous amendment, if not clarification. Vesenkha's and STO's decrees, together with several other *ad hoc* orders promulgated during the following autumn and winter, advanced the proposition of a limited form of *laissez faire* and confirmed administrative devolution, but in ways far removed from

---

[29] Anglo-Russian Cotton Factories Ltd., *Report of Proceedings at Annual General Meeting of Shareholders held at Company Offices*, 28 June 1921, pp. 3–4; 22 June 1922, p. 4, GL L69.55 MS11–760.

[30] The 1922 eleventh party congress once more stated that unions should have no part in running the factory and made a firm commitment to individual management: I. Deutscher, *Soviet Trade Unions: Their Place in Soviet Labour Policy* (1950), p. 62.

[31] Y. Avdakov, V. Borodin, *USSR State Industry During the Transition Period* (1977), p. 147; V. N. Bandera, 'Market orientation of state enterprises during NEP', *Soviet Studies*, 1, 1970, pp. 111–18; Conyngham, *Industrial Management*, p. 20.

[32] V. T. Pikhalo, 'Trestirovanie promyshlennosti SSSR v 20-e gody', *Istoriia SSSR*, 4, July–August 1971, p. 22; V. M. Selunskaia, ed., *Izmeneniia sotsial'noi struktury sovetskogo obshchestva 1921 – seredina 30–kh godov* (1979), p. 25.

the free-booting activities of shock committees. Trusts were given the right to manage their own material and financial resources, and enjoined to buy and sell on the open market and keep profit and loss accounts. The April 1923 Decree on Trusts systematized many of these points while simultaneously reducing local competence. Henceforth STO price guide-lines became increasingly binding on these supposedly autonomous organizations – in theory anyway. Four years later, in summer 1927, the Statute on Trusts apparently resolved once and for all the uncertain relationship between centre and periphery: trust functions were limited to technical supervision while Vesenkha, recently reorganized, fixed prices and handed down production targets. Confusingly, the 'unions', which had been a feature of the War Communism years, again began to play an active role, though so powerful was the textile syndicate (discussed below) that it blocked moves to resurrect *Glavtekstil'* until December 1927.[33]

Trustification proceeded very rapidly in textiles. The industry accounted for nine of the original twenty-three registered with Vesenkha in December 1921, and by the following autumn there were fifty-two textile trusts encompassing 484 mills and employing over a quarter of a million workers. The biggest were in the cotton sector; a Vesenkha exhibition staged in October 1922 attracted displays from eighteen cotton trusts which between them employed just over 200,000 workers and office personnel.[34] Subsequently cotton trusts grew as more factories were reactivated but it is clear that the largest mills were put to work first; in 1924 trusts employed around nine-tenths of the total cotton workforce but were using only just over half of the country's mill stock.[35] In the early NEP years recovery was accompanied by endless reorganizations; only in mid-decade did trust structure take on some definite shape and thereafter changes seem to have been made much more slowly. Three, the First, Second and Third, were designated trusts of 'All-Union significance' and placed directly under Vesenkha's control. All others were regionally based

[33] Bandera, 'Market orientation', pp. 111–18; Carr, *Bolshevik Revolution*, 2, pp. 306–7; E. H. Carr, R. W. Davies, *Foundations of a Planned Economy*, vol. 1, part 1 (1969), p. 355; Conyngham, *Industrial Management*, p. 20; M. Dewar, *Labour Policy in the USSR 1917–28* (1956), pp. 90–1; *Tekstil'shchik, k stanku*, 10 September 1921.

[34] Dobb, *Soviet Economic Development*, pp. 134–5; Iu. A. Lavrikov *et al.*, *Ocherk ekonomi-cheskogo razvitiia leningradskoi industrii za 1917–1967gg* (1968), pp. 35–6; *Na novykh putiakh*, p. 1; Pikhalo, 'Trestirovanie promyshlennosti', pp. 23–4; *Postoiannaia prom-yshlennaia pokazatel'naia vystavka VSNKh. Vystavka tekstil'nykh trestov, 16 oktiabria 1922g* (1923), pp. 282–329; A. C. Sutton, *Western Technology and Soviet Economic Development* vol. 1 (1968), p. 225.

[35] *BI-VGSB*, 9, 1925, p. 2.

and their administration shared between Moscow and the localities. In Ivanovo guberniya, for example, Ivanovo-Voznesensk State Textile Trust was run by Vesenkha: *Ivtekstil'*, centred on the provincial capital, by the RSFSR, and Ivanovo-Voznesensk Guberniya Trust by the local economic council.[36]

While trusts resembled in some ways War Communism's defunct regional unions, the All-Union Textile Syndicate was something like the Provisional government's *Tsentrotkan'*. It held a key position in the national economy because it came to be the main channel for the supply of consumer goods to the peasantry,[37] and it lasted just as long as NEP. Founded out of the ruins of *Glavtekstil'* and abolished late in 1929 it was, in effect, a joint-stock company functioning under state auspices.[38] Although the initial reason for its creation was to prevent excessive price cutting amongst competing trusts, the syndicate's objectives soon fanned out to include the co-ordination of storage, procurement, and finance; state orders were distributed through it and foreign purchases organized by it. In a further move against the market the syndicate gradually assumed the role of wholesale agent; by 1926 more than two-thirds of all textile output passed through its hands and a year earlier Ivanovo State Textile Trust had agreed to dispose of its entire production this way. In February 1927 all stores were placed under syndicate control, all sales administered by the syndicate and all advance orders channelled through the syndicate. Next year all retail co-operatives were obliged to give the syndicate six months' notice of their requirements for cloth. After 1927 the syndicate also began to take on planning functions.[39]

If the preceding paragraphs give the impression of an orderly transition from a system characterized by a relatively free market to one dominated by planning, one where the syndicate interposed itself between the trust and the market – or even of a series of tensions contained within a more or less well-defined bureaucratic structure – this is the penalty which must be paid for abbreviation. It was most certainly not the case in reality. For a start trustification created as many problems as it solved since mills grouped together under the

---

[36] Ivanovo-Voznesensk State Textile Trust, with 54,000 workers, was the biggest in the country in 1922. Big mills, like the Tverskaia which accounted for 60 per cent of a single trust's output, virtually ran themselves: Carr, *Bolshevik Revolution*, 2, p. 307: Carr, Davies, *Foundations*, 1, 1, pp. 379–80.

[37] Carr, Davies, *Foundations*, 1, 1, pp. 373–4.

[38] Z. K. Zvezdin, 'Vsesoiuznyi tekstil'nyi sindikat v 1922–1929gg', *Istoricheskie zapiski*, 88, 1971, pp. 8, 55.

[39] *Ibid.*, p. 9; Avdakov, Borodin, *USSR State Industry*, pp. 171–93, 226–34; Dobb, *Soviet Economic Development*, pp. 159–60; Carr, Davies, *Foundations*, 1, 1, p. 219.

NEP variant of socialism had not evolved together under the tsarist variant of capitalism. As NEP unfolded the fixed assets and product range of a given trust often bore little relationship to the tasks imposed on that trust, and in spite of the régime's wishes, the market sometimes located those mills best fitted to serve consumers' needs.[40] Beyond this the party constantly and confusingly cut across evolving lines of communication and control. Although the eleventh party congress asserted that local party organs should not meddle with economic administration, central committee instructors and all manner of *ad hoc* plenipotentiaries extended their powers during the 1920s. As a by-product of the succession struggle the 1923 twelfth party congress partially reversed the devolutionary tendencies previously in fashion and restated the party's right to interfere in decision making. The drift towards recentralization and line-over-staff policy-making became clear in 1925 when the party's organizational department, and not the competent specialist bodies, decreed the administrative structure of the industry, and it became more evident still throughout the following two years when the same Politburo sub-committee led the campaign for lower prices and rationalization.[41] But it was not just the party's central committee which, from time to time, and particularly at moments of crisis, dictated to the industry. Because cotton was so important many other organizations – the Commissariats of Labour and Finance, the Young Communist League (Komsomol), the textileworkers' union and its local branches, as well as what might be called pressure groups like the union's Taylorist institute – felt that they ought to have a finger in the pie. They were all issuing 'orders' or making recommendations which were supposed to be put into effect in the mill. It is not that the chain of command for the industry was complex – legally and formally the structure, given time and patience, could be understood and described. Rather, it seems that the cross-currents were so wayward and unpredictable that much of the time no single organization knew clearly what was really happening in the industry, even to the extent of not knowing what the factories were producing. The crises afflicting cotton mills which loom so large in this study, therefore, were – to some extent at least – the result of the regime's inability to grasp what was going on. So it is not too surprising to discover that central responses were sometimes based on illusions and misunderstandings, frequently cobbled together at the last minute, and often informed by a sense of frustration and panic.

[40] Glebov, Letukov, *Ivanovo*, p. 25.
[41] Conyngham, *Industrial Management*, pp. 10–17, 21.

2   Workforce

Where are they, our textile workers? In every corner of our Soviet land you can find workers from Orekhovo-Zuevo and our other textile districts . . . after four years of cold, hunger and disease they're scattered everywhere.

A worker's letter in *Tekstil'shchik, k stanku*, 16 September 1921

Numbers and location

The 1926 census classed some 5.6 million out of a total Soviet population of 147 million as workers. Of these about 2.3 million were to be found in large-scale industry. The vast majority – 1.7 million – lived in the RSFSR and were concentrated in Leningrad, the CIR, and the Ural region, 45 per cent in the Moscow/Leningrad axis alone. If the Russian Federation accounted for approximately three-quarters of the country's factory workers, virtually all the rest were resident in the Ukraine. White Russia, Transcaucasia, Uzbekistan and Turkestan took the remainder – 4.6 per cent. The number of factory workers had doubled since 1920 and more or less reached pre-war levels.[1]

It is not difficult to situate cotton within these figures; decline and recovery were a function of the industry's changing fortunes described briefly in chapter 1. As against 480,000 in 1913, the mills employed about 137,000 in 1921, 182,000 in the following year, 231,000 in 1923, 296,000 in 1924, 406,000 by mid-decade, 419,000 at the time of the first All-Union census, 438,000 in 1927, 477,000 in 1928 and 496,000 in 1929.[2]

[1] Y. S. Borisov *et al.*, eds., *Outline History of the Soviet Working Class* (1973), p. 82; A. A. Matiugin, *Rabochii klass SSSR v gody vosstanovleniia narodnogo khoziaistva (1921–1925gg)* (1962), pp. 205–9; L. I. Vas'kina, *Rabochii klass SSSR nakanune sotsialisticheskoi industrializatsii. (Chislennost', sostav, razmeshchenie)* (1981), pp. 11, 21–4.

[2] A. M. Korneev, *Tekstil'naia promyshlennost' SSSR i puti ee razvitiia* (1957), p. 111; *Sotsialisticheskoe stroitelstvo SSSR* (1934), p. 134; *Vsesoiuznaia perepis' naseleniia 1926 goda* (1930), tom XXXIV, table 3 pp. 22–6 (hereafter *1926 census*).

The geographical concentration of the industry was matched by the geographical concentration of the workforce; according to the 1926 census 96 per cent of all operatives lived and worked in the RSFSR. They represented a substantial and slightly increasing proportion of the total factory population throughout the 1920s, starting at just below and rising to just over one-quarter of the total.[3] For women workers alone the trend is the same, although the percentages are higher throughout – 32.2 per cent of all women employed in large-scale industry worked in textiles in 1923, 40.6 per cent five years later. In parts of the CIR where textiles were all but the monopoly employer – Ivanovo, Vladimir, Iaroslavl' and Kostroma guberniyas – mills absorbed virtually all female workers.[4] Moscow also took a disproportionate share of employed women, particularly of the young. In 1925, in the city and guberniya respectively one-quarter and four-fifths of all working girls under eighteen were to be found in mills. The textile-workers' union was far and away the largest union in the region, taking over 22 per cent of all union members in 1925; its nearest rival, the shopworkers' union, had only half that proportion.[5]

Enough has been said about the industrial structure of Ivanovo to render detailed elaboration superfluous. Cotton was central to the economic life of the provincial capital, and the province had the highest concentration of proletarians of all the guberniyas of the CIR – 22.5 per cent of the total guberniya population.[6] In 1923/24 Ivanovo State Textile Trust employed three-quarters of these and *Ivtekstil'* employed a further 13 per cent. Eighty per cent of the textile workforce was registered in the union's cotton section[7] and roughly the same proportions are evident three years later, in 1927/28. By then cotton mills employed 84 per cent of a total industrial workforce of just over 158,000.[8] The same pattern was repeated wherever large mills were

[3] *Ten Years of Soviet Power in Figures, 1917–1927* (n.d), pp. 292–3; Vas'kina, *Rabochii klass*, p. 117.

[4] A. G. Rashin, *Zhenskii trud v SSSR*, vyp. 1 (1928), p. 6; 92 per cent of these four provinces' 192,800 women workers in 1929: *Rabochii krai*, 11 July 1929.

[5] *Otchet TsK vsesoiuznogo professional'nogo soiuza tekstil'shchikov k VI vsesoiuznomu s"ezdu tekstil'shchikov. Okt. 1922–okt. 1924g* (1924), p. 124 (hereafter *TsK VPST 1922–24*); *Rabota moskovskogo gubernskogo soveta profsoiuzov s oktiabria 1924g po ianvar' 1926g* (1926), p. 7; *Okhrana truda v tekstil'noi promyshlennosti* (1927), p. 59; M. Ia. Vydro, *Naselenie Moskvy (po materialam perepisei naseleniia 1871–1970gg)* (1976), tables 7, 9, 10 pp. 21, 23.

[6] *Iz istorii rabochego klassa SSSR* (1967), p. 153; Ia. E. Shostak, *Zabolevaemost' tekstil'shchikov g. Ivanovo-Voznesenska v 1927 godu* (1931), table 5 p. 15.

[7] *Otchet gubernskogo otdela soiuza 15-mu gubernskomu s"ezdu tekstil'shchikov ivanovo-voznesenskoi gubernii (ap. 1924g–mart 1925g)* (1925), p. 12; *Voprosy truda*, 3, March 1925, p. 153.

[8] *Biulleten' ivanovo-voznesenskogo gubernskogo statisticheskogo biuro*, 19, 1929, table 1 p. 8 (hereafter *BI-VGSB*).

situated deep in the countryside. In Iaroslavl' guberniya, for example, three cotton mills employed about 14,000 workers in 1924/25, the remaining 22,000 industrial workers were scattered throughout 215 enterprises.[9]

New and established operatives

It is worth emphasizing that established workers were schooled to labour in large factories; in 1913 just over four-fifths of all operatives worked in mills employing 500 or more.[10] That they returned to their shops after the settlement of 1921, forming a link – a mediating agency – for all manner of cultural traits between the pre- and post-revolutionary mill, is not in doubt. Nor is there much point in questioning the evidence which suggests that many stayed on at the factory during the worst years of economic collapse, even though figures often seem too high – it would be interesting to know, for example, what the 40 per cent of Moscow guberniya's 1913 textile workforce were actually doing in their mills in 1920/21.[11] Operatives who did not remain at the frame during War Communism, or at least on the nominal pay roll of the mills, sometimes returned to work after service in the Red Army. The total number in uniform fell to 526,000 in 1924, releasing 3.5 million into civil life. Just under 500,000 drifted back to industry between 1921 and 1924.[12] Between 1922 and 1929, 10,000-odd textile workers returned to Leningrad's mills from the Army, 5,500 to Moscow city's mills, 48,000 to those in the province and 55,000 to Ivanovo guberniya. In all cases the vast majority, over 80 per cent of the numbers cited above, returned between 1922 and 1925.[13] For other established operatives revolution and war meant flight to the land. Here they shared an experience common to all industrial workers, but for cotton hands, as will become evident later, there are reasons which suggest that the experience was less traumatic than for others. Although they formed the biggest single group of industrial workers in the Empire in 1913,[14] cotton operatives were not clearly divorced

9 *Iaroslavskii statisticheskii vestnik*, 8, 1924, table 13 p. 53; 7, September 1925, p. 113.
10 10.6 per cent worked in mills in the 501–1,000 range, 77.6 per cent in the 1,000+ range: P. A. Khromov, *Ocherki ekonomiki tekstil'noi promyshlennosti SSSR* (1946), pp. 52–3.
11 The figure is from *Fabrichno-zavodskaia promyshlennost' g. Moskvy i moskovskoi gubernii, 1917–27gg* (1928), table 3 p. 15.
12 Matiugin, *Rabochii klass*, p. 216; V. M. Selunskaia *et al.*, eds., *Izmeneniia sotsial'noi struktury sovetskogo obshchestva 1921 – seredina 30–kh godov* (1979), p. 26.
13 Matiugin, *Rabochii klass*, p. 215, table 5 p. 218.
14 *Istoriia rabochego klassa SSSR. Rabochii klass Rossii, 1907–fevral' 1917g* (1982), table 2 p. 36, pp. 44–5.

from the village. In many cases mills situated in the countryside did not form the nuclei of towns: frequently they were only industrial settlements. This was particularly so in Vladimir and Ivanovo,[15] and not far from 'proletarian' Leningrad it is still possible to see places like them today: factories set deep in the woodland surrounded by workers' barracks.

Like ex-soldiers, the majority of industrial workers who temporarily became farmers returned to their factories. Although in some industries, notably metals, established workers sometimes stayed in the countryside until the beginning of the First Five Year Plan, virtually all available cotton operatives had been drawn back within the first years of NEP.[16] Frequent complaints from administrators and directors support this assertion. Leningrad's trust reported serious shortages of skilled spinners and weavers in 1924/25.[17] In 1925 *Golos tekstilei*, the union's newspaper, began to carry reports of labour shortages which were little more than thinly disguised advertisements placed by directors seeking experienced workers. By August the newspaper anticipated that within eight weeks there would be a national shortfall of 70,000 spinners and 11,000 weavers, and predicted a demand for 20,000 spinners and 38,000 weavers the following year.[18]

By then there were vacancies for 10,000 skilled operatives in Ivanovo guberniya alone[19] and they had to be filled somehow. In 1928, of all textile workers in the provincial capital's hinterland, about one-third had started work in the mills sometime during the preceding decade, the biggest influx occurring between 1922 and 1925, probably to make up for the losses sustained since 1914. For the Moscow district, which exhibited the same pattern, the proportion was just over 40 per cent.[20] To the north, 60 per cent of Leningrad's textile workforce was new to the industry in 1925/26.[21] Looking back from the end of the decade a survey based on a sample of 119,000 cotton workers taken from major textile districts found that over 40 per cent of the city's mill hands started work after 1922. A book

15 See chapter 3.
16 Matiugin, *Rabochii klass*, pp. 213–18; Selunskaia, *Izmeneniia sotsial'noi struktury*, p. 11; *Iz istorii rabochego klassa SSSR* (1962), pp. 79–80.
17 *Otchet za 1924–25g. Leningradskii gosudarstvennyi tekstil'nyi trest 'Leningradtekstil''* (1925), p. 6 (hereafter *Lentekstil' 1924–25*).
18 See *Golos tekstilei* for spring 1925 and 11 August 1925.
19 *Voprosy truda*, 1, January 1926, p. 126.
20 Ia. M. Bineman, ed., *Trud v SSSR 1926–30gg* (1930), p. xii, table 28 p. 26; *Puti industralizatsii*, 1, 1930, p. 37; *Vladimirskii tekstil'shchik*, 20 April 1926.
21 *Pod znamenem kommunizma*, 2 February 1927, p. 71.

drawing on the 1929 industrial and trades union census came to much the same conclusion.[22]

Although this post-1917 influx was made up of various social elements, many new workers came from the countryside. Nationally, the number arriving from the village in search of work in industry or construction (and probably including seasonal migrants) stood at 2.8 million in 1924/25, 3.3 million in the following year, 3.8 million in 1926/27 and four million in 1927/28.[23] About one-quarter of new recruits to Leningrad's mills in the three years after 1922 were peasants, roughly one-third in Moscow and Ivanovo guberniyas. Almost all the rest were from workers' families. In 1926 peasants again provided about a third of new entrants to the industry and thereafter numbers rose sharply.[24] For each year of the eleven years after 1917, in the survey of 119,000 cotton workers mentioned above, about one-third of new recruits came from peasant families.[25] Officials of the Tver' and Orekhovo trusts noted a significant influx of peasants into their mills after 1922; interestingly, these were peasants who kept their land and came into the factories because they were unable to make ends meet without industrial wages.[26]

Social characteristics

The 1926 census reveals that in common with other countries Soviet mills relied heavily on female labour, about 70 per cent of the total nationally.[27] There is little to be gained from stressing the point by referring to local statistics; throughout NEP all districts had roughly the same proportion of women workers.[28] Russia shared in the general European tendency for women to substitute for men on the shop floor during the Great War and for men to displace women when hostilities ended: in Moscow guberniya numbers of women in the mills fell between February 1921 and July 1924 as soldiers returned

[22] Bineman, *Trud v SSSR*, table 28 p. 26; *Puti industrializatsii*, 1, 1930, p. 37.
[23] L. S. Rogachevskaia, *Iz istorii rabochego klassa SSSR v pervye gody industrializatsii (1926–1927gg)* (1959), pp. 55–6; L. S. Rogachevskaia, *Likvidatsiia bezrabotitsy v SSSR 1917–1930gg* (1973), p. 144.
[24] Matiugin, *Rabochii klass*, pp. 221, 228–9; N. V. Poliakova, 'Bor'ba rabochikh-tekstil'shchikov za povyshenie proizvoditel'nosti truda v 1921–1925gg. (Po materialam Moskvy i moskovskoi gubernii)', *Voprosy istorii*, 6, July 1959, p. 22.
[25] *Puti industrializatsii*, 1, 1930, p. 38.   [26] Matiugin, *Rabochii klass*, p. 212.
[27] *1926 census*, tom XXXIV, table 3 pp. 22–6.
[28] Of the mass of statistical detail on this point see for example N. L. Brodskii *et al.*, *Tekstil'shchik (istoriia, byt, bor'ba)* (1925), pp. 85–7; *Izvestiia tekstil'noi promyshlennosti i torgovli*, 19–20, October 1927, p. 13; *Voprosy truda*, 3, March 1925, pp. 48–9; 2, February 1928, table 3 p. 37.

from the front.[29] Thereafter the trend reversed; the number of women employed in textiles nearly doubled between 1923 and 1926.[30]

Gender and age interacted to produce marked differences in the mills. Overall the cotton workforce was becoming younger, and in general women were younger than men: 50.1 per cent of males and 68.9 per cent of females were in the age range 18 to 39 in a sample for 1918, 62.7 per cent and 73.9 per cent respectively in 1926, and 65.4 per cent and 73.1 per cent three years later. After 1918 the number of young teenagers fell as Soviet labour legislation began to bite, similarly the elderly declined as a proportion of the total. Moreover, teenagers as well as women were displaced by returning soldiers,[31] but the decline of the under-eighteens as a proportion of the labour force may have started before the Revolution.[32] The union tried to counter youth unemployment by setting recruitment targets for young workers; the figures are not very clear, but these instructions were, it seems, often ignored.[33] But whatever the case most statistics are probably unreliable. The scramble for jobs encouraged teenagers to falsify their age, sometimes with the connivance of local officials; in Vladimir guberniya in 1922 one local party committee issued documents to twelve- and thirteen-year-old children listing their age as sixteen in order to help them find work in nearby cotton mills.[34] In any event recruitment frequently had nothing to do with official bodies – aspiring workers often relied on kinship networks or patronage in their search for a job.[35]

Length of service in industry can be dealt with quickly. Looked at from the stand-point of 1929, a survey conducted by the statistician A. G. Rashin found that about half the textile workforce started work before 1918. This source also lends weight to the view that new workers came in increasing numbers after mid-decade;[36] established workers, therefore, were back in place by 1925 and formed a respectable proportion of the total. Thereafter expansion pulled in people

[29] I. M. Aleshchenko, 'Iz istorii rabochego klassa Moskvy v vosstanovlennyi period (1921–1925gg)', *Istoriia SSSR*, 1, January–February 1959, p. 112.

[30] E. D. Emel'ianova, *Rabota kommunisticheskoi partii sredi trudiashchikhsia zhenshchin v vosstanovitel'nyi period* (1961), p. 15.

[31] Aleshchenko, 'Iz istorii', p. 112.

[32] See *Rabochii klass Rossii, 1907–fevral' 1917g*, p. 54; F. F. Kilevits, *Tekstil'naia promyshlennost' i rabochie tekstil'shchiki* (1928), p. 7; Poliakova, 'Bor'ba rabochikh-tekstil'shchikov', p. 24.

[33] On recruitment targets for young workers see *BI-VGSB*, 2, November 1922, p. 36; *Khoziaistvo i upravlenie*, 2, February 1925, p. 51; *Nashe khoziaistvo* (Vladimir), 11–12 (52–53), November–December 1925, p. 39; *Voprosy truda*, 1, January 1926, p. 127.

[34] *Rabochaia zhizn'*, 8, 22 September 1922, p. 3.   [35] See chapter 5.

[36] A. G. Rashin, *Sostav fabrichno-zavodskogo proletariata SSSR* (1930), pp. 8, 58, 64, 66.

who had no experience of the pre-revolutionary mill. Skill profile is more problematic. Rashin's 1929 sample contradicts data from the 1926 census which listed 53 per cent of the textile workforce as skilled, 40 per cent as semi-skilled and 7 per cent as unskilled.[37] It is necessary to add immediately, however, that these categories, regardless of any statistical variations, are virtually useless in order to try to understand what workers did and how they thought of themselves and each other. The highly skilled and unskilled were doubtless service personnel and auxiliary workers respectively, but 'skill' seems to have had no clear meaning. Thus Ivanovo guberniya was short of the following skilled workers in 1920: weaving-room foremen and overlookers, ring-frame and mule spinners. Five years later Leningrad's textile trust wanted more skilled overlookers, flyer-frame spinners and weavers, and in 1925/26 the union's central committee predicted a shortfall of 72,000 skilled weavers, flyer- and ring-frame operatives.[38] This gamut of skilled workers represents almost the entire range of trades in a cotton mill, so the term is either a social construct which cannot be deduced from technology, or is related to work in some other way. Most probably it meant experienced. One Soviet historian, for instance, writes that among women cotton workers in 1923, 43 per cent were unskilled, 37 per cent semi-skilled and 20 per cent skilled. And yet in a sample of 114,474 cotton operatives taken in mid-decade, divided into the three categories and then cross-referenced with age, length of service in industry, gender and education, the main determinants of skill turn out to be age and length of service in industry.[39] In some way, therefore, it seems that workers became skilled by staying in the mill for a long time, regardless of the particular trade in which they were engaged.

In just the same way the importance of social origin should not be overstressed. While it is true that some workers had been on the shop floor for a long time and others had only recently come from the village, it is not possible, without falling victim to a particularly barren form of sociological determinism, to deduce workers' responses by appealing to a set of social antecedents. Commentators often got themselves into a semantic mess by trying to ram operatives into their chosen categories – here is the union's central committee struggling

[37] Ibid., pp. 76–7; Vas'kina, Rabochii klass, pp. 116, 123. This book is a useful extended review of the 1926 census.
[38] Dostizheniia i nedochety tekstil'noi promyshlennosti SSSR (Po materialam tekstil'noi sektsii NK RKI SSSR) (1926), p. 197; Lentekstil' 1924–25, p. 52; Rabochii krai, 21 November 1920; 24 November 1920.
[39] Bineman, Trud v SSSR, table 32 p. 32; Matiugin, Rabochii klass, p. 252.

with women workers in 1924: 'for as long as the female operative is not fully developed as a worker it is difficult to speak of the general class maturity of the textile proletariat, because women form the predominant part of the union's membership'.[40] Of course the central committee had its own ideological axe to grind; for the purposes of this study it is enough that women were on the shop floor – that made them workers. To anticipate for a moment, it will become clear that many workers' children held land and many peasant immigrants were landless; nevertheless it is difficult to believe that the former did not consider themselves to be workers, just as the latter probably thought they were peasants. This is not to say that social origin was unimportant, but to experience work in a mill was to experience change – in the case of NEP Russia rapid change – and change often causes a re-valuation of past experience: structure forms the beginning of analysis, not the end of it. To put it another way, home is where they started from, not where they ended up.

Despite the tendency of Soviet historians to view the history of their country's working class as a history of heavy industry, the cotton workforce merits attention.[41] Concentrated in large concerns, situated in the heartland of the Russian Industrial Revolution and vital to the *smychka*, it was, however, without many of those *machismo* traits reflected in the myth of the Soviet worker. Most obviously, women played an exceptional role in cotton working. Equally, whilst many were established workers, the number and proportion of new operatives drawn from the peasantry was considerable. Lastly, the juxtaposition of large, well-established mills in a plainly rural setting renders problematic the equation sometimes drawn between industrialization, urbanization and proletarianization.

[40] *TsK VPST 1922–24*, p. 74.
[41] On the size of the metal and textile labour forces see E. B. Genkina, 'Ob osobennostiakh vosstanovleniia promyshlennosti v SSSR (1921–1925gg)', *Istoriia SSSR*, 5, 1962; Matiugin, *Rabochii klass*; O. I. Shkaratan, *Problemy sotsial'noi struktury rabochego klassa SSSR (Istorichesko-sotsiologicheskoe issledovanie)* (1970); Vas'kina, *Rabochii klass*.

Part II

The mill

Our factory is a patriarchal factory.

Mel'nichanskii, 1926

3   Field and factory

When agricultural taxes were raised the rural part of the workforce said, 'The proletariat has it easy, they pay nothing to the state . . .' On such occasions a quarrel develops about who lives better, pure proletarians or those connected with the countryside.

Letter to the central committee of the textileworkers' union
from a mill in Moscow guberniya, sometime in the 1920s

The problem of 'tie with the land'

The cotton industry exhibited all the features that should lead to proletarianization: the substitution of capital for labour, concentration of the workforce in big enterprises, separation of the workers from the means of production and wage labour. But not all operatives were totally dependent on wages. Many divided their time between field and factory. There is, therefore, a temptation to try to work out if the labour force, or some part of it, exhibited a 'working-class' consciousness or a 'peasant mentality'. These are the categories which contemporaries habitually used to try to understand the situation, the two opposing poles of worker and peasant, but they are highly tendentious. In the first place it is not at all easy to discover how many workers had an interest in agriculture, most obviously because those who were farming would be reluctant to tell the truth about their economic circumstances; the more they revealed the more likely they were to be taxed. Even the detailed study by Rashin published in 1930 ends up by invalidating much of its own material. Rashin acknowledges under-recording of 'tie with the land' and guesses the true proportion of landholding cotton workers to be around one-quarter of the total workforce.[1] This is the best available source for the 1920s but it is far from comprehensive; sixty-one large mills were investigated

[1] A. G. Rashin, *Sostav fabrichno-zavodskogo proletariata SSSR* (1930), pp. 24–5.

with a combined worker population of 119,000, amounting to about 25 per cent of the national total, and the sample was drawn exclusively from Moscow (three mills with 5,440 workers), Leningrad (six mills with 10,296 workers), and Moscow and Ivanovo guberniyas (twenty-three mills with 48,320 workers and twenty-nine mills employing 54,930 respectively). Admittedly these were the main textile districts, but the country had more than 300 working cotton factories in mid-decade, many of them small enterprises scattered across the CIR.[2] Trades union handbooks and newspapers, syndicate journals and trust reports can help make good these deficiencies, and taken together with Rashin's survey they can point towards some common-sense judgements about operatives in, for example, Leningrad and the little industrial villages fanning out from Moscow, but it is hard to press statistical analysis much beyond this.

Of course it is equally clear that it would be wrong to ignore the evidence to hand. It should be possible to imagine how workers felt about their situation and how they were likely to react to change by looking at their relationship to off-mill income. That there are no perfect sources for such an inquiry is scarcely the point; the residua of the past were not designed for the consumption of the present. The second, major, problem is not one of sources but one of conceptualization.

In a useful article published in 1961 the Soviet historian A. A. Matiugin considered that textile operatives in general had more varied links with the rural economy than any other group of workers in large-scale industry.[3] These links might – and did – mean anything from possession of a thriving farm to living in a village or renting a room from a peasant. It is necessary, therefore, at once to modify the image of the cotton workforce as one distinguished by this or that number of 'peasant-workers'. The concept is too inexact. What has to be dealt with is not a discontinuity between worker and peasant but a continuum between mill and village, and one having two axes; the first measuring the level of 'wage dependence' on or financial independence from the mill, the second measuring the physical distance of the operative's home from the factory, what might be called 'time dependence'. Apart from its descriptive efficacy, this idea suggests ways in which the impact of change can be understood more clearly. The dynamics of NEP, and they touched the mill in many different ways, had different potentials for different workers depend-

[2] *Ibid.*, pp. 2–3; *Tekstil'nye fabriki SSSR* (1927), lists 433 textile mills of all kinds.
[3] *Izmeneniia v chislennosti i sostave sovetskogo rabochego klassa* (1961), p. 91.

ing on their position on the dual axis. Of course responses and reactions cannot be plotted on these vectors in a predictive fashion; rather, it is necessary to think in terms of predispositions, tendencies and affinities. Land, residence, gender, age, length of service in industry and past experience – as well as the irreducible complexities of individual temperament – were woven together in an intricate and evolving pattern. All that is being suggested is that it may be possible to tease out a few more historical threads from an imperfectly understood whole.

Notwithstanding the displays of official polemics which will be cited in a moment, friction and conflict were not generally characteristic of the relationship between field and factory, although they could arise if new policies were initiated in agriculture or industry. Instead, mill and village existed in a kind of symbiotic rapport. They had to. Excluding the old Imperial capital, mills were often constructed in the countryside. By 1917 many had been there for half-a-century or so,[4] and it was still possible to find new factories under construction in rural districts not long before the Revolution. In Vladimir guberniya in 1911:

> Near half-forgotten outposts and stations, among tiny hamlets and villages are mushrooming all kinds of workshops and factories, and sometimes whole manufacturing establishments with leviathan-size complexes. And where hitherto not more than a field track was ambling along, through which here and there a single creaking peasant cart might make its rare appearance, [the air] is filled with the din and whistle of many-storied factory buildings, towards which lines of carts are converging from all sides[5]

When an English traveller visited one of these enterprises around 1920 he was struck by the poverty of the soil, the vast brilliant-blue sky and the mill's remote situation, it stood alone on the edge of a forest.[6] Consequently the rhythms of factory and village life developed in syncopation, with long spring and summer breaks to allow workers to return to their fields. Here is a glimpse of Morozov's Nikol'skaia complex at Orekhovo-Zuevo near Moscow just before the Revolution:

> The mill hands of Russia are better fed and healthier than their fellows in England, but this is due to the fact that they live part of the year in their villages ... Between eighty and ninety per cent of the

---

4 Before 1917 peasants often needed off-farm employment to keep their farms going. See P. Mathias, M. Postan, eds., *The Cambridge Economic History of Europe*, vol. 7, part 2 (1978), p. 413; R. E. Johnson, *Peasant and Proletarian. The Working Class of Moscow in the Late Nineteenth Century* (1979), pp. 39–40, 50.
5 Cited in O. Crisp, *Studies in the Russian Economy before 1914* (1976), p. 46.
6 H. N. Brailsford, *The Russian Workers' Republic* (1921), pp. 11–12.

adult male workers own land and cottages in the village commune to
which they are attached, and to which they frequently return.[7]

Bolshevik complaints about pre-revolutionary 'backward' work
practices or over-manning should be seen as another aspect of the
Russian symbiosis: because labour was static, plentiful and cheap,
there was little incentive for entrepreneurs to chase profits by efficiency
drives or expensive capital substitution.[8] On a broader canvas,
although transport networks were weak by European standards –
many mills had no canal link, let alone railway halt – there were plenty
of peasants willing to hire out their carts on a casual basis.[9] 'Nests' of
domestic workers, the persistence of handloom weaving, and the
propensity for members of peasant families to seek work in the mills
have already been mentioned in part I.[10] Old Russia, therefore, already
had a *smychka*, one characterized by deeply embedded economic and
social links. Much of this latticework of interdependence survived into
NEP. Mills still tended to work to the agricultural calendar, thread was
still spun for handloom weavers and domestic workers still fabricated
machine parts.[11] Indeed, because of the depression in heavy industry
in the early 1920s, the number of small local concerns catering for the
cotton industry's needs was probably rising.[12]

In advancing the connected notions of a continuum of workforce
relationships to land and a symbiotic relationship between the mill and
the rural economy there is, of course, a danger of missing tensions and
incompatibilities. In both cases deliberate attacks or accidental dislocations could result in disruption and instability. Much was expected
of the cotton industry in terms of the *smychka*, and the régime soon
came to believe that there would have to be radical changes inside the
mill to appease the hunger for cloth. Moreover, Bolsheviks were not
content to restore and replicate the old world. They wanted to change
it, to 'modernize' Russia. They wanted their workers to be proletarians

---

[7] J. F. Fraser, *Russia of To-day* (1915), pp. 180–81, 187.
[8] A similar point was made by Fedotov at the 'Industrial Party' trial: see p. 262.
[9] Only 20 per cent of mills listed in *Tekstil'nye fabriki SSSR* (1927), had a canal link or
rail-head on site, the remainder were supplied by animal-drawn carts.
[10] See pp. 11, 13–14, 23–4, 27.
[11] *Izvestiia tekstil'noi promyshlennosti i torgovli*, 23–24, December 1927, p. 6 (hereafter
ITPT). When the Rodnikovskaia went over to three shifts in 1928 things went badly
because someone forgot to order more loom weights from local domestic workers: I.
S. Belinskii, A. I. Kucherov, *Tri mesiatsa raboty semichasovykh fabrik. (Opyt perevoda i
raboty semichasovykh fabrik v ivanovo-voznesenskoi gubernii)* (1928), p. 8.
[12] Small-scale metal, wood and leather working all increased in importance in Ivanovo
between 1913 and 1925: *Biulleten' ivanovo-voznesenskogo gubernskogo statisticheskogo
biuro*, 15, 1927, table 14 p. 39; A. Kaufman, *Small-scale Industry in the Soviet Union*
(1962), table A–2 pp. 66–72.

and in the long run they wanted to get rid of the peasants altogether. As strains became evident in NEP measures were taken which menaced the links described above. With speed-ups, rationalization drives and shift changes came increasing pressure for operatives to choose between field and factory. In the second half of the decade domestic workers and small enterprises supplying parts to the mills came under attack from new imported foreign technologies, and more especially from the creation of a home-based engineering sector fabricating machine parts.[13] As will become apparent peasants increased their charges to lodging workers. They were also 'turned against the factory' because mills relied less and less on the casual hiring of peasant carts.[14] Nevertheless, it is worth emphasizing continuum and symbiosis, if only as counterweight to the dysfunctions which historians are inclined to dwell on and as a corrective to the hostile bias of the sources. Looking at the problem this way also raises the possibility that field and factory may have been reaching towards a new accommodation under NEP, but this is not our immediate concern. Instead we will concentrate on the idea of the dual-axis continuum.

Tie with the land and wage dependence

In 1927 the Vysokovskaia mill's factory committee reported thus on the social composition of the enterprise's labour force: 'about 30 per cent of those living in the countryside are old workers, workers who began their careers before 1917. Most have union cards dating from 1917–1918.'[15] Next year *Pravda* published this letter from a Danilovskaia mill hand: 'all the old workers have been in the mill for thirty or forty years, and each family has its own smallholding in the countryside, with which it is intimately concerned'.[16] The latter mill is in central Moscow, about half a mile from what is now the Kursk station, the former in a small settlement in the guberniya's Klinskii district which, in 1923, had only 6,000 inhabitants.[17] Late in the decade a foreigner got into conversation with an operative in the Tsindel's factory barracks, also deep in the city, about a mile from the Kursk

[13] See p. 53.
[14] M. O. Braginskii, *Zhilishchnyi vopros v tekstil'noi promyshlennosti* (1927), p. 10.
[15] Cited N. Semenov, *Litso fabrichnykh rabochikh, prozhivaiushchikh v derevniakh, i politrosvetrabota sredi nikh. Po materialam obsledovaniia rabochikh tekstil'noi promyshlennosti tsentral'no-promyshlennoi oblasti* (1929), p. 11.
[16] *Pravda*, 9 February 1928.
[17] *Trudy tsentral'nogo statisticheskogo upravleniia*, tom XVII, vyp. 1 (1924), table 4 pp. 31–2 (hereafter *1923 census*).

station. While chatting he was busy making a fishing net to use when he returned to his native village.[18] These examples show that the continuum of land and residence was not related in any straight-forward way to length of service in the industry or urbanization; urban-based workers could have an interest in the village just as the rural-based could be part of the established workforce. An investigation carried out late in the decade made just this point: rural-based operatives often had considerable factory experience.[19]

Using Rashin's estimate of 25 per cent as a rough-and-ready guide for the decade gives some indication of how many workers held land. Of the total number of cotton workers listed in chapter 2,[20] 25 per cent comes out as follows: 34,250 (1921), 45,550 (1922), 57,750 (1923), 74,000 (1924), 101,500 (1925), 104,750 (1926), 109,500 (1927), 119,250 (1928) and 124,000 (1929). Of course, if there was some decline in landholding during NEP these estimates are wrong, but in fact Rashin's survey suggests that there was not much change. Excluding Leningrad, even amongst new recruits the percentage of landholders coming into the mill throughout the decade holds up remarkably well. Sharp declines are restricted to the years 1913–17; the 1920s were evidently a period of stabilization with numbers falling by only a couple of percentage points or so.[21] An article in Vesenkha's house journal points in the opposite direction; connection with agriculture rose in the CIR after 1922 and fell back, though not to the pre-1922 level, between 1926 and 1929.[22] Thus it appears from this source that links with agriculture were being strengthened throughout the 1920s, and this is far from unlikely, not least because NEP gave anybody connected with the village a powerful incentive to invest time and effort in the land. More than any other sector of the Russian economy, agriculture benefited from the concession to *laissez faire* methods. In any event the difference between the Vesenkha and Rashin figures can be resolved by looking closely at what kind of questions workers were asked. Rashin's questionnaire asked 'do you have land?'[23] so his respondents would be landholding workers only and thus his figures take no account of any other forms of connection with the village economy. 'Connection with agriculture', Vesenkha's definition, is not the same thing. Some of those turning up in Vesenkha's figures, therefore, were probably

[18] N. Farson, *Seeing Red Today in Russia* (1930), pp. 3–4.
[19] Semenov, *Litso fabrichnykh rabochikh*, p. 53.
[20] See p. 20.   [21] Rashin, *Sostav*, p. 30.   [22] *Puti industrializatsii*, 1, 1930, p. 43.
[23] V. V. Il'inskii, *Ivanovskii tekstil'shchik. Sostav i sotsial'naia kharakteristika rabochikh-tekstil'shchikov ivanovskoi promyshlennoi oblasti* (1930), p. 25.

landless mill hands, workers maintaining other economic links with the countryside.

This brings us back to the continuum, for whatever the exact percentages holding land, rural links remained important right up into NEP. Although the *Cambridge Economic History of Europe* surmises that from as early as the 1880s over 90 per cent of workers in the fifteen largest mills around Ivanovo-Voznesensk were permanent and stable, this is not necessarily evidence of a declining interest in the village. The deterministic assertion that modern technology necessitates continuous production except for a few weeks devoted to overhauling the machinery[24] does not preclude simultaneous agricultural work – the Nikol'skaia's operatives seem to have managed well enough – and there are a whole host of references in the NEP literature to simultaneous working, but the issue is horribly complicated by regional and local variations. In three of the Moscow guberniya mills investigated by Rashin, 11, 4 and 2 per cent of workers held land, but in another five the figure was over 80 per cent. Half the 10,000-odd workers in Iaroslavl's giant Krasnyi Perekop mill had 'close connections' with the countryside in the early 1920s. About one-third of all new operatives hired by Ivanovo State Textile Trust throughout 1924/25 had an active interest in farming, in some other mills in the guberniya the percentages were significantly higher, occasionally over 80 per cent. For the Trekhgornaia (Moscow, opposite the Ukraine hotel) the proportion was two-thirds in 1924.[25] Leningrad can be dealt with quickly. As in so many other ways it was quite different from the other cotton districts. A tiny 4.4 per cent of Rashin's sample, 449 workers, held land in 1929, and there is no evidence that proportions ever approached those apparent in the CIR.[26]

Operatives certainly used the land. In September 1921 workers in Ivanovo guberniya's Iakhromskaia mill were tilling the fields adjacent to their factory. Simultaneously all textile workers were excluded from food ration entitlement. Three years later the Moscow guberniya branch of the textileworkers' union told workers laid off due to the 'concentration of production' to protect themselves by 'temporarily returning to field work'. It is notable that the Iakhromskaia's workers

24 H. J. Habakkuk, M. Postan, eds., *The Cambridge Economic History of Europe*, vol. 6, part 2 (1965), p. 823.

25 *Izmeneniia v chislennosti i sostave*, p. 91; *Otchet o rabote ivanovo-voznesenskogo gubernskogo otdela vsesoiuznogo soiuza tekstil'shchikov za vremia s apr. 1925g–mart 1926g. 16-mu s"ezdu soiuza* (1926), p. 6; Rashin, *Sostav*, p. 26. Workforce total for Krasnyi Perekop from *Tekstil'nye fabriki SSSR* (1927).

26 *ITPT*, 22–23, December 1927, p. 5; *Puti industrializatsii*, 1, 1930, p. 79; Rashin, *Sostav*, pp. 30, 139.

may have envisaged themselves as farmers for rather longer than one season, not only were they cultivating a variety of crops, they were also busy with dairying.[27] Some seven years after this a building intended for oil storage in Kaluga guberniya's Trud mill was being used as a cattle shed[28] – an ironic example of symbiosis.

The union recommendation cited above was good advice. To many workers made sceptical by the disasters of 1914 to 1921 the stabilization engendered by NEP must have seemed precarious, and not without reason. Wages were often in arrears, and a generally accepted currency became available only in 1924.[29] Moreover, any mill was likely to be shut down at any time due to shortages of fuel, raw materials or machine parts, or because of capricious changes in policy, or some sudden catastrophe in the economy at large. Wage dependency on the mill left the workers' family dangerously exposed, so a place on the continuum was a sound form of insurance, far more reliable than the state's work schemes or dole payments.[30] The uncertainties of NEP therefore, together with the influx of new workers from the village and the destruction of the old estates attendant on war and revolution, probably gave a new lease of life to the landed worker in the textile industry.[31] If the regime's benign attitude towards private farming is added to these considerations the case becomes stronger still: by mid-decade agriculture was prospering as never before under socialism.

Statistical evidence for these assertions comes from a study of textile workers around Ivanovo carried out by V. V. Il'inskii and based on Rashin, but Il'inskii's booklet goes into more detail on land usage and breaks down the region's mills into three groups. Group I covered city factories, those in 'more or less significant towns', such as Ivanovo-Voznesensk and Shuia; group II mills in industrial villages; and group III rural-based enterprises. The proportion of workers holding land in 1929 was 5.7, 18.4 and 44.1 per cent respectively for groups I, II and III. Il'inskii thought that the figure for group III was too high and therefore included other connections with the rural economy,[32] but there is

---

[27] Y. S. Borisov et al., Outline History of the Soviet Working Class (1973), pp. 77–9; Otchet o rabote moskovskogo gubernskogo otdela vsesoiuznogo professional'nogo soiuza tekstil'shchikov mai 1923g–mart 1924g (1924), p. 135; Tekstil'shchik, k stanku, 16 September 1921.

[28] Golos tekstilei, 26 May 1928.   [29] See p. 159.

[30] Before 1917 land was often regarded as a form of social insurance. See T. von Laue, 'Russian peasants in the factory, 1892–1904', Journal of Economic History, 20, 1, 1961, pp. 61–80.

[31] Post-1917 redistributions encouraged workers to return to their villages to claim a share in the land. See G. Yaney, The Urge to Mobilize. Agrarian Reform in Russia, 1861–1930 (1982), pp. 469–75.

[32] Il'inskii, Ivanovskii tekstil'shchik, pp. 9, 25.

Table 1. *Sources of labour on cotton workers' land 1929*

	Percentage of all landed with arable land	Of them, percentage using:			
		Own and family labour	Own and non-family labour	Non-family labour only	None of these
Moscow	93.8	84.8	13.0	2.1	1.1
Moscow district	77.6	78.2	19.3	0.7	1.8
Ivanovo district	90.3	81.8	16.1	1.2	0.8

Source: A. G. Rashin, *Sostav fabrichno-zavodskogo proletariata SSSR* (1930), p. 43

no reason to accept this reservation; averaged out, groups, I, II and III come to 22.7 per cent, in effect Rashin's estimate. Matiugin, writing of the period 1921–25, categorizes operatives in much the same way.[33] If Il'inskii's and Matiugin's estimates are combined there is evidence of a very strong landed presence in all but 'significant' towns and a remarkably intensive utilization of land across mill groups.[34] Il'inskii's group differentiations also support the common-sense assumption that landholding was unevenly distributed throughout the labour force; those in metropolitan districts (Leningrad, Moscow) the least likely to hold land, those in provincial centres or small towns rather more likely, those in the countryside exhibiting the greatest degree of attachment. But even the small numbers in Ivanovo's group I mills were actively farming; right up to 1929 the local press carried regular advertisements placed by private nurseries raising seed for crops, fruit trees and vegetables.[35] That intensive land use was the case generally in the CIR becomes even more clear from an examination of Rashin's sample. Again, excluding Leningrad's insignificant number, the landed were not leasing their fields or leaving agricultural work to other kin. Instead they were engaged in cultivation with their family, and to a lesser but somewhat surprising extent, they used labour drawn in some way from outside the family (see table 1).[36] Moreover,

[33] *Izmeneniia v chislennosti i sostave*, p. 93.
[34] Il'inskii, *Ivanovskii tekstil'shchik*, pp. 28–30.
[35] See the back page of *Rabochii krai* for 1929.
[36] Legal confirmation of the right to lease land and hire labour came in 1922–23: E. H. Carr, *The Bolshevik Revolution 1917–1923*, vol. 2 (1966), pp. 289, 296–7; O. A. Narkie-

most were tax-payers; over 80 per cent of the CIR landed in all Rashin's and Il'inskii's categories. Finally, the landed were not drawn exclusively from peasant backgrounds, nor were they particularly young.[37] It is therefore possible to deduce inheritance inside established worker families and there is additional evidence to suggest that long-serving workers were holding on to their land in the 1920s.

In 1928 *Golos tekstilei* castigated those who came into the mills 'thinking most of all of their own business, of buying a horse, etc.' Six years previously Ivanovo's local branch recognized that for many operatives, who were also domestic workers or peasants, factory labour was merely an additional source of income. Union officials in Vladimir guberniya lamented the fact that too many workers were 'temporary guests in the mill', as did *Rabochii krai*, Ivanovo's local paper, in 1927: 'many of these semi-peasants or semi-proletarians regard production as temporary, auxiliary work for wages'. In 1926 the syndicate's journal blamed falling productivity on those connected with land 'who arrive for work at the mill exhausted'.[38] At the end of the decade a wide-ranging sociological investigation elaborated the point with reference to CIR mills:

> a significant fall in output during the summer months is the normal seasonal phenomenon in our mills, and this is partly explained by the fact that workers with an interest in the peasant economy, in our mills more than fifty per cent of the total, reduce their output in the summer months. They come straight from the fields where they've been working ... usually two to three hours before dawn and the start of the morning shift ... You can see them in the shops making tea, 'I'm so tired, I come here to rest, not to work'.[39]

There is little doubt that these workers should be subsumed under the optic 'landed'. They represent what, for want of a better term, could be called the 'kulak-end' of our wage-dependence continuum, workers least dependent on wages.

It is far less easy to get a grip on mill hands who had more tenuous links with the village, those for whom agriculture came a poor second

---

wicz, *The Making of the Soviet State Apparatus* (1970), p. 49. Before the war many CIR cotton workers kept livestock in their homesteads close to the mill: V. A. Kungurtsev, *Tekstil'naia promyshlennost' SSSR* (1957), p. 23.

[37] Il'inskii, *Ivanovskii tekstil'shchik*, p. 31; Rashin, *Sostav*, pp. 44–5. 31 per cent of Rashin's landholders came from worker backgrounds. 38 per cent were younger than twenty-nine, 47 per cent older than forty: *ibid.*, pp. 35–6.

[38] *Golos tekstilei*, 17 November 1928; *ITPT*, 3, 23 January 1926, p. 10; *Rabochii krai*, 25 June 1922; 22 June 1927; *Rezoliutsii i postanovleniia (8-go) vladimirskogo gubernskogo s"ezda soiuza tekstil'shchikov, 13–18 dek. 1925g* (1925), p. 13.

[39] Semenov, *Litso fabrichnykh rabochikh*, pp. 44–5.

to wage labour. They certainly existed but it is impossible to estimate their numbers. Instead, the existence of the continuum's 'mill-end' has to be deduced from scattered, incidental references to off-mill working. In 1923, for example, the textileworkers' union central committee noted that in some places where the scissors crisis had resulted in shut-downs 'the majority of established long-service workers now unemployed have some connection with agriculture'.[40] The 1926 census recorded 24,000 cotton workers for whom wage labour was the main, but not the only source of money income.[41] Next year a survey found that amongst textileworker families in Vladimir guberniya where the woman was the main bread-winner 'the peasant economy' was less important than the shop floor.[42] Another investigator thought that throughout the decade following the October Revolution the majority of operatives in Ivanovo's cotton factories simultaneously engaged in non-industrial pursuits looked to the mill as their primary source of money income.[43]

Nevertheless, even amongst such mill-end workers village ties could still be very strong. Speaking at the fourteenth party congress in December 1925 Tomsky complained about commitment to industry. Specifically referring to the Ivanovo district he continued, 'most new workers are pure peasants ... young peasant girls ... These new workers consider themselves to be temporary guests in the factories. At weekends they go home to the countryside and return the following Monday', often 'with a sack, in which they carry bread, potatoes and other foodstuffs for the week'.[44] Although these young girls were almost certainly landless they helped to strengthen the *smychka* between mill and village. Through such channels information about housing and work opportunities could be conveyed to the general mill population, and vice versa. In 1923, for instance, *Rabochii krai* mentioned that operatives in one of the region's mills commonly worked for local peasants during the summer shut-down, even when they were 'pure proletarians'. And when in 1928 the chairman of another mill's factory committee called a general meeting to declare that the enterprise would be shutting for a month because there were no raw materials, workers 'greeted the announcement with general

[40] *Rezoliutsii 3-go plenuma TsK soiuza tekstil'shchikov (12–15 aprelia 1923g)* (1923), pp. 59–60. For the scissors crisis see chapter 7.
[41] L. I. Vas'kina, *Rabochii klass SSSR nakanune sotsialisticheskoi industrializatsii. (Chislennost', sostav, razmeshchenie)* (1981), p. 119.
[42] *Bol'shevik*, 4, 15 February 1927, p. 42.
[43] *Ivanovo-Voznesenskaia guberniia za desiat' let oktiabr'skoi revoliutsii (1917–1927gg)* (1927), p. 47.
[44] *Golos tekstilei*, 8 January 1926.

applause'. Questioned afterwards, they said they were pleased because they would get half pay while working on the land.[45] A writer in the syndicate's journal doubtless spoke from experience when he stated quite bluntly that it was futile to try to keep CIR workers on the shop floor during the summer months and went on to urge trusts and managers to work in harmony with the rhythms of village life.[46]

Residence patterns and time dependence

Population growth and economic recovery were the prime factors influencing throughout the 1920s.[47] The population of the Russian Federation, the heartland of the cotton industry, grew by 6.8 per cent between 1914 and 1926. In general this was probably the result of a rise in the birth rate, but in towns, where numbers rose by five million from 1923 to 1926, two-thirds of the increase was due to rural immigration; peasants were flooding into the towns in search of work.[48] The 1926 census provides a useful starting point for a more detailed discussion of cotton workers' residence patterns. The census grouped operatives into three residential categories: those living in provincial capitals, those in other towns, and those in the countryside. Averaging out the figures for the main CIR cotton guberniyas (Moscow, Ivanovo, Vladimir, Iaroslavl' and Tver') reveals that about 34 per cent lived in provincial capitals, 43 per cent in other towns and 23 per cent in the countryside.[49]

Urban areas (proximate to urban-based mills) and factory barracks represent the 'mill end' of the housing continuum. Crippled by years of neglect they were ill-equipped to deal with the problems raised by the contagion of numbers.[50] During the Revolution people tended to seize property close to their work, but under War Communism, where everybody was responsible, nobody was responsible; abandoned dwellings quickly decayed and appropriated housing fell into disrepair. In line with the general ethos of NEP public indifference gave ground to private virtue, but in ways which were of little benefit to

---

[45] *Rabochii krai*, 21 July 1923; Semenov, *Litso fabrichnykh rabochikh*, p. 45.

[46] *ITPT*, 22–23, December 1927, pp. 4–6.

[47] Braginskii, *Zhilishchnyi vopros*, p. 3.

[48] A. A. Matiugin, *Rabochii klass SSSR v gody vosstanovleniia narodnogo khoziaistva (1921–1925gg)* (1962), p. 227; *Ten Years of Soviet Power in Figures, 1917–1927* (n.d.), p. 32.

[49] *Vsesoiuznaia perepis' naseleniia 1926 goda*, tom XIX (1929), table 4 pp. 124, 415, 427, 438, 512, 547.

[50] For overcrowding in Moscow in 1923 see L. Lawton, *The Russian Revolution 1917–1926* (1927), p. 276.

workers. Although about one-quarter of Moscow's and Leningrad's housing stock had been demunicipalized by 1924 local soviets often let *en bloc* to the unscrupulous and shared in the high rents subsequently charged.[51] But it was not only the two capitals that suffered from overcrowding and rack-renting. As the dispersed drifted home and the dispossessed left the wreckage of their former lives in search of work, old regional centres reasserted their influence. Many of these ancient towns – Serpukhov is a prime example – owed much of their nineteenth-century growth to cotton. The rapid and early recovery of the industry, therefore, led to astonishing population surges in established textile centres.[52] Newspaper revelations about conditions in and around these areas strike one with all the force of the British Parliamentary Blue Books of a century or so earlier.[53] Mill barracks acted like clearing houses for disease; even industrial illnesses specific to particular shops were generalized throughout the factory population.[54] Iaroslavl's biggest mill had 12,000 workers and their families crammed into two blocks in 1926; in the same year both were flooded out and needed extensive repair. Six years earlier the same factory had been ravaged by a typhoid epidemic.[55] Further south in Vladimir guberniya one-quarter of all workers in the Sokolovskaia mill had malaria in 1921. In the Karabanovskii Combine half the children had tuberculosis or malaria. In both cases insanitary housing was blamed. 'We have more sick than healthy people', commented the province's representative to the textileworkers' union central committee in 1925, 'two-thirds of our young workers are ill'.[56]

Although most trusts had organized housing co-operatives by mid-decade, all areas continued to complain about the acute shortage

---

51 *Ibid.*, p. 272; *Russia: the Official Report of the British Trades Union Delegation to Russia and Caucasia. November and December 1924* (1925), p. 129; *Trud*, 13 June 1923.

52 For towns with a significant cotton presence growth rates between 1920 and 1926 were as follows: Leningrad, 128.6 per cent; Serpukhov, 100 per cent; Moscow, 97 per cent; Orekhovo-Zuevo, 96.8 per cent; Ivanovo-Voznesensk, 91.3 per cent; Vladimir, 73.9 per cent; Tver', 66.1 per cent; Iaroslavl', 56.1 per cent; Kostroma, 54.1 per cent and Smolensk, 38.5 per cent. Calculated from C. D. Harris, *Cities of the Soviet Union. Studies in their Functions, Size, Density, and Growth* (1970), table 27 pp. 256–7. Even though much of this marked recovery – repopulation – the point remains that the housing stock had decayed.

53 See for example *Golos tekstilei*, 2 February 1926; 23 February 1926; *Pravda*, 9 February 1928; *Trud*, 17 March 1928.

54 *Nashe khoziaistvo* (Tver'), 7–8, July–August 1925, p. 21.

55 *'Krasnyi Perekop.' Priadil'no-tkatskaia fabrika v Iaroslavle. Proizvodstvennyi al'bom* (1926), p. 34; 'Obzor arkhivnykh materialov po istorii fabriki "Krasnyi Perekop" (1722–1929gg)', *Krasnyi arkhiv*, 63, 1934, pp. 106–23.

56 *Golos tekstilei*, 20 November 1925; *Tekstil'shchik, k stanku*, 30 July 1921; 16 September 1921.

of decent living space near to their mills.[57] But it was not just economic recovery and population growth which made life difficult – three other factors intervened to complicate matters. The first of these was the social disorientation occasioned by revolution and civil war. At the start of NEP many people living in mill accommodation had nothing whatsoever to do with the industry – they had simply got hold of housing somehow or other over the previous few years.[58] In some areas social dislocation led to systematic discrimination as factories struggled to cope with the housing crisis. By 1928 an 'unwritten law' had evolved in Vladimir guberniya: working men with unskilled partners or housewives were allocated living space, but not working women with husbands outside the industry. In another district youngsters bore the brunt of discrimination, receiving 'the least desirable corners of rooms'.[59] Secondly, policy decisions taken in Moscow often had unintended results which made things worse: a case in point was the response of Ivanovo's trusts to the government's 1926 'regime of economy'. Forced to save money, administrators decided to cut the housing budget.[60] Finally, the defensive reflexes of local communities played a part in exacerbating the overall situation for individuals and families caught in particular localities: when a mill in Iuzha (Ivanovo guberniya) temporarily closed in 1923, workers who went to Sereda in search of work were told that there were no spaces for them in the factory barracks, even though at that time there were. Somewhat later a large mill in Rodniki was reluctant to house 600 temporarily unemployed Iuzha operatives, who subsequently complained that factory committees and local union officials were unhelpful and hostile.[61]

If there were acute problems towards the continuum's mill end – that is, in towns and factory barracks – a few examples will show how 'village-end' operatives were physically distanced from their factories. In 1922 half the operatives near Shchelkovo, Moscow guberniya, lived with local peasants.[62] Three years later a similar proportion were found to be living more than two miles distant from their place of work in Ivanovo guberniya,[63] though in some districts, like Rodniki, the proportion rose to three-quarters.[64] A year after this more than half the operatives in a Moscow guberniya mill lived over three miles distant

---

[57] *ITPT*, 23, 10 July 1925, p. 9.   [58] *Tekstil'shchik, k stanku*, 20 May 1921.
[59] *Golos tekstilei*, 9 February 1928; *Komsomol'skaia pravda*, 28 February 1928.
[60] *Trud*, 17 December 1926.
[61] *Golos tekstilei*, 18 July 1924; *Rabochii krai*, 28 August 1923.
[62] *Tekstil'shchik, k stanku*, 25 June 1922.   [63] Braginskii, *Zhilishchnyi vopros*, pp. 9–10.
[64] *Kommunistka*, 8, August 1925, pp. 55–6.

Table 2. *Residence patterns of rural-dwelling textile workers, Vladimir guberniya 1925–6*

Data covering 24,869 rural-dwelling operatives from 31 mills		
Distance from mills in km	Number of villages in each distance group	As % of total number of villages
Less than 1	68	6.7
1–3	169	16.6
3–5	252	24.6
5–10	293	28.8
More than 10	235	23.1

Source: N. Semenov, *Litso fabrichnykh rabochikh, prozhivaiushchikh v derevniakh, i politrosvetrabota sredi nikh. Po materialam obsledovaniia rabochikh tekstil'noi promyshlennosti tsentral'no-promyshlennoi oblasti* (1929), pp. 12–13

from their work, and one-third of the 53,000 employed in thirty-one Vladimir guberniya mills were commuting seven miles to their shops.[65] A more detailed breakdown of the figures from this source shown in table 2 reveals just how complex the symbiosis between field and factory could be. Elsewhere the very success of individual mills in recovering from economic collapse created problems; in the Ramenskaia, a large factory in Moscow guberniya, many had to travel seven to ten miles to work in 1926. Two years later it was not uncommon for these workers to travel thirteen miles every day.[66] Another survey found that in 1926/27 about 40 per cent of textile hands in the Ivanovo, Vladimir and Moscow guberniyas were rural residents.[67] Of those in Vladimir, only one-third were in the countryside because they held land. For this guberniya alone 70 per cent of the workforce from forty-five mills were housed in rural districts.[68] That same year the central committee of the textileworkers' union calculated that one-third of its entire membership were rural dwellers.[69] Finally, in another survey conducted in 1927, 4,344 workers – that is, half the total for eight textile and three metal factories in Vladimir guberniya – were drawn from 136 villages. The author of this survey

[65] Semenov, *Litso fabrichnykh rabochikh*, pp. 12–13.
[66] *Golos tekstilei*, 2 February 1926; 16 March 1926; 9 October 1926; *Trud*, 1 August 1928.
[67] Braginskii, *Zhilishchnyi vopros*, p. 11; Semenov, *Litso fabrichnykh rabochikh*, p. 10.
[68] *ITPT*, 22–23, December 1927, p. 5; *Bol'shevik*, 4, 15 February 1927, pp. 42–3.
[69] *Golos tekstilei*, 5 March 1927.

thought that the sample was typical of the province as a whole.[72] *Golos tekstilei's* 1926 assertion that 'many workers are obliged to live with the peasantry, several versts away from their mills',[71] only reinforces the point.

Once more it will be appreciated that in the CIR, although not in Leningrad, field and factory were not sharply differentiated one from the other, but even in the old capital continuum lineations can be detected; the local union branch found that the housing crisis was pushing its members out and away from their mills.[73] It is possible, therefore, that in metropolitan districts some mills' residential catchment areas were expanding, but if we turn our attention to changing catchment areas in the CIR the position is more complex. Here sources on housing costs provide a clue. Operatives living in private accommodation close to Sereda's mills paid 30 to 40 per cent of their wages in rent in 1926; 'free' flats around one mill, complained workers, cost ten to fifteen roubles a month. Rent inflation was a specific grievance of Rodniki's workers in 1926, and in the Drezna, a Moscow guberniya mill where most operatives lived with local peasants, workers paid twelve roubles a month in 1928 'for the right to place a mattress on the floor' compared with six roubles a year previously.[73]

At first glance it might seem that much of this was caused by immigration. As outsiders found jobs in the industry rents would tend to rise, but in fact pressure on rented accommodation appears to have been partially offset by increasing home ownership amongst these new workers. Whereas in 1924 just under one-quarter of all members of the union owned a house, next year over one-third of new entrants, the majority of them living in the countryside, were house owners. The union drew the obvious conclusion that home ownership was increasing, but it is inconceivable that textile workers were buying property in significant numbers. Rather, new workers from peasant backgrounds and with houses were inflating the total number of house owners. The rest were already renting or had to find rooms as best they could. And though peasants were increasing their rents, this does not seem to have been in response to rising demand alone; in the second half of the decade the union's central committee worried about the constantly widening financial gap between those in mill barracks

---

[70] *Bol'shevik*, 4, 15 February 1927, pp. 41, 43. Housing for Vladimir guberniya's mill workers was particularly bad in the second half of the decade. See E. H. Carr, R. W. Davies, *Foundations of a Planned Economy*, vol. 1, part 2 (1969), p. 615.

[71] *Golos tekstilei*, 2 February 1926.   [72] *Leningradskii tekstil'shchik*, 2 February 1926.

[73] *Golos tekstilei*, 2 February 1926; 23 February 1926; 16 March 1926; 6 April 1928.

and workers in rented accommodation. They concluded that rents were rising partly because of the success of NEP – because the 'material position of the peasantry has improved . . . they do not need to let out housing space'.[74]

Before the Revolution large rural-based mills sometimes developed as fully-fledged industrial communities.[75] Take for example J. F. Fraser's observations on Morozov's Nikol'skaia, again around 1915:

> The population of 22,000 living on the firm's property have lodging, lighting and heating provided free, whilst the workpeople who live in their own villages, four, five or six versts away and cycle to and fro, get a monthly sum in lieu of lodging . . . There are almshouses for old people, or if they go back to their villages they are pensioned.

In addition the complex had three hospitals, two schools with more than forty teachers, a kindergarten, compulsory insurance schemes, parks and picnic areas, theatres and amateur dramatic societies, athletic clubs, reading rooms, lecture halls, one brass band, two string bands and four choirs.[76] Even provincial centres do not seem to have had this range of amenities;[77] Ivanovo-Voznesensk was little more than an overgrown village surrounded by cotton mills:

> Half of Ivanovo is 'old Russian' small town pure and simple. It has long, wide streets, each independent of all others and like a village mainstreet. Most . . . have no roadway, but a wide, unbroken lawn that separates the two lines of houses one from another . . . Its houses are single-storied wooden houses . . . standing back from the grass centre-walk behind wooden gates and palings. Down most such streets one might be in a small primaeval village of a couple of hundred inhabitants.

This was in the early thirties, when the town had over 200,000 inhabitants. The other half, the suburbs, was swallowed up by mills.[78] There was no mains water supply until 1925 and no trams or buses until the following decade.[79] Iuzha was a typical industrial settlement; thirty-three miles from the nearest railway halt and forty miles from the nearest town, Shuia, which in 1923 had only 26,000 inhabitants

---

[74] Braginskii, *Zhilishchnyi vopros*, pp. 10–11.
[75] See Kungurtsev, *Tekstil'naia promyshlennost'*, p. 25; T. von Laue, 'Russian labor between field and factory, 1892–1903', *California Slavic Studies*, 3, 1964, p. 62; M. S. Miller, *The Economic Development of Russia, 1905–1914* (1926), p. 251; R. M. Odell, *Cotton Goods in Russia* (1912), p. 12.
[76] Fraser, *Russia*, pp. 184–6. It was not unusual for workers to retire back to their villages: Mathias, Postan, *Cambridge Economic History of Europe*, 7, 2, p. 367.
[77] See Johnson, *Peasant and Proletarian*, chapters 3, 4.
[78] H. Griffith, *Seeing Soviet Russia* (1932), pp. 132–3.
[79] Iu. F. Glebov, T. N. Letukov, *Ivanovo* (1981), pp. 25, 29.

and 5,500 houses. Cold in winter, hot and dusty in summer, there was no centre apart from the Iuzhskaia, surrounded by the workers' barracks 'like an ocean around the island of the mill'. Iuzha had a population of just under 10,000 in 1923. Four years later the mill housed 2,000 workers and 3,500 family members, but a further 1,500-odd lived in the countryside.[80]

By the 1920s the Nikol'skaia must have been very different and much more like the Iuzhskaia. It is hard to imagine that the paternalistic benefits, which mimicked urban life and were enjoyed by Morozov's workers, survived the Revolution. It is in such circumstances that the resonance of 'tie with the land' set alarm bells ringing in the minds of official commentators. New workers coming onto the shop floor around mid-decade after recovery had soaked up existing unemployment, or in 1928 when some rural mills went over to three-shift working, were 'dark people', easily led astray by class enemies. Their 'class consciousness' was 'low'. They were connected with 'the mood of the countryside' and their presence in the shops caused a 'decline in the social composition of the workforce'.[81] One trade union activist called them 'ballast', and asked rhetorically why they should be allowed to vote in factory committee elections. Another, at the 1922 twentieth Vladimir guberniya party conference, was equally dismissive: 'I consider that this group of workers takes no part in the life of the union, the party, or the factory. They simply work for eight hours a day.'[82] The central committee of the union expressed its worries in rather more measured tones in a 1926 circular: 'a characteristic peculiarity of our union is that the majority of our mills are situated in rural areas, and thus a significant number of union members do not live by their mills, but in nearby villages or in the countryside'. It was hoped that they could be orientated towards the regime's goals by bringing them into close contact with formal institutions, but unfortunately 'at the end of the working day these workers leave the factory's vicinity, and thus are not under the influence of the union'.[83]

If those possessing land were the most secure because they were not completely wage dependent, those with a house were equally

---

[80] *Rabochii krai*, 12 July 1923; 12 June 1927; *1923 census*, table 4 pp. 27–8.
[81] *Golos tekstilei*, 4 October 1926; 17 November 1928; *Otchet TsK vsesoiuznogo professional'nogo soiuza tekstil'shchikov k 7-mu vsesoiuznomu s"ezdu tekstil'shchikov. Iiul' 1924g–ianv. 1926g* (1926), p. 3; *Puti industrializatsii*, 1, 1930, p. 43.
[82] Cited Semenov, *Litso fabrichnykh rabochikh*, pp. 41–2, 57.
[83] *Informatsionnaia svodka TsK vsesoiuznogo profsoiuza tekstil'shchikov*, 8(20), 5 October 1926, p. 6.

fortunate because they were free of urban overcrowding, factory rookeries or rack-renting peasants. Indeed, the industry sometimes unwittingly encouraged workers to add a rural dimension to their lives; no plans were made to provide workers with barracks when Vladimir guberniya's Lakin mill underwent major repair in 1926,[84] so local peasants with their own houses and not unemployed workers from other districts, would be likely to take on the new jobs, thus strengthening the links between field and factory. But a place on the continuum contained a latent penalty clause, one far more worrying than the disapproval of the party or the union. When the Iuzhskaia temporarily closed many workers were simply left stranded in their villages.[85] Regardless of whether they were 'proletarians' renting a room or 'peasants' using the mill to earn extra money their response would probably be the same; unemployment followed by a review of sources of off-mill income and more concentration on field work. They would surely be hesitant about giving up their auxiliary work when the enterprise reopened. Similarly the strains attendant on rationalization and speed-ups, common after 1924, could be severe. Many people, complained Golos tekstilei in spring 1925, 'come into the mill to rest. Having laboured for eight hours at home and walked four or five miles to the factory, they are not fit for work. Some do a double shift and take the following day off ... After twelve hours their attention wanders from the machine and they begin to nod off'.[86] Be they 'peasants' or 'proletarians' the new emphasis on time-work discipline obviously created real difficulties. Three years later Moscow began to panic over falling grain deliveries. Consequently, in an attempt to maintain market equilibrium and strengthen the official smychka, some rural mills were hurriedly switched to seven-hour/three-shift working. This led to 'a struggle amongst the workers'; some living far from their mills wanted continuous shifts, others living nearby were willing to accept split shifts.[87] Once more these divisions cannot be subsumed under the nostrum 'tie with the land': those distant from the factory – again, be they 'peasants' or 'proletarians' – shared a common problem of time-dependency, whereas operative-farmers and wage labourers living close by did not.

Thus when the regime began to blunder into the intricate symbiosis of field and factory cotton operatives were not very likely to divide along simple fault lines – 'backward' peasant-workers versus 'pro-

---

[84] Golos tekstilei, 2 October 1926. [85] Rabochii krai, 12 July 1923.
[86] Golos tekstilei, 19 May 1925. See also chapter 10.
[87] Sputnik agitatora, 6, March 1928, p. 27. See also chapter 12.

gressive' proletarians. Instead, fissures should be expected to run in crooked, and in terms of a notional peasant/worker polarization, seemingly random directions. The predispositions latent in the complex interaction of land, residence and mill became manifest when change was imposed on the industry, but workers' responses depended partly on mill location, partly on the range of continuum gradations and partly on the type of change introduced.

4 Machines and trades

> The policy ... of engaging Englishmen as managers and using English methods in the mills, is a striking feature of the industry to-day ... Many of the mills I visited were like English mills transferred to Russian soil.
>
> R. M. Odell reporting to the American Secretary of State for Commerce and Labor in 1912

The technological context

According to a Russian textile engineer the equipment in a standard 80,000-spindle cotton spinning mill in the 1920s was as listed in table 3. The end process, fine spinning, which produced thread for weaving or sewing, was carried out either by the 'continuous' method using ring-frames, or the older 'intermittent' method using selfactors. The balance between the two techniques differed between trusts and mills. Generally speaking, Leningrad's pre-revolutionary entrepreneurs had shown more willingness to buy ring-frames than had the more conservative-minded CIR cotton magnates,[1] and taking the country as a whole in October 1928 about one-third of the active spindle stock was on selfactors, the rest on ring-frames.[2] Weaving sheds sometimes existed as separate enterprises or were included in large manufactories or combines. Here wide technical differences were common. In mid-decade, for example, Ivanovo guberniya's Bol'shaia Kokhomskaia's sheds housed 1,260 looms; they were of two types, Lancashire and Jacquard, but there were sub-divisions within these categories.[3] Depending on the scale of production mills might

[1] See O. Crisp, *Studies in the Russian Economy before 1914* (1976), p. 47; R. E. Johnson, *Peasant and Proletarian. The Working Class of Moscow in the Late Nineteenth Century* (1979), chapter 1.
[2] *Planovoe khoziastvo*, 10, October 1928, p. 304.
[3] *Bol'shaia Kokhomskaia tekstil'naia manufaktura. Proizvodstvennyi al'bom 1925g* (1925), p. 24.

Table 3. *Machinery in a typical Soviet cotton-spinning mill 1924*

Initial processing rooms	
Cotton bale opener	1
Scutching machines – first	2
– second	2
Carding machines	90
Preparatory departments	
Drawing frames	48
Flyer frames – slubbing	580 spindles
– intermediate	2,000 spindles
– fine	8,000 spindles
Fine spinning halls	
Selfactors and ring-frames	80,000 spindles

Source: V. I. Feoktistov, *Ekskursiia na bumagopriadil'nuiu fabriku* (1924), p. 18

also have had auxiliary sections, and there were also variations if they specialized in a particular cotton count (thread thickness) or cloth type.[4]

There was nothing particularly 'Russian' about this arrangement. The basic mill design – a central engine house and multi-storey building with belt-drive power transmission – came from Britain.[5] 'At the time of the October Revolution', claimed the president of Leningrad's textile trust in 1925, with some exaggeration, 'the industry was dominated by England ... almost all Leningrad's textile production was owned by Englishmen ... ninety per cent of engineers and foremen were English'.[6] British influence was not confined to the capital. The Morozovs installed James Charnock as manager and partner at the Nikol'skaia and initially all the machinery came from Hetherington's of Manchester.[7] Reviewing the origins of work organization in Russia's mills in general a specialist noted that 'Englishmen played a big part in establishing many of our spinning and weaving

[4] D. D. Budanov, *Obshchie poniatiia o NOT'e v chastnosti v tekstil'noi promyshlennosti* (1926), p. 72.

[5] S. I. Krichevskii, *Sbornik lektsii chitannykh na proizvodstvenno-ekonomicheskikh kursakh pri TsK soiuza tekstil'shchikov*, vyp. 3 (1926), p. 9; M. S. Miller, *The Economic Development of Russia, 1905–1914* (1926), p. 250.

[6] *Golos tekstilei*, 2 June 1925. Only seven of the city's twenty-nine mills had Russians as their major shareholders in 1914 and all mills spun high counts from Egyptian cotton, invariably on British frames: A. M. Korneev, *Tekstil'naia promyshlennost' SSSR i puti ee razvitiia* (1957), pp. 27–8.

[7] J. F. Fraser, *Russia of To-day* (1915), pp. 179, 182–3.

factories. Not only was the machinery from Britain, the organizational form was also British'. He went on to write that this was 'still so' in 1926.[8]

That the Empire's cotton kings looked to Britain for their equipment is not in doubt.[9] Domestic production before the Revolution was insignificant and Soviet attempts to create a base for machine manufacture hesitant.[10] By mid-decade about eleven factories made parts, but a determined effort to build complete frames began only in 1926. Even then enterprises continued to rely on Britain for parts and fittings for final assembly;[11] in spite of a rather defensive claim by *Golos tekstilei* that parts made in Tula or Leningrad were 'no worse' than those from England, native equipment was thought to be too expensive and of indifferent quality.[12] Imports increased after mid-decade but were still limited in comparison with pre-war times.[13] This did not prevent trusts from reverting to their traditional suppliers when they undertook major repairs or extensions (the new corpus of Moscow guberniya's Glukhovskaia mill, for example, completed in 1928/29, was fitted out by the Lancashire firms Platt and Saco-Lowell) nor did it stop brand new mills from looking overseas. Krasnaia Talka, the first new Soviet cotton mill, purchased its machines from England.[14]

A. A. Nol'de, engineer, specialist, and a frequent commentator on the textile industry, advised mills with equipment that was so old that parts were no longer available not to waste time by stopping frames when matters could be solved by stripping other machines.[15] Elsewhere he put the issue in its historical context: 'the majority of Russian mills grew slowly from small spinning rooms or weaving sheds. As the years passed new extensions were added and new machines installed, but old buildings and equipment continued to function alongside the new. Many mills thus resemble museums of

[8] *Izvestiia tekstil'noi promyshlennosti i torgovli*, 33–34, 15 September 1926, p. 1 (hereafter *ITPT*).

[9] *Tekstil'nye novosti*, 8–9, August–September, 1929, p. 453.

[10] *Golos tekstilei*, 13 January 1925; 20 November 1925; 9 October 1926; A. A. Matiugin, *Rabochii klass SSSR v gody vosstanovleniia narodnogo khoziaistva (1921–1925gg)* (1962), p. 204.

[11] *ITPT*, 3, 23 January 1926, p. 21; *Leningradskie rabochie v bor'be za sotsializma. 1926–1937gg* (1965), p. 28; *Tekstil'nye novosti*, 8–9, August-September 1929, p. 454.

[12] *Ekonomicheskoe obozrenie*, March 1926, pp. 67–71; *Golos tekstilei*, 18 June 1924.

[13] See A. C. Sutton, *Western Technology and Soviet Economic Development*, vol. 1 (1968), p. 227.

[14] A. Pis'mennyi, *Na Glukhovke za 20 let. Glukhovskii khlopchatobumazhnyi kombinat im. V. I. Lenina* (1937), pp. 31–3; *Trud*, 8 September 1928.

[15] A. A. Nol'de, *NOT v tekstil'noi promyshlennosti* (1924), p. 11.

Plate 1 British influence in Russian mills. Left to right; the Anisimov, Nikol'skaia, Krasnyi Tekstil'shchik and Savinskaia mills, from Hetherington's catalogues for 1906 and 1931

Plate 2 British influence in Russian mills. Left to right; the Khalturin, Vozhd' Proletariata, Nogin and Kutuzov mills, from Howard and Bullough's catalogue for 1925.

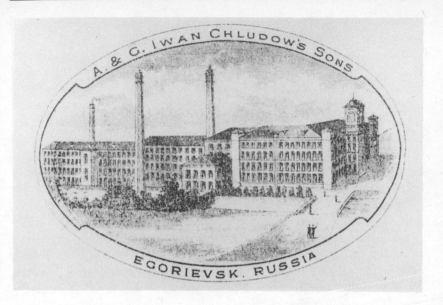

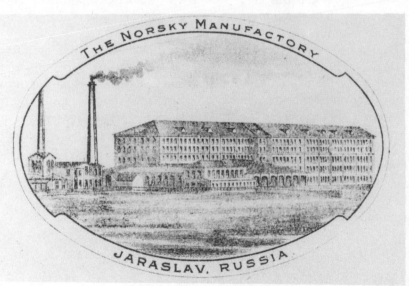

the textile industry spread over many years.'[16] Iaroslavl's biggest mill was a case in point; founded in 1722 and enlarged piecemeal in 1861, 1878 and 1882, it 'violated the elementary rules of the rational distribution of equipment'.[17] The mill is still there today. A short history of Moscow guberniya's Reutovskaia published in 1928 includes a fold-out plan showing old and new buildings in which selfactors and ring-frames were sometimes in separate rooms and sometimes jumbled together, and in another mill in Ivanovo-Voznesensk a plethora of spinning and weaving frames were mixed in on the same floors, and even in the same rooms.[18] *Rabkrin* (the Workers' and Peasants' Inspectorate) lamented the 'abnormal distribution of machinery' in the industry at large in 1926, but nothing had changed four years later; mills still had 'in one and the same shop machines of various construction, speed and age'.[19] If anything the limited market policies of NEP encouraged technological idiosyncrasy and localism: frames offered for sale by the Karl Marks enterprise in 1926, for instance, could not be manufactured to one standard pattern. A Vesenkha commission noted this curious fact with dismay; 'separatism' arose because trusts insisted on introducing design variations at the behest of particular mills.[20]

The consequences of eclectic capital purchases, technological idiosyncrasy and the gradual accumulation of worn-out machinery were predictable; the extraordinary technological diversity apparent in the industry frustrated managers and technicians who wanted to reform the production process. 'Methods of work in various trusts and even within enterprises of the same trust are quite different', asserted a weaving engineer; in general 'each mill established its own technical norms', observed Nol'de, 'depending on particular circumstances'.[21] Systematic accounting and control over work on the shop floor was thus a real problem for specialists like the weaving engineer A. Abramov:

> The factory shop consists of a collection of operatives engaged in the same work. It is the basic production unit of the mill, and thus it

[16] L. Ia. Shukhgal'ter, ed., *Vnutrizavodskii kontrol' kachestva. Sbornik statei i instruktsii* (1927), p. 5.

[17] 'Krasnyi Perekop.' *Priadil'no-tkatskaia fabrika v Iaroslavle. Proizvodstvennyi al'bom* (1926), *passim*.

[18] M. B. Itsikson, *Reutovskaia priadil'naia fabrika. Ocherk* (1928), pp. 12–13.

[19] *Dostizheniia i nedochety tekstil'noi promyshlennosti SSSR. (Po materialam tekstil'noi sektsii NK RKI SSSR)* (1926), p. 113; *ITPT*, 1–2, January–February 1930, p. 45.

[20] *Ekonomicheskaia zhizn'*, 20 July 1928; *Predpriiatie*, 10, October 1927, pp. 60–3.

[21] Shukhgal'ter, *Vnutrizavodskii kontrol'*, pp. 6–7; A. F. Ziman, *Normirovanie tkatskogo stanka. (Kratkoe prakticheskoe rukovodstvo)* (1926), p. 3.

follows that systematic control of the work of these production cells is the barest minimum required for efficiency's sake. Nevertheless, we know of shops where it is known only that they exist – how they work is known to scarcely anyone.[22]

Control was decentralized, traditional, elusive; almost, one is tempted to say, a trade secret inherited by successive generations of workers of a particular locality or job as they were initiated into the mill: 'in every mill there is some kind of accounting', lamented Abramov, 'but in many mills things carry on as they were first introduced half-a-century ago. Such methods may be termed "accounting by eye"'.[23] Localism and tradition also pervaded trade terminology and demarcation: 106 textile trades were identified by the Commissariat of Labour and the central committee of the textileworkers' union in 1920,[24] and there is no evidence of any reduction in subsequent years. Writing of just eight Vladimir guberniya mills in the course of an investigation into industrial illness in 1925, a doctor discovered that 'in this or that factory the naming and details of each profession are different'.[25] The union's first tariff handbook for the industry in NEP, originally published in 1922 and reissued in an expanded form late in 1925, contained 1,261 paragraphs which tried to define pay scales for 588 trades, and when a new handbook came out in 1928, it listed sixty-four shops and departments and 544 trades for cotton mills alone.[26]

Initial processing rooms

Reviewing each of the main departments of a cotton mill shows that idiosyncratic work organization was the corollary of technological idiosyncrasy. When baled cotton arrived in the mill it was taken first to sorting rooms, and because the bales were heavy most of the carrying was done by men.[27] Elsewhere jobs were allocated by gender for social, not technical reasons. On the 'opener' one male directed the work of three or four female operatives who fed the

---

22 A. Abramov, *Nagliadnyi uchet v tekstil'noi promyshlennosti* (1926), p. 87.
23 *Ibid.*, p. 8.
24 *Tekstil'shchik*, 6–7 (20–21), September–October 1920, pp. 31–2.
25 *Nashe khoziaistvo* (Vladimir), 7–8 (48–49), July–August 1925, p. 19.
26 *Tarifnyi spravochnik tekstil'shchikov* (1926) (hereafter *1925 spravochnik*); *Tarifno-spravochnik rabochikh khlopchato-bumazhnogo proizvodstva* (1928).
27 N. A. Rozenbaum, *Gigiena truda v bumagopriadil'nom i bumagotkatskom proizvodstvakh* (1928), p. 13.

machine.[28] Depending on the scale of production sources list a welter of auxiliary workers restricted to one part of the process: waste sorters, waste processors, bin stackers, carriers, labellers, greasers, and so forth.[29] Norm setters found it all but impossible to arrive at standard definitions of work routines, not least because fluctuations in the quality of cotton coming into the mill with each delivery made calculations very difficult.[30] In addition, there is just a hint that individualized, and perhaps pre-literate forms of superintendence persisted well into NEP, keeping control decentralized and checking interference by specialists. In Tver's largest mill, for example, there were no reference tables of any kind for the multifarious types of raw cotton worked up in the factory in 1926, and this meant that – as in Lancashire – experienced sorters were probably making judgements and grading cotton on the basis of their own knowledge.[31]

Scutching machines beat and crushed cotton and wound the resultant fleecy mass on to drums for use in carding rooms.[32] Workloads varied considerably, usually one female operator to one, two or three scutchers, and one overlooker and one engineer to between twenty-five and thirty machines. But whatever differences there may have been in terms of the number of workers to a machine, control over production was clearly defined, hierarchical, and gender specific. Regular cleaning and minor repairs were the operative's responsibility, but only in partnership with mechanics and the assent of foremen, to whom all technical questions were supposed to be referred.[33] In theory machine speeds and loadings depended on cotton sort and weight, but in practice the 'condition of raw materials and the skill of the worker' was what really mattered.[34] As foremen held the cover keys for machine adjustment there was probably a large measure of informal shop-floor bargaining over work routines and

[28] V. I. Feoktistov, *Ekskursiia na bumagopriadil'nuiu fabriku* (1924), p. 26; *Ozdorovlenie truda i revoliutsiia byta* (1924), pp. 37–40; A. M. Zaikov, *Na khlopchatobumazhnoi fabrike* (1926/27), pp. 22–3, 27–8.

[29] *1925 spravochnik*, pp. 11–12; A. F. Shvarabovich, *Kak uberech' sebia ot neschastnykh sluchaev v khlopchatobumazhnom proizvodstve* (1926), pp. 11–12, 16; A. A. Tikhomirov, *Odin den'na priadil'noi fabrike* (1927), p. 16.

[30] A. F. Ziman, *Tekhnicheskoe normirovanie priadil'nogo proizvodstva. Chast' 1. Otdely: sortirovochnyi, trepal'nyi, chesal'nyi* (1928), pp. 11, 17–18, 52–3.

[31] *Golos tekstilei*, 23 February 1926; and see L. H. C. Tippett, *A Portrait of the Lancashire Textile Industry* (1969).

[32] C. Singer et al., eds., *A History of Technology: The Industrial Revolution c.1750 to c.1850*, vol. 4 (1958), pp. 283–6.

[33] Rozenbaum, *Gigiena truda*, p. 13; *Ozdorovlenie truda*, p. 46; Zaikov, *Na k–b fabrike*, pp. 15, 22–3; Ziman, *Chast'* 1, pp. 109, 112.

[34] *Rezoliutsiia 1-go vsesoiuznogo s"ezda otdelov truda i T.N.B. tekstil'noi promyshlennosti (20–26/IX-1925g)* (1926), p. 16 (hereafter *TNB 1925*); Ziman, *Chast'1*, pp. 52–3, 62, 88–9.

Plate 3 Drawing-frame room in a Soviet mill, late 1920s. Clearly a propaganda photograph, since the room is far too clean and tidy.

work loadings; in the early 1920s scutchers in Rodniki were run at different speeds.[35]

Carding frames, developed in Manchester to cut labour costs by

[35] *Initsiativnyi sovet po nauchnoi organizatsii truda pri tsentral'nom komitete soiuza tekstil'sh-chikov. Kratkii otchet* (1924), p. 15 (hereafter *ISNOT*); Shvarabovich, *Kak uberech' sebia*, pp. 17–18; Ziman, *Chast' 1*, p. 109.

substituting unskilled female operatives for male carders, combed cotton fibres into roughly parallel lines for preparatory spinning.[36] Here work was simple but the allocation of functions particularized, partly because workers inherited different machines of different ages from different countries with corresponding differences in operating technique. Three operatives working as a team dealt with up to fifteen frames, but some had to be stopped and cleaned down twice a day – by men. As in sorting rooms, carders were surrounded by swarms of auxiliaries: greasers, needle solderers, needle setters, comb strippers, can boys and a card-grinding team made up of first, second and third grinders ranging from experienced workers to adolescent trainees. Because work was not labour intensive, and presumably because servicing and supervisory functions predominated, carding rooms were thought to be reasonably pleasant places in which to work.[37]

Preparatory departments

Like carders, drawing-frame operatives were exclusively and traditionally female. The work was simple and required no substantial physical strength, but this does not mean that the usual appellation 'unskilled' should be accepted without some reservations; a monograph on industrial accidents in cotton mills asserted that workers were, or should be, 'experienced female operatives'.[38] Carding drums were loaded at one end of the machine and thick slivers of cotton drawn off at the other and fed into large cans for primary spinning. Machine banks were long, able to take up to forty-eight drums, and work tasks were confined to walking along the banks to load up drums and join up broken slivers of cotton.[39] Perhaps because drawing-frame rooms never became a major target for rationalizers there are very few of the scattered, casual references in the sources which help to build up a montage of variations in work practices. Auxiliary trades seem to have been limited to can carrying and greasing, and as elsewhere foremen and overlookers were invariably male.[40] Engineers agreed

[36] C. Singer et al., eds., A History of Technology: The Late Nineteenth Century c.1850 to c.1900, vol. 5 (1958), pp. 570–6.

[37] 1925 spravochnik, pp. 13–14, 18–19; Feoktistov, Ekskursiia, pp. 27–8; Singer, History of Technology, vol. 4, pp. 283–6; Rozenbaum, Gigiena truda, p. 13; Zaikov, Na k-b fabrike, pp. 33–8; Ziman, Chast' 1, pp. 115, 159.

[38] Okhrana truda, 3 (44), March 1929, p. 5; Rozenbaum, Gigiena truda, p. 13; Shvarabovich, Kak uberech' sebia, p. 29; Zaikov, Na k-b fabrike, pp. 38–40.

[39] Rozenbaum, Gigiena truda, p. 13; Tikhomirov, Odin den', p. 32.

[40] Sistema i organizatsiia, 8, 1925, p. 22; Zaikov, Na k-b fabrike, pp. 38–40.

Plate 4 Operative replenishing a very well kept Soviet made flyer-frame in Ivanovo-Voznesensk, late 1920s.

that two women worked a single frame, but perhaps this was an ideal; in Shuia until late in the decade there were three to a machine.[41]

In cotton mills the scale of production increases as the unit size of semi-finished goods decreases; large aggregates of workers, therefore, make their first appearance in flyer-frame rooms. Developed in the 1820s, the flyer-frame de-skilled the manipulative processes attendant on producing rovings – thick-spun cotton suitable for use on selfactors or ring-frames. Slivers were crushed through rollers and thread given its initial twist, and considerable dexterity was needed to 'doff off' full bobbins and 'piece up' broken ends quickly.[42] Diverse technology and inexact Russian terminology makes it difficult to uncover the structure of work, but there are clear parallels between the definitions and usages of nineteenth-century Britain and NEP Russia: slubbing frames had somewhere between 80 and 100 spindles, intermediates between 100 and 300, and what were variously known as jack-, roving- or fine-roving frames around 300. Because thread became progressively

---

[41] I. S. Belinskii, A. I. Kucherov, *Tri mesiatsa raboty semichasovykh fabrik. (Opyt perevoda i raboty semichasovykh fabrik v ivanovo-voznesenskoi gubernii)* (1928), table 2 p. 15; Feoktistov, *Ekskursiia*, p. 28; A. F. Ziman, *Tekhnicheskoe normirovanie priadil'nogo proizvodstva. Chast' 2. Lentochno-bankabroshnyi i vaternyi otdely* (1931), p. 79.
[42] Feoktistov, *Ekskursiia*, p. 28; Singer, *History of Technology*, vol. 4, pp. 283–6; *Ozdorovlenie truda*, p. 59; Zaikov, *Na k-b fabrike*, pp. 40–5; Ziman, *Chast'* 2, pp. 10–11.

finer as it passed down the production chain, spindle speeds increased on each subsequent frame group, but were modified to take account of fluctuations in cotton quality and changed depending on whether or not the spinning was for warp or weft threads. On slubbing frames, prior to 1925 or so, one or two women operated one machine, or two women shared two frames, or one woman worked on two frames alone. Adolescent girl helpers were added to intermediate and jack-frames because doffing occurred more frequently, but numbers still varied: the range of sources for this section of the mill indicate one helper for every one or two frames, one spinner and one assistant for four frames, or one spinner and two girls for four frames.[43] If machine and count are held constant there is little evidence of standardized work practices between different regions; equally, when one mill with varied machinery is isolated the same lack of pattern is evident.[44] As in other rooms there were considerable numbers of auxiliary workers: bobbin sorters, bobbin strippers, loaders, machine repairers and their assistants, and roving sampler and cleaner teams, each with experienced and ranking members.[45]

But if the division of labour was highly localized, particular to a region or trust, or an individual mill within a region or trust, the allocation of functions by gender was rigidly felt. Apart from repairers all the trades described here were usually listed with the feminine form of the noun. Even when the Krasnaia Talka came on stream demarcation was inflected into the brand-new corpus: *Rabochii krai* complained that 'the men don't want to work on flyer-frames. According to them that's "women's work". Twenty [trainees] have already handed in their notice.'[46] Supervisory staff, however – foremen, senior overlookers and their assistants – were invariably male; the single female overlooker found in one mill in 1929 was looked on as a curiosity.[47]

Fine spinning halls

Although in a minority, selfactor or 'mule' spinners held a unique position in the post-revolutionary mill. Sources always use the masculine form of the noun when referring to them because spinners

[43] Belinskii, Kucherov, *Tri mesiatsa raboty*, table 2 p. 15; Feoktistov, *Ekskursiia*, p. 28; *Sistema i organizatsiia*, 8, 1925, p. 25; *TNB 1925*, pp. 16–17; Ziman, *Chast' 2*, pp. 17–20, 203, 245.
[44] *Predpriiatie*, 7, July 1928, p. 19; *Sistema i organizatsiia*, 8, 1925, p. 24.
[45] *Ozdorovlenie truda*, pp. 57–8; *Trud i proizvodstvo*, 3, March 1925, pp. 14–15; Ziman, *Chast' 2*, pp. 17–20.
[46] *Rabochii krai*, 20 July 1929.   [47] *Okhrana truda*, 3 (44), March 1929, p. 5.

as well as supervisors were men. The selfactor work team, or *komplekt*, had a long history. Mule frames were among the first factory-based machines to be introduced into Russia, appearing within a dozen years or so of their invention in England. Many Soviet mills had frames well over half-a-century old, and some had been working from as early as the 1840s.[48] Almost all were British. Platt and Asa Lees are the makes most frequently mentioned in the Ivanovo area in 1918 and a time-and-motion investigation of 1930 takes a 1908 Platt selfactor as standard.[49] But as the selfactor reached its peak of technical perfection only in the 1880s[50] there were some variations in the structure and functioning of Soviet frames.

This brings us closer to a consideration of the complex relationship between technology and work in Russian selfactor rooms and the unusual status of the Soviet selfactor spinner. The assertion of a 1926 source that men controlled mules because of 'the difficulty of walking with the carriage' is disingenuous.[51] While the spinner might have to cover thirty to forty feet per minute, women were sometimes employed as piecers, whose production tasks were similar to those of the spinner.[52] Moreover, the physical burden of selfactor work was paralleled in other mill rooms where women predominated. That there was a choice of technique for selfactor spinning will become clear, but proponents of rationalization in Soviet mills never really managed to impose an alternative. This is at first sight surprising, as it was thought that the elimination of the traditional work team would have created conditions for a significant rise in productivity. Furthermore, the attack could have been mounted within the discourse of economic efficiency in the factory and sexual equality at the frame, a seemingly irresistible combination. The problem, therefore, is to dissect the exact nature of work on selfactors and thus illuminate the field of action for alternative techniques. To do this we must first of all try to understand the history of the social and technological parameters of mule spinning.

[48] There is a vast incidental literature on machine ages and dates of installation. This example is from *ITPT*, 1–2, January–February 1930, p. 49.
[49] A. M. Buras, *Osnovy tekhnicheskogo normirovaniia v tekstil'noi promyshlennosti* (1930), appendix for p. 263; *Spisok fabrik, zavodov i drugikh promyshlennykh predpriiatii ivanovo-voznesenskoi gubernii. Po dannym vserossiiskoi promyshlennoi i professional'noi perepis' 1918 goda* (1919), pp. 58–84 (hereafter *I. gub. ind. census 1918*).
[50] H. Catling, *The Spinning Mule* (1970), p. 10.
[51] Budanov, *Obshchie poniatiia*, p. 73.
[52] W. H. Lazonick, 'Production relations, labor productivity, and choice of technique: British and U.S. cotton spinning', *Journal of Economic History*, 41, 3, September 1981, p. 493.

Plate 5 The origins of the Russian selfactor *komplekt*. A mule pair in early nineteenth-century England. On the left the spinner is preparing to draw a frame and on the right a piecer is repairing the yarn. A doffer is sweeping up under the yarn sheet.

The selfactor arose on the basis of an eighteenth-century domestic frame designed to de-skill the simultaneous actions of twisting and stretching rovings while at the same time spinning a very fine count which would allow English entrepreneurs to break into profitable high-fashion markets currently dominated by Indian muslins. On the domestic mule, yarn spindles for building up cops of fine spun cotton were attached to a sliding carriage sitting in a fixed frame. Roving bobbins were slotted onto the frame. When roving ends were attached to the spindle shanks the carriage was moved out and away from the roving bobbins while the yarn spindles were simultaneously rotated at high speed, thus putting twist and stretch into the thread at the same time. Both actions, carriage movement and spindle turn, were set in motion by the operative turning a large wheel attached to the spindles and carriage by belt-drive. 'Drafting rollers' were situated directly in front of the rovings and adjusted to retard the draw of the thread. This 'gain on the carriage' allowed for finer spinning. The spinner controlled the motion of the wheel with his right hand, the 'faller wire', a device for steadying the 'yarn sheet', with his left. At the point of full carriage 'draw', that is, when the carriage reached the end of its run of five feet or so, the motion was reversed, or 'backed off', and fine-spun cotton wound onto the cops. A slow draw progressively thinned the rovings as they passed through the drafting rollers, giving a high count; conversely a fast draw resulted in a thick yarn and a low count. For very fine counts one carriage draw might take four minutes, for coarse counts there might be five draws a minute. The workload, therefore, depended on count and in the last resort on market demand for fine or coarse cloth and the quality of the cotton. Everything was connected to the wheel by belt-drive, so there was a syncopated motion between carriage, yarn spindles, roving bobbins and drafting rollers. Eventually, after several draws, the roving cops would be exhausted and the spindle shanks full. The machine was then stopped and doffed off prior to starting the cycle of operations again.

Carriage sizes were rapidly increased (see plate 5) and 600 to 1,200 spindles per frame became common after steam-powered fly-wheels had been added to give inertial assistance to the spinner's wheel. The traditional layout of a selfactor 'pair' arose as these semi-automatic mules migrated to the first factories in the 1790s, continued long after technical parameters had changed, and was standard for Russian mills in the 1920s. Two mules were placed facing each other, thus allowing the spinner to back-off one while the other was drawing automatically: all the spinner had to do was to turn on his heel in order to be facing

Plate 6 A Hetherington's selfactor from the company's 1906 and 1931 catalogues for export sales. Slots for roving bobbins (next to the belt drives) and spindle shanks on the carriages (beneath the belt drives) can be seen stretching each side of the 'wheel'.

one or the other of the fly-wheels. As the carriages moved back and forth auxiliary workers walked between the frames to piece up the yarn sheets or crawled beneath the carriages to sweep up loose cotton fibres.[53]

It will be appreciated that since the quality of the finished thread still depended on individual touch, domestic and semi-automatic mules were only partially successful in de-skilling the spinner's work. Moreover, the temptation to 'stretch out' frames by adding more and more spindles – by the first quarter of the nineteenth century carriage lengths were already approaching 100 feet – meant that ever more strength was needed to turn the wheels, and so there was little chance of replacing expensive male spinners with women or children.[54] Only a fully automatic or *selfacting* mule would allow cotton masters to reduce their labour costs to any significant degree.

[53] This account of the working of the mule is taken from Catling, *Mule*, pp. 32–4, 44–9; W. English, *The Textile Industry* (1969), p. 177; Lazonick, 'Production', p. 493; Singer, *History of Technology*, 4, pp. 278–80.

[54] Singer, *History of Technology*, 4, pp. 278–80; R. L. Hills, *Power in the Industrial Revolution* (1970), pp. 116–19, 126–7.

Although technological evolution may in some cases be self-generating, the immediate incentive for the development of the selfactor, as Andrew Ure pointed out in 1835, was the desire of Lancashire mill owners to break a spinners' strike following the repeal of the Combination Acts eleven years previously:

> During a disastrous turmoil of the kind at Hyde, Stayley-bridge, and the adjoining factory townships, several of the capitalists, afraid of their business being driven to France, Belgium and the United States, had recourse to the celebrated machinists Messrs. Sharp and Co., of Manchester, requesting them to direct the inventive talents of their partner, Mr. Roberts, to the construction of a self-acting mule, in order to emancipate the trade from galling slavery and impending ruin.[55]

Marx too was alive to the fact that the new technology was conceived in strife: 'it would be possible to write quite a history of the inventions, made since 1830, for the sole purpose of supplying capital with weapons against the revolts of the working class. At the head of these in importance stands the self-acting mule, because it opened up a new epoch in the automatic system.'[56] Successful patents were registered by Roberts in 1825 and 1830, and the attraction of the new machine resided not in its technical sophistication but in its purported ability to reduce labour costs and allow masters to gain control over work processes on the shop floor: Roberts' original prospectus envisaged the elimination of the highly paid male spinner and the substitution of unskilled operatives; three female piecers to a selfactor pair supervised by one male overlooker to every four or five pairs.[57]

Something like this organization of work was to be found in New England's mills in the latter half of the nineteenth century. A spinner and 'back boy' kept two pairs of mules supplied with creels (roving bobbins) and also cleaned and oiled the frames. Two or three doffers and two 'tubers', who placed paper tubes over the spindle shanks to prevent cops unwinding when doffing, were employed for every ten or so mules. Highly paid mechanics did all the technical work. Most importantly they, and not the spinner, fixed count and adjusted machine speeds. These New England spinners never built up any craft traditions or elaborated methods of control at the workplace through restrictive practices; as in other areas of American industry

---

[55] A. Ure, *Philosophy of Manufacturers* (1835), pp. 366–7.
[56] K. Marx, *Capital*, vol. 1 (1906), pp. 475–6.
[57] W. H. Lazonick, 'Industrial relations and technical change: the case of the self-acting mule', *Cambridge Journal of Economics*, 3, 1979, pp. 237–44.

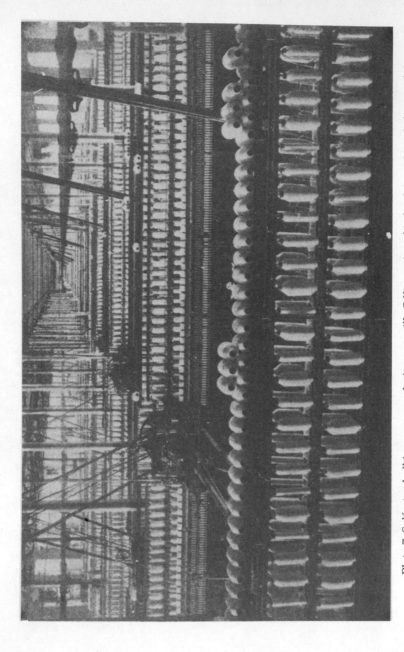

Plate 7 Selfactor hall in a pre-revolutionary mill. Offset pairs of 'wheels', with each frame of the pair facing the other, can be seen receding into the distance.

the spinner's defence rested on the ease with which he could quit and move on. Piece rates were uniform across mills so the major variant encountered by spinners was not low pay but 'bad spinning'; the use of inferior cotton which increased workloads and retarded output since more time had to be spent piecing. The most competent therefore tended to drift away from factories using inferior cotton in order to protect their earnings. Employers found that there was little to be gained from purchasing poor cotton: bad spinning only served to attract inferior spinners.[58]

An approximation to the New England pattern of work organization could have readily taken root in Russian soil. There was no technical reason why peasant women from the CIR or workers' wives in St Petersburg should not have been put to the selfactor as piecers and their children employed as back boys. From the owners' perspective problems of labour discipline could have been internalized within the family and scarce male technical personnel distributed around the rooms as overlookers; patriarchal traditions would surely have guaranteed the acquiescence of the piecers. Moreover, in a country with no bed-rock of guild traditions, the spontaneous generation of craft unionism was inconceivable. Capitalists could even have obliged operatives to bear the cost of bad spinning; the relative immobility of labour, before and after emancipation, would have checked the final defence of moving on possessed by American spinners. Nothing of the kind happened, and much of the pressure from specialists and rationalizers in the NEP years can be interpreted as an attempt to enforce in Soviet mills the kind of techniques envisaged by Roberts a century or so earlier.

The organization of the labour process on mules in NEP Russia was found to be clear and hierarchical – sources record that teams were always made up of spinner, piecers and doffers and point out that a pair was always worked[59] – but investigators had great difficulty in penetrating the mysteries of the *komplekt*. Vesenkha made a start with a 1925 order requesting information from mills on 'how the *komplekt* is distributed on a pair of selfactors'. The order also tried to fix standard work routines and arrived at the following description: 'production processes' were listed as doffing, creeling, setting up bobbins, placing paper tubes and piecing; 'technical processes' were described as

58 Lazonick, 'Production', pp. 506–9.
59 Buras, *Osnovy*, appendix for p. 263; N. T. Pavlov, *Sel'faktor* (1926), p. 116; *Tekstil'nye novosti*, 1, January 1930, p. 52. The only exception seems to have been one room in the Trekhgornaia where four frames were worked by four spinners and twenty-two piecers: *Ozdorovlenie truda*, pp. 77–9.

dusting, periodic general cleaning, oiling and greasing and changing the leather sleeves on the drafting rollers; 'adjustment and repair' included changing weights, belts and cones and making small running repairs 'etc.'.[60] The spinner controlled the timing, distribution and organization of all these tasks: 'the chief person on a pair of machines is the spinner. He is responsible for his own pair and for the correct functioning of them. Under his direct orders are the piecers and doffers whom he instructs and who must obey his orders.'[61] The spinner's production task was to walk with the carriage and piece up broken ends. The main duty of the piecer, the spinner's 'chief assistant', was fast and accurate piecing. When the spindle shanks were full or the roving bobbins exhausted, the spinner stopped the machine while doffers removed completed cops and creelers replaced rovings. In free moments doffers helped with piecing and cleaned down the frame.[62] That there were many variations on this basic pattern[63] only reinforces the point that although the *hierarchy* of work was well established and clearly defined, the *division* of labour was a matter for the individual spinner. In fact about 20 per cent of his working day was taken up with 'work subsidiary to production' compared with 9 per cent for ring-frame spinners and 2 per cent for weavers, which shows that for spinners managerial tasks were just as important as production tasks.[64]

If the examination of the *komplekt* is pressed still further we can begin to appreciate how lines of power and authority reached out into the spinning halls. Sources on the selfactor are vague in their estimations of *komplekt* numbers. One 1925 investigation cites spinner, piecer and creeler as standard for two 1,200-spindle frames in the CIR prior to the First World War. Another records spinner, piecer, doffer and creeler for the mid-1920s. Four to six to a pair are mentioned in 1924, four in 1926 and 'usually' five in 1927.[65] In fact the *komplekt* could be much larger than these examples suggest. It could include first, second and third piecers and first and second creelers. These were subordinate to the spinner, who also directed the activities of the following auxiliary workers when they walked through the 'jenny-gates' – the entrances at each end of the long corridor separating the two frames: one tube sorter, three to four roving carriers, four ropers

[60] *Sistema i organizatsiia*, 10, 1925, pp. 7–9.   [61] Pavlov, *Sel'faktor*, p. 117.
[62] *Ibid.*, pp. 119–20; Budanov, *Obshchie poniatiia*, p. 73; Rozenbaum, *Gigiena truda*, p. 15.
[63] *Sistema i organizatsiia*, 10, 1925, pp. 7–9.   [64] *ITPT*, 1, January 1928, pp. 44–5.
[65] Buras, *Osnovy*, pp. 262–4; Feoktistov, *Ekskursiia*, p. 30; Pavlov, *Sel'faktor*, p. 116; Sistema i organizatsiia, 8, 1925, p. 22; Tikhomirov, *Odin den'*, p. 44.

(supplying ropes and belts) and four thread carriers.[66] Some spinners, therefore, exercised primary authority over more than fifteen operatives on the shop floor at various moments throughout the working day. But it was not only the direction of subsidiary personnel that assured spinners authority at the workplace. Their competence fanned out beyond the process hitherto described; they appropriated the controls which, in America, were invested in mechanics. Spinners, it was asserted in 1924, 'must fully understand the complex workings of their machines' and carry out auxiliary servicing; they were 'in command' of machine repair. They, and not technical personnel, decided when the pair would be halted for cleaning and adjustment, and they, and not engineers, were responsible for ensuring correct count and quality.[67] In addition trade terminology was often muddled and inexact, a further indication of weak managerial control.[68]

There is much here which suggests that the size of the work team was increasing throughout NEP, but it is not enough to assign *komplekt* inflation to some vague tendency for manning levels to rise because of the breakdown of managerial authority after 1917. And even if it were possible to deduce the particular from the general we would still be left with the problem of power, of exactly where definitions of appropriate manning levels came from.

Here we must return to England. The internal ramifications of the *komplekt* and the appropriation of control by the spinner were not native developments, although they were refracted through Russian culture and affected by post-revolutionary conditions. To put it another way, English machinery did not come to Russia as neutral technology.

As with the transition from domestic spinning to the semi-automatic mule in the late eighteenth century, the introduction of the selfactor in England in the second quarter of the nineteenth century confounded the predictions and expectations of Marx and Ure. It did not result in the elimination of the highly paid male spinner. The launch of Roberts' machine fortuitously coincided with a period of intense competition in cotton manufacture which set a premium on uninterrupted high-quality spinning. Lancashire masters were not inclined to risk conflicts which would lead to poor quality output or bankruptcy by experi-

[66] *1925 spravochnik*, pp. 17–18.
[67] Budanov, *Obshchie poniatiia*, p. 73; *Golos tekstilei*, 23 October 1926; Pavlov, *Sel'faktor*, pp. 117–18; *Ozdorovlenie truda*, p. 79; Shvarabovich, *Kak uberech' sebia*, p. 43.
[68] I. G. Andreev, *Nevskie priadil'shchiki. Kratkii ocherk istorii priadil'no-nitochnogo kombinata im. S. M. Kirova* (1959), pp. 34, 50; Pavlov, *Sel'faktor*, pp. 116, 120; Rozenbaum, *Gigiena truda*, p. 15.

menting with the substitution of unskilled and non-unionized labour. Instead, selfactor 'minders' were drawn from the pool of common-mule spinners and adolescent or child piecers placed under their authority. This hierarchical organization of work resigned the problem of shop-floor discipline to the minder, who replicated familial and patriarchal modes of control at the bench. The subsequent long-term attachment of a minder to his machines – most stayed with a pair for twenty or thirty years and senior piecers expected to inherit their 'wheels' or take on a new pair as the industry expanded – meant that technical control inexorably devolved into their hands. As each mule pair developed its own idiosyncrasies the continued employment of an established minder on that pair became progressively advantageous to owners and managers. Mule spinners grasped the opportunities thus afforded, and used the demand for good minders created by the long boom of the 1850s and continued cut-throat competition between small employers, to consolidate the hierarchical, gender-based structure of shop-floor relations and to construct a powerful craft union predicated on their control over labour and machinery.[69]

Manufactured in Lancashire, installed by English engineers for English managers in shops subsequently run by English foremen, the selfactors exported to Russia before the Revolution thus embodied assumptions about how they should be worked. Expatriates brought with them habits and conventions which had evolved in north-western England throughout the last seventy-five years of the old century and imposed them on Russia's newly recruited factory labour force. That their influence persisted for decades can be seen by glancing at materials relating to mule spinning in the Soviet Union for the 1920s; 'in spite of the great experience of Russian technicians with the selfactor', notes one source, 'the more experienced technicians and workers' must study nineteenth-century English manuals. This article itself was a straight reprint from a pre-war journal.[70] Lancashire's experience also helps us to discover why there were variations in *komplekt* sizes. Nineteenth-century English craft unions negotiated lists which gave highly detailed guidance to master and minder alike on how to fix manning levels and the rate for the job,[71] and fragments of this arrangement seem to have been carried abroad by expatriates,

[69] P. Joyce, *Work, Society and Politics: The Culture of the Factory in Later Victorian England* (1980), chapter 3; Lazonick, 'Production', pp. 500–1.
[70] N. A. Vasil'ev, ed., *Sel'faktor (dlia gladkoi i pushistoi priazhi)* (1922), p. 170; *Vestnik manufakturnoi promyshlennosti*, 31/7 (1911–12).
[71] Lazonick, 'Production', pp. 493–5.

transplanted to Russia, and embodied in the union's rule book after the Revolution.[72]

Thereafter local factors supervened. Selfactors were best for spinning fine to medium counts with good quality cotton. Although they could spin coarse counts this resulted in bad spinning; rovings were exhausted more quickly, the rate of carriage draw accelerated and there were more breakages on the yarn sheet which meant more time spent piecing. Consequently Anglo-Russian practices dictated that there should be more piecers to a spinner and an increase in the number of creelers and doffers as a proportion of the *komplekt*. Equally, *komplekt* sizes rose if the quality of the raw cotton fell.[73]

These two factors – the production of coarse counts leading to bad spinning and a fall in the quality of raw cotton coming into the mill – were endemic throughout NEP. Seven years of war and revolution had swept away the social foundations which underpinned the call for fine spinning; it is unlikely that the new 'instant' bourgeoisie which flourished in the guise of carpet-baggers and petty traders – the *nepmeny* – could have filled the gaps in the demand for high fashion left by the departed aristocracy and middling ranks. In addition, the disruption of overseas cotton supplies engendered by economic collapse and isolation became a chronic feature of the 1920s. So as cotton quality fell coincidentally with a tendency to concentrate on low counts – *smychka* counts for the peasantry – the cost of mule-spun cloth rose, *komplekt* sizes increased, and consequently the grip of the mule spinner on the shop floor tightened.

The sense of exclusiveness which *komplekt* working fostered radiated outwards and was reflected back in the spinner's dealings with others. Standard forms which rationalizers hoped to introduce in the mid-1920s were designed for completion by the spinner and not by room foremen or technical personnel. The spinner was referred to by full name – first name, patronymic and surname – the other *komplekt* members, to be listed by him, by surname alone. Later attempts by rationalizers to collect information about work tasks as a strategy for gaining control over production similarly deferred to knowledge and authority; they were to be completed by the spinner and merely counter-signed by shop foremen.[74] As in England the organization of

[72] *Tarif tekstil'shchikov* (1922), p. 47.
[73] *Ibid.*, p. 515; Feoktistov, *Ekskursiia*, pp. 30–1; T. Williams, ed., *A History of Technology: The Twentieth Century c.1900 to c.1950*, vol. 6 (1978), p. 639; *Sistema i organizatsiia*, 10, 1925, pp. 7–9; Tikhomirov, *Odin den'*, p. 44.
[74] Abramov, *Nagliadnyi uchet*, pp. 94–5; *Tekstil'nye novosti*, 2–3, February–March 1930, pp. 140–3.

work ensured that spinners 'grew and aged with' and became 'partisans of their own machines',[75] but post-revolutionary conditions meant that Russia's mule spinners probably expanded the area of control at work to an even greater extent than did their Lancashire counterparts. It was not just that a bewildering variety of selfactors were scattered throughout the country; the acute shortage of technical personnel together with the lack of specialist maintenance (one source mentions no general repair for forty years) indicates that machine idiosyncrasy proceeded apace, and that the spinner's competence extended far beyond routine servicing.[76]

Recruitment into the *komplekt* implied commitment to a life-long trade with the expectation of progression through the ranks, as one example from the 1920s will show: A. I. Shevarev, a spinner from Tver' aged fifty-three, 'worked in the mill for forty years. Two years as a doffer, twelve as a piecer, twenty-six as a spinner'.[77] In Petrograd in 1917 twelve-year-old boys were recruited as junior piecers for what were later to be called the Sovetskaia Zvezda and Krasnaia Nit' factories;[78] if they survived, these youngsters would become established spinners in the following decade. Slow rise through the *komplekt* remained the convention throughout NEP. Adolescent doffers and creelers were trained by established spinners,[79] and advancement to piecer status occurred only 'after three or four years' satisfactory work' gathering experience of the workings of a pair.[80] Newer mule spinners were often objects of derision; their seniors regarded them as spinners 'only in inverted commas' because of their lack of 'professional' experience.[81] On the shop floor minders were discouraged from leaving their frames because 'labour discipline is weakened while the spinner is absent'.[82] Spinners also commanded obedience at the frontier between home and factory. Post-holiday absenteeism was a 'mass phenomenon' in Leningrad's Ravenstvo mill in 1928, 'in the mule rooms the selfactors stood idle while the rest of the factory was

[75] M. Shaginian, *Nevskaia nitka* (1925), p. 16.
[76] *Golos tekstilei*, 7 June 1927; *ITPT*, 8–9, August–September 1930, pp. 112–13. Twelve engineers worked in the Iartsevskaia in 1913, but only four remained in 1925; D. I. Budaev, *Estafeta pokolenii. Ocherki istorii k 100 letiiu iartsevskogo kh. b. kombinata* (1973), p. 53.
[77] *Vek truda i bor'by. Dokumenty i materialy po istorii kalinskogo khlopchato-bumazhnogo kombinata 1858–1958gg* (1961), p. 302.
[78] Andreev, *Nevskie priadil'shchiki*, pp. 34, 50.
[79] *Leningradskii tekstil'*, 15 February 1928, p. 9; *Nashe khoziaistvo* (Tver'), 1(9), January 1923, p. 85; Shvarabovich, *Kak uberech' sebia*, p. 36.
[80] Pavlov, *Sel'faktor*, p. 119.   [81] *Leningradskii tekstil'*, 7, 1 April 1928, p. 6.
[82] Abramov, *Nagliadnyi uchet*, p. 78.

working flat out'.[83] But on the other hand that same year many operatives in the city's mills worked for an extra unpaid hour because spinners insisted that mule shifts should come in early to set up stores of rovings for their machines.[84]

To some extent the Soviet Union shared in the world-wide drift away from mule spinning after World War I.[85] The proportion of thread spun on selfactors in the Ivanovo area fell from just over one-third to one-quarter of the total between 1913 and 1922.[86] Moreover, because of the decline of selfactor purchases and the inflation of *komplekt* sizes, not all who began work on the mule could hope to get their own wheels; promotion increasingly depended on the retirement of existing spinners. Something like the 'piecer problem' current in England may thus have been generating new strains in the *komplekt*[87] – aside, that is, from any caused by the exclusive right of men to become spinners. In fact acceptance of male hegemony appears to have been widespread, as there are only occasional criticisms of the sexual division of functions. One is from Ivanovo where an operative wrote to complain that women were not being trained to work on selfactors;[88] another comes from Ramenskoe in Moscow guberniya: 'in the spinning rooms, where around three thousand people are employed, selfactors are worked exclusively by men in spite of the fact that women operated these machines during the war. When the men returned from the front the women lost their places, because it's considered that such work is a male right.'[89]

Notwithstanding these few complaints and the initial fall in the number of working frames, Soviet conditions deflected the full impact of technological obsolescence and arrested the decline of the selfactor after the first few years of NEP. Diplomatic isolation and the Republic's withdrawal from free participation in international trade protected Russian mills from the blast of far-eastern competition which decimated other European producers; the lacuna of unsatisfied peasant demand revealed and stimulated by NEP was to be met

[83] S. Zhukovskii *et al.*, *Pervaia udarnaia* (1931), pp. 8–9.
[84] *Golos tekstilei*, 11 November 1928.
[85] For the global decline of the mule see Catling, *Mule*, p. 10; D. A. Farnie, 'Platt Brothers & Co. Ltd. of Oldham, machine makers to Lancashire and the world: an index of production of cotton spinning spindles 1880–1914', *Business History*, 23, March 1981, p. 85.
[86] *Trud* (Ivanovo-Voznesensk), 5, May 1923, p. 21.
[87] Rozenbaum, *Gigiena truda*, p. 15. The 1926 census showed that whilst doffers were younger than spinners, spinners and piecers were of much the same age: *Vsesoiuznaia perepis' naseleniia 1926 goda* (1930), tom XXXIV, table 3-a pp. 91–3 (hereafter *1926 census*). See also below pp. 238–9.
[88] *Golos tekstilei*, 6 April 1926.   [89] *Okhrana truda*, 3 (44), March 1929, p. 5.

Plate 8 Ring-frame hall in a Soviet mill, late 1920s, with generous spacing between the frames. By the time this photograph was taken a *komplekt* would be expected to look after at least two of the long machine banks.

almost entirely from internal resources, from utilization of the machinery to hand. For the same reason the purchase of foreign ring-frames (discussed below) could, in the short run, never really threaten the operation of existing mules. Imports depended on the availability of an acceptable means of exchange, the general international situation, and the credit and goodwill afforded by western manufacturers. Apart from this there were distinct advantages in keeping selfactors on stream. Selfactors produced a complex cop: a self-contained thread package with no internal spindle which unwound easily for the weaver. Increasing the number of ring-frames invited difficulties in weaving sheds, because the selfactor and the Lancashire power loom, the standard Russian loom, had evolved simultaneously within the context of nineteenth-century English capitalism and constituted a single integrated production unit.[90] Automatic looms suitable for ring-frame cops were common in America where the selfactor quickly gave ground to the ring-frame, but they were rare in NEP Russia. In the long run, if automatic looms replaced Lancashire looms, productivity would rise,[91] but in the short run ring-frames made work more difficult for the weaver and slowed the rate of cloth production. Thus mule spinning was enmeshed within an all-embracing protective network of technological interdependence inside the mill, and there were also wider social and political factors in its favour – since the *smychka* had to be maintained at almost any cost, cloth had to be produced at virtually any price.[92]

While the survival of the mule put the industry and the *smychka* at cross purposes because sustained output for the peasant market could be achieved only with a simultaneous rise in labour costs, this was not the case for the other machine found in fine-spinning halls, the ring-frame. The compromise between labour and capital worked out in Lancashire around 1850 did not end the search for ways of substituting unskilled for skilled labour; rather, it stimulated the development of alternative technologies which would bypass control over the shop floor imposed by minders and reopen freedom of action for employers. The Russian name for the ring-frame, *vater-mashina*, betrays its ancestry; a virtually forgotten eighteenth-century machine, Arkwright's water frame, was resurrected and modified for use in

---

[90] Catling, *Mule*, p. 77.   [91] Shaginian, *Nevskaia nitka*, pp. 33–6.
[92] This annoyed someone at the 1928 eighth textileworkers' union congress: 'In our factories there's a directive to the effect that obsolete mule frames are to be replaced by more profitable ring-frames. But what do we see? Once again we buy mules from abroad and install them in the mills.' *Golos tekstilei*, 8 April 1928.

mills driven by steam or electricity, but not until the mid-nineteenth century was it capable of fine spinning.[93]

Like their counterparts elsewhere, Russian entrepreneurs began to turn away from the mule in the late nineteenth century; nine-tenths of all ring-frames listed in 1927 had been installed after 1890.[94] Continuous and intermittent spinning expanded simultaneously until the end of the century, and thereafter the selfactor stock remained virtually stable while the number of ring-frames continued to increase.[95] One further point is evident from the sources. Because ring-frame purchases occurred in conditions of rapid expansion there was no friction between alternative technologies, no institutional or social blocks to ring-frame installation. The British expatriates who created the mule *komplekt* were not motivated by any wish to defend craft or status. They simply introduced patterns of work which were, for them, self-evident. When new technologies came along which gave them the chance to organize work differently, they had no reason to ignore designers' original intentions. We should not be surprised, therefore, to find ring-frame halls populated by women.

Sources habitually refer to ring-frame spinners as unskilled, or insist that 'less skilled' operatives would do,[96] but in fact the job did require specific skills. On the ring-frame, as on the mule, rovings passed through rollers, but there was no moving carriage. Stretching and twisting were effected by placing a rotating arm on top of the spindle: tension between rollers and a 'traveller' put in the stretch, and circular motion round the arm added twist. Count was changed by retarding the delivery of the rovings. Machine speeds were fast, up to 15,000 spindle turns per minute by the mid-1920s. Piecing, doffing and cleaning were often carried out while the frames were still running, a dangerous practice encouraged by labour intensification. When spinners stopped their banks the shut-down time for a full doffing (involving in excess of 700 spindles) was supposed to be three to four minutes. Not only did the doffing have to be done quickly, but conditions in ring-frame halls left little margin for error – Moscow's Trekhgornaia had only five feet between machine rows and two-and-a-half between adjacent banks. Spinners, therefore, had to be atten-

[93] English, *Textile Industry*, pp. 70, 166.
[94] Shukhgal'ter, *Vnutrizavodskii kontrol'*, p. 5; *Tekstil'nye novosti*, 10–11, October–November 1927, p. 365.
[95] P. A. Khromov, *Ocherki ekonomiki tekstil'noi promyshlennosti* (1946), pp. 45, 48.
[96] Rozenbaum, *Gigiena truda*, pp. 12–13.

tive to their work and needed good visual judgement to prevent spindles over-running.[97]

Ring-frame spinners were surrounded by the usual range of fetching and carrying trades we have seen in other rooms.[98] Spinner and doffers, sometimes with assistant spinner, made up the *komplekt* itself, and as on the mule the *komplekt* was more than just a work team: 'the doffers who work under the direction of the ring-frame spinner, these immediate candidates for the post of spinner, are interested in the acquisition of corresponding practical skills at work'.[99]

One or two banks of 720 spindles per work group seem to have been common up to mid-decade, but there is evidence of substantially higher loadings before the Revolution – one spinner to four banks in an Ivanovo-Voznesensk mill, for instance.[100] Spinner and piecers helped with the doffing but the division of functions was not so strictly delineated as on the mule; assistants were sometimes responsible for cleaning and doffers occasionally and temporarily took on assistants' work. Control at the frame and patterns of authority inside the *komplekt* were also different; frame adjustment was in the hands of shop-floor management, foremen and overlookers sometimes directed workers to other machines, undertook small repairs themselves, and kept daily records of machine output and *komplekt* performance.[101] Theoretically, ring-frame spinners were allowed only fifteen to twenty-five minutes' stoppage time in total for 'occasional elements' every day,[102] but Leningrad's operatives, at least, frequently stopped their work for ten or fifteen minutes to ask the foreman some question or other.[103] Discretion at the frame was thus limited, and the spinner's authority over girls in the *komplekt* far from absolute; in Leningrad they were supervised jointly by the spinner and the overlooker.[104]

While these features of ring-frame working might make it easier for rationalizers to gain control over the details of production, they were, for other reasons, no more welcome than those obtaining on the

[97] I. G. Eremin, *Trudovaia distsiplina v tekstil'noi promyshlennosti* (1929), pp. 20–1; *Ozdorovlenie truda*, pp. 60–2; Shvarabovich, *Kak uberech' sebia*, p. 36; Tikhomirov, *Odin den'*, pp. 38–41; Zaikov, *Na k-b fabrike*, p. 50; Ziman, *Chast'* 2, p. 367.

[98] Ziman, *Chast'* 2, pp. 281–5.

[99] Ia. Kvasha, F. Shofman, *Semichasovoi rabochii den' v tekstil'noi promyshlennosti* (1930), pp. 54–5.

[100] *Sistema i organizatsiia*, 8, 1925, p. 22; *TNB 1925*, p. 17.

[101] Kvasha, Shofman, *Semichasovoi rabochii den'*, pp. 54–5; *Ozdorovlenie truda*, pp. 60–2; Ziman, *Chast'* 2, pp. 395, 401–4.

[102] Ziman, *Chast'* 2, p. 319.   [103] *Golos tekstilei*, 17 June 1926.

[104] *Sistema i organizatsiia*, 8, 1925, p. 22.

selfactor: 'as is evident', complained one engineer, 'the vast majority of stoppages result from the failure of foremen and over-lookers to keep control over the workers and their machines, and from poor servicing work on the machines themselves.'[105] Failure to keep control probably arose partly because machine diversity encouraged *komplekt* specialization: the permanent allocation of spinners to frames they had learned to master. One example of this comes from a large mill in Kokhma, Ivanovo guberniya, where 100 ring-frames originated from three different European companies.[106] Equally, the ageing of the entire national stock of spindles attendant on the hiatus in capital investment could only serve to accelerate the drift away from standardization; on average, the country's ring-frame stock was thirty-five to forty years old in 1926.[107]

If the manufacture of Soviet frames was unlikely to reverse this trend,[108] patterns of recruitment, training and remuneration reinforced a sense of group solidarity quite unrelated to technological considerations.[109] Nevertheless, it remains the case that the sinews of power on the ring-frame *komplekt* were weaker than those on the selfactor, and that in general control passed from operative to foreman, from female to male. That the press reported the presence of female overlookers – 'already' two in one mill in Ivanovo-Voznesensk in 1926 – is an indication of their rarity. Only in Leningrad, perhaps because industrial diversity traditionally offered wider choices for male employment and thus weakened gender demarcation in cotton, is there any evidence of substantial female penetration of male supervisory roles; 'planners' who kept an eye on the frames for doffing were, according to one worker, almost all women in the city's mill, in contrast to the CIR where this was a man's trade.[110]

Weaving sheds

Although tensions arose between all departments over the use of inferior cotton, weavers felt the full impact of declining standards. In June 1927 the union's newspaper ran a series of letters on this issue which developed into a heated wrangle between mills in Leningrad and the Orekhovo-Zuevo district. Weavers complained that the yarn they received bore no relationship to the official count, mule weft being

[105] Ziman, *Chast'* 2, p.373.   [106] *Bol'shaia Kokhomskaia*, p. 30.
[107] *Golos tekstilei*, 9 October 1926.
[108] See page 58.
[109] See chapters 5, 12 and pp. 169–71.
[110] *Golos tekstilei*, 8 January 1926; 23 February 1926.

Plate 9 The weaving shed in Leningrad's Rabotnitsa mill, 1928. A revealing amateur photograph.

particularly bad, and that quality was at its lowest level in living memory. A year earlier Leningrad's Nogin mill attributed high waste rates, up to 25 per cent, to the receipt of poor warp and weft, and in 1924 shop delegates from the Nikol'skaia's weaving sheds demanded to know why their raw materials were of such low quality. Four American engineers, invited by the syndicate to comment on broadcloth output in four Soviet mills in 1929, reported that 60 to 70 per cent should be declared waste by their standards.[111] These were not isolated instances. A glance through *Golos tekstilei* reveals that scarcely a week passed without the problem of bad spinning receiving an airing somewhere or other. And though the authors of one 1925 factory history were not deceiving their readers when they remarked on the 'simple' processes attendant on power-loom weaving 'in all likelihood recognized by anyone who knows how to use a hand loom', they were somewhat short of the mark as far as most districts were concerned.[112]

[111] *Golos tekstilei*, 1 August 1924; 23 February 1926; 2 June 1927; 7 June 1927; 23 October 1929.
[112] *Bol'shaia Kokhomskaia*, p. 32.

Whilst it is true that in ideal conditions the technical demands of weaving were slight, revealing, incidentally, how the CIR's domestic weavers could be so readily absorbed into the mills,[113] the rapid spread of bad spinning in NEP serves as a caution against dismissing weavers' work as entirely standardized or unskilled.

The power, or Lancashire loom, developed by Roberts, Hill & Co. a century previously (the same Roberts responsible for the selfactor), made it possible for one weaver to work several frames simultaneously; operatives' functions were reduced to shuttle threading, checking warp and weft tensions and attending to breakages. Throughout NEP virtually the entire loom stock comprised simple one-shuttle Lancashire looms. Of the 70,000 listed in Ivanovo guberniya in 1918, only 551 were Jacquard frames for complex pattern weaving, and a mere 166 of the fully automatic variety.[114] This was the great weaving centre of the cotton industry. In mid-decade Ivanovo State Textile Trust alone, excluding the thirteen mills in the provincial capital and the forty-seven administered by the local economic council, accounted for just under one-third of all active looms in Russia,[115] so it is reasonable to take Ivanovo as characteristic of the whole country. In fact just 3 per cent of the national total were automatic multi-shuttle looms in 1928 compared with 85 per cent in America, the Soviet percentage remaining exactly the same as two years previously. Leningrad's Karl Marks enterprise had managed to produce only 708 in toto by autumn 1927, and occasional and rare foreign purchases were sometimes frustrated by unfamiliarity with the new technology: 100 English auto-looms stood idle in one Vladimir guberniya mill because the trust failed to buy the right spools.[116]

At first sight the automatic loom appears to be the very embodiment of rationalizers' dreams. Developed in the 1890s by the American Draper Corporation, the frame marked the high point in the displacement of labour by capital in weaving sheds, reducing the weaver to the status of piecer and shuttle-changer. But in reality it is doubtful if the machine was applicable to the social and economic milieu of NEP Russia. Capital costs were three times higher than for Lancashire looms, and the machine did not have the product range of its older

---

[113] See pp. 90–1.

[114] Singer, *History of Technology*, vol. 4, pp. 299–303; vol. 5, pp. 585–6; Figures from *I. gub. ind. census 1918*, pp. 58–84.

[115] *Trudy pervogo vsesoiuznogo s"ezda po ratsionalizatsii v tekstil'noi promyshlennosti. 19–24 maia 1926 goda* (1926), p. 100; *ITPT*, 21, 7 June 1926, p. 4; *Tekstil'nyi fabriki SSSR* (1927), pp. 38, 58–64.

[116] *Golos tekstilei*, 9 October 1926; 17 May 1928; *Predpriiatie*, 10, October 1927, p. 61; *Tekstil'nye novosti*, 8–9, August–September, 1929, p. 454.

rival – an important point, as will become evident. Moreover, it was best suited to combines spinning exclusively on ring-frames, and we have already seen that one-third of spindles were on mules.[117] Finally, the automatic loom required high-quality yarn and would not tolerate bad spinning: even in American mills, where ring-frame predominance ensured a perfect technical fit between spinning and weaving, thread arriving from the spinning halls often had to be re-wound in weaving sheds.[118]

Like most other equipment in Russia's mills the loom stock was old; in 1927 at least seven out of ten had been installed before 1910,[119] and as in some other shops weavers had reduced their work loads after the Revolution. Four looms to an operative was normal in the Iaroslavl' and Serpukhov districts before the war, compared with two per weaver in most mills before the mid-1920s.[120] The real workload also decreased because weavers were at the end of the production chain and thus completely dependent on the efficiency of all the other rooms in the mill: 'in our factory', commented a worker from Ivanovo's Bol'shevik, 'it often happens that the thread runs out. Then the weavers stroll around and wait for a delivery while the looms stand idle.'[121] Foremen fixed 'loom stroke', the number of beats on the cloth, which generally ranged from 175 to 240 each minute, depending on cotton sort and count, and shuttle faults were supposed to be corrected by overlookers, but rigid implementation of the formal division of responsibilities could lead to a further fall in output. In Moscow, for instance, weavers were in the habit of stopping their looms for long periods while mechanics were found to undertake some minor adjustment or repair.[122] *Golos tekstilei* lampooned these habits in 1926: 'weaver Ivanovich needs a new shuttle ... first he goes to the overlooker, then from the overlooker to the foreman, then from the foreman to the storeman, then from the storeman to the director ... when all the signatures are collected – by the end of the following day – everything's fine.'[123]

[117] See p. 51.
[118] Singer, *History of Technology*, vol. 5, pp. 585–6; vol. 6, p. 639; W. H. Lazonick, 'Competition, specialization and industrial decline', *Journal of Economic History*, 41, 1, March 1981, pp. 31–4; W. H. Lazonick, 'Factor costs and the diffusion of ring spinning in Britain prior to World War One', *The Quarterly Journal of Economics*, 46, 1, February 1981, pp. 94, 100.
[119] Shukhgal'ter, *Vnutrizavodskii kontrol'*, p. 5; *Tekstil'nye novosti*, 10–11, October–November 1927, p. 365.
[120] *Khoziaistvo i upravlenie*, 5, 1925, p. 55; *Sistema i organizatsiia*, 8, 1925, p. 22.
[121] *ISNOT*, p. 3.
[122] *Golos tekstilei*, 17 June 1926; Ziman, *Normirovanie tkatskogo stanka*, pp. 21, 26.
[123] *Golos tekstilei*, 29 June 1926.

Weavers responded to the high incidence of bad spinning, the advanced age of the loom stock and bureaucratic controls at the frame by modifying their work practices. In some parts of Moscow guberniya they became responsible for finding and fitting new parts for their frames,[124] but rationalizers took a jaundiced view of the gradual encroachment of such non-standard work routines: 'in the majority of mills in the Soviet Union weavers not only work at their machines, they also have to watch over the frames, because most of them are in poor condition – thread breakages necessitate much hand-work.'[125] Another textile engineer complained about the 'irrational' use of the weaving labour force; skilled weavers had to fetch their own thread and other materials, 'and it even happens that they have to adjust and trim the looms themselves'.[126]

In particular mills at particular times the control exercised by weavers may have increased still more if the quality of shop-floor management was felt to be low; in one district of Ivanovo guberniya in 1927, for example, not more than half the overlookers were considered to be properly qualified.[127] The devolution of control over work, however, could occur only in a hesitant, sporadic fashion. Lancashire looms had none of the mystique surrounding the mule, and there was no British tradition of craft in power-loom weaving which could have been grafted onto the Russian mill. Sometimes authority was demonstrated in a potent and unambiguous manner: when overlookers in Tomna, Ivanovo guberniya, struck in autumn 1920 they brought the weaving sheds to a halt by forcibly shutting down the looms of those weavers who refused to join them.[128] Patterns of control were, no doubt, also conditioned by gender and culture. Because weaving sheds were a natural entrée into the mill for a peasant population with a still-existing or very recent tradition of domestic working, patriarchal authority could easily be exercised by male supervisors to extract obedience from women, but one caveat needs to be entered here: although weaving was dominated by women, it was not their exclusive preserve. Weaving sheds are the one place in the mill where trade allocation by gender was somewhat blurred.[129]

If the epidemic of bad spinning reduced the attraction of the automatic loom and throws into doubt assumptions about standard work routines on the Lancashire loom, the industry's product range

[124] *ISNOT*, pp. 21–2.   [125] Budanov, *Obshchie poniatiia*, pp. 77–8.
[126] Abramov, *Nagliadnyi uchet*, p. 78.
[127] *Rabochii krai*, 7 April 1927.   [128] *Rabochii krai*, 4 November 1920.
[129] *1926 census*, tom XXXIV, table V p. 124, table 8 pp. 190–1.

demonstrates the irrelevance of the newer technology and the diversity of work carried out on the old. In 1924 the syndicate tried to summarize what had been happening to the industry over the previous quarter century. Before the Revolution the Moscow district produced better cloths for urban consumers while Vladimir and Ivanovo guberniyas ran up cheap calicos for the peasant market. During and after the collapse residual output went to the military and specialization vanished. The resurrection of the market after 1921 reversed this trend, but established area specialization failed to reappear; instead, as part of the 'reaction against the cage' of War Communism mills fine-tuned their output to their own perceptions of the market. Cloth sorts multiplied, 'often without the knowledge of the trusts'.[130] In the first half of the 1920s cloth diversification reached staggering proportions – or rather proportions quite normal in a western *laissez faire* economy. One source claims that by 1924 a total of 2,600 lines were being produced, and a figure of this order of magnitude seems reasonable when the average number of looms per cloth sort in Ivanovo State Textile Trust in 1922 was only 38.5. For a single mill in Tver' in 1924 and 1927 two sources agree on a figure of 500 cloth sorts. That a third insists that there were just sixty-nine in summer 1924[131] serves to reveal the confusions buzzing in the minds of some observers, and the tendency for decision making to shift to the primary level of the individual mill. Even after the 1925 rationalization drive the evidence belied the official claim that there should be only three sorts in 1926.[132]

Three points are clear. First, mills exhibited few of the features associated with standardization, even when technologies appear at first glance to be standard; secondly, it would be far from easy to rationalize the rich and complex world of the shop floor. Thirdly, as far as workers are concerned little is to be gained by imagining that it is possible to conjure up the past by reference to the presence of a supposedly common technical inheritance. But while one can try to delineate the broad matrix of forces present in a given room, their particular and specific combination remains elusive. Large chunks of the delicate latticework of interaction on the shop-floor are lost to the

[130] V. M. Makarov, A. A. Fedotov, eds., *Trudy soveshchaniia proizvodstvennikov v tekstil'noi promyshlennosti. Moskva, 2–4 iiunia 1924g* (1925), p. 5.
[131] M. Dobb, *Soviet Economic Development Since 1917* (1966), p. 17; *Golos tekstilei*, 5 August 1924; 20 August 1927; *Sistema i organizatsiia*, 1–2, 1926, pp. 67–8.
[132] *Trudy pervogo vsesoiuznogo s"ezda*, p. 100; *ITPT*, 21, 7 June 1926, p. 4.

historian forever. The sources simply refuse to speak beyond a certain threshold of experience.

Nevertheless, enough has been said for us to appreciate that the Revolution bequeathed to the Bolsheviks a vast lumber room of equipment which was neither neutral nor value free. In many rooms a choice of working technique, which allowed some operatives some degree of autonomy at the frame, had already been made over half a century previously and in another country: their inheritance came cheaply; the struggles had taken place elsewhere. Thereafter the story of the interrelationship between technology and technique was projected in shadow-play on the Russian screen, but the shadows took on substance and developed a life of their own. Well after the Revolution factory, shop, and even machine loyalties were still very strong: in 1925 Ivanovo guberniya's Bol'shaia Kokhomskaia proudly listed the medals it had won in St Petersburg, Paris and Chicago between 1849 and 1900;[133] *Golos tekstilei* ran frequent campaigns where one mill was picked out and criticized for some failing (the usual response to which was for each shop to blame the other); after late payment of wages the biggest single cause of strikes in the Moscow district in 1922/23 was 'shop demands',[134] and somewhat later (1927), an article on tensions in Ivanovo guberniya singled out 'demands from one group of workers in one shop' as a significant cause of conflict. That year, when the issue of 'shop narrowness' came up at the province's seventeenth textileworkers' union congress a delegate found 'nothing strange' in its existence.[135] Two years on the guberniya's party conference thought it expedient to point out the necessity of moving textile workers away 'from group, shop and individualistic feelings' towards a 'general class consciousness'.[136] But loyalty to one frame or machine group was almost bound to occur in the conditions pertaining in NEP, if only because movement from supposedly standard frames could affect wages. 'Right up to the present day', noted the union's president in 1929, 'textile workers are still wedded to their own machines . . . and they don't want to be moved . . . If an operative has been working on one [group] for ten or fifteen years, it seems to her that if she transfers to others she won't be able to manage them.'[137]

[133] *Bol'shaia Kokhomskaia*, p. 10.
[134] *Otchet o rabote moskovskogo gubernskogo otdela vsesoiuznogo professional'nogo soiuza tekstil'shchikov mart 1922g–mart 1923g* (1923), p. 127.
[135] *Rabochii krai*, 17 June 1927; 26 June 1927.   [136] *Rabochii krai*, 1 January 1929.
[137] *Rabochii krai*, 23 March 1929.

5 Making an operative

If the son of a weaver is always a weaver, the son of a foreman always a foreman, the son of an engineer always an engineer, then the children of unskilled workers will always remain unskilled.

> Letter to *Golos tekstilei*, 24 March 1927, complaining about job inheritance

Recruitment

The regime's answer to the problems of unemployment and labour allocation was the Bureau of Labour. Abolished after a brief existence in 1918 and resurrected under the auspices of the Commissariat of Labour in 1922, it gradually established a network of offices throughout the country. By 1926 there were some 250 labour exchanges with about 1,000 affiliated 'correspondence points', or local branches, in the countryside. Broadly speaking they were charged with the twin duties of distributing unemployment benefit and placing workers in industry.[1] Our concern is with their latter function. Initially the bureaux exercised monopoly control over the labour market, but as industry recovered they were found to be incapable of handling the vast number of demobilized soldiers, returning workers and migrating peasants looking for jobs. Local registers, which supposedly listed vacancies, the number of unemployed and their particular skills, quickly became fictions bearing little relationship to the real state of the market. Faced with these problems enterprises responded by hiring workers directly, 'at the factory gate'.[2] In August 1923 the Commissariat of Labour tacitly recognized the efficacy of this

[1] L. S. Rogachevskaia, *Likvidatsiia bezrabotitsy v SSSR 1917–1930gg* (1973), pp. 95–6; K. I. Suvorov, *Istoricheskii opyt KPSS po likvidatsii bezrabotitsy, 1917–1930gg* (1968), p. 101.
[2] Y. S. Borisov, *et al.*, eds., *Outline History of the Soviet Working Class* (1973), p. 90; *Russia: the Official Report of the British Trades Union Delegation to Russia and Caucasia, November and December 1924* (1925), p. 153.

practice by cancelling their monopoly; thereafter 'direct employment' turned the exchanges into recording agencies. The trades unions were left to influence matters in the localities as best they could by negotiating clauses restricting hiring to members of their particular union when collective agreements were drawn up with employers. The Central Council of Trades Unions seemed to have won a major victory in December 1926 when restrictive hiring was made binding on all employers, but there was a widely exploited let-out clause which stated that especially skilled workers in short supply did not have to be union members.[3]

The Central Council's December resolution was probably caused by disquiet over the declining influence of the unions. There was certainly unease in the textileworkers' union. A month previously *Golos tekstilei* had started a vigorous campaign against current practices: 'time and again', complained a Moscow correspondent, 'collective agreements have stated that workers must be hired only through the labour exchanges' while managers continued to flout the union and look elsewhere. In the same issue editorial staff revealed that in the first three months of 1926 only half of all new workers in the region were recruited via the bureaux, and that most of the rest did not even have a union card.[4] Complaints were not confined to the CIR. A Leningrad worker believed that the majority of operatives recruited between January and July 1926 were taken from the factory gate and that most did not belong to the union.[5]

Directors had sound reasons for preferring non-union labour. During NEP, when trusts had to cope with erratic raw material supply and the sporadic eruption of efficiency drives – which invariably turned out to be campaigns against overmanning, mills might have to close down or cut their workforce at very short notice. Non-union labour could be dismissed without prior union consultation and without depleting enterprise or trust funds, since compensation, severance, or half-pay applied to union members only.[6] It would be a mistake, however, to characterize the issue of direct employment as a straightforward conflict between mill managers and a free market in labour on one side and local union branches and the workforce on the other. Hiring without recourse to the exchanges and in contravention of collective agreements was sometimes a matter of collusion between

[3] Borisov, *Outline History*, p. 91; S. M. Schwarz, *Labor in the Soviet Union* (1953), pp. 39–43.
[4] *Golos tekstilei*, 13 November 1926.   [5] *Golos tekstilei*, 23 October 1926.
[6] M. Dewar, *Labour Policy in the USSR 1917–28* (1956), pp. 91, 96–117, 142, 246, 256, 259.

local union branches and factory managers: Mel'nichanskii, who replaced Kutuzov as union president in 1926, reported that year that in some parts of Ivanovo guberniya 'peasants are enrolled in batches into the union from the nearby areas. Then they go to the mills with their union card and the factory committees take them on. Needless to say, this doesn't help those on the books of the labour exchanges'.[7] Frolov, president of Ivanovo State Textile Trust, put the problem from the employers' side in an exasperated condemnation of the new bureaux in 1922: 'now they say we don't have the right to hire from the villages. We must take pure proletarians from the bureaux of labour . . . but take skilled weavers as an example, where do they come from? They have always come from the villages.'[8] Nor, once again, was the practice confined to the CIR. When Shaginian, a popular writer of the period, visited Leningrad and chatted to the mule spinners she also noticed that 'old, experienced women with a history of work in the industry are not to be found in the labour exchanges. Instead there are young city girls with hungry faces, but "without particular skills" and without any experience.'[9] Replying to *Golos tekstilei*'s campaign, the director of a Moscow mill insisted that the factory would continue to make its own arrangements for hiring weavers from the countryside because the exchanges were unable to meet his requirements for competent labour.[10]

The notion of symbiosis helps to explain why the industry tended to ignore official recruitment channels. The survival of handloom weaving and the inability of this vigorous domestic sector to get enough thread to meet its needs has already been sketched out.[11] Factory competition and supply discontinuities thus checked the expansion of handloom weaving at the same time as mills were anxiously looking for a constituency capable of rapid assimilation on to the shop floor, and some new workers from peasant families could adapt just as quickly to the technical demands of production (if not to time–work discipline) as the offspring of worker families removed from the rural economy, children and adolescents whose contact with the world of work was restricted by current legislation. This was

[7] *Golos tekstilei*, 16 October 1926.
[8] *Stenograficheskii otchet 1-go vserossiiskogo s"ezda rabotnikov tekstil'noi promyshlennosti v Moskve, 12–16 okt. 1922g* (1923), p. 37.
[9] M. Shaginian, *Nevskaia nitka* (1925), p. 23.   [10] *Golos tekstilei*, 13 November 1926.
[11] See pp. 11, 14. See also *Planovoe khoziastvo*, 2, February 1927, p. 23; S. P. Sereda, ed., *Kustarnaia promyshlennost' SSSR*, vyp. 1 (1925), p. 92.

particularly so in weaving: witness remarks from Ivanovo guberniya's Bol'shaia Kokhomskaia cited above.[12]

But if 'proletarian' background did not presuppose immediate workplace competence, it is also the case that we cannot re-jig the forces underpinning direct employment by imagining that trust and mill administrators, local union officials, and peasant families with some interest in handloom weaving were united in a conspiracy against established workers who then languished on the books of the labour exchanges. Prospective cotton workers of all kinds, whether 'peasants' or 'pure proletarians' – a distinction, as we have seen, of limited value – took action which bypassed the Commissariat of Labour's rules and undermined the union's collective agreements. In 1927 a member of the union's central committee remarked that before the Revolution operatives often worked in family groups and that wages were paid to the family head. Something of this survived into NEP. 'Right up to the present time', he continued, 'it would be difficult to find a mill where there are not whole families working in the same factory.'[13] More will be said about this later on, but the union's preference for positive discrimination in favour of established workers' children, based on the hope that proletarian elements in the mill would be strengthened, also boosted this tradition. The unease which family-based hiring subsequently generated was partly due to the difficulty of clarifying the practice in terms of class or egalitarianism. This conundrum does not concern us, but the sparks of irritation and confusion which found their way into the press have left a multitude of traces which reveal the importance of kin-related hiring.

In the first few months of NEP the union's central committee had started to worry about mill workers' children. Because many were neither at school nor at work some lived from hand to mouth as speculators.[14] By 1926 concern over low skill levels had led one syndicate author to a sharp awareness of the role of the family: 'self-possessed, disciplined, hereditary workers, formed by the environment of the mill, were scarce before the War and are even more scarce now'. This was in stark contrast to the English operative, who was congratulated on having had 'more than a century to develop his skills. There spinning and weaving skills were handed down from father to son.'[15] Nevertheless, Shaginian found that such generational

---

[12] See p. 83.   [13] *Golos tekstilei*, 24 March 1927.
[14] *Tekstil'shchik, k stanku*, 20 July 1921.
[15] *Izvestiia tekstil'noi promyshlennosti i torgovli*, 33–34, 15 September 1926, p. 1 (hereafter *ITPT*).

links were not entirely absent from Russia. In Leningrad the parents of a textile workers' child were 'not only its mother and father, but the mill . . . from childhood onwards they stand in a special relationship to their parents and the factory. They became their parents' assistants.'[16] Elsewhere there is evidence of kin recruitment. The author of a book on women workers in the industry reported enthusiastically that from mid-decade onwards 'the number of textile workers [drawn] from amongst the families of existing textile workers' was everywhere increasing. This was in contrast to recruitment from the village,[17] a comparison of dubious validity since there is little reason to think that many peasants and handloom weavers did not also have family in the mill. Support for blurring the distinction between peasant and pro-letarian families comes from a Iaroslavl' source of 1924. In this overwhelmingly rural province the local union branch encouraged workers, drawing no distinctions as to background, to bring their sons and daughters into the mills in order to teach them their trades.[18] The issue came up again in 1927 when the union in Moscow guberniya unconditionally condemned family-based hiring. In January and March *Golos tekstilei* published disapproving cartoons lampooning direct employment through the family or via 'recommendation' by showing a prospective worker passing through the factory gates holding a large envelope marked 'private', but later on the paper reported, without adverse comment, that workers were petitioning management to allow job vacancies to be filled by members of their own families.[19]

'Recommendation' should properly be included under the heading *magarych*. In modern Russian the word means 'wetting a bargain', but earlier in the century it had a much stronger cultural resonance.[20] All

---

[16] Shaginian, *Nevskaia nitka*, p. 19. Kindergarten shortages may have helped to socialize children into production. The union thought them to be an urgent necessity, not only to combat child neglect but also to free women's attention from their offspring so they could get on with their work, a hint that youngsters were on the shop floor. In Vladimir guberniya's Kommunisticheskii Avangard at least, children played in the storerooms and shops: *Golos tekstilei*, 8 June 1926; *Rezoliutsii i postanovleniia 6-go s"ezda professional'nogo soiuza tekstil'shchikov* (1924), p. 43.

[17] V. Borodin, *Zhenskii trud v Sovetskoi tekstil'noi promyshlennosti* (1926), p. 9.

[18] *Golos tekstilei*, 8 August 1924. A few days later someone from the Nikol'skaia complained that brothers and sons of employed workers were being hired 'over the heads' of well-qualified operatives out of work for two years or more: *Golos tekstilei*, 12 August 1924.

[19] *Golos tekstilei*, 6 January 1927; 12 March 1927; 17 March 1927; 18 March 1927. See also chapter 12.

[20] A way of getting a job through inside 'contacts', it was a popular target of NEP satirists: in Il'f and Petrov's *Svetlaia lichnost'* hiring via *magarych* becomes impossible only when the prospective candidate is rendered invisible.

references to *magarych* are hostile, making it difficult to uncover the true nature of its extent, but, according to one author, in cotton it was universal: '*magarych* is not an occasional or episodic thing, not something that happens in the odd mill or with the odd foreman. The system and tradition of *magarych is still a powerful force in mills and amongst foremen.*' The 'law of *magarych*', he went on, extended to all textile factories in the Ivanovo-Voznesensk district. In the Sereda 'from shop to shop, from spinning rooms to weaving sheds, from ring-frames to flyer-frames ... everywhere I've experienced this unpleasant atmosphere.'[21] Although the union's central committee was predictably 'decisively against' it,[22] the open discussion of *magarych* in the textile press hints at widespread application. *Magarych* had its roots in the old pre-revolutionary mill, averred a correspondent in 1928, but is now becoming ever stronger, with shop foremen at the centre of the system: 'pay, and you'll be given work – don't pay, and you'll be unemployed'.[23] When managers in Vladimir guberniya posted up notices about vacancies at the mill gates they were closely followed by shop foremen who 'selected' their workers and then passed on their details ('union membership, etc.') to the factory committees. In the Shuia and Nerl' districts of Ivanovo guberniya hopeful recruits distributed vodka to foremen and overlookers in order to secure places. A 1926 cartoon shows a worker being hired after becoming the drinking partner of a foreman.[24]

Training

As will become apparent *magarych* also played a part in training, but the formal method of placing recruits in particular trades was the *fabrichno-zavodskoe uchenichestvo*, or factory school attached to the mill. As more settled conditions obtained after the end of War Communism economic recovery exposed gaps in the labour market occasioned by war and revolution and the general weakness of the tsarist apprenticeship system. This misalliance between industry's

---

21 *Komsomol'skaia pravda*, 27 February 1927 [stress in the original].
22 *Informatsionnaia svodka TsK vsesoiuznogo profsoiuza tekstil'shchikov*, 13(25), 5 March 1927, p. 4.
23 *Golos tekstilei*, 19 May 1928. Before 1917 workers moving back and forth from village to factory were expected to bring gifts to their foremen and punished if they did not, and according to von Laue 'extortion and graft' characterized relations between foremen and workers at the turn of the century: R. E. Johnson, *Peasant and Proletarian. The Working Class of Moscow in the Late Nineteenth Century* (1979), p. 37; T. von Laue, 'Russian labor between field and factory, 1892–1903', *California Slavic Studies*, 3, 1974, p. 57.
24 *Golos tekstilei*, 13 November 1926; 18 April 1928; 19 May 1928.

Table 4. *Factory schools in ten Ivanovo guberniya cotton mills June 1923*

Mill [a, b]	Factory school pupils in June 1923 [c]	Approximate mill population in 1918[b]	1925[a]
Boniachenskaia	42	?	5,659
Kamenskaia	19	?	shut
Bol'shaia Kokhomskaia	50	1,332	6,062
Navol'skaia	40	?	3,664
Rodnikovskaia	62	9,881	9,115
Seredskaia	36	11,740	9,784
Bol'shevik	35	4,934	6,343
Tomna	50	5,940	4,604
Shuiskaia	40	6,000	5,934
Iuzhskaia	30	shut	4,487

Sources:
[a] *Tekstil'nye fabriki SSSR* (1927), pp. 14–15, 60–1.
[b] *Spisok fabrik, zavodov i drugikh promyshlennykh predpriiatii ivanovo-voznesenskoi gubernii. Po dannym vserossiiskoi promyshlennoi i professional'noi perepis' 1918 goda* (1919), pp. 60–3, 66–73, 76–7.
[c] *Vosstanovlenie tekstil'noi promyshlennosti ivanovo-voznesenskoi gubernii, 1920–1925gg* (1966), pp. 133–5.

needs and the skill profile of the adolescent population received attention at the eleventh party congress in 1922,[25] but in cotton the factory school movement never kept pace with the industry's recovery. Although the union in Ivanovo guberniya announced its intention to arrange for the training of all fourteen to eighteen year olds in the industry in October 1921, almost simultaneously the central committee predicted that shortages of skilled workers would oblige factories to disperse potential instructors to the shop floor to act as a leaven raising the competence of the unskilled,[26] and despite the union's hopes there is little evidence that factory schools played much part in training recruits. A mere fifty were registered for courses in the large Tomna mill in 1922, for example, and only four of them were girls.[27] Next year Moscow announced plans similar to those of

[25] N. V. Poliakova, 'Bor'ba rabochikh-tekstil'shchikov za povyshenie proizvoditel'nosti truda v 1921–1925gg. (Po materialam Moskvy i moskovskoi gubernii)', *Voprosy istorii*, 6, July 1959, p. 24.
[26] *Tekstil'shchik, k stanku*, 10 September 1921; *Vosstanovlenie tekstil'noi promyshlennosti ivanovo-voznesenskoi gubernii, 1920–1925gg.* (1966), p. 126 (hereafter *VTPI-VG 1920–25*).
[27] *VTPI-VG 1920–25*, p. 129.

Ivanovo, factory schools for all cotton trades, but by March there were only thirty-seven schools in the guberniya with 2,185 trainees on role.[28] Twenty-six schools were established in Vladimir guberniya throughout 1923 but many turned out to be ephemeral.[29] In regions where production was concentrated in a few large combines, thus giving administrators the chance to concentrate their resources, performance was no better. The Iartsevkaia was the single functioning cotton mill in Smolensk guberniya in the early 1920s, nevertheless, in 1923 when the mill employed over 7,000 workers, more than half of them women, the school trained only twenty-three adolescents, twenty-one of them males.[30] By mid-decade when CIR mills were experiencing a second wave of recruitment following the ebb occasioned by the scissors crisis and the first serious attempts at labour intensification, the failure of the movement was thrown into sharp relief. The weak level of courses in Ivanovo guberniya in 1923 – courses which should have been providing skilled workers for the coming years – is evident from table 4. In December 1923 a survey showed that only two out of twenty-four mills sampled in the guberniya had a majority of their youngsters in schools,[31] and in spring 1924 *Rabochii krai* revealed that a mere 150 adolescents were on courses in the province.[32]

In fact from the mid-1920s onwards it appears that the union considered individual or brigade training, methods whereby a skilled worker trained up a group of adolescents or an individual on the shop floor, to be just as important as the schools, particularly as the latter were sometimes criticized for not taking on girls.[33] Figures published by *Golos tekstilei* in April 1926 give rough idea of the balance between the various types of instruction in Moscow guberniya's cotton mills in the mid-NEP years: forty-nine schools were training 8,503 youngsters, 105 brigades 2,996 adolescents, while another 5,782 were in the hands

---

[28] *Otchet o rabote moskovskogo gubernskogo otdela vsesoiuznogo professional'nogo soiuza tekstil'shchikov mart 1922g–mart 1923g* (1923), table 10 pp. 147–8.

[29] Iu. F. Iakovlev, *Vladimirskie rabochie v bor'be i ukreplenie soiuza s krest'ianstvom v 1921–1925 godakh* (1963), p. 24; *Nashe khoziaistvo* (Vladimir), 11–12, November–December 1925, p. 41.

[30] *Golos tekstilei*, 3 March 1927.

[31] *Otchet o rabote ivanovo-voznesenskogo gubernskogo otdela vserossiiskogo professional'nogo soiuza tekstil'shchikov za vremia s 1 iiunia 1923g po 1 apr. 1924g. XIII–XIV s"ezd* (1924), table 13 p. 42 (hereafter *I–V gubotdel VPST 1923–24*).

[32] *Rabochii krai*, 4 March 1924.

[33] *Rezoliutsii i postanovleniia 7-go gubernskogo s"ezda soiuza tekstil'shchikov, 25–27 okt. 1924g* (1924), pp. 19–20; *Rezoliutsii moskovskogo gubotdela soiuza tekstil'shchikov za period oktiabr' 1924g–fevral' 1925g* (1925), p. 13.

of individual masters. The rest – 1,003 – were listed as receiving no instruction whatsoever.[34]

Shop-floor training had been discussed by the union's central committee in 1923. Interestingly, worries were expressed about the potential loss of control should training migrate to the bench; the adopted resolution primly stated that places should be allocated to youngsters 'of the right character', that 'exact accounts' should be kept and 'clear guide-lines' issued to instructors.[35] By 1925 such concerns were receding into the background. A speaker at the first congress of norm setters in the textile industry advocated recasting the role of the schools. Because the workforce was growing rapidly they should use only highly skilled instructors and be reserved for potentially highly skilled operatives; the rest should pick up their skills at the bench.[36] There was also much disquiet over the competence of graduates. Someone from Egor'evsk attending a conference of young textile workers in Moscow guberniya in 1928 lambasted the 'devil may care' attitude of the young who came straight from the classroom, claiming that they would not 'even become average, let alone good workers'. Youngsters at the Nikol'skaia 'did not go straight to the machines, as they should, but to the kitchens, or to work as cleaners or stokers'.[37]

Because the sources invariably classify workers by skill or pay level, at first glance it appears that the schools offered youngsters the only chance of advancement. An investigation of twenty-one Ivanovo guberniya mills in December 1923, for instance, found that 70 per cent of all adolescents were in unskilled jobs and 11 per cent in skilled trades; the factory schools were training a further 19 per cent to take up skilled positions.[38] *Rabkrin* and the union's central committee also drew a sharp distinction between adolescents in factory schools who would become skilled workers and the majority condemned to low skills and low pay,[39] but it is far from the case that the schools offered courses for all cotton trades, skilled or otherwise. Iaroslavl' had none for ring-frames or looms, the Central Institute of Labour in Moscow offered instruction on ring- and flyer-frames only, and in Shuia,

---

[34] *Golos tekstilei*, 16 April 1926.
[35] *Rezoliutsii 3-go plenuma TsK soiuza tekstil'shchikov (12–15 aprelia 1923g)* (1923), pp. 45–6 (hereafter *3-go plen TsK VPST 1923*).
[36] *Rezoliutsii 1-go vsesoiuznogo s"ezda otdelov truda i T.N.B. tekstil'noi promyshlennosti (20–26/IX–1925g)* (1926), pp. 24–5 (hereafter *TNB 1925*).
[37] *Trud*, 11 September 1928. For other complaints about incompetence see *Golos tekstilei*, 11 August 1925; 4 September 1925; 8 September 1925; 20 November 1925; *Khar'kovskii tekstil'shchik*, 1925, p. 4; *Tekstil'nye novosti*, 1, January 1929, p. 45.
[38] Calculated from *I–V gubotdel VPST 1923–24*, table 3, p. 42.
[39] *Khoziaistvo i upravlenie*, 2, February 1926, p. 66.

Ivanovo-Voznesensk, and in Leningrad courses were incomplete.[40] The absence of any mention at all of formal training procedures on selfactors in these sources is confirmed by a plenum of the union's central committee in 1925.[41]

In reality many of those outside the orbit of the schools and notionally unskilled were attached to work teams, and were, of course, receiving training. They were moving up the *komplekt*, albeit slowly. Others were waiting to inherit jobs which belonged to the family. In March 1927 a weaver from a rural mill, himself the son of a weaver, made a point similar to the one set at the head of this chapter. Four months later *Golos tekstilei* devoted half a page to workers' letters on this issue. Job inheritance necessarily led to the rigid stratification of the workforce, complained a Moscow operative: the unskilled cannot break through because 'masters will transmit the secrets of their trade only to their own children'. Family training inevitably results in the reinforcement of traditional work practices, remarked another.[42] Two old women writing in 1963 recalled their time in Leningrad's Ravenstvo mill during NEP: 'we were trained in the old ways without instruments . . . by women who were sometimes reluctant to pass on the secrets of their skills'.[43]

Officials viewed the problems of on-the-job training with some hesitation. In 1925 a speaker at the norm setters' congress limited himself to recommending shop-based 'schemes' where the semi-skilled trained the unskilled, together with a campaign to entice back any skilled workers who had still not returned from the countryside.[44] Although way back in 1921 the union's central committee had predicted that the 'difficult position' of old workers – those past retirement age with scarcely enough to live on – would be resolved easily by using them to pass on their knowledge,[45] the various enticements subsequently offered appear to have held little attraction. 'Part of the workforce doesn't fully understand how important it is to train skilled workers', reported a Leningrad newspaper in 1925. That year skilled operatives who agreed to take on trainees were recommended for 10 per cent pay rises, pushed up to 15 per cent in 1926; nevertheless, *Golos tekstilei* made much of a story about a master

---

[40] *Golos tekstilei*, 18 June 1926; 28 April 1927; *Leningradskii tekstil'*, 1, January 1926, p. 26; *Nauchnaia organizatsiia truda, proizvodstva i upravleniia, 1918–1930gg* (1969), pp. 251–2; Simchenko-Sosnovkin, *Tekstil'naia molodezh' na profrabote i v proizvodstve. Rabota soiuza tekstilei sredi molodezhi* (1926), pp. 7, 11; *Tekstil'nye novosti*, 4, April 1930, pp. 204–6.
[41] *3-go plen Tsk VPST 1923*, pp. 38–42.   [42] *Golos tekstilei*, 12 July 1927.
[43] *Zhenshchiny goroda Lenina* (1963), p. 197.
[44] *TNB 1925*, p. 25.   [45] *Tekstil'shchik, k stanku*, 1 December 1921.

spinner who refused to train up a youngster.[46] *Rabkrin* and the central committee of the union urged the industry to make brigade and individual training 'more expedient'; workers were 'indifferent' to youngsters, there should be some 'stimulus' to encourage them.[47] Elsewhere it seems that operatives were not so indifferent. Speaking to a plenum of Moscow guberniya's local union branch in 1927 Zorin, a member of the central committee, asserted that 'the question of unemployment amongst young mill hands, and the question of their training, is now regarded even more seriously by operatives with families than the question of pay'.[48] Next year, on the other hand, indifference was still in evidence; a factory committee in Ramenskoe reported that foremen and overlookers were not interested in training novices.[49]

The explanation for all these confusions is fairly simple. Writers generally shied away from the social dimension of the subject. To be successful it was preferable if shop-floor training was rooted in some underlying bond. Ivanovo district again: 'if you want to begin something, if you want to learn or understand – *magarych*, money, vodka is necessary ... if you don't play along you can study for two hundred years, but nothing will ever get started'.[50] There individual apprenticeship was everywhere linked to *magarych* – 'trainees pay what they must and keep quiet'.[51] In Sereda weavers were expected to reward their overlookers upon qualification. Recruits to another mill were invited to buy vodka for the foremen in order to secure a decent loom. Those who refused were also allocated the worst warp and weft, and all trainees were advised to make a contribution to the overlookers' drinks cupboard if the factory committee was not to be told that their recruitment and training were unofficial.[52] Nor was the link between *magarych* and training confined to the CIR. It was widespread in Leningrad's Krasnyi Tkach according to a correspondent in *Golos tekstilei* in 1928,[53] and in that and the previous year the paper published cartoons showing adolescents approaching a mill loaded down with food, drink and money while members of the factory committee looked on through their fingers.[54]

At its best *magarych* could probably be called patronage. Youngsters

[46] *Golos tekstilei*, 16 February 1926; 5 October 1926; *Leningradskii tekstil'shchik*, 1 December 1925; *3-go plen TsK VPST 1923*, p. 19.
[47] *Khoziastvo i upravlenie*, 2, February 1926, p. 68.   [48] *Golos tekstilei*, 18 March 1927.
[49] *Trud*, 28 July 1928.   [50] *Komsomol'skaia pravda*, 27 February 1927.
[51] *Rabochii krai*, 11 March 1927.
[52] *Komsomol'skaia pravda*, 27 February 1927.
[53] *Golos tekstilei*, 19 May 1928; 31 May 1928; *Rabochii krai*, 23 July 1927.
[54] *Golos tekstilei*, 12 July 1927; 19 May 1928.

without other connections who were otherwise likely to receive indifferent training had at least paid their dues and could expect something in return. At its worst it was little more than a protection racket. In Ivanovo guberniya's Varentsova the highly skilled formed themselves into a sort of mafia. 'Membership fees' ranged from five to twenty-five roubles, and before the secret police broke the ring it had spread to include the party and Komsomol.[55] Just as menacingly, the system could provide an excuse for the sexual exploitation of women on the shop floor.[56]

But whatever *magarych* was it seems to have functioned as an alternative to the family. When Zorin made his speech in 1927 he also said that many adolescents received skilled training through the system *magarych* because 'not every young worker has parents who are skilled workers'.[57] A few years earlier another central committee functionary, this time from Ivanovo, made the link between the systemic and social advantages of kin-based training. Two problems beset the industry in his region: the shortage of skilled workers and the shortage of housing. As many thousands of girls were listed as unskilled on the files of the exchanges and thus were of no use to the mills, mothers should bring their daughters into the factory to pass on their own skills.[58] An *émigré* textile engineer confirmed that during NEP factory schools were to be found only in the largest mills, and that elsewhere individual training was usually based on kinship networks.[59] There is also a rather sour observation from the Egor'evsk-Ramenskoe region in 1925 on what looks like the same phenomenon:

> Now the mills have started to take the grown-up youngsters of established textile workers into their shops, adolescents between the ages of nineteen and twenty-four. They're given only five weeks instruction. The factory management think they're killing two birds with one stone – solving the problem of skill shortage and the housing problem – because these youngsters continue to live with their parents.[60]

To the extent that such adolescents could be subsumed in the general family economy pay levels could be kept down. Delegates to the 1926 conference of young textile workers learned that they earned on average only half the adult wage. In Ivanovo-Voznesensk some

[55] *Komsomol'skaia pravda*, 27 February 1927.
[56] See *Golos tekstilei*, 23 June 1926; 17 May 1927; 16 February 1928; 30 May 1928; *Trud*, 7 October 1928.
[57] *Golos tekstilei*, 18 March 1927.   [58] *Golos tekstilei*, 18 June 1924.
[59] V. A. Kungurtsev, *Tekstil'naia promyshlennost' SSSR* (1957), p. 43.
[60] *Golos tekstilei*, 11 August 1925.

earned nothing at all.[61] An anonymous letter of 1927 commented on the 'open secret' that formal methods of training were very bad, and that therefore it was better to let workers instruct their own children. In such circumstances training was effective and cheap because workers did not demand extra pay – Zorin mentioned this too.[62] At least one operative from a mill in Ul'ianovsk guberniya held that 'youngsters are better taught by their own parents, or by other members of their own family', a sentiment echoed in Leningrad where it is also hinted that the extended family might be the relevant unit. When new recruits were expected in the Vyshnevolochek district of Tver' guberniya parents petitioned that they should be drawn from amongst their own children because this was an expedient way of replicating a skilled workforce. Such events were a 'daily occurrence' in Ivanovo's Iakhromskaia, particularly as workers objected to the hiring of peasants[63] – presumably, that is, peasants who did not already have kin in the mill.

Indeed, if families were split up inside the factory production was sometimes disrupted, because kin-based training was inextricably mixed up with job inheritance. Parents working in Ramenskoe in 1928 'rushed away' from their own machines to instruct their offspring allocated to other rooms.[64] An operative from the Ozerskii Trust reported a 'mass demand' from weavers to be allowed to train their own children in 1927. 'Parents consider this their right', he continued, and laconically mentioned that family influence embraced the labour exchange and the local insurance office as well.[65] Letters received by *Golos tekstilei* in March that year from the Glukhovskaia, Livers, Shcherbakov and Zvonkov mills in Moscow guberniya, the Rabochii in Leningrad, the Iakhromskaia in Ivanovo, the Kutuzov in Iaroslavl', the Abel'man in Vladimir and the Aseev in Saratov all confirm the link between relatives, direct hiring, shop-floor training and job inheritance: women operatives in the northern part of Tver' guberniya passed their looms on to their daughters when they retired.[66]

As a general rule throughout the 1920s training for doffers took between two weeks and three months, depending on their position in the hierarchies of various work teams. Drawing-frame operatives received three months' instruction, flyer-frame workers two. Weavers, until the latter part of the decade, spent a month sharing a loom with

61 *Golos tekstilei*, 2 October 1926.   62 *Golos tekstilei*, 12 March 1927; 18 March 1927.
63 *Golos tekstilei*, 12 March 1927; 24 March 1927.   64 *Trud*, 28 July 1928.
65 *Golos tekstilei*, 12 March 1927.
66 *Golos tekstilei*, 24 March 1927; 21 February 1928.

an experienced worker, five or six more in a brigade and six months alone on a pair before qualifying.[67] These were all 'entrance-point' trades suitable for adolescents – selfactor and ring-frame spinners and selfactors piercers, it will be remembered, qualified by seniority. Given such time scales it is possible that relatives were brought in to keep jobs warm while operatives left for a while to undertake seasonal work on their own land, or women to have children. This may explain the curious variant which operated in the mills of Vyshnevolochek district. There women petitioned the factory committee to let them hire and train members of their own families so they could leave their work 'to rest' for a few months.[68]

Whether or not things went as far as this in all regions, the organization of work in the industry generally could be very flexible. Looking back over the decade as a whole one investigation noted that:

> on a two shift system, that is, where each machine or group of machines is operated by two workers at different times, each shift member can easily estimate the effectiveness of the other's work. Moreover, the selection of shift members was comparatively simple, and frequently members of one and the same family worked on the same machines on different shifts.[69]

More will be said about the implications of this for pay in chapter 9. For the moment let us concentrate on the possibility of time sharing implicit here, a point made explicit by the managers' journal in 1927:

> In many factories where women operate the same machines on a two shift system, not unnaturally, they produce half the necessary minimum monthly output each. Furthermore, by private arrangement amongst themselves – and sometimes with the agreement of the foreman – they alter the distribution of their hours so that one or the other of them can attend to some business of her own.[70]

It is mildly surprising to learn that even in an industry as rich in surprises as this one, it was, apparently, not always necessary to ask the permission of the foreman; presumably the practice was in some places so common as to be taken for granted by all concerned. This was certainly the case in at least one mill in Vladimir guberniya, in which the shifts reorganized themselves every week.[71]

---

[67] I. S. Belinskii, A. I. Kucherov, *Tri mesiatsa raboty semichasovykh fabrik. (Opyt perevoda i raboty semichasovykh fabrik v ivanovo-voznesenskoi gubernii)* (1928), p. 11.
[68] *Golos tekstilei*, 12 March 1927.
[69] Ia. Kvasha, F. Shofman, *Semichasovoi rabochii den' v tekstil'noi promyshlennosti* (1930), p. 73.
[70] *Predpriiatie*, 2, February 1927, p. 66.   [71] *Golos tekstilei*, 10 March 1927.

The shop floor

Having tried to disentangle the various elements that went into the making of an operative, it is now possible to relate them more generally to the world of the shop floor. Work in a textile factory was hard, wrote one pamphleteer, although it might seem to be a matter of simply watching and controlling machinery, 'this is only at first glance. It is not at all easy to stand eight hours a day, day after day, for the whole year by the machine . . . How is this possible? . . . It is the product of habit, but habit does not come as a gift to the body.'[72] Training was thus predicated on physical and mental subordination, so for many, factory discipline and family discipline mutually strengthened one another because habit was learned by allocating and enforcing executive and subordinate roles within a traditional framework of gender and age. Hints of this underlying social condition sometimes surfaced in the press. In 1928 textile workers training their own offspring reasoned that 'the trade might come in handy someday, and besides, it distracts the children from hooliganism', a throwback to sentiments expressed by the central committee of the union in 1921. Intra-family training was popular in Leningrad because 'hooliganism does not occur',[73] and the steadying influence of cross-generational interaction can be sensed in Shaginian's acute observations of the city's mills in mid-decade: while the worker who spent his formative years in the disintegrating muddle of war and revolution was 'tired and without hope . . . he doesn't read the newspapers, he doesn't attend factory meetings. If you chat to him you'll hear a constant stream of loud complaints', older, pre-revolutionary workers were 'aristocrats' and 'professionals' who reached over to influence the third generation.[74]

These professionals were the '*na glazakh*' masters (masters who did things 'by eye'), against whom no one could argue; 'old masters of some kind accepted by the workers in their section' whose relationship with a shop's population was thought by this writer in 1930 to

[72] A. Lavrova, *Kak zhivut i trudiatsia rabochie-tekstil'shchiki* (1926), p. 17.
[73] *Golos tekstilei*, 24 March 1927; *Trud*, 28 July 1928. A note on the Karabanovskii Combine lends support to the view that the *komplekt* worked best if operatives felt some sense of mutual responsibility: 'At the moment things are going better in the weaving sheds, but discipline is worse in the spinning halls where collectives operate the machines and each person relies upon the other': *Tri goda raboty vladimirsko-aleksandrovskogo tresta khlopchatobumazhnykh fabrik, 1922–24gg* (1925), p. 107 (hereafter *V-A Trust 1922–24*). And see above p. 92.
[74] Shaginian, *Nevskaia nitka*, p. 18.

have a fundamental effect on output and general attitude.[75] Here
personal idiosyncrasy was the corollary of technological idiosyncrasy.
Working by eye meant that foremen kept notebooks drawn from their
own experience: 'such notes take, for example, the following form:
"weft count sixty sort II on 400-spindle frame turns out in six hours ten
minutes" or "five doffers clear 160-spindle ring-frame in three
minutes"'. But 'if the master leaves the factory the norm leaves too,
and if the master is ill the norm is ill'. Notebooks could not simply be
picked up by other foremen, and foremen could not transfer their
notes to other mills because 'major and minor' differences obtained:
'Master Ivan might give an entirely different output norm to Master
Petr – if it were possible to hold a conference of all masters to establish
output norms, we should have no norms at all.' Nevertheless, this
author was forced to admit that such methods were often expedient,
and day in and day out men like these passed the old methods on to
their recruits.[76] This was particularly so because a significant minority of workers – about one-quarter of the total textile workforce in
large-scale industry in 1926 – were illiterate.[77]

Komplekt working, kinship networks, technological and individual
idiosyncrasy and the uneven level of literacy thus combined to
reproduce and transmit a traditional culture of work across generations, and they allowed subtle, fluid arrangements to form and
re-form under the official crust of rules and regulations. The Central
Council of Trades Unions' newspaper ruminated on one aspect of
customary practice in 1928:

> The Russian textile worker has virtually no experience of individual
> piece work; on single shifts he receives a fixed portion of the wage of
> three or four workers who look after a bank of spindles or group of

[75] A. M. Buras, *Osnovy tekhnicheskogo normirovaniia v tekstil'noi promyshlennosti* (1930),
p. 27.
[76] *Ibid.*, pp. 26–8. See also *Sistema i organizatsiia*, 7, 1927, p. 12; *Sputnik kommunista*,
16(97), 1929, p. 79.
[77] L. I. Vas'kina, *Rabochii klass SSSR nakanune sotsialisticheskoi industrializatsii. (Chislennost', sostav, razmeshchenie)* (1981), p. 123. But, as might be expected, there were wide
variations concealed within this overall figure. In all shops men were more literate
than women and the rate declined from metropolitan to rural areas: while in 1928
three-quarters of Moscow's operatives were literate, with proportions of roughly the
same order for Ivanovo guberniya the following year, from as early as 1924 four-fifths
of all Leningrad's mill hands could read and write. Literacy campaigns in CIR mills
were constantly undermined by the influx of new recruits from the countryside:
Partiia v period stroitel'stva sotsializma i kommunizma (1977), p. 85; *Otchet leningradskogo
gubernskogo otdela vsesoiuznogo professional'nogo soiuza tekstil'shchikov. Okt. 1924–1925gg*
(1926), prilozhenie 2 p. 15; A. G. Rashin, *Sostav fabrichno-zavodskogo proletariata SSSR*
(1930), p. 97; *Trud i proizvodstvo*, 1, February 1927 pp. 28–30; *Vsesoiuznaia perepis'
naseleniia 1926 goda*, tom XXXIV (1930), tables 3–9, pp. 91–3.

looms. On two or three shifts machines are shared by all shifts over a twenty-four hour period, so skilled and experienced operatives lose out, especially in those work groups which include novices.[78]

But only for those who came via the factory schools. And it is worth emphasizing once more that schools did not cover all trades in all regions. Novices whose low competence levels pulled down earnings could be tolerated and disciplined if they were relatives or faces made visible by *magarych*. In the former case they would eventually add to the family's income and perhaps inherit the job; in the latter money and gifts helped to offset the instructor's reduced wage packet. In both cases arrangements allowed *komplekt* members some discretion over the distribution of work-time, an important consideration should the operative have off-mill interests.

Direct hiring also reversed cultural flow. Not only did the mill stamp its image on the recruit, recruits brought their own world to the shop floor. The textile syndicate elaborated the point in 1926. Newcomers from the countryside were 'in the majority of cases domestic workers accustomed to a low return on their work. To expect from such operatives American output levels without creating for them American conditions of life . . . is impossible.'[79] There was no shortage of comment, editorializing, letter writing and speech making on this matter throughout the 1920s. One pamphlet noted that 'the peasants, given the backward state of our agricultural technology, have had little contact with machinery. They imagine that the workers' tasks are much easier than the peasants', that the machine does all the work, and that looking after the machine is not very difficult.'[80] At the seventh textileworkers' union congress of 1926 a Moscow delegate complained of the 'great influx of new workers from the countryside. They come to the mill knowing nothing about machinery, and consequently there are many accidents.'[81]

Another cultural feature, readily transmitted to new entrants, strengthened by discontinuities in production, and abetted by rural immigration, was the widespread indifference to time-work discipline.[82] 'Here and there they say that we have reverted to pre-war

---

[78] *Trud*, 28 July 1928.   [79] *ITPT*, 33–34, 25 September 1926, p. 3.
[80] Lavrova, *Kak zhivut*, p. 2.
[81] *Golos tekstilei*, 18 May 1926.
[82] For remarks that peasants experienced difficulties because of the seasonal nature of agriculture see *Golos tekstilei*, 26 June 1926; 29 June 1926; *ITPT*, 3, 23 January 1926, p. 10; 33–34, 25 September 1926, p. 3; Lavrova, *Kak zhivut*, p. 2; *Rezoliutsii i postanovleniia (8-go) vladimirskogo gubernskogo s"ezda soiuza tekstil'shchikov, 13–18 dek. 1925g* (1925), p. 13.

forms of labour discipline', reported the directors of Vladimir-Aleksandrov Trust in 1925,

> but this is not the issue. We must raise labour discipline, but what methods can we use? . . . We have a Labour Code . . . and each worker knows for how long he can be absent. If he's absent for three days in a row, of course, he won't come to work anymore. If he's absent for any six days in a month it's also the case. But of course they're absent for just under six days a month, and never three days in a row.[83]

As the Commissariat of Labour confirmed in 1926, once inside the mill custom proved to be more influential than central decrees: orders had been issued by

> the Commissariat of Labour of the Russian Federation and the Workers' and Peasants' Inspectorate . . . the Supreme Economic Councils of the Soviet Union and the Russian Federation . . . the Commissariats of Trade of the Soviet Union and the Russian Federation . . . [and] the All-Union Textile Syndicate . . . lateness is controlled by a list which lays on a table in each shop, theoretically until 9.30 am. At 9 o'clock no one is there. At 9.05 one person has arrived, at 9.10 half-a-dozen more. The rest drift in during the following two hours. There is no accounting of lateness and absence.[84]

Additionally, much time was wasted collecting pay. This usually took twenty to thirty minutes, but workers sometimes started leaving their machines for the cash point one-and-a half hours before the official time. Equally, dinner breaks normally extended both sides of the official time and precious minutes were lost at the beginning and end of each shift:

> After the factory hooter has sounded and ten or fifteen minutes have slipped by the workers drift into the mill, disperse to their shops, smoke, chat to their friends and generally get themselves sorted out, so that another fifteen or twenty minutes pass . . . In many factories lateness has evidently come to be accepted as normal practice, so much so that lateness 'norms' have been established.[85]

The frustrations felt by rationalizers probably gave rise to a measure of exaggeration, nevertheless, here traces of the land/residence continuum have been located from another angle, and we can appreciate

---

[83] *V-A Trust 1922–24*, pp. 107–8. The Kommunisticheskii Avangard connived at up to forty-five days' absence, perhaps for field work: *Sbornik postanovlenii pravleniia soiuza, prezidiuma i soveshchanii pri prezidiume gubotdela (za mart–apr. 1925g)* (1925), p. 18.

[84] *Voprosy truda*, 10, October 1926, pp. 4–5.

[85] *Initsiativnyi sovet po nauchnoi organizatsii truda pri tsentral'nom komitete soiuza tekstil'shchikov. Kratkii otchet* (1924), pp. 23–4.

their impact inside the mill. But to return to the main point of the chapter: though cultural traits from outside the factory gates impinged on the mill, many aspects of recruitment practices, training techniques and shop-floor culture in general provided interstices within which tradition and customary practice could flourish unchecked – unless fundamental change was attempted.

6   Workers' institutional commitments

[They] feel that it's their own holiday and not the Bolshevik holiday.
From a secret police report on preparations for Easter 1929 in the
Iartsevskaia mill, Smolensk guberniya

The party

Few cotton operatives were party members.[1] At the very end
of NEP, as table 5 shows, they were everywhere less inclined to overt
political commitment than almost all other groups of industrial
workers. Rashin's sample also indicates that a clear distinction should
be drawn between urban and rural mills. Membership was significantly higher in metropolitan areas. Evidence from earlier in the
decade bears out this general picture. Overall Ivanovo guberniya had a
mere 3,300 full and candidate members in January 1923, rising by 425
throughout the next ten months. For the economic year 1923/24,
however, numbers increased by 6,414. Of these 'Lenin enrolment'
recruits, 86 per cent (5,516) were classed as workers, and 82 per cent
(4,523) came from transport depots, textile mills and other large-scale
enterprises, but this figure looks much less impressive when set
against the guberniya's cotton workforce for that year – 66,677.[2] In
contrast the party was rather more successful in Leningrad. By October
1925, 15.1 per cent of operatives in the Khalturin, 16.6 per cent in
Krasnyi Maiak, 17.7 per cent in Krasnyi Tkach and 20.1 per cent in
Krasnoe Znamia had joined. Some three years after this the city's mills
trailed behind metal and engineering factories, print works and

[1] As opposed to managers, directors, trust employees or union officials. See *Komsostav krupnoi promyshlennosti. (Po materialam orgraspred. otdela TsK RKP)* (1924), pp. 10, 32, 36.
[2] *Leninskii prizyv RKP(b)* (1925), p. 170; *Otchet TsK vsesoiuznogo professional'nogo soiuza tekstil'shchikov k VI vsesoiuznomu s"ezdu tekstil'shchikov. Okt. 1922g–okt. 1924g* (1924), table 6 pp. 16–17 (hereafter *TsK VPST 1922–24*).

Table 5. *Party membership amongst industrial workers 1929*

Industry	Worker sample	Percentage in party
Oil	6,730	30.9
Metalworking and engineering	40,883	19.5
Metallurgy	33,633	13.0
Coal mining	52,513	11.1
Cotton		
Leningrad	10,298	11.8
Moscow	5,429	10.3
Ivanovo region	54,932	7.1
Moscow region	48,314	5.8
Totals and averages for cotton	118,973	8.7

Source: calculated from A. G. Rashin, *Sostav fabrichno-zavodskogo proletariata SSSR* (1930), p. 126

chemical plants, but the proportion of communists – 13.2 per cent – was still considerably higher than in the other textile districts sampled by Rashin a year or so later.[3] Moscow guberniya displayed the same features as Ivanovo guberniya. Only 2,604 communists were to be found in the region's mills in spring 1923, and although 94 per cent of the 24,662 enrolled next year were classed as workers, textiles, by far and away the guberniya's largest employer, accounted for under one-quarter of the number. In fact for the entire Soviet Union all textile industries contributed just 19,760 to the Lenin enrolment out of 190,000 transport and industrial workers; 10.4 per cent of the total and a figure greatly at variance with their proportional strength in the Soviet economy. Collectively they ranked last out of nine major sectors enrolling workers throughout 1924.[4]

Regional imbalances were mirrored by variations inside the work-

[3] *Leningradskie rabochie v bor'be za sotsializma 1926–1937 gg* (1965), p. 40; S. I. Tiul'panov, ed., *Istoriia industrializatsii SSSR. Dokumenty i materialy. Zavershenie vosstanovleniia promyshlennosti i nachalo industrializatsii severo-zapadnogo raiona (1925–1928gg)* (1964), p. 229. Four other Leningrad mills were reported to have above average membership in 1924 – the Rabochii, Rabotnitsa, Nogin and Samoilovskaia: calculated from *Otchet leningradskogo gubernskogo otdela vsesoiuznogo professional'nogo soiuza tekstil'shchikov. Okt. 1924–1925gg* (1926), prilozhenie 4 p. 16; *Tekstil'nye fabriki SSSR* (1927).
[4] *Leninskii prizyv*, table 2 p. 9, table 3 p. 20, pp. 135–7; *Otchet o rabote moskovskogo gubernskogo otdela vsesoiuznogo professional'nogo soiuza tekstil'shchikov mart 1922g–mart 1923g* (1923), pp. 10, 12 (hereafter *Moskgubotdel VPST 1922–23*).

Table 6. *Gender and party membership of cotton workers 1929*

	Total female sample	Percentage in party	Total male sample	Percentage in party
Leningrad	7,622	9.5	2,676	18.1
Moscow	2,988	5.6	2,431	16.0
Ivanovo region	35,428	4.4	19,504	12.1
Moscow region	29,807	3.5	18,507	9.8

Source: calculated from A. G. Rashin, *Sostav fabrichno-zavodskogo proletariata SSSR* (1930), p. 128

force. Our source on the Lenin enrolment records that in total in 1922 about two-fifths of all members were women, with two-fifths of them again taken from the bench, but next year in Moscow guberniya's mills female labour accounted for over half the total workforce but contributed under one-fifth of the membership, a mere 514 out of 2,064. On average 11.6 per cent of Lenin enrolment recruits in textiles were women, with figures of much the same order for other textile regions.[5] Five years on less than one-quarter of the membership was female in the cotton mills of Vladimir, Ivanovo, Kostroma and Iaroslavl' guberniyas.[6] Thus throughout NEP, although women were everywhere in a majority in cotton factories, they were even less likely to join the party than their male co-workers; moreover, the higher membership levels for women evident in metropolitan regions were matched by still higher levels amongst men (see table 6).

These gender disproportions require little explanation. As elsewhere in Russian society male chauvinism effectively restricted women's choices.[7] Disapproving spouses and the demands attendant on the division of labour enforced in the household often deterred them from political activity. When a girl married into a textile worker's family, complained Moscow's party branch in 1928, she was expected to stay at home with the children; 'the husband goes to meetings, to the club, etc.'[8] Kindergartens and communal dining rooms were sometimes canvassed as a solution. It was hoped that they would

[5] *Moskgubotdel VPST 1922–23*, pp. 10, 12; *Leninskii prizyv*, p. 98. Leningrad 18 per cent, Ivanovo guberniya c.16 per cent. Moscow guberniya c.10 per cent: *ibid.*, p. 100.

[6] *Rabochii krai*, 10 July 1929.

[7] In the Glukhovskaia, however, there were 'women-only' club evenings: *Golos tekstilei*, 2 June 1925.

[8] *Sputnik kommunista*, 23(80), 20 December 1928, p. 53.

release the ambitious and the committed from the burdens of child rearing,[9] but as the figures cited above show, they had little effect.

Age differences were also marked. A delegate to the 1928 Ivanovo guberniya party conference lauded the political enthusiasm shown by adolescent cotton workers, including girls,[10] but in 1929 Rashin found the highest membership levels amongst young adults in the age group twenty to twenty-nine. If we assume that the majority of these operatives started work at about sixteen years old, then the most committed entered the factory somewhere between 1916 and 1925. Analysed in terms of length of service in industry all textile regions recruited most successfully from amongst those coming into the mills before mid-decade, and all but Ivanovo region had more success with workers who began their careers before NEP was introduced.[11]

After gender, age and geography the fourth major variant affecting the distribution of party membership was skill. Two clear gradients are apparent in Rashin's samples. Firstly, whatever the region, the skilled and highly skilled minority were much more likely to be in the party than the semi-skilled and unskilled; secondly, the skill/membership gradient descended from urban to rural areas, Leningrad consistently recording the highest levels, the provincial hinterland of Moscow the lowest.[12] Unfortunately, Rashin gives no definition of skill, but as the party was dominated by men it is reasonable to assume that there was considerable overlap between male-dominated trades and political commitment.

The fading afterglow of 1917 may help to explain the party's relative popularity in the two capitals, and it is equally likely that metropolitan areas received more than their fair share of attention from the few agitators scattered across the country.[13] But there were other reasons for the indifference of the countryside. In the first place the experience of industrialization varied from region to region; secondly, in many districts cotton mills overlaid a long tradition of artisanal endeavour, and lastly many CIR operatives kept one foot in the village. Rashin's survey shows that the land/residence continuum visibly affected recruitment levels. Whereas only 4.8 per cent of a sample of 17,427

---

9 See *Rezoliutsii i postanovleniia 7-go gubernskogo s"ezda soiuza tekstil'shchikov, 25–27 okt. 1924g* (1924), p. 19; *TsK VPST 1922–24*, pp. 132–3.
10 *Rabochii krai*, 1 January 1929.
11 A. G. Rashin, *Sostav fabrichno-zavodskogo proletariata SSSR* (1930), p. 135.
12 *Ibid.*, p. 137. Of all Lenin enrolment workers 62 per cent were listed as skilled, 18 per cent as semi-skilled and 20 per cent as unskilled: *Leninskii prizyv*, p. 21.
13 On the party's weakness outside the main towns see T. H. Rigby, *Communist Party Membership in the USSR, 1917–1967* (1968).

landed operatives were in the party, nearly twice that figure – 8.9 per cent from a sample of 101,546 without land – were members in 1929.[14]

Several instances of official anxiety over and disapproval of the provincial cotton workforce have already been mentioned in chapter 3. Given such attitudes it is not surprising that there were problems away from metropolitan districts: 'there are times', said Mel'nichanskii at a joint plenum of Ivanovo's party and union branches in 1929, 'when the director or foreman behaves in a different way towards a communist worker and a non-party worker. The non-party workers say, "For you – you communists – everything's possible."'[15] Four years earlier, in a scathing report commissioned by the local committee into conditions in a mill outside Moscow, 'mechanical group enrolments' in 1924 were blamed for a 'fall in discipline'. Cells were vague about their functions, failed to keep financial accounts and proper records, and neglected to liaise with the union and Komsomol. 'Loud and long speeches that go on for hours' did nothing to strengthen political consciousness and drunkenness and absenteeism added to indifference and depressed morale. Little interest was shown in recruiting women and communists had no clear idea of the duties of a party member. Similar sentiments were expressed to the east; they have failed to establish a 'comradely connection' between themselves and non-party workers, reported the twentieth Ivanovo party conference of its members.[16]

These anxieties were symptoms of a general malaise afflicting the party at the start of NEP,[17] a malaise which continued throughout the 1920s and was inflected through the social and geographical parameters described above. Although recruitment was unimpressive in all textile districts, once War Communism gave way to NEP, and once the old socio-economic symbiosis reasserted itself, an egalitarian city-based ideology had little resonance outside the two capitals. Enrolments were particularly low in rural mills, amongst women and amongst those characterized as less skilled – collectively the majority of the workforce – and this was only marginally offset by increased recruitment amongst adolescents towards the end of the decade.

---

[14] Rashin, *Sostav*, p. 139.   [15] *Rabochii krai*, 23 March 1929.

[16] *Rezoliutsii 20-i ivanovo-voznesenskoi partiinoi konferentsii (1–4 iiulia 1925g)* (1925), pp. 13–14; *Vybory i predlozhenie po dokladu o sostoianie partraboty na sukonnoi fabrike im. tkacha Petra Alekseeva (vysh. Iokish)* (1925), pp. 3–6.

[17] The tenth party congress ordered the mobilization of cadres to counter the activities of the Workers' Opposition and other factional groups in Moscow's mills. See N. V. Poliakova, 'Bor'ba rabochikh-tekstil'shchikov za povyshenie proizvoditel'nosti truda v 1921–1925gg. (Po materialam Moskvy i moskovskoi gubernii)', *Voprosy istorii*, 6, July 1959, pp. 25, 27.

These groups – those labelled unskilled, women, and workers in rural mills – tended to be all of a piece. 'The vast majority of women textile workers', reported the women's section of the party of Moscow guberniya in 1922, 'have only average skills; weavers, piecers, ring-frame spinners, etc.' and nothing had changed two years later.[18] And when, after a further two years, the local branch of the textileworkers' union reported that in the eighty or so mills run by three trusts in Ivanovo guberniya all but twenty weaving-shed foremen, fourteen master spinners, eight spinning room overlookers and one spinning room foreman were men,[19] it was only reinforcing the point that this was the constituency from which the majority of party members were drawn.

The union

> Thousands of workers go home each day to the countryside. These workers take almost no part at all in factory life. They never attend conferences or meetings ... for rural workers union membership simply means possessing a union card, without which they would be sacked.[20]

This letter from the Likino mill in Moscow guberniya tells us that joining the union was a matter of routine, a means of securing a job. Even though operatives found themselves in what was over-whelmingly a 'workers' union,[21] membership implied no particular commitment to socialism or to the regime.[22] Union growth throughout the 1920s, encompassing 99 per cent of the workforce in 1923, 97.6 per cent in 1924 and 95.8 per cent in 1925, simply kept pace with economic

---

[18] *Kommunistka*, 10–11, October–November 1922, p. 51; *Professional'nye soiuzy SSSR 1922–1924gg. Otchet VTsSPS k VI s"ezdu profsoiuzov* (1924), p. 152.

[19] *Otchet o rabote ivanovo-voznesenskogo gubernskogo otdela vsesoiuznogo soiuza tekstil'shchikov za vremia s apr. 1925g–mart 1926g. 16-mu s"ezdu soiuza* (1926), p. 28 (hereafter *I–V gubotdel VPST 1925–26*). Calculations in relation to mill totals from *Tekstil'nye fabriki SSSR* (1927).

[20] *Golos tekstilei*, 19 February 1927.

[21] The number of office workers fluctuated around 7 to 9 per cent of the membership in 1923/24, by far the lowest for any industrial union. Ivanovo had special sections for handloom weavers: *Golos tekstilei*, 1 September 1925; L. Magaziner, *Chislennost' i sostav professional'nykh soiuzov SSSR* (1926), pp. 29, 39; *Rabochii krai*, 2 July 1927; *Trud* (Ivanovo-Voznesensk), 5, May 1923, p. 43.

[22] Although 65.6 per cent of provincial union functionaries were communists in 1922, 89.9 per cent of delegates at the May 1924 fifth Moscow guberniya congress and 80 per cent at the October 1926 sixth guberniya congress were non-party: *Itogi raboty moskovskogo gubernskogo otdela profsoiuza tekstil'shchikov s 1 apr. 1924g po 1 okt. 1925g* (1926), p. 51 (hereafter *Moskgubotdel VPST 1924–25*); *Otchet TsK vserossiiskogo professional'nogo soiuza tekstil'shchikov sent. 1922g–sent. 1923g. K IV vseross. konferentsii soiuza 1923g* (1923), p. 16.

Table 7. *Gender divisions amongst factory- and shop-delegate committees in twenty-five Vladimir guberniya cotton mills 1923*

	Male	Female	Percentages	
			Male	Female
Mill population	12,563	17,897	41.2	58.8
Shop delegates	581	787	42.5	57.5
Factory committee plenums	102	20	83.6	16.4

Source: Calculated from *Otchet o rabote valdimirskogo gubernskogo pravleniia professional'nogo soiuza tekstil'shchikov s sent. 1923g po sent. 1924g. K 7-mu gubernskomu s"ezdu soiuza* (1924), pp. 6–9

recovery; by then cotton operatives accounted for 413,328 out of the union's total of 436,114. In the same way branch size merely reflected the industry's pre-revolutionary location; in 1924 membership was more or less equally divided between major cities (23.9 per cent), provincial towns (26.7 per cent), and urban settlements and the countryside (24.7 per cent each).[23] Similarly the union mirrored the workforce's gender divisions, but as was to be expected women played but a small part in the central bureaucracy and a secondary role in the local apparatus. The twenty-five strong central committee included just two women in 1924.[24]

Individual factories were represented at national congresses either via direct election or, in the case of large mills, through delegate conferences, committees made up of workers chosen from each shop who then put forward members on behalf of the entire workforce.[25] Delegate conferences first appeared at the end of 1921 and three years later the central committee established ratios of one delegate to between ten and forty workers for the industry.[26] Here, in contrast to provincial and central bureaucracies, women were much more in evidence, with percentages on a par with their proportional strength in the workforce (see table 7). It is also worth noting that a dispropor-

[23] *Biulleten' podotdela statistiki TsK vsesoiuznogo professional'nogo soiuza tekstil'shchikov, 3,* October 1925, table 9 pp. 16–17; Magaziner, *Chislennost' i sostav,* pp. 42, 45.
[24] *Biulleten' ivanovo-voznesenskogo gubernskogo statisticheskogo biuro,* 19, 1929, table 4 p. 30.
[25] R. Dunn, *Soviet Trade Unions* (1928), pp. 67, 177.
[26] *Rezoliutsii i postanovleniia 6-go s"ezda professional'nogo soiuza tekstil'shchikov* (1924), p. 20; *Otchet TsK vsesoiuznogo professional'nogo soiuza tekstil'shchikov k 7-mu vsesoiuznomu s"ezdu tekstil'shchikov. Iiul' 1924g–ianv. 1926g* (1926), p. 43 (hereafter *TsK VPST 1924–26*).

tionate number of shop delegates were party members, over 25 per cent in the Vladimir, Ivanovo and Moscow guberniyas around mid-decade.[27] Nevertheless, the sources betray a sense of indifference and constraint. 'The Revolution is now five years old', wrote an operative from Sereda, 'but women workers in our textile industry remain sunk in darkness. Apart from their own immediate concerns the majority of them are uninterested in the union.'[28] A letter from 'the dumb' of Iaroslavl's Krasnyi Perekop pointed out that there were 300 shop delegates for the mill's 11,000 workers, half of whom were women, but no general meetings for women alone. If there were, she continued, 'they would speak out about the things which they now only mutter about in their shops'.[29] Family pressures, domestic work and male scepticism – the belief that the union was 'no business' of women[30] – thus conspired to restrict the ambitions of some and perpetuate a psychology of subservience amongst others: 'I don't want to be a delegate!', grumbled someone from Vladimir guberniya who was unwittingly elected in her absence.[31]

In fact shop delegates were secondary links in the union's transmission belt from the centre to the provinces. They had no power beyond voicing grievances at congresses. They relayed information to the factory committees, the 'basic organs of the trade union in the localities', but were subordinate to them.[32] According to the 1922 Labour Code factory committees were the primary link with the leadership and it was they who liaised with management, foremen

---

[27] *Otchet o rabote bogorodskogo uezdnogo otdeleniia tekstil'shchikov za period s okt. 1925g po ianv. 1927g* (1927), p. 12; *I–V gubotdel VPST 1925–26*, pp. 19–20; *Otchet o rabote moskovskogo gubernskogo otdela vsesoiuznogo professional'nogo soiuza tekstil'shchikov avg.–okt. 1923g* (1923), table 13 p. 28 (hereafter *Moskgubotdel VPST Aug–Oct 1923*); *Moskgubotdel VPST 1924–25*, pp. 51–2; *Otchet o rabote vladimirskogo gubernskogo pravleniia professional'nogo soiuza tekstil'shchikov s sent. 1923g po sent. 1924g. K 7-mu gub. s"ezdu soiuza* (1923), p. 21 (hereafter *Vladgubotdel VPST 1923–24*); *Otchet o rabote vladimirskogo gubernskogo pravleniia professional'nogo soiuza tekstil'shchikov okt. 1924g–okt. 1925g. K 8-mu gubenskomu s"ezdu soiuza* (1925), p. 28 (hereafter *Vladgubotdel VPST 1924–25*).

[28] *Rabochii krai*, 25 June 1922.   [29] *Golos tekstilei*, 23 February 1926.

[30] *Rabochii krai*, 4 June 1920. Only 23.7 per cent of delegates elected from mills to the fifth Moscow guberniya congress in May 1924 were women. As for the party there were complaints that the lack of kindergartens, communal washing facilities and canteens kept women away from union work: *Golos tekstilei*, 8 October 1927; *Otchet o rabote moskovskogo gubernskogo otdela vsesoiuznogo professional'nogo soiuza tekstil'shchikov okt.–dek. 1924g* (1925), p. 6.

[31] *Golos tekstilei*, 1 June 1926.

[32] *TsK VPST 1924–26*, pp. 43–4. After 1923 all mills with fifty or more workers were to have factory committees. Size depended on mill population; three members in mills with between fifty and 300 workers rising to nine for mills with more than 5,000 workers: *Polozheniia i instruktsii fabkomam i komissiiam* (1923), p. 3.

Table 8. *Gender divisions in the union's factory committees 1924*[a]

Branch	Total number of factory committees	Percentage male membership
Tver'	32	79.1
Vladimir	236	78.7
Moscow	830	74.5
Iaroslavl'	75	72.4
Ivanovo	233	70.2
Kostroma	33	65.0
Leningrad	135	51.3

[a] Averaged from figures for May and July
Source: Calculated from *Otchet TsK vsesoiuznogo professional'nogo soiuza tek-stil'shchikov k VI vsesoiuznomu s"ezdu tekstil'shchikov. Okt. 1922g–okt. 1924g* (1924), p. 78

and overlookers.[33] They checked the implementation of collective agreements and watched over questions pertaining to pay, labour protection, social insurance and specialist clothing. They participated in hiring and firing and they organized clubs and literacy drives. In short they touched on, or could touch on, virtually every aspect of the worker's daily life in the mill.[34]

Given their latent powers, it comes as no surprise to find that they were dominated by men to a far greater extent than delegate conferences (tables 7 and 8). Even though women were making some slight inroads throughout NEP,[35] as late as 1929 just over 82 per cent of Ivanovo's factory committee chairmen were male.[36] Two further pieces of evidence from the provinces emphasize the point. In Vladimir, regardless of mill size or the gender balance of the factory's population, there was scarcely any variation in the number of women

[33] E. H. Carr, *Socialism in One Country*, vol. 1 (1970), p. 444; E. H. Carr, *The Bolshevik Revolution 1917–23*, vol. 2 (1966), p. 329; M. Dewar, *Labour Policy in the USSR 1917–28* (1956), pp. 288–90.
[34] *Instruktsii fabkomam*, pp. 4–6. This source runs to forty-eight pages under eight headings on the rights and duties of factory committees in textile mills.
[35] See *Golos tekstilei*, 24 May 1927; 'Krasnyi Profintern' bumago-priadil'naia, tkatskaia i otdelochnaia fabrika v s. Tezino, ivanovo-voznesenskoi gubernii. Proizvodstvennyi al'bom (1926), pp. 8, 32–3; *Leningradskii tekstil'shchik*, 1 May 1925; *Moskgubotdel VPST Aug–Oct 1923*, tables 7–10 pp. 20–2; *Otchet o rabote moskovskogo gubernskogo otdela vsesoiuznogo professional'nogo soiuza tekstil'shchikov mai–iiul' 1923g* (1923), p. 27; *Trud* (Ivanovo-Voznesensk), 7, 1 August 1924, p. 4; *TsK VPST 1922–24*, pp. 27, 78; *Vladgubotdel VPST 1924–25*, p. 25.
[36] *Rabochii krai*, 11 July 1929.

on factory committees, whilst in the urban regions of Ivanovo – Ivanovo-Voznesensk, Kineshma, Shuia, Sereda – numbers were only fractionally greater than in rural districts.[37] In exactly the same way gender disproportions were carried over into factory committee sub-sections which multiplied in cotton mills after 1923-4. Assessment and conflict commissions, which settled disputes arising from the implementation of collective agreements and were in continuous contact with management rather in the style of nineteenth-century English craft unions, were dominated by men, whereas in other sub-committees – cultural commissions and labour protection – women had more scope.[38]

Although, as for the party, there is no direct evidence to indicate which trades were represented on factory committees, it appears that male hegemony produced marked imbalances. The majority of union activists in flyer- and ring-frame rooms, wrote a worker from Ivanovo in 1926, were men;[39] operatives in these shops, of course, were women. Even the party's central committee, ruminating in distant Moscow on the joint failure of party and union in the textile industry in 1929, could discern the discriminatory effects of trade disproportions; more 'flyer- and ring-frame spinners, more bobbin carriers and thread winders and more female weavers' should be brought into responsible positions in both institutions.[40]

Indeed, male hegemony in the union was reinforced by political hegemony. The party was overwhelmingly male and textileworker factory committees exhibited a very high level of party saturation: 62.6 per cent in July 1924.[41] It is therefore hard to avoid the conclusion that since men were over-represented in the party and on factory committees, by extension certain trades were over-represented in both organizations: foremen and overlookers in cotton processing rooms, preparatory departments, flyer-frame rooms, ring-frame rooms and weaving sheds, male weavers in weaving sheds, and selfactor spinners in mule-frame rooms.[42]

---

[37] Otchet o rabote ivanovo-voznesenskogo gubernskogo otdela vserossiiskogo soiuza tekstil'shchikov za vremia s 1 iiunia 1923g po 1 apr. 1924g. XIII–XIV s"ezd (1924), table 7 pp. 34–5; Vladgubotdel VPST 1923–24, pp. 6–9.

[38] TsK VPST 1922–24, p. 86. Labour protection commissions operated as a troika – one member from the factory committee, one from management and one elected from general meetings: Spravochnik po voprosam okhrany truda v tekstil'noi promyshlennosti (1924), p. 5.

[39] Golos tekstilei, 23 February 1926.   [40] Golos tekstilei, 31 March 1929.

[41] Second only to the mining industry: TsK VPST 1922–24, p. 27.

[42] According to the press the social factors which prevented women from standing for factory committee elections were the same as those which stopped them from joining the party. See Golos tekstilei, 3 October 1924; 8 September 1925.

Religion

When Patriarch Tikhon looked out over Holy Russia shortly before his death in 1925 he saw his Church deserted by the young and all but dead in the towns. In the countryside, however, and amongst the old and middle-aged, the faith still flourished.[43]

No one knows how many Christians there were in Russia, but Tikhon's observations give a rough impression of the contours of religious commitment amongst cotton workers. Of the fifty or so instances located in the sources which touch on religion in specific enterprises, only one comes from what is clearly a metropolitan environment.[44] On the other hand high absenteeism around Church holidays was frequently reported from those mills towards the rural extremities of the land/residence continuum and was often linked to time off for field work.[45] Five large mills were picked out as being under the sway of religion in spring 1924, all of them in non-metropolitan areas of the CIR.[46] Elsewhere in the countryside and throughout the decade lamps festooned mill gates, icons were carried into general meetings, paraded through workers' barracks with an orchestra, or reverentially hung in the family flat. 'Red corners' were sometimes shared by secular and supernatural deities; in the Kutuzov in Iaroslavl' guberniya a portrait of Lenin and an icon stared across the room at each other. In another district the entire workforce from several mills regularly attended services every Saturday and Sunday.[47] The Central Council of Trades Unions detected widespread religious sentiment in Tver' guberniya in 1925; the local trades council responded by stepping up the level of anti-religious propaganda, particularly in the Tverskaia mill.[48]

But if these fragments support the Patriarch's contentions what is missing is the dimension of gender, for women certainly seem to have formed the core of believers; 'the basic cadre of the textile industry', as a delegate to the 1929 Ivanovo Congress of the Godless put it, 'and the

---

[43] L. Lawton, *The Russian Revolution 1917–26* (1927), p. 230.
[44] Leningrad's Samoilovskaia, where workers voted to move the spring break from Easter to May Day: *Golos tekstilei*, 27 April 1924. This was one of the mills with high party membership: see note 3 above.
[45] S. I. Belinskii, A. I. Kucherov, *Tri mesiatsa raboty semchasovykh fabrik. (Opyt perevoda i raboty semichasovykh fabrik v ivanovo-voznesenskoi gubernii)* (1928), p. 42; *Golos tekstilei*, 17 July 1925; 26 June 1926; 22 October 1927.
[46] *Moskovskii tekstil'shchik*, 25 April 1924.
[47] *Golos tekstilei*, 12 August 1924; *Moskovskii tekstil'shchik*, 11 January 1924; *Pravda*, 9 February 1928; *Rabochii krai*, 17 April 1923; 22 June 1923; 1 March 1930.
[48] *Trud*, 25 October 1925.

chief victims of religious thought'.[49] Press reports from the CIR cite work stoppages by women in their weaving sheds for organized worship or the observance of Church festivals throughout the decade, and sharp quarrels between established operatives and young girls reared in the new atheism.[50]

All this was little more than an affront to Bolshevik sensibilities and an additional, if minor, irritant for administrators worried about absenteeism and labour discipline. What was more unsettling was the evident willingness of many cotton workers outside Moscow and Leningrad to support the Church with their time and money. Throughout the second half of the decade Christians in Smolensk guberniya's Iartsevskaia raised money for church repairs. Priests relied on the financial generosity of the Lenin mill's workforce in Ul'ianovsk guberniya, and while union dues remained scandalously in arrears in Penza guberniya's Krasnyi Oktiabr' operatives amassed 18,000 roubles for the construction of a new church. Further north workers in Rodniki provided the wherewithal for a new peal of bells, and by 1927 two organizations, a 'League of Believers' and a 'Church Soviet', both based in the shops of Vladimir guberniya's Kommunisti-cheskii Avangard, had collected enough money from subscribers to pay for the construction of an Orthodox church next door to the mill.[51]

Equally disquieting was the poor response to the anti-religious campaigns mounted in Ivanovo-Voznesensk towards the end of the decade. Late in 1928 *Rabochii krai* published a series of 'workers' petitions' against the two remaining churches in the city, but of the fifty-one offices, factories, shops and departments agitating for closure in October and November, only seven petitions originated from cotton mills. Both churches were still open twelve months later.[52] Elsewhere there was little enthusiasm for atheism. Five thousand icons were taken from workers' barracks attached to mills in the Bogorodsk region in 1930 and burnt, but this appears to have been done by a minority of young activists; photographs show a large bonfire half-surrounded by grinning youths wearing caps and leather jackets, the

[49] *Rabochii krai*, 16 October 1929.
[50] In the Krasnaia Roza and Naro-Fominsk (Moscow guberniya), and the Shagov and Shuiskaia (Ivanovo guberniya): *Golos tekstilei*, 12 August 1924; 1 January 1925; *Rabochii krai*, 13 April 1923; 26 October 1928.
[51] *Biulleten' TsK vsesoiuznogo profsoiuza tekstil'shchikov*, 30(42), 18 October 1928, p. 23; *Golos tekstilei*, 29 January 1926; 9 November 1926; 8 January 1927; 21 July 1927; 13 April 1928; 18 April 1928.
[52] *Rabochii krai*, 24 October 1928; 25 October 1929.

unofficial uniform of the Komsomol. Women standing nearby seem to be weeping.[53]

Far more alarming was the confluence of religious sentiment and political opposition. During the first half of 1922 many of the industrial districts of Ivanovo guberniya seem to have been in some turmoil. Early in February Chernov, the chairman of the party's guberniya executive committee, introduced a series of emergency measures against 'banditry', a common euphemism for social or political unrest. Next month saw the imposition of martial law and a curfew. A war commissar was appointed to the province and a military commandant to the capital. Some weeks later the sixteenth local party conference discussed the 'serious situation' in the region. Many 'enemies of the working class' were posing as friends, and communists had lost all influence. Simultaneously *Rabochii krai* demanded the recruitment of more militiamen to 'defend the Revolution'.[54]

Trouble appears to have centred on three mills, the Iuzhskaia, Shuiskaia and Seredskaia, the former deep in the countryside, the latter two in small towns, but details are frustratingly vague. On March 1 the local press reprinted articles from *Pravda* and *Izvestiia* which condemned the Socialist Revolutionary Party as a counter-revolutionary organization. Two weeks later a demonstration, probably spontaneous but with some SR participation, took place in Shuia's town centre to protest against the government's seizure of Church valuables. Next day the Iuzhskaia's workers held an open-air meeting in support of those suffering in the Volga famine. Everything was 'serious and sober' (a hint that this was not the case elsewhere) and a collection was taken. On April 21 the 'Shuia Affair' began – the trial of twenty-four priests and laity who had refused to release liturgical artifacts to the state sometime earlier. All were subsequently convicted and sentenced to between one and five years' imprisonment.[55]

Perhaps this was Chernov's answer to the March demonstration and one local instance of the current conflict between Church and state.[56] It is not clear if the Iuzhskaia's workers knew of the events in Shuia the day before their meeting, but the news was now public and unrest evidently continued. June 1 saw *Rabochii krai* printing 'workers' petitions' against the SRs but none originated from cotton mills. On

[53] *Rabochii krai*, 14 February 1930.
[54] *Rabochii krai*, 11 February 1922; 17 March 1922; 22 March 1922.
[55] *Rabochii krai*, 1 March 1922; 21 March 1922; 24 April 1922; 28 April 1922; 20 June 1922; 22 June 1922.
[56] Carr, *Socialism in One Country*, 1, pp. 48–57.

the following day one was from a textile factory, the Balashov, but on June 3, when the SRs were revealed as the people's 'enemies', neither of the two covering petitions had anything to do with the local cotton industry. A week later the paper gave considerable space to the big SR show trial in Moscow, and ten days after this an unsigned letter from seventy-six Shuiskaia 'delegates' demanded an investigation into 'the activities of the PSR in our mill'. SRs, continued an editorial, were 'in theoretical opposition to the leadership of the working class'. A few days later the newspaper purported to discover SR 'centres' in the three mills named above, in the Shuiskaia persisting from 1918 onwards. Shortly afterwards activists were instructed to prepare talks on the necessity of handing over Church valuables to the state and on the iniquity of the SRs as revealed in the Moscow show trial. At the end of the month an anti-SR petition appeared over the names of twenty-nine enterprises and offices, but these included only two cotton mills, the Varentsova (1,440 signatures) and the Staro-Posadskaia (42 signatures).[57]

Tenuous evidence invites caution, but it does seem apparent that the coincidence of religious and political persecution touched off some kind of explosion in the guberniya and that local SRs took the opportunity to link the two together. It also appears that Ivanovo's cotton workers were, at the very least, unenthusiastic supporters of government policy,[58] and in the case of not less than three mills, actively opposed to it. Moreover, *Rabochii krai* believed that the Shuiskaia for one had a history of SR sympathies, and this was one of the mills where women were holding religious meetings in their weaving sheds a year later.[59]

Except in such unusual circumstances we should not expect to find the Russian clergy stimulating or articulating discontent amongst cotton workers. The Orthodox Church was not a proselytizing church and so toleration of the peasant's God, grudgingly accepted by the party in 1923, was just possible, and it lasted just as long as the

---

[57] *Rabochii krai*, 1 June 1922; 2 June 1922; 3 June 1922; 10 June 1922; 20 June 1922; 22 June 1922; 25 June 1922; 29 June 1922.

[58] And perhaps not only in Ivanovo. In an unspecified Moscow weaving mill only 10 per cent of the 400-strong workforce could be mustered for an anti-SR demonstration in the summer 1922, all of them communists. No petitions against the SRs were printed in the national textileworkers' union press; the editor was 'unable . . . for technical reasons . . . to reproduce the many resolutions received from workers' general meetings demanding strict measures against the SRs': *Sotsialisticheskii vestnik*, 15(37), 2 August 1922, p. 8; *Tekstil'shchik, k stanku*, 10 June 1922.

[59] See note 50 above.

smychka.[60] In addition, intimidation played its part. Once turbulent priests and laity had been removed to the Solovki prison camps after local initiatives like the Shuia affair, once local SRs had been terrified into silence by the Moscow show trial,[61] and once the Patriarch had abjured his flock to compromise with the regime, the ground was cleared for what Trotsky called, in a slightly different context, 'an ecclesiastical NEP'.[62] It was in these circumstances that mill congregations were allowed some latitude throughout the high NEP years.

It was not so easy to tame dissenting congregations, and on these information is scarce indeed. The journal of the Moscow party organization ran a brief article on sectarians in March 1927 discussing both Old Believers and foreign schismatics: Spiritualists, Baptists, Evangelicals and Seventh Day Adventists. These latter groups were said to have been recruiting heavily in the 1920s.[63] Their remarkable resilience in the face of persecution during and after the 1930s is well known,[64] but this source gives some glimpse of equally principled defiance for the earlier period; 'in a whole series of places' many sectarians refused service in the Red Army, and after the introduction of NEP there was some organized refusal to pay agricultural taxes.[65]

According to the article most sect members were peasants or shopkeepers and tradesmen, but occasionally 'groups of workers'.[66] Some of these were certainly cotton operatives. In 1928 a few workers from the Vyshnevolochek mill complex in Tver' guberniya complained that their factories were 'overrun' with evangelicals. While the local union branch and the Union of Atheists had done nothing 'to

[60] When the party was most conciliatory towards the peasants it was also most tolerant of the Church: E. H. Carr, *The Interregnum 1923–24* (1969), p. 95; Carr, *Socialism in One Country*, 1, pp. 54, 56.

[61] Leading SRs were tried in Moscow between 8 June and 7 August; fourteen were condemned to death and others to imprisonment. Krylenko, the prosecutor, regarded the sentences as 'directives' for the guidance of provincial courts: A. Solzhenitsyn, *The Gulag Archipelago*, vol. 1 (1974), p. 354; vol. 2 (1976), pp. 29, 31, 39.

[62] Cited in Carr, *Socialism in One Country*, 1, p. 52. *Veselyi tkach*, published in Ivanovo-Voznesensk and specializing in vicious lampoons of capitalists, *nepmeny*, kulaks and the Church much in the style of *Krokodil*, abruptly ceased publication in 1924 after only one issue.

[63] *Sputnik kommunista*, 6(39), 30 March 1927, p. 27. For estimates of the number of dissenters see K. Borders, *Village Life Under the Soviets* (1927); *Sots. vest.*, 3(193), 9 February 1929, p. 15.

[64] See A. Solzhenitsyn, *The Gulag Archipelago*, vol. 3 (1978), pp. 105–109, 515–17.

[65] *Sputnik kommunista*, 6(39), 30 March 1927, p. 30. Shortly after the February Revolution a national congress of sects resolved to have nothing further to do with the Great War: *ibid.*, p. 30.

[66] *Ibid.*, p. 28.

struggle against this dangerous sect', they had opened a chapel in the main street of a nearby town.[67]

It is very tempting to draw parallels with low church movements in nineteenth-century England. If the Moscow party organization's writer was correct, they appealed to the same kind of constituency, the poor and those on the margins of poverty, and in the same conditions of social, political and economic insecurity. 'Pre-millennialism is widespread', observed an American visitor to Russia in the late 1920s, 'as might be expected among devout believers who have passed through the last decade in Russia'. Such congregations were typically closely integrated; tightly knit sub-groups generating a high degree of mutual trust which served to support a distinctive and often dissenting version of social reality. More than this, some were proselytizing, 'witnessing' congregations, fusing demonstrative piety with everyday life in a way quite alien to the resignation characteristic of much Orthodox practice.[68] In England they often provided the organizational and spiritual backbone of the early labour movement, and it is at this point that they are of particular interest to us in their Soviet context. There is a little evidence to suggest that they acted as a channel of communication between mills and mill districts and provided a rough-and-ready framework for industrial action in the latter part of the decade.[69]

[67] *Trud*, 14 October 1928.
[68] See Borders, *Village Life*, pp. 139–40. For the wider links between industry and dissent see W. L. Blackwell, *The Beginnings of Russian Industrialization 1800–1860* (1968), pp. 212–40; O. Crisp, *Studies in the Russian Economy Before 1914* (1976), p. 14.
[69] See pp. 257–8.

Part III

The crisis of 1923 and its consequences

If we, who in essence . . . have a state super-monopoly, do not push, press and whip our cadres, spurring them on to cheapen the cost of production, then . . . we have before us all the prerequisites of monopolistic decay. The role played by competition in a capitalist society . . . must with us be played by the constant pressure arising from the needs of the masses.

Bukharin, 1925

7 The market collapses

Socialism is accounting.

Textileworkers' union slogan, 1921

The market

Lenin's final collapse and withdrawal from public life coincided with the emergence of chronic unemployment in large-scale industry and the virtual collapse of NEP. All three signalled the beginning of a confused struggle for political mastery compounded by bitter personal rivalries.

There had been alarms in 1922 as Russia painfully adjusted to the new dispensation. Demand was sluggish and the countryside only beginning to recover from famine and the depredations of the procurement squads. In addition retail networks, never impressive in relation to the potential market and severely damaged by war and revolution, could not cope with the sudden switch to private trading. Mills began to approach normal working in November 1922. A month previously, at the fifth textileworkers' union congress, Kutuzov, the current union president, pointed out that supply problems were easing now that the civil war was over.[1] The remaining cotton stacked in the warehouses of Turkestan's farms thus quickly became cloth packed into the storerooms of Russia's mills. Frantic to increase the circulation of a debased currency and to reach the consumer and preserve the *smychka*, factories disgorged their remaining stocks of finished goods. Cotton mills took the lead, dumping cloth onto the market at grossly deflated prices.[2] Some trusts were auctioning off at 50 per cent below the cost of production. Managers set up makeshift kiosks outside their mill gates or haggled over margins with carpet-

[1] N. L. Brodskii, *et al.*, eds., *Tekstil'shchik (istoriia, byt, bor'ba)* (1925), pp. 258–9.
[2] *Na novykh putiakh. Itogi novoi ekonomicheskoi politiki 1921–22gg*, vyp. 3 (1923), p. 17.

baggers in order to get the better of rival enterprises.[3] Communists were being taught how to trade. Later the secret police would take its revenge in a series of raids on fashionable night clubs and restaurants patronized by the *nepmeny*.[4]

The events of 1922 were only the harbinger of a much more serious dislocation, ironically triggered by administrative devices cobbled together to forestall the recrudescence of *razbazarivanie* (literally 'squandering at the bazaar'). In an effort to impose order trusts were reorganized and placed under the newly created syndicate,[5] but these new fixities stood in contradiction to *laissez faire* in agriculture. Now, as factories hoarded labour and pushed up retail prices, consumers found themselves the victims of industrial monopoly. Moreover, the famines of the previous few years had reduced the number of mouths which had to be fed in the village. Fine weather added the finishing touch. Grain marketings rose and grain prices tumbled as commodity prices soared, and the peasantry began their reflexive retreat from the market.[6]

When Trotsky arrived from the State Planning Commission (Gosplan) and displayed his diagram showing the price 'scissors' to delegates assembled for the twelfth party congress in April 1923,[7] the crisis still had several months to run. At first it seemed difficult to understand and not particularly threatening. Industry was becoming more profitable and agriculture had obviously recovered. Kalinin talked of 'the most calm, the most business-like year in the existence of the Soviet Republic'.[8] Even in September, when the storm had already broken, Nogin, then chairman of the textile syndicate, went on denying that there was a sales crisis at all. Rather, he placed all the blame on the Commissar of Finance's obsession with a balanced budget, the gold rouble and tight money. In any case the syndicate was by no means averse to mills securing high prices for their products. Nogin was not alone in his misapprehensions.[9] Lenin's absence from the congress must have been deeply felt, and in view of

3 E. H. Carr, *The Bolshevik Revolution 1917–23*, vol. 2 (1966), p. 313; R. Day, *Leon Trotsky and the Politics of Economic Isolation* (1973), pp. 72, 80; M. Dobb, *Soviet Economic Development since 1917* (1966), pp. 103, 113, 149, 154–61.
4 J. B. Sorenson, *The Life and Death of Soviet Trade Unionism 1917–28* (1969), p. 183.
5 See chapter 1. 'Trusts sprang up like mushrooms', remembered one old official, 'they took almost no notice of Vesenkha': N. Valentinov, *Novaia ekonomicheskaia politika i krizis partii posle smerti Lenina* (1971), p. 95.
6 Dobb, *Soviet Economic Development*, pp. 157, 164.
7 E. H. Carr, *The Interregnum 1923–24* (1969), p. 29.
8 Cited in *Izmeneniia v chislennosti i sostave sovetskogo rabochego klassa* (1961), p. 85.
9 Carr, *Interregnum*, pp. 16–17; E. H. Carr, *Socialism in One Country*, vol. 1 (1970), p. 357; Dobb, *Soviet Economic Development*, pp. 171–2.

the hostility and passion generated by the succession struggle, it was unfortunate that it should have been Trotsky who made one of the two speeches that seriously tried to get to grips with the problem. The other came from Sokol'nikov, captivated by the possibilities of financial orthodoxy current in the Finance Commissariat, who pressed his novel idea that the *smychka* should be viewed as part of a system of international exchange. 'How is it possible', he asked his opponents,

> to provide cotton for our industry . . . ? It is only possible in the following manner . . . until Turkestan's cotton production is restored we must export grain and use the currency to purchase cotton abroad. Thus we will ensure the production of the textile industry and these products will return to the peasant. To be sure this is a . . . complex cycle. But in my view, even though the cycle between industry and agriculture must pass through the world market it does not constitute a *smychka* between the peasant and Western European or American capital . . . the idea that we might exist in isolation from the world market – this idea, if it is an idea at all, is a reactionary utopia.[10]

In fact hopes for commodity intervention had received something of a set-back twelve months earlier at the international conference at Genoa. The Soviet Union was not particularly welcome as a trading partner. Foreign investors were still waiting for the tsar's debts to be honoured.[11] Only by concluding a last-minute agreement in the nearby village of Rapallo with that other pariah of the international community, Weimar Germany, did Chicherin manage to avoid coming home empty-handed. Nevertheless, the Finance Commissar's arguments had the force of logic, especially in view of the state of native cotton supply.[12]

Sokol'nikov's jibes were probably aimed at Piatakov (vice president of Vesenkha), Preobrazhensky and, at this stage of his career, Trotsky, all of whom pointed to the neglect of heavy industry under NEP. Krasin was still absorbed in dreams involving foreign concessions and huge loans from abroad, and Zinoviev and Bukharin busy advancing the interests of the peasantry. Though something like two groupings emerged at the congress, neither took any notice of Trotsky's insist-

[10] Cited in Day, *Leon Trotsky*, p. 85.
[11] See for example Anglo-Russian Cotton Factories Ltd., *Report of Proceedings of Annual General Meeting of Shareholders at Company Offices*, London, 28th June 1921; *Report of Proceedings of Annual General Meeting of Shareholders at Company Offices*, London, 3rd June 1924, Guildhall Library L69.55 MS11, 760.
[12] Though sown area increased throughout NEP, so did cotton imports: E. H. Carr, R. W. Davies, *Foundations of a Planned Economy*, vol. 1, part 2 (1969), table 1 p. 940, table 39 p. 972.

ence that planning, rationalization, the concentration of production and redundancies should accompany an accelerated drive to export grain. Instead the assembly broke up without giving any clear policy directives. Only in summer did the Politburo suddenly become aware of the enormity of the crisis.[13] The *smychka* might snap. Urban food shortages and rural unrest might lead to a third revolution.

The scissors crisis proved to be a seminal event, forcing Old Bolsheviks to re-think their view of Russia's relationship to the outside world, their strategies for advancing towards socialism, and even their very conception of what socialism might be. Throughout the remaining years of NEP only Trotsky persisted in championing economic integration with the west. By a curious twist of fate he came to adopt almost all Sokol'nikov's initial premises as the latter executed a spectacular *volte face*. For Zinoviev and Kamenev 'face to the countryside' turned out to be just one more political wobble; two years later at the fourteenth party congress the Leningrad party secretary was to throw his weight behind those advocating an end to the 'kulak deviation' and a forward policy for industry.[14] Bukharin began to develop Lenin's last notes on the peasantry and co-operation into what was eventually to become a kind of theoretical prototype for market socialism.[15] As leaders groped towards a new understanding of their situation, political *faux pas* – 'enrich yourselves', 'primitive socialist accumulation' – were in plentiful supply, allowing Stalin to enhance his reputation for moderation and caution.

But whichever side of the problem shifting groupings stressed – peasants or workers, industry or agriculture, town or country – the new orthodoxy was isolationist. Just as the European Revolution had failed to come to Russia's aid, so capitalist Europe declined the invitation to strengthen socialism. The misplaced optimism of the early integrationists gradually gave way to an equally exaggerated sense of foreboding. Capitalism's ability to recover without benefit of the Soviet market was seen as the precursor to a renewed assault on socialism. Extensive trade with the west, therefore, now supposedly

[13] Carr, *Interregnum*, pp. 23–25; Day, *Leon Trotsky*, pp. 51–65, 81–90; Dobb, *Soviet Economic Development*, p. 174.

[14] The slogan 'face to the countryside' was a launched by Zinoviev in *Leningradskaia Pravda* in August 1924. A few months later he was beginning to criticize Bukharin and Stalin for surrendering to the 'rural bourgeoisie': M. Lewin, *Russian Peasants and Soviet Power* (1968), p. 143.

[15] Sympathetically described in S. F. Cohen, *Bukharin and the Bolshevik Revolution: a Political Biography 1888–1938* (1975). Lenin's hints are contained in *On Co-operation*, written 4–6 January 1923.

involved the risk of colonial subjugation.[16] Out of these confusions was born the deceptively simple formula of 'socialism in one country'.

It took time for Bukharin to elaborate the theory and for Stalin to enforce it as party dogma. Meanwhile, the fact of Russia's isolation and the threat posed to the *smychka* required instant action. On 3 October 1923 the Commissariat of Internal Trade hastily instructed a protesting textile syndicate to effect an immediate 20 per cent cut in the retail price of cotton cloth, the first to receive such an order.[17] The central committee of the union seconded the syndicate's complaints with its own populist version of the causes of the sales crisis: 'excessive financial burdens occasioned by various kinds of taxes, the imperfect state of the retail structure, a significant increase in staffing, especially ˙ in the organs of management, and an insufficiency of workers in comparison with the vast number of clerical staff, have led to price increases in textile goods'.[18] But the union bowed to the inevitable. Two slogans were adopted by the emergency conference convened in Ivanovo-Voznesensk as the scissors yawned still wider: 'closer to the masses' and 'closer to production'. 'Improve the working-class standard of living' came but a poor third.[19] Similarly the syndicate accepted interference in its sphere of competence. Textile executives meeting in Moscow the following summer under the auspices of Vesenkha listened as two board members, Fedotov and Makarov, reminisced about the dangers so recently overcome: 'in the autumn of 1923 the high cost of cloth pressed against and lowered the purchasing power of the population. Economic – yes, and no less political considerations – necessitated a rapid and decisive fall in retail prices.' A second price cut was imposed in March 1924,[20] this time as workers began to experience directly the consequences of isolation.

Vesenkha had been pressing the cotton industry about the need for efficiency ever since *razbazarivanie*. A speaker at the 1922 congress of textile executives put matters quite bluntly:

> The question of closing factories is extremely painful, and this is a question of *concentration*. It does not get a sympathetic hearing . . . because concentration involves expense, transferring personnel, and a series of other organizational problems. Nevertheless, the Pres-

[16] Day, *Leon Trotsky*, pp. 81–6, 94–7, 119, 174.   [17] Carr, *Interregnum*, pp. 119–20.
[18] *Rezoliutsii 3–go plenuma TsK soiuza tekstil'shchikov (12–15 aprelia 1923g)* (1923), pp. 14–25 (hereafter *3–go plen TsK VPST 1923*).
[19] Cited *Profsoiuz tekstil'shchikov (kratkii istoricheskii ocherk)* (1963), p. 89.
[20] V. M. Makarov, A. A. Fedotov, eds., *Trudy soveshchaniia proizvodstvennikov v tekstil'noi promyshlennosti. Moskva, 2–4 iiunia 1924g* (1925), p. 5. Between October 1923 and October 1924 the retail price of cloth fell by 40 per cent: Dobb, *Soviet Economic Development*, pp. 174–6.

idium of Vesenkha considers this question to be the most important one facing our congress, because ... *cheapening the cost of production must be seen in the context of the concentration of production.*[21]

The syndicate made a further round of trust amalgamations in July 1923 but management fudged the issue of internal reorganization until goaded into action by the party's alarm over scissors. In cotton mills around Moscow, for example, concentration was not at first accompanied by overall reductions in manning levels,[22] though short-time working swept across the industry in late summer, this was still only a response to immediate necessity. Stocks of home-grown raw cotton, plentiful throughout the previous eighteen months, were now exhausted and the industry faced its first peace-time supply crisis. Outright closures soon followed. The number of working mills fell by nearly one-fifth between autumn 1923 and February 1924.[23] As hopes for commodity intervention faded price cutting was effected through the 'hard, very hard nut' of redundancies referred to by Trotsky in his speech to the twelfth party congress.[24]

The problem of unemployment

Just as they emphasized Russia's isolation, so *razbazarivanie* and scissors focused attention on the labour market. The union in particular worried over the implications of recent events. 'Unfortunately', predicted the central committee in February 1924, 'constant shortages of raw materials mean that unemployment is likely to be a long-term phenomenon'. In fact the picture was not as clear as this, and the number without work remained comparatively low

---

[21] *Stenograficheskii otchet 1–go vserossiiskogo s"ezda rabotnikov tekstil'noi promyshlennosti v Moskve, 12–16 okt. 1922g* (1923), p. 4 [stress in the original].

[22] *Tri goda raboty vladimirsko-aleksandrovskogo tresta khlopchatobumazhnykh fabrik, 1922–24gg* (1925), pp. 20–1; *Otchet o rabote moskovskogo gubernskogo otdela vsesoiuznogo professional'-nogo soiuza tekstil'shchikov mai–iiul' 1923g* (1923), table 13 p. 43 (hereafter *Moskgubotdel VPST May–July 1923*).

[23] *Moskgubotdel VPST May–July 1923*, pp. 45–6; *Nashe khoziaistvo* (Tver'), 1, 1923, p. 81; *Otchet o rabote moskovskogo gubernskogo otdela vsesoiuznogo professional'nogo soiuza tekstil'shchikov mai 1923g–mart 1924g* (1924), pp. 137–8; *Otchet TsK vsesoiuznogo professional'nogo soiuza tekstil'shchikov k VI vsesoiuznomu s"ezdu tekstil'shchikov. Okt. 1922g–okt. 1924g* (1924), pp. 94, 168 (hereafter *TsK VPST 1922–24*); *Rabochii krai*, 5 April 1923; *3–go plen TsK VPST 1923*, pp. 5–6; *Vosstanovlenie tekstil'noi promyshlennosti ivanovo-voznesenskoi gubernii, 1920–1925gg* (1966), p. 159. An additional problem was caused by the currency reform. Central Asian growers soon learned to refuse *sovznaky* and would accept nothing but *chervontsy*: M. S. Farbman, *After Lenin. The New Phase in Russia* (1924), p. 121.

[24] Cited in Carr, *Interregnum*, p. 26.

throughout the next two years or so,[25] because those operatives with a scarce trade had good employment prospects. As early as May 1923 the union's Moscow branch reported that most of the jobless were unskilled.[26] CIR mills were short of flyer-frame, selfactor and ring-frame spinners and experienced weavers, but in the exchanges, wrote one correspondent in summer 1924, 'we have mainly auxiliary workers, the majority of whom are not closely connected with the textile industry . . . temporary workers from the countryside'.[27] 'In the bureaux of labour', reported another a few months later, 'there remain only those who've never worked before or who're completely unskilled.' Things were much the same in Ivanovo guberniya. Of the 25,832 mill hands out of work in October 1925 less than one-third were classed as skilled, a proportion which fell to one-seventh within four weeks.[28] These biases were reflected at national level. Speaking at the November 1924 sixth textileworkers' union congress a member of the central committee reported that the 'vast majority' of union members without work were unskilled. Two months later bureaux listings for the entire country included only eighty-three flyer-frame operatives, 234 mule *komplekt* workers, 659 ring-frame spinners and 1,524 weavers.[29] Even as the 'regime of economy' began to take effect in 1926 shortages of skilled workers rose coincidentally with unemployment.[30]

All cotton districts recorded high unemployment levels amongst female operatives, that is, the unskilled. On average for 1922/23, for example, 86.9, 77.6, 77.5, and 73.5 per cent of the unemployed in the union's Petrograd, Moscow, Ivanovo and Vladimir branches respectively were women, as were two-thirds of the nation's jobless mill hands late in 1926.[31] The relationship between gender, skill and

[25] *Golos tekstilei*, 1 February 1924; 16 October 1926; *Otchet TsK vsesoiuznogo professional'-nogo soiuza tekstil'shchikov k 7-mu vsesoiuznomu s"ezdu tekstil'shchikov. Iiul' 1924g–ianvar. 1926g* (1926), p. 17 (hereafter *TsK VPST 1924–26*); L. S. Rogachevskaia, *Likvidatsiia bezrabotitsy v SSSR 1917–1930gg* (1973), p. 88.

[26] *Tezisy, priniatye plenumom gubotdela 12 maia 1923g. (Materialy k 5–mu moskovskomu gubs"ezdu tekstil'shchikov)* (1924), p. 13.

[27] *Moskovskii tekstil'shchik*, 5 August 1924.

[28] *Golos tekstilei*, 23 September 1924; L. E. Mints, I. F. Engel', eds., *Statisticheskie materialy po trudu i sotsial'nomu strakhovaniiu za 1925–26g* (1927), table 1 p. 6; *Trudi i proizvodstvo*, 1, January 1926, p. 6.

[29] *Rezoliutsii i postanovleniia 6–go s"ezda professional'nogo soiuza tekstil'shchikov* (1924), p. 40; *Voprosy truda 7–8*, July–August, 1925, p. 47.

[30] *Golos tekstilei*, 2 October 1926; 12 October 1926; *Professional'nye soiuzy SSSR 1924–1926gg. Otchet VTsSPS k VII s"ezdu profsoiuzov* (1926), p. 26; Rogachevskaia, *Likvidatsiia bezrabotitsy*, p. 88; *TsK VPST 1924–26*, p. 17.

[31] L. E. Mints, I. F. Engel', eds., *Statisticheskie materialy po trudu i sotsial'nomu strakho-vaniiu za 1926–27g*, vyp.1 (1927), table 1 p. 7; *Otchet TsK vserossiiskogo professional'nogo soiuza tekstil'shchikov sent. 1922g–sent. 1923g. K IV veross. konferentsii soiuza 1923g* (1923), pp. 70–1.

redundancy often clouded the minds of contemporaries anxious to promote equality on the shop floor. 'Where the number of workers must be reduced there should be no dismissal of women merely because of their sex,' insisted one worker in 1925, 'It's wrong to say that women should sit at home, look after the children and cook the dinner.'[32] Shortly after the introduction of NEP the women's section of the party had condemned 'the reduction of female labour in state enterprises and the consequent growth of female unemployment'. By 1922 it was coming round to the idea that dismissal was predicated on skill, although 'not only for [these] objective reasons'. A year later low skill levels, physical weakness and the demands of raising a family were ranked before outright male prejudice as reasons for lay-offs.[33]

To some extent the alarm evident in the women's section of the party was misplaced. Many women looking for jobs had probably never worked before or had worked only for a short time.[34] In any case the curve of female unemployment in cotton peaked early in NEP, in 1922–3.[35] There are two possible explanations here. Either those women seeking work in cotton factories were quickly absorbed as the industry recovered, or female registration should properly be seen as a marginal, opportunistic element in the labour market. There is very little evidence to suggest that chronic unemployment, regardless of gender, was a feature of the industry. In comparison with other sectors of the economy cotton took a diminishing share of the jobless throughout the first half of the decade.[36]

The meaning of unemployment

It is not easy to get beyond these generalizations. The sheer volume of tables, graphs, percentages and absolutes disgorged year after year seems impressive, but it is important to bear in mind that all were collected and compiled by a welter of competing bureaucracies, each one still in the process of formation, and each one anxious to define and occupy some niche within emerging administrative structures. As late as 1928 the Central Council of Trades Unions and the

32 *Golos tekstilei*, 9 January 1925.
33 *Biulleten' otdela TsK RKP(b) po rabote sredi zhenshchin*, 15, 1921, p. 18; 4(20), 1922, pp. 9–10; 5, 1923, p. 38 (hereafter *B Tsk RKP (b) Zh*).
34 Women substituted for men on the shop floor after 1914: Rogachevskaia, *Likvidatsiia bezrabotitsy*, pp. 86–7.
35 K. I. Suvorov, *Istoricheskii opyt KPSS po likvidatsii bezrabotitsy, 1917–1930gg* (1968), p. 121.
36 *Golos tekstilei*, 12 October 1926; Rogachevskaia, *Likvidatsiia bezrabotitsy*, p. 88; *TsK VPST 1924–26*, p. 17.

Central Statistical Agency could not even begin to approach consensus on the figures for total unemployment,[37] and the Commissariat of Labour was never really happy with the functioning of its exchanges and correspondence points, especially after compulsory registration was abandoned. 'Cleaning' the books became an annual ritual; somewhere around one-third to one-quarter were struck off between December 1922 and January 1923. In Ivanovo guberniya the purge sought to identify the 'genuine' unemployed and clear out domestic workers, people who registered to avoid paying taxes, and those quaintly described as 'dead souls'; an exercise repeated at national level in July 1924.[38] Central assessors uncovered a situation in one major cotton town five years later which would have delighted NEP's satirists:

> An investigation into the Bureau of Labour at Ivanovo-Voznesensk was concluded on 1 July 1929 and covered 7,614 of the city's 13,283 registered unemployed. Of these ... 1,558 had left the town for unknown destinations, 3,101 were not to be found at their registered addresses, 867 had left for the countryside or other towns, thirty-seven were in the Red Army, twenty-eight were invalids, twenty-five were in jail and sixteen were dead. In all, 5,748, or 75.5 per cent of the sample taken, were falsely registered.[39]

Given such cautionary tales the very meaning of registered unemployment becomes problematic.[40] Local factors and the relative advantages enjoyed by particular regions complicate the story in other ways. We have already seen how workers in provincial mills could be left stranded by closures.[41] Where operatives could not move, either because they had some investment in agriculture or because railways were too distant, it should be possible, in principle, to construct a reasonably accurate map of the local distribution of unemployment. But even in the most isolated districts there was some relationship between the length of a mill's shut-down and the likely dispersal of its labour force after many had abandoned all hope of getting help from

---

[37] On 1 January 1928 the Central Statistical Agency listed 1,352,800 unemployed, the Central Council of Trades Unions 2,036,800: Sorenson, *Soviet Trade Unionism*, pp. 222–3.

[38] A. A. Matiugin, *Rabochii klass SSSR v gody vosstanovleniia narodnogo khoziaistva (1921–1925gg)* (1962), p. 192; Rogachevskaia, *Likvidatsiia bezrabotitsy*, p. 81; Suvorov, *Istoricheskii opyt*, p. 107; *Trud* (Ivanovo-Voznesensk), 2, February 1923, p. 51; 5, May 1923, p. 79.

[39] Cited in Rogachevskaia, *Likvidatsiia bezrabotitsy*, pp. 258–9.

[40] A point made in Carr, *Socialism in One Country*, 1, pp. 388–9.

[41] See pp. 44, 48–9.

their local exchanges. In February 1923 Ivanovo trades council listed the following unemployment black-spots: Shuia 4,164, Ivanovo-Voznesensk 2,740, Vichuga 735, and Sereda 551. Three months later some of these operatives were starting to register for work in other guberniyas.[42] Perhaps some eventually got as far as Ramenskoe in Moscow guberniya, where in 1925 the director of a large mill told immigrants seeking jobs 'we've plenty of our own unemployed in the province'.[43] A year later two Ivanovo delegates at a plenum of the union's central committee complained about reverse migration, the 'uninterrupted wave' of job seekers flooding into their guberniya. When there were lay-offs in Moscow and Leningrad, Ivanovo suffered: 'Why? Because it's forbidden to travel to Moscow but possible to come to Ivanovo-Voznesensk . . . The system [of help for redundant operatives] works like this. "Here's five roubles, go where you want!"'[44]

The consequences of scissors did not affect all cotton districts to the same extent. In line with the general drift of policy giant mills with modern equipment were favoured at the expense of smaller, obsolescent enterprises.[45] For several reasons this arrangement naturally benefited Leningrad. On the whole the old capital's factories were larger and more efficient than those around Moscow.[46] Moreover, although Krasin's grand vision of import substitution and concessions was not to be realized,[47] the exchange of goods between town and country could not be maintained without cotton. Sokol'nikov's notion of an international *smychka* would thus remain valid until productivity could be raised in Turkestan.[48] With this in mind Nogin had been sent abroad late in 1923 to seek out foreign suppliers. He returned early in February 1924 with an agreement to ship cotton from New Orleans backed up by credits from the Chase National Bank. Imports were to be routed via Murmansk, ice-free throughout the winter. Cotton could thus reach Leningrad's spinning halls much more quickly than mills

[42] *Trud* (Ivanovo-Voznesensk) 2, February 1923, p. 52; 5, May 1923, p. 22.
[43] *Golos tekstilei*, 11 August 1925.
[44] *Golos tekstilei*, 16 October 1926.
[45] *Tekstil'nye fabriki SSSR* (1927), *passim*; *3–go plen TsK VPST 1923*, p. 5.
[46] See R. E. Johnson, *Peasant and Proletarian. The Working Class of Moscow in the Late Nineteenth Century* (1979), chapter 1; R. M. Odell, *Cotton Goods in Russia* (1912).
[47] See Krasin's speech in July 1924 in Day, *Leon Trotsky*, p. 144.
[48] A good cotton crop depended on melted snow running down to the Central Asian Plain from the Tian'-Shania mountains on the Chinese border. Irrigation was crude; *chigiri* – endless bucket chains driven by camels – distributed water into ditches: A. M. Zaikov, *Na khlopchatobumazhnoi fabrike* (1926/27), pp. 10–11.

elsewhere,[49] and in contrast to Moscow guberniya the number of workers there rose steadily after 1923.[50]

Thus CIR mills were likely to bear the brunt of the concentration of production. As early as 1921 the Commissariat of Labour ordered a 25 per cent reduction in the workforce of Penza guberniya's mills. The first to go were youngsters, temporary workers and 'peasants'. Mills in the Serpukhov district of Moscow guberniya fired those 'predatory on the factory'.[51] Unemployment was not only caused by supply problems, wrote the union's central committee in October 1924; peasant immigration, demobilization and the concentration of production should now be added to the list.[52] These sentiments are in line with accepted wisdom. That unemployment rose as the economy expanded is a commonplace of Soviet and western historiography. The first wave seeking jobs was made up of demobilized soldiers and workers drifting back to the cities; the second, and far larger, of peasants pulled in by the lure of urban life and high wages or pushed off the land by over-population. In addition the ebb and flow of seasonal workers always left some flotsam on the shores of Moscow, Leningrad and provincial centres. Lastly, the shattered remnants of the old middling ranks forever lapped and eddied around the doors of the exchanges. Swirling amongst all these was the country's established proletariat, those with no means of subsistence beside wage labour.

The Commissariat of Labour's purging bureaucrats wished to separate out hard-core proletarians from others seeking work, but in many cotton districts established workers could not be distinguished from non-proletarian elements – mill hands defy easy classification.[53]

[49] *En route* Nogin visited Bremen and the Liverpool Cotton Exchange, and before the Revolution American cotton usually came via Liverpool, Bremen and Hamburg to St Petersburg, the traditional entrepôt for English and American cotton goods. Between 1923 and 1925 the percentage of home-grown cotton worked up in Leningrad fell from 42.1 to 32.8 per cent of the total while the amount imported from America rose from 15.6 to 28.1 per cent. Almost all the rest came from Egypt: *Biulleten' vserossiiskogo tekstil'nogo sindikata*, 7/8(101/102), 26 February 1924, p. 1; *Golos tekstilei*, 15 February 1924; 24 June 1924; 2 December 1924; 2 July 1925; Odell, *Cotton Goods*, pp. 11, 23; *Otchet za 1924–25g. Leningradskii gosudarstvennyi tekstil'nyi trest 'Leningradtekstil'* (1925), p. 12; A. C. Sutton, *Western Technology and Soviet Economic Development*, vol. 1 (1968), p. 266.
[50] L. I. Derevnina, *Rabochie Leningrada v period vosstanovleniia narodnogo khoziaistva: chislennost', sostav i material'noe polozhenie* (1981), table 1 pp. 34–5; *Fabrichno-zavodskaia promyshlennost' g. Moskvy i moskovskoi gubernii, 1917–1927gg* (1928), table 9 p. 28, table 11 p. 44, table 13 p. 62.
[51] *Tekstil'shchik, k stanku*, 16 September 1921; 15 October 1921.
[52] *TsK VPST 1923–24*, pp. 59–60.
[53] 'Why', complained some of the Penza peasants mentioned above, 'are we being pushed out when our fathers worked here before us?' *Tekstil'shchik, k stanku*, 16 September 1921. For a fuller discussion of job inheritance see chapter 5.

Although one author noted that in 1923 unemployment in Ivanovo guberniya was 'due to the influx of poor peasants into the factories', another blurred the distinction between peasants with sources of off-mill income and jobless proletarians reliant on wage labour by insisting that many cotton hands without work were not truly unemployed because of their connections with the village. A third pointed to the real difficulty. During summer shut-downs in 1922 and 1923 the guberniya's operatives frequently occupied themselves with farm labour or handicrafts, but because such work was precarious they often registered at the exchanges in order to find a place on the shop floor later on. That was why there were periodic fluctuations in bureau registrations.[54]

One of the authors cited above noticed how rumours affected statistics: 'the moment mills begin to produce, the number of regis- tered unemployed workers rises, and falls in the following month'.[55] To put it another way, the population of a given district was likely to try to second guess the immediate future of nearby mills. Potential operatives appear to have balanced the relative advantage of wasting time queuing and registering against the likelihood of a mill, a shop or a department coming back on stream.[56] Second-guessing is neatly revealed in a statistical series prepared by the union's central commit- tee covering the period January 1923 to July 1924. Whilst the total number of union members rose as employment increased, the reverse is also evident; union membership fell back as employment decreased. If there had been a fixed number of operatives seeking work then union membership should have remained more or less constant, or risen steadily. Instead, membership rose and fell in time with changes in employment prospects.[57] This kind of response was particularly characteristic of women. The national percentage employed and belonging to the union remained more or less static throughout the twenty-two months following October 1922; however, the number of

[54] *Trud* (Ivanovo-Voznesensk), 2, February 1923, p. 52; 5, May 1923, p. 22; 6–7, June–July 1923, p. 5.

[55] *Trud* (Ivanovo-Voznesensk), 5, May 1923, p. 22.

[56] For time wasted in this way in Moscow see Rogachevskaia, *Likvidatsiia bezrabotitsy*, pp. 79, 99. For CIR cotton operatives, whose nearest correspondence point might be a train journey away and whose nearest station might be several miles distant, such a routine would be even more of a burden.

[57] *TsK VPST 1922–24*, table 1 p. 10. One contemporary noted the effect of closures on would-be workers from Tver' in 1923–24: 'In the last two years men of the *volost* have started to go off elsewhere, but during 1923 some of them who had gone returned; they were on the point of establishing themselves when there were "redundancies". So back to the village.' A. M. Bol'shakov, 'The Soviet countryside 1917–1924: its economics and life', [1924], *Journal of Peasant Studies*, 4, 1, October 1976, p. 59.

unemployed women (better described as women seeking work) fluctuated sharply.[58] Moreover, there were differences within regions
where mill locations were split between town and countryside. In
April 1922 women made up 70.7 per cent of the unemployed in
Ivanovo-Voznesensk, but in the guberniya only 58.4 per cent. The
most likely explanation is that the guberniya's women were marginally unemployed, women perhaps with an interest in agriculture,
whereas in the city they probably had fewer employment opportunities outside the mill.[59]

Statistical series, therefore, cannot be accepted as evidence of a
simple construct called unemployment. Rather, registration was a
function of stop–go production in the cotton industry intermingled
with local perceptions of the job market. That *razbazarivanie* and
scissors caused sharp fluctuations in the level of bureau registrations is
beyond doubt.[60] It is less clear that they reflected really significant
levels of redundancy amongst established workers or measured long-
term unemployment. In one sense both crises were temporary aber-
rations, in another, they were but the most severe symptoms of a
general problem. Although the amount of cotton harvested inside
Russia rose consistently throughout NEP mills were never able to
break free of their reliance on imports,[61] and the very nature of the
international cotton trade – involving many different companies and
countries estimating crop levels and shipping costs several months in
advance – conspired against steady employment. Foreign dealers
tended to utilize the financial expedient of long-term credits. The
government's agents were thus obliged to compete on the open
market in a decade riven by diplomatic conflict between the Soviet
Union and the west and characterized by doubts about the regime's
internal stability and credit-worthiness.[62] On top of this, where
broadening home demand pressed on restricted supply and the state
reacted nervously to every subsequent threat to the *smychka* by hastily
attempting to increase output, maladministration and transport

[58] *TsK VPST 1922–24*, table 7 p. 18.   [59] *B TsK RKP (b) Zh*, 5, 1923, p. 40.
[60] See the figures in *TsK VPST 1922–24*, p. 61.
[61] See P. A. Khromov, *Ocherki ekonomiki tekstil'noi promyshlennosti SSSR* (1946), pp. 45,
58; A. Santalov, L. Segal, eds., *Soviet Union Yearbook* (1928), p. 278; (1929), p. 285;
(1930), p. 285.
[62] Before the war American cotton was purchased two to three months in advance. Bills
of exchange might run for months. In 1922 hesitations over the party's attitude to the
trade monopoly created problems with foreign merchants, and in 1926 Trotsky
warned against buying cotton and machinery and then opting out of payment: Day,
Leon Trotsky, p. 163; M. Lewin, *Lenin's Last Struggle* (1975), pp. 36–7; Odell, *Cotton
Goods*, p. 23. Trotsky's warning must have been alarming for firms dealing with the
Soviet Union.

bottle-necks resulted in sudden, inexplicable shortages on the shop floor.

If in spite of all this the numbers employed in the cotton industry rose consistently throughout NEP,[63] what was the meaning of unemployment? For established workers it meant sporadic redundancy: a phenomenon sparked off by the 1923 rationalization drive and subsequently fuelled by dislocations in supply. Registration figures obscure the industry's chronic hunger for skilled workers – or rather experienced operatives. Many rural immigrants and women were not unemployed operatives but people seeking work for the first time, or individuals dropping in and out of the exchanges in response to local perceptions of the chances of work. And in the CIR's cotton factories unemployment was not experienced in the same way as it was in metropolitan districts. It cannot be separated from that complex symbiosis between field and factory. There, short-time working and lay-offs could affect almost any mill at any time.[64] If cost factors worked against Central Russian mills,[65] it was also the case that provincial workers could be laid off, if not with impunity, then at least in the realization that they would be much more likely to have some means of livelihood outside the mill gates than would their metropolitan counterparts.[66]

[63] See p. 20.
[64] For low stocks see *Biulleten' ivanovo-voznesenskogo gosudarstvennogo tekstil'nogo tresta*, 16/7, March 1926, pp. 5–6; *Golos tekstilei*, 16 March 1926; 23 March 1926; 14 October 1926; *Izvestiia tekstil'noi promyshlennosti i torgovli*, 20, 31 May 1926, p. 3. For this reason short-time working became common in 1926–28: Sutton, *Western Technology*, p. 226; *Tekstil'nye novosti*, 1, March 1926, p. 38.
[65] Moving raw cotton from the Baltic to the CIR added 5 per cent to costs before 1914: calculated from Odell, *Cotton Goods*, pp. 22–3.
[66] N. V. Poliakova, 'Rabochie-tekstil'shchiki Moskvy i moskovskoi gubernii v bor'be za vosstanovlenie promyshlennosti v periode perekhoda na mirnuiu rabotu, (1921–1925gg)'(1952), *passim*. See also chapter 3.

8   Organizing Taylorism: production

No one, of course, speaks against accounting. Everyone agrees that it's necessary. But when we start to talk about ways and means, differences of opinion multiply.

A textile engineer writing in 1926

The origins of NOT

Several practitioners and commentators before Marx – Jean-Baptiste Colbert, Charles Babbage, Peter Gaskell, Andrew Ure – had been gifted with some presentiment of the productive forces slumbering in the lap of social labour, but the world envisaged by Frederick Taylor's Soviet disciples makes even Adam Smith's liberal-capitalist prognosis seem positively benign. 'The essence of NOT [the 'scientific organization of work'] is the study of the complete production process', wrote Nol'de in 1924,

> of each motion, even the smallest. Introducing scientific organizational principles into a mill demands not only that [workers'] mechanical actions . . . harmonize with the machine, but that during working hours a person should subordinate his psychology, his emotions and feelings, to the tempo and character of the machine . . . The whole enterprise should resemble a finely-tuned clock, where each part is interconnected with the other . . . [And] where the working of the whole depends on the efficient working of the part . . . no single unit can stop or slow down without disrupting the entire mechanism[1]

Doubtless events predisposed the Bolsheviks towards Taylorism. In the first place two wars and two revolutions had seriously weakened the country's economic infrastructure. Secondly, 1917 swept away

---

[1] A. A. Nol'de, *NOT v tekstil'noi promyshlennosti* (1924), pp. 5–6, 9. Machine metaphors run throughout this source.

much of the old pattern of authority and discipline which maintained production in the tsarist factory. Thirdly, big industry, without which, according to Lenin, socialism was impossible, was the natural arena for Taylorist experimentation.[2] Moreover, NEP was predicated on the *smychka* which in turn gave rise to the search for commercial efficiency in industry, and if costs were to be lowered, authority, discipline, and accounting – however organized – were necessary. Nevertheless, it is almost incredible that not one political leader tried to articulate a critical sociology of the labour process by developing the libertarian strand in Marxism.[3]

Scientific management had been in the air long before 1923 and was one aspect of American culture which found a ready response amongst European capitalists worried by growing international competition.[4] Bolsheviks were ambivalent in their attitudes. In spite of some early doubts Lenin never shook off his fascination with Taylorism. After the Revolution he came round to the view that its 'refined brutality', if properly managed by specialists under the watchful eye of the workers' state, could be transmogrified into a value-free technique for the good of all.[5] With this in mind the Central Institute of Labour had been established in Moscow in 1920. Under the enthusiastic guidance of Alexei Gastev conferences and manifestos quickly followed. Late in 1923 the Institute created the NOT Council which was charged with the duty of implementing NOT in state enterprises. Simultaneously Kerzhentsev founded the Time League. Unlike the Institute and the Council this putative mass movement wished to initiate a cultural revolution in the country at large: nothing less ambitious than teaching Russians to be punctual.[6]

Propagandizing the textile industry pre-dated the formation of the NOT Council. *Rabochii krai* began running articles on Taylorism a few days before the tenth party congress in 1921, but there is little evidence

---

[2] S. A. Smith, 'Bolshevism, Taylorism and the technical intelligentsia: the Soviet Union, 1917–41', *Radical Science Journal*, 13, 1983, pp. 9–15.

[3] It was left to the writers. Zamyatin, in his novel *My*, saw the nightmare behind the dream.

[4] See H. Braverman, *Labor and Monopoly Capitalism. The Degradation of Work in the Twentieth Century* (1974).

[5] *Immediate tasks of the Soviet Government* (1918) contains Lenin's fullest discussion of the role of Taylorism under socialism.

[6] This account of the early history of NOT is taken from K. E. Bailes, *Technology and Society under Lenin and Stalin: Origins of the Soviet Technical Intelligentsia, 1917–41* (1978); Smith, 'Bolshevism, Taylorism'.

of any particular sense of urgency.[7] Pressing problems inside the country and party meant that pamphlets and leading articles in the provincial press were not enough to guarantee implementation. In any case the cotton industry appeared to be doing quite well. The Central Institute would probably have survived as a curiosity had not events, in the shape of the scissors crisis, given the theorists their chance. The NOT Council and the Time League did not emerge out of nothing. In cotton, for instance, the concentration of production had not initially resulted in any marked reduction of the workforce, nor had there been much reduction of manning levels.[8]

In retrospect it all seemed clear. In 1926 weaving engineer Abramov reminded his readers that scissors had given everyone a salutary lesson:

> lowering the cost of production permits us to maintain the *smychka* between town and country, upon which to a considerable degree depends the well-being and further development of our industry and national economy . . . Nobody will deny the tremendous importance of proper accounting and rational management . . . Is there anyone who does not know that cheap retail prices depend directly on the ability of mills to overcome time-wasting, the incorrect use of machinery, labour resources, semi-finished goods and . . . raw materials?[9]

Others offered a pot-pourri of social, economic and historical justifications for NOT. Cotton was the first industry to be transformed by the machine, wrote one professor, and played the most important role in spreading cheap goods and industrialization throughout the world. But Russian mills had never been subjected to scientific analysis. Studying the processes of production prior to the rationalization of the industry was therefore 'an urgent task of the present time'. When the norm-setters held their first congress in 1925 one delegate believed that further advance depended on abandoning pre-war techniques, 'mass production' could be achieved only 'by means of more simplified methods of work, by drawing into production large numbers of less

---

[7] *Rabochii krai*, 23 February 1921. The series tailed off after a few months. It took two years for the local union branch to make some obeisance to the principle of scientific management: *Vosstanovlenie tekstil'noi promyshlennosti ivanovo-voznesenskoi gubernii, 1920–1925gg* (1966), p. 143.

[8] N. L. Brodskii *et al.*, *Tekstil'shchik (istoriia, byt, bor'ba)* (1925), p. 17; *Otchet TsK vsesoiuznogo professional'nogo soiuza tekstil'shchikov k VI vsesoiuznomu s"ezdu tekstil'shchikov. Okt. 1922g–okt. 1924g* (1924), p. 175 (hereafter *TsK VPST 1922–24*).

[9] A. Abramov, *Nagliadnyi uchet v tekstil'noi promyshlennosti* (1926), pp. 5–7.

skilled operatives'.[10] Nol'de declared that the market could not be satisfied unless Taylorism transformed the mill. Low productivity was largely due to 'unfamiliarity with normal work routines, with the necessity for enterprises to stay working for a definite number of hours each day, for machines to have a specific work-load and for operatives to work intensively'. But, he cautioned, many difficulties faced the industry. War and revolution had ruined buildings, disrupted work routines and supply networks and damaged machinery. There were too few skilled workers, hardly any trained technicians and not enough machine parts. Labour productivity, pay, work stoppages, shop-floor interaction between operatives, technicians and managers and working conditions were all of a piece, hence the entire macro-economic system should be investigated, starting with the mill.[11]

ISNOT and the problems of rationalization

In the midst of the scissors crisis – October 1923 – the union's emergency conference resolved to rationalize production and reduce manning levels. On December 13 the central committee discussed Taylorism and created a temporary commission to consider the matter. Fourteen days after this the paperwork was handed over to the labour department.[12] For the next two months nothing further happened, and it seemed that the whole issue might simply fade away. The final stimulus came from abroad. Nogin's trip as head of the syndicate gave him the opportunity to visit foreign enterprises. He and his associates were mightily impressed, particularly with the American mills. Their startled appreciation of Americanism and their insistence that Soviet mills should emulate American organizational forms galvanized the union into action.[13] The Initiative Council for

[10] D. D. Budanov, *Obshchie poniatiia o NOT'e v chastnosti v tekstil'noi promyshlennosti* (1926), pp. 61–2; *Rezoliutsii 1-go vsesoiuznogo s"ezda otdelov truda i T.N.B. tekstil'noi promyshlennosti (20–26/IX–1925g)* (1926), p. 13.

[11] *Sistema i organizatsiia*, 3, 1925, pp. 3–4; Nol'de, *NOT*, pp. 6, 10–14, 18–19, 24. Tsarist Russia had just two research and training institutes – the Ivanovo-Voznesensk School of Colour and the Moscow Spinning and Weaving College: N. V. Poliakova, 'Bor'ba rabochikh-tekstil'shchikov za povyshenie proizvoditel'nosti truda v 1921–1925gg. (Po materialam Moskvy i moskovskoi gubernii)', *Voprosy istorii*, 6, July, 1959, p. 24.

[12] *Initsiativnyi sovet po nauchnoi organizatsii truda pri tsentral'nom komitete soiuza tekstil'shchikov. Kratkii otchet* (1924), pp. 6–7 (hereafter *ISNOT*); *Rezoliutsii 4-oi vserossiiskoi konferentsii soiuza tekstil'shchikov, 23–27 oktiabria 1923g* (1923), pp. 5–6.

[13] *Biulleten' vserossiiskogo tekstil'nogo sindikata*, 7/8 (101/102), 26 February 1924, p. 4 (hereafter *BVTS*); *ISNOT*, pp. 6–7. *Sistema i organizatsiia*, 1, 1927, pp. 2–3, makes it plain that Nogin's foreign trip was the catalyst for action.

NOT in the Textile Industry (ISNOT) was founded on 24 February 1924, held its first meeting on 8 April and issued its first circular to all trusts and union branches sixteen days later advising them to begin a 'broad and energetic' movement by establishing special committees in every factory. By the end of the summer shut-down all mills were supposed to have NOT cells.[14]

The principles which lay behind the formation of ISNOT were a compromise. Gastev's elitist conception and Kerzhentsev's preference for mass participation jostled each other in the text of the organization's founding principles. Whilst on the one hand the country's economic difficulties required 'the most efficient and intensive methods of work to cut the cost of production', on the other mills should increase their productivity with regard to 'existing circumstances', and NOT would, 'as a part of its implementation', effect improvements in working conditions, and 'in our state must involve the broad mass of workers' through production conferences.[15] ISNOT's head office at the Palace of Labour on Moscow's Solianka Street quickly amassed a library of books and pamphlets for use in local cells, encouraged lectures and reports in mills and sponsored publications.[16]

Democratic accountability and popular participation, however, were at a discount. ISNOT had strong corporatist overtones. Pamphlets emerging in the autumn and winter of 1924 were usually published under the joint imprint of ISNOT, the central committee of the union and Vesenkha. Although theoretically under the union's control,[17] not one branch delegate, let alone factory committee chairman or textile worker, sat on ISNOT's central bureau, the presidium, or the presidium of scientific-technical commissions. A solitary woman found a place on the thirty-five strong governing council. In contrast, engineers, the trusts, the syndicate, Vesenkha and the Central Council of Trades Unions were well represented. 'Strict' planning was to accompany the foundation of special departments attached to each mill for studying output and productivity. In due

[14] *Sistema i organizatsiia*, 1, 1927, pp. 2–3; *ISNOT*, pp. 4–7; *Nauchnaia organizatsiia truda, proizvodstva i upravleniia* (1969), pp. 238–9; Nol'de, *NOT*, pp. 26–7, 30–3; TsK VPST 1922–24, pp. 231–2.
[15] *Nauchnaia organizatsiia*, p. 240. For a disagreements between Gastev and Kerzhentsev see Smith, 'Bolshevism, Taylorism', pp. 18–19.
[16] In *BVTS, Golos tekstilei, Predpriiatie* and *Vremia* (the Time League's journal). S. Kaplun, *Ukazatel' literatury na russkom iazyke po NOT i smeshnym voprosam* (1924), lists over 2,000 NOT publications.
[17] *TsK VPST 1922–24*, p. 229. *Trudy pervogo vsesoiuznogo s"ezda po ratsionalizatsii v tekstil'noi promyshlennosti. 19–24 maia 1926 goda* (1926) gives a short account of ISNOT's early development.

course these were to tell operatives how to work their machines, supervise the working day, and define the rights and duties of managers, technicians and operatives. Elites dominated the scientific-technical commissions which were to oversee departmental work, and they conducted their business well away from the masses; experiments directed towards de-skilling took place in laboratories borrowed from the Commissariat of Labour.[18]

Equally production conferences soon lost whatever popular dynamism they may at first have had. They seem to have grown out of the All-Russian Bureau for Productivity Propaganda. Founded in January 1921 with some help from the Central Council of Trades Unions, the bureau worked through the unions and local soviets and tried to systematize the spontaneous activity of workers.[19] In January and February 1924 the thirteenth party conference and the party's central committee pointed out the need for workers to get involved in productivity and rationalization drives, and specifically for them to form discussion circles to advise management. The Central Council of Trades Unions and *Rabkrin* designed model statutes in May, the Moscow region responded in October with conferences, commissions and meetings, and in November the sixth Central Council of Trades Unions and sixth textileworkers' union congresses stressed their importance, a theme reiterated at the fourteenth party congress in 1925.[20]

Although production conferences had been established in a number of mills from 1923 onwards (twenty-eight in the Moscow district by mid-summer 1924, for example[21]) there were soon complaints from the shop floor: 'I've been in this mill for thirty years,' wrote one worker, 'and now you want to tell me how to work.'[22] Others voiced their suspicions that the whole business threatened wages and conditions,[23] and many more commented on formalism in the meetings and the consequent lack of interest shown by operatives;[24] more 'significant' questions should be put to the conferences, averred one worker, 'real' questions about planning.[25] This may imply that

18 *Golos tekstilei*, 18 July 1924; *ISNOT*, p. 5; Nol'de, *NOT*, pp. 9–10, 38–40.
19 L. S. Rogachevskaia, *Sotsialisticheskoe sorevnovanie v SSSR. Istoricheskie ocherki* 1917–70gg (1977), pp. 20–1, 55.
20 E. H. Carr, *Socialism in One Country*, vol. 1 (1970), p. 427; Poliakova, 'Bor'ba rabochikh-tekstil'shchikov', pp. 30–1; *Rezoliutsii i postanovleniia 6-go s"ezda professional'nogo soiuza tekstil'shchikov* (1924), pp. 10–12 (hereafter *VI Congress VPST*).
21 I. P. Ostapenko, *Uchastie rabochego klassa SSSR v upravlenii proizvodstvom: proizvodstvennye sovershchaniia v promyshlennosti v 1921–1932gg* (1964), p. 26.
22 *Golos tekstilei*, 18 November 1924.   23 *Golos tekstilei*, 26 November 1924.
24 *Golos tekstilei*, 9 January 1925; 11 August 1925; *Rabochii krai*, 6 January 1924.
25 *Postanovleniia 2-go plenuma TsK vsesoiuznogo soiuza tekstil'shchikov 21–23 maia 1925g v Leningrade* (1925), p. 15.

operatives were indifferent because the conferences were but a pale shadow of the old idea of workers' control, but in any event, because the movement was bound up with the concentration of production and the rationalization drive,[26] cotton operatives had little reason to consider the conferences as anything other than an adjunct of management.

In fact one of ISNOT's first tasks was to persuade management of the necessity for NOT. Consequently in June 1924 Vesenkha and the syndicate called a national meeting of textile managers and executives, 'the first step on the road to rationalizing production', remarked one participant, 'let us hope it is not the last'.[27] The man primarily responsible for its convocation was the old textile engineer A. A. Fedotov, employed jointly by Vesenkha and the syndicate and a member of ISNOT's presidium. Fedotov had a long tradition of radical sympathies. Years before he had resigned as a director of Morozov's company in order to be free to attend the funeral of those workers killed in the 1905 strikes, but he was fully committed to raising productivity under socialism, even if it meant that workers would have to bear the subsequent burdens.[28] The conference devoted its time exclusively to discussing the need for efficiency, which was defined soberly in terms of the concentration of production and holding down wages.[29]

Stretching across the middle years of NEP it is possible to trace the shadowy outlines of a grand design for the cotton industry. The old engineers provided the first and essential element – men trained to resist waste and inefficiency. 'Is it not well known to many workers, foremen and (let's face it) administrators', wrote Nol'de,

> that shutting down a factory while parts are purchased for machinery is an excuse; a way of escaping from the necessity of proper accounting and of being satisfied with the bare minimum from operatives and machines, and that meanwhile the factory stands idle while investment and capital are squandered? . . . All over the mills are machines with signs hanging from them – 'stopped due to lack of oil', . . . etc.

Though many pressures worked against implementing NOT, continued Nol'de – insufficient funds, the supply crisis, competing

[26] See *Otchet o rabote moskovskogo gubernskogo otdela vsesoiuznogo professional'nogo soiuza tekstil'shchikov mai 1923g–mart 1924g* (1924), p. 135; *Rezoliutsii 3-go plenuma TsK soiuza tekstil'shchikov (12–15 aprelia 1923g)* (1923).

[27] V. M. Makarov, A. A. Fedotov, eds., *Trudy soveshchaniia proizvodstvennikov v tekstil'noi promyshlennosti. Moskva, 2–4 iiunia 1924g* (1925), p. 6; *TsK VPST 1922–24*, p. 238.

[28] See N. Valentinov, *Novaia ekonomicheskaia politika i krizis partii posle smerti Lenina* (1971), p. 25; A. Solzhenitsyn *The Gulag Archipelago*, vol. 1 (1974), p. 389.

[29] Makarov, Fedotov, *Trudy soveshchaniia, passim*.

priorities – a start could be made by undertaking a general survey of resources and by each trust rationalizing a couple of mills with workers' participation.[30] The second element was the consensus that cloth types and cotton counts should be reduced and standardized;[31] the third the union hierarchy's acceptance of some form of rationalization, signalled by the formation of ISNOT and its formal ratification by the sixth textileworkers' union congress in November 1924.[32] The fourth was the regime's general predisposition towards planning, enshrined in Gosplan's victory at the 1925 party congress, and its new-found respect for technical expertise. Both raised the engineers' confidence and self-esteem.[33]

The last element was the growing sense of realism in the highest echelons of the party-state. But only two Politburo members, ironically bitter enemies, demonstrated a determined willingness to get to the root of the matter. In January and April 1925 Bukharin published two candid articles on economic policy, both similar to positions advanced by Trotsky. The west had recovered from the instabilities caused by the Great War, wrote Bukharin, and even if there were to be European revolutions in the near future, Russia could expect no help from that direction for some considerable time. There would be civil upheavals and economic disruption. Either way the lesson was the same. More emphasis should be placed on the *smychka*, the rate of capital turnover should increase, and workers should concentrate on producing cheap goods for the peasants.[34] Like Bukharin, Trotsky was alive to the dangers and possibilities inherent in monopoly. Ever since the ill-fated attempt to impose some form or order in locomotive repair shops during the civil war his interest in standardization had been growing. Specialization and standardization would clear the way for the efficient production of the 'democratic' commodities now required, and limited integrationism – grain exports for hard currency – would give the peasantry some purchasing power and allow the state to buy foreign machinery. This would at once stimulate and satisfy mass demand and provide a simple technique for capital accumulation earmarked for investment in heavy industry. But there should be a measure of efficiency, something other than the acid test of com-

30 Nol'de, *NOT*, pp. 9–12, 23.
31 Budanov, *Obshchie poniatiia*, p. 72; *Tekstil'nye novosti*, 10–11, October–November 1927, pp. 375–6; L. Ia. Shukhgal'ter, ed., *Vnutrizavodskii kontrol' kachestva. Sbornik statei i instruktsii* (1927), p. 7.
32 *VI Congress VPST*, p. 15.   33 Shukhgal'ter, *Vnutrizavodskii kontrol'*, p. 12.
34 M. Lewin, *Russian Peasants and Soviet Power* (1968), p. 140; R. Day, *Leon Trotsky and the Politics of Economic Isolation* (1973), pp. 101, 103.

petition and the free market. Trotsky's solution was a system of equivalents expressed as co-efficients between Soviet and foreign commodities. A poor co-efficient would signal a weakness in Soviet industry and act as an automatic guide for planners, telling them where and how to intervene in production.[35]

'The difficulties are great', warned Nol'de in 1925, 'new machines have been installed in western countries, but in our mills ... old machines have worked on with insufficient repair.'[36] Were they insuperable? The question deserves a moment's speculation. Had the grand design been consciously realized and then translated into a definite plan it would have been a compromise; a composite of limited integrationism and limited Taylorism predicated on existing technologies. From Serpukhov to Shanghai, from Salford to Salem, factories operated British machinery; thus all the techniques used to measure output and productivity – count, cotton type, cloth type – were known, not only to every European and American mill owner, Russian textile executive, manager, engineer and worker, but also to virtually every handloom weaver who had ever produced a yard of calico. Considered imaginatively, the Lancashire equipment and expertise inherited from tsarism added up to more than a mass of obsolescent buildings, looms and spindle banks. By 1924 no one could doubt cotton's central role in the scheme of things; it would have been a good candidate for testing Trotsky's system of international equivalents and co-efficients.

The chief problem was that confusion reigned throughout the cotton districts. As demand became firmer and mills re-opened, so districts, trusts and individual enterprises hired and trained workers as best they could and arranged their shifts in response to immediate necessity or local conditions. Some mills opened as others closed and few were able to utilize all their machinery.[37] One Petrograd factory managed to bring on only 10 per cent of its 2,000 looms in 1922 because the roof leaked.[38] Nine other Leningrad cotton mills silent for half a decade started producing between 1924 and 1926 and the old Samsonev'skia was finally reopened in February 1927 after an eight-year shut-down.[39] Accumulated rust obliged workers to force the Ravenst-

---

[35] Day, *Leon Trotsky*, pp. 36, 114, 140–42.   [36] *Sistema i organizatsiia*, 3, 1925, p. 3.
[37] *TsK VPST 1922–24*, p. 175.
[38] Anglo-Russian Cotton Factories Ltd. *Report of Proceedings of Annual General Meeting of Shareholders at Company Offices, London*, 3 June 1924, MS11,760, p. 2.
[39] *Golos tekstilei*, 14 August 1925; 3 February 1927; *Leningradskaia promyshlennost'.za 50 let* (1967), p. 308.

vo's doors in 1921.[40] Moscow district's mills were running somewhat less than two-thirds of their spindles in 1923,[41] while those around Rodniki in Ivanovo guberniya ran barely 50 per cent, but this was on average. The Rodnikovskaia managed 51.1 per cent of spindles and 59.1 per cent of its looms, the Tezinskaia all spindles, the Varentsova no spindles but all looms, the Tomna 61.6 per cent of spindles, the Bol'shevik 40 per cent of spindles and 45.3 per cent of looms and the Bol'shaia Kokhomskaia 62.2 per cent of spindles and 88.3 per cent of looms.[42] The syndicate wanted a 20 per cent rise in output for 1925–6 which meant that another twenty-three mills would have to be pressed into service somehow or other.[43] In March 1925 Ivanovo State Textile Trust and the local economic council responded by reopening eighteen mills closed for many years.[44]

The industry's pre-revolutionary history also affected matters. There had never been a standard shift system in cotton. Before the Revolution cheap labour and expensive capital encouraged some entrepreneurs to opt for two shifts. Way back in 1888 several mills in Tver' and Moscow guberniyas were running their frames for fourteen hours a day, but in St Petersburg, where labour was comparatively scarce and mills had to compete with other industries, managers preferred one stretch of between nine and eleven hours. Nor had there ever been a standard working day.[45] The impact of the immediate past confused things still more. During the Civil War manning levels had failed to fall in time with the industry's collapse, a tendency repeated in 1923 with the first moves towards the concentration of production.[46] These idiosyncratic features continued as NEP took hold. Some, but by no means all of the cotton mills in Leningrad and the CIR went over to two shifts in 1924 to try to keep up with demand.[47]

40 Rabochie Leningrada. Kratkii istoricheskii ocherk 1703–1975gg (1975), p. 188.
41 Dostizheniia i nedochety tekstil'noi promyshlennosti SSSR. (Po materialam tekstil'noi sektsii NK RKI SSSR) (1926), p. 112.
42 Otchet ivanovo-voznesenskogo gosudarstvennogo tekstil'nogo tresta za 1923–24gg (1925), table 1 p. 113; Trud (Ivanovo-Voznesensk), 5, May 1923, p. 20.
43 Golos tekstilei, 6 January 1925; 1 September 1925.
44 Otchet gubernskogo otdela soiuza 15-mu gubernskomu s"ezdu tekstil'shchikov ivanovo-voznesenskoi gubernii (ap. 1924g–mart 1925g) (1925), p. 8 (hereafter I–V gubotdel VPST 1924–25).
45 O. Crisp, Studies in the Russian Economy before 1914 (1976), p. 40; Iu. I. Kir'ianov, Zhiznennyi uroven' rabochikh Rossii (konets XIX – nachalo XXv) (1979), table 1 pp. 44–5, table 5 p. 59; R. M. Odell, Cotton Goods in Russia (1912), pp. 23–4.
46 See p. 132. In 1920 around one-third of the 1913 workforce produced 5 per cent of the 1923 cloth output: P. A. Khromov, Ocherki ekonomiki tekstil'noi promyshlennosti SSSR (1946), p. 67.
47 Itogi raboty moskovskogo gubernskogo otdela profsoiuza tekstil'shchikov s 1 apr. 1924g po 1 okt. 1925g (1926), p. 111; Otchet o rabote moskovskogo gubernskogo otdela vsesoiuznogo

Given such conditions the avalanche of information triggered by ISNOT frustrated the reformers. In October 1925 the central committee of the union revealed that the average output of finished cloth per person per working day for twelve cotton trusts in June was 212.3 kg. Iaroslavl' produced the highest – 248.9 kg, Orekhovo-Zuevo the lowest – 117.3 kg.[48] But where chaotic shift working, machine idiosyncrasy and the general decay of *materiel* rendered meaningful comparisons all but impossible, statistics like these were of little use. When Nol'de addressed the seventh textileworkers' union congress in 1926 his sense of disappointment was plain for all to hear: 'it's not that they [in the west] have new machinery, they know how to organize the work of a factory correctly, how to organize machinery and people'.[49]

The upshot of all this was an early and understandable propensity to point the finger at one factor of production – labour – especially after visiting a few foreign factories. 'We are still far from those successes we have seen in English mills', lamented N. M. Matveev, syndicate member, candidate member of the union's central committee, president of the Orekhovo-Zuevo Trust, and a member of the Nogin delegation:

> there more attention is paid to labour saving, and English mills are themselves a long way from the ideal in organization and working practices. In some mills we have ten or eleven operatives per 1,000 spindles, and we've set ourselves the task of reducing this to nine. [But] in English mills . . . for every 1,000 spindles there are only 2.25 workers.[50]

Mill directors had made similar observations two years earlier at their first national congress in 1922:

> in textile production we use three times as much fuel as in pre-war times but produce five times less, because not all our mills are working . . . [nevertheless] we know that the individual productivity of skilled workers has fallen significantly, while at the same time we have many auxiliary workers in the mills, representing a huge percentage [of the workforce] that we never had before the War.[51]

professional' nogo soiuza tekstil' shchikov okt.–dek. 1924g (1925), pp. 40–1 (hereafter *Mosk-gubotdel VPST Oct–Dec 1924*); *Otchet za 1924–25g. Leningradskii gosudarstvennyi tekstil'-nyi trest 'Leningradtekstil'* (1925), p. 6; *Tri goda raboty vladimirsko-aleksandrovskogo tresta khlopchatobumazhnykh fabrik, 1922–1924gg* (1925), p. 34.

[48] *Biulleten' podotdela statistiki TsK vsesoiuznogo professional' nogo soiuza tekstil' shchikov*, 3, October 1925, table 42 pp. 74–5.

[49] *Golos tekstilei*, 15 May 1926.   [50] *Golos tekstilei*, 5 December 1924.

[51] *Stenograficheskii otchet 1-go vserossiiskogo s"ezda rabotnikov tekstil'noi promyshlennosti v Moskve, 12–16 okt. 1922g* (1923), pp. 3–4.

Exaggeration must be allowed for in the surveys prompted by ISNOT; even so there is no doubt that Russian mills were inefficient by international standards, and had been for decades. In 1927 the ubiquitous Nol'de unearthed an article criticizing Russian mills for time wasting and inefficiency; it had been published seventy years previously.[52] Foreigners were struck by the substitution of labour for capital. In 1915 J. F. Fraser reckoned up ten Russian operatives in Morozov's Nikol'skaia complex for every six in England. Eleven years later the chairman of the British Calico Printers' Association visited Russia and estimated that Soviet mills used, on average, five times as many workers for a given production process as those in Lancashire.[53] One Soviet engineer gave the following averages in 1924: 8.5 operatives per 1,000 spindles in Russia before 1914 rising to seventeen in 1917 and twenty-two in 1922, compared to 5.5 per 1,000 spindles abroad before 1914,[54] but these global figures concealed wild fluctuations and considerable regional variations, particularly between Leningrad and the CIR.[55] Not surprisingly the productivity of labour was low, somewhere around two-thirds of the 1912 level in 1922.[56] And there would have been scant comfort for the specialists had the results of a survey presented to the United States' Secretary for Commerce in 1912 become known to them. Special agent Odell reported that it was almost impossible to measure productivity in Russia's cotton industry, because 'the percentage [of machines run at optimum speeds] varies considerably in different factories and the wide range of yarns spun makes it difficult to secure accurate data'.[57]

Absenteeism was also a problem; 14 per cent for the industry in October 1923, 9.6 per cent in January 1924, 9 per cent in April and 12 per cent in July.[58] 'Time and again', thundered *Golos tekstilei* on its

---

[52] *Sistema i organizatsiia*, 1, 1927, p. 1.
[53] J. F. Fraser, *Russia of To-day* (1915), pp. 183, 189; *Textile Recorder*, 44, 520, 15 July 1926, p. 42.
[54] V. I. Feoktistov, *Ekskursiia na bumagopriadil'nuiu fabriku* (1924), p. 21.
[55] *Ibid.*, p. 21; *Na novykh putiakh. Itogi novoi ekonomicheskoi politiki 1921–1922gg*, vyp. 3 (1923), p. 14; *Trud i proizvodstvo*, 1, January 1925, p. 7; *TsK VPST 1922–24*, p. 177; *Vosstanovlenie promyshlennosti Leningrada (1921–1924gg)* (1963), p. 169.
[56] S. G. Strumilin, *Zarabotnaia plata i proizvoditel'nost'truda v russkoi promyshlennosti za 1913–1922gg* (1923), appendix 13 p. 87.
[57] Odell, *Cotton Goods*, p. 16. In October 1921 *Glavtekstil'* tried to establish norms for spinning rooms; thirty workers of all kinds per 1,000 spindles, revised down to twenty-four in June 1922. These were, of course, averages. Very specific instructions were sometimes issued: for 1921/22, for example, there should be no more than 16.5 workers of all kinds per 1,000 ring-frame spindles spinning count 20 on two shifts, and so on. One wonders if anyone even read them: *BVTS*, 9, 11 May 1922, p. 2; Feoktistov, *Ekskursiia*, p. 20; *Sistema i organizatsiia*, 11, 1925, p. 23.
[58] *TsK VPST 1922–24*, p. 159.

front page, 'we hear from factory directors that the percentage of absentees is rising month by month.' Later the paper claimed that operatives manipulated official visits and the rules on sickness to escape from the shop floor.[59] Stoppages in the Ivanovo district were put down to absenteeism and slackness. Spindles and cotton were left lying around on the floor while overlookers spent the day reading the paper. Although time-keeping improved in those factories recently opened, after a while the percentage of absentees started to rise.[60] Waste and poor workmanship were endemic in the Egor'evsk-Ramenskoe district, absenteeism high in Leningrad and Moscow guberniya.[61] Vladimir-Aleksandrov Trust discovered that it had 13.2 workers of all kinds per 1,000 spindles in 1923/24, and an astonishing 10.8 for every loom; thus harassed local administrators like I. G. Eremin probably had little time to speculate about the finer points of Taylorism: 'we have some interesting figures which show how many workers there were in our factories before the war, in all, 20,000 . . . Now we have almost 18,000, that is, 80 per cent of the pre-war level. And output? Do we have an 80 per cent output level? No, not in one mill'.[62]

Trotsky's hopes and the specialists' prognoses needed time. Effective intervention required an honest appraisal of the industry's real potential, a detailed industrial census followed by careful experiment and much persuasion; 'reorganizing a factory is not a matter of a day or a week', warned Nol'de.[63] But one can appreciate that given the fixities imposed by all manner of shortages, dislocations, and bureaucratic inefficiencies, compounded by the refusal to countenance integrationism, circumstances would probably have resulted in the eventual degeneration of NOT in any case. Labour appeared to be the only free factor in production. Circumstances, however, never had a chance to work their way through. Cotton's NOT enthusiasts were spared the pangs of disillusionment by the Politburo's collective impatience, seconded by Dzerzhinskii and Piatakov in Vesenkha. Taylorism was never officially abandoned – NOT publications and NOT propagandizing continued unabated throughout NEP[64] – but the

---

59 *Golos tekstilei*, 22 April 1924; 3 June 1924.
60 *Rabochii krai*, 26 March 1922; *Trud i proizvodstvo*, 1, January 1925, p. 8; 1, January 1926, p. 25.
61 *Dostizheniia i nedochety*, p. 195; *Golos tekstilei*, 18 July 1924; 2 January 1925; 23 June 1926.
62 *Tri goda raboty*, pp. 42, 87.   63 Nol'de, *NOT*, p. 23.
64 A great number of Taylorist articles were published in 1925: see *Sistema i organizatsiia* for that year. *Trud* (Ivanovo-Voznesensk) joined in rather late; NOT propaganda started to appear only at the end of January 1925, after the eclipse of pure NOT. The

movement rapidly collapsed into a chaotic welter of speed-ups, sudden unplanned increases in workloads and *uplotnenie* – 'tightening up the working day'.

The beginnings of the *uplotnenie* drive

These developments took place against a background of uncertainty in the countryside. The regime could not (or would not) level out peaks and troughs in the national economy by trading in food and consumer goods on the international market; thus economic, social and political stability depended on chance. Although first returns for 1924 indicated a bumper harvest, drought afflicted south-eastern Russia and the Volga district in mid-summer. The government reacted by suspending grain exports. Inside the country prices began to soar, and went on rising until May 1925. Price control was abandoned the previous November. With good reason, therefore, leaders were worried about relationships with the peasantry and anxious to broaden NEP, and as the threat of grain shortages grew so the party's concern increased. In May 1924 the union's central committee reaffirmed its commitment to the *smychka*.[65] Two months previously Moscow's local party conference discussed the need for rationalization and higher labour productivity in industry, a sentiment echoed by the central committee in Moscow in August. In November 1924, just as price control over grain was abandoned, the sixth Central Council of Trades Unions' Congress put labour productivity at the head of the agenda. Strikes were not to be tolerated and there were to be special bonuses for technical personnel. Efficiency and discipline were the watchwords. Rykov spoke of the threat of another scissors crisis.[66] Twenty-four hours after the delegates dispersed *Golos tekstilei* came out with the headline 'Towards Working Three Looms!' Underneath appeared a battery of figures from British and American mills – yet another legacy of Nogin's trip.[67]

Well before the sixth textileworkers' union congress, delayed for a few days to accommodate the Central Council of Trades Unions, a slow but steady drift towards labour intensification was already under-

journal was renamed *Trud i proizvodstvo* to emphasize 'the great importance . . . of raising the productivity of labour': *Trud i proizvodstvo*, 1, 31 January 1925, p. 1.

[65] Lewin, *Russian Peasants*, pp. 82, 114; Carr, *Socialism in One Country*, 1, pp. 205–9.

[66] Carr, *Socialism in One Country*, 1, p. 209; M. Dewar, *Labour Policy in the USSR 1917–28* (1956), pp. 119–22; Poliakova, 'Bor'ba rabochikh tekstil'shchikov', pp. 23, 30; J. B. Sorenson, *The Life and Death of Soviet Trade Unionism 1917–28* (1969), p. 217.

[67] *Golos tekstilei*, 19 November 1924.

way in the cotton industry. *Rabkrin* circularized the union, factory committees, and all its local branches on 21 May, emphasizing the importance of lowering production costs. Next month Dzerzhinskii sent out telegrams to the trusts encouraging them to raise individual workloads.[68] Krasno-Presnensk Trust called for the abolition of demarcation – cautiously, however, only for auxiliaries – and on July 18 Egor'evsk-Ramenskoe Trust announced its intention to lay off auxiliary workers. The union's president was not impressed. A week later he wrote that sacking assistant operatives – 'ballast' – was an easy option for executives. It made the figures on labour productivity look better than they really were. What was needed was labour discipline, labour intensification and the abolition of overtime so that the eight-hour day could be measured properly.[69] In October the union's Vladimir branch responded by promising 'full enforcement' of the working day, and *Golos tekstilei* took up the struggle for raising labour productivity – 'one of our basic tasks'.[70] Sometime between October and the end of the year Moscow guberniya's union branch discussed the possibility of three-loom working in order to cut costs, overcome shortages of skilled workers and shortfalls in housing. On November 1 a new collective agreement covering operatives in the Ivanovo area also made much of *uplotnenie*.[71] Kalinin and Dzerzhinskii turned up to address the union's congress, an indication of élite preoccupations with cotton's place in the *smychka*, and insisted that time-keeping and work schedules be tightened up. Concluding speeches from the platform stressed the importance of NOT, now interpreted as the rapid growth of labour productivity through labour intensification.[72]

As union delegates made their way home the government's alarm became evident. The sources are worth extensive quotation. For a start executives suddenly found Vesenkha's 'Telegram Number 40' on their desks:

> To All Cotton Trusts. I order immediately: (1) The transfer from one to three, and where possible to four [looms per weaver]. If you have automatic looms, transfer to ten. (2) Transfer ring-frame spinners to three spindle banks ... on other types of machinery [transfer workers] to four machines. (3) Where explanations are required this telegram is to be made known in my name. If the reasons for the

[68] *Sistema i organizatsiia*, 11, 1925, p. 23.
[69] *Golos tekstilei*, 18 July 1924; 25 July 1924; 30 September 1924; *Obzor deiatel'nosti krasno-presnenskogo tresta za 1924–1925 operats. goda* (1925), p. 31.
[70] *Golos tekstilei*, 14 October 1924; *Rezoliutsii i postanovleniia 7-go gubernskogo s"ezda soiuza tekstil'shchikov, 25–27 okt. 1924g* (1924), p. 26.
[71] *I–V gubotdel VPST 1924–25*, p. 57; *Moskgubotdel VPST Oct–Dec 1924*, p. 36.
[72] *Golos tekstilei*, 26 November 1924; 30 November 1924.

transfer are not fully understood, explain them. On the 1st and 16th of every month each director of each mill is to communicate the progress of this work to me. (Piatakov.[73])

Piatakov's terse instruction probably stemmed from his superior's involvement in a state commission for raising labour productivity. Dzerzhinskii's commission discussed fixed assets, labour resources, management, costs, and the chances of labour intensification, particularly on looms and ring-frames, and also prepared 'basic documents' for each mill shop 'containing general instructions on rationalization'. It is just possible, but not very likely, that these reached the factories before November. The commission was convened in October 1924 and sat seven times before its dissolution in February 1925.[74]

Vesenkha's vice-chairman stirred up a hornet's nest. Five months into 1925 *Rabkrin* concluded that *uplotnenie* was far from easy because standard work practices were incompatible with variations arising from local conditions. Piatakov should have known this. Instead 'there was no appreciation of the difficulty . . . [the] big mistake in the well-known telegram of November 1924 . . . was to couch the instruction in the form of a military command'.[75] But somehow or other factories responded, or at least persuaded *Golos tekstilei* that they were doing something. Throughout December the paper began to print workers' letters announcing the switch in their mills. To add to the confusion Vesenkha started to back-pedal almost at once – Circular 15, sent to the cotton industry on December 10:

> It is impossible to contemplate for the present the mass transfer of all weavers to three looms . . . and all ring-frame spinners to three spindle banks. This can only be done after a reduction in the types of . . . cloth produced and a reduction in the number of counts spun . . . [Meanwhile] managers must: (1) Become familiar with the technical paradigms of machinery in their mills. (2) Agitate for higher productivity amongst middle and high ranking technical personnel. (3) Carry out a re-organization of the labour process and eliminate those operations not demanding much skill . . . [and] dismiss assistant workers whose jobs require no basic skills. (4) Begin to reduce cloth types. (5) Prepare plans for speed-ups in spinning halls. (6) Give the most serious attention to waste and poor workmanship in spinning rooms.[76]

---

[73] *Khoziaistvo i upravlenie*, 5, 1925, p. 50.
[74] F. E. Dzerzhinskii *et al.*, eds., *K probleme proizvoditel'nosti truda*, vyp. 3 (1925), p. 51. For an earlier commission on wages see p. 173.
[75] *Khoziaistvo i upravlenie*, 5, 1925, pp. 49–50.   [76] *Ibid.*, p. 50.

Five days later Piatakov, the Central Council of Trades Unions, the union's president and the syndicate dispatched a soothing letter to all mills and their factory committees. Although *uplotnenie* was necessary, and the best way was to re-organize unskilled work and switch workers to running more than two looms and two spindle banks, there must be planning and no unnecessary haste. That it could be done was demonstrated by successes in the Naro-Fominsk's spinning halls in Moscow guberniya. There three-bank working had been in operation since 1922. Stress was laid on benefits to workers. There was to be a big campaign in the mills.[77]

[77] *Golos tekstilei*, 19 December 1924.

9　Organizing Taylorism: wages

> Some local branches work in such a way that it seems that we have
> not a united union, but some kind of federation, and one where each
> part does not always fit with the whole.
>
> Lebedev, secretary of the textileworkers' union, writing in *Golos*
> *tekstilei*, 18 August 1925

Wage levels and wage scales

If NOT enthusiasts could take little comfort from their
growing awareness of the industry's human and material complexities, still less could be drawn from an examination of the system of
remuneration, or rather the lack of system. Indeed, as far as pay is
concerned, war, revolution and fiscal and economic collapse have
turned the early Soviet period into a dark age. We will probably never
know the exact balance of gains and losses for particular communities. The union thought that the average wage of all textileworkers
had more or less reached its 1914 level by 1924 after sinking to its
lowest point in 1920.[1] Whether or not the exact figures are reliable,
the general impression of rapid recovery after 1921 makes sense. Textiles were a lead industry in early NEP, and a series produced by
Rashin for 1922–4 showing fairly continuous recovery with slight falls
in the early summers of 1923 and 1924 can also be accepted as reasonable.[2] We would expect a drop for 1923; the scissors crisis put the
union at a disadvantage and negotiations for wage increases were
unsuccessful.[3] The falls of the following year probably signalled the

[1] *Otchet TsK vsesoiuznogo professional'nogo soiuza tekstil'shchikov k VI vsesoiuznomu s"ezdu
tekstil'shchikov. Okt. 1922g–okt. 1924g* (1924), p. 106 (hereafter *TsK VPST 1922–24*).

[2] S. G. Strumilin, ed., *Naemnyi trud v Rossii i na zapade 1913–25gg* (1927), table 1 p. 9; A. G.
Rashin, *Zarabotnaia plata za vosstanovitel'nyi period khoziaistva SSSR. 1922/23–1926/27gg*
(1927), table 2 p. 234.

[3] *Otchet o rabote moskovskogo gubernskogo otdela vsesoiuznogo professional'nogo soiuza
tekstil'shchikov mai–iiul' 1923g* (1923), pp. 46–7; *Otchet o rabote moskovskogo gubernskogo*

first move against auxiliary workers after February's round of negotiations secured a general wage rise of 15 per cent.[4]

What is more interesting, if no less problematic, is the way central
policy, market forces and tradition interacted to affect differentials.
From 1919 onwards the industry operated on the basis of a thirty-five
point wage scale, reduced to seventeen in the new handbook
published by the union in 1922. Both included allowances in kind, a
principle gradually abandoned as collective agreements took hold; in
October that year the fifth union congress ratified a new directive of
the Central Council of Trades Unions' committing Soviet industry to
all-money wages and left the problem of implementation to the
provinces.[5] Before the Revolution factory owners outside the two
capitals often assumed the burden of social overhead costs, one of the
reasons why cotton appeared to be an exceptionally low-wage industry.[6] Abolition of payment in kind and communal services certainly
seem to have affected living standards adversely, but on the other
hand the state had now, in principle, assumed responsibility for a
whole range of social services never previously provided. Whatever
the case, although the simultaneous switch from trade to gold roubles
complicated re-scaling, most areas had, it seems, converted to all-
money wages by January 1923.[7] Late in 1923 there was another
change. Now the Central Council's simplified 'unified tariff', based on
skill, working conditions and the 'relationship between the workforce
and the labour market' was to apply to all large-scale industry, and
therefore to all cotton operatives. Overlookers, for example,
previously on point seven with adjustments for type and size of
machines in their shops, found themselves on points eight and nine
with no adjustments. Weavers moved up a point, from three to four.[8]

The Central Council's order on the unified tariff cut across union
research directed towards establishing yet another new tariff for
textileworkers as events undermined the seventeen-point scale. In
fact the 1922 scale had been breached from the start and the provinces
simply ignored the Council's order. Leading from behind, the central

otdela vsesoiuznogo professional'nogo soiuza tekstil'shchikov mai 1923g–mart 1924g (1924),
pp. 104, 137 (hereafter Moskgubotdel VPST 1923–24); TsK VPST 1922–24, pp. 94–5.
[4] Golos tekstilei, 26 February 1924.
[5] Tekstil'shchik, 1/2 (15–16), April–May 1920, pp. 17–18; TsK VPST 1922–24, p. 101.
[6] R. M. Odell, Cotton Goods in Russia (1912), pp. 12–14, 25, 37.
[7] Otchet TsK vserossiiskogo professional'nogo soiuza tekstil'shchikov sent. 1922g–sent. 1923g. K
IV vseross. konferentsii soiuza 1923g (1923), pp. 123–5, 128, 198–9 (hereafter TsK VPST
1922–23); A. G. Rashin, ed., Trud v SSSR. Statistiko–ekonomicheskii obzor, oktiabr'
1922g–mart 1924g) (1924), p. 77; TsK VPST 1922–24, pp. 97–8, 105–6.
[8] TsK VPST 1922–24, pp. 97–100; Tarifnyi spravochnik tekstil'shchikov (1926), p. 3.

committee of the union subsequently argued that sub-divisions on the old 1919 thirty-five point system were an important means of rewarding skill.[9] Ivanovo's branch successfully defended its unilateral division of seventeen points into fifty-six sub-categories – so as to match skill and established patterns of work – before an extraordinary commission in October 1922.[10] Differentials widened. Those on point one had their wages calculated from a base-line 6.05 roubles, those on nine from 23.94. Five months later this had become 6.93 and 27.88 respectively.[11] Though it provides the best example of the industry's centrifugal tendencies, Ivanovo was not the only region to snub the Central Council. Throughout 1923/24 Tambov and some other districts sub-divided by quarters, and co-efficients between scale points also varied.[12] Local deviations continued well into NEP. Ivanovo preserved its special scales up to, and possibly beyond, January 1926, and although by then twenty-three branches had transferred to the unified tariff, these accounted for only 13.2 per cent of the textile workforce.[13]

Even these official rates only hint at the real extent of localism. Collective agreements for October–December 1923 show twenty-one trusts varying between 5.9 and 7.6 trade roubles for scale point one, for example. Twelve enterprises in the Vladimir district split between three trusts had about 144 variations on point one in September 1923,[14] and over 230 different classifications of point six applied in Moscow guberniya's mills. There factories and trusts accepted individual agreements with skilled workers which caused some to depart significantly from the tariff. Wages should depend not only on general economic conditions and the profitability of each mill, said the local union branch, but on the economic potential of each trust department. Special commissions were established to try to sort out the

[9] *Golos tekstilei*, 2 February 1928; *TsK VPST 1922–23*, p. 125; *TsK VPST 1922–24*, pp. 100–02.

[10] *Golos tekstilei*, 25 August 1925; *Trud* (Ivanovo-Voznesensk), 5, May 1923, p. 70.

[11] *Trud* (Ivanovo-Voznesensk), 5, May 1923, p. 123; *Rezoliutsii 3-go plenuma TsK soiuza tekstil'shchikov (12–15 aprelia 1923g)* (1923), p. 11 (hereafter *3-go plen TsK VPST 1923*). Large pay rises for the guberniya's skilled workers are mentioned in summer 1923: *Trud* (Ivanovo-Voznesensk), 6–7, June–July 1923, pp. 4–5.

[12] A common choice was 2:2.5, 3:3.5, etc., but 1:3 in Moscow guberniya; 1:2.8 in Vladimir; 1:2.6 in Tver'; 1:2.5 in Iaroslavl' and 1:2.3 in Leningrad: *Golos tekstilei*, 25 July 1924; 2 February 1928.

[13] *Otchet TsK vsesoiuznogo professional'nogo soiuza tekstil'shchikov k 7-mu vsesoiuznomu s"ezdu tekstil'shchikov. Iiul' 1924g–ianv. 1926g* (1926), p. 97 (hereafter *TsK VPST 1924–26*).

[14] *Golos tekstilei*, 12 February 1924; 19 February 1924; *Otchet o rabote vladimirskogo gubernskogo pravleniia professional'nogo soiuza tekstil'shchikov s sent. 1923g po sent. 1924g. K 7-mu gubernskomu s"ezdu soiuza* (1924), p. 59 (hereafter *Vladgubotdel VPST 1923–24*).

Table 9. *The wage hierarchy in the cotton trade c.1910–1923/24*

	Wage index (selfactor spinner = 100)	
	*c.*1910[a]	1923/24[b]
Preparatory departments		
Drawing-frame operatives	35	64
Flyer-frame operatives	36	62
Fine spinning rooms		
Ring-frame spinners	34	58
Selfactor *komplekt*		
spinners	100	100
senior piecers	40	74
doffers/creelers	26	43
Weaving sheds		
Weavers	43	66

Sources: Calculated from
[a] R. M. Odell, *Cotton Goods in Russia* (1912), p. 25
[b] S. G. Strumilin, ed., *Naemnyi trud v Rossii i na zapade 1913–1925gg* (1927), table 16 pp. 23–4.

mess,[15] but nothing further was ever heard from them. 'The old [1922] tariff gave no real guidance', remembered one union official, 'as a result each area established its own system, and different rates for the same job arose.'[16]

Nationally, the vast majority of mill hands were classed as unskilled. Only 9 per cent of men and 0.1 per cent of women were above scale point eight in January 1923.[17] No more than a minority – most of them men – would therefore benefit from individual agreements, but this did not preclude the continued rapid multiplication of differentials. The geographical variations which appeared were no less marked than those predicated on skill and were probably symptomatic of local labour shortages. Examples are legion,

---

[15] By the new year some workers on scale points fifteen and sixteen were receiving 50 per cent in excess of official pay under overtime deals. Throughout Soviet industry generally official rates were a fiction at this time: *Golos tekstilei*, 18 January 1924; E. H. Carr, *The Interregnum 1923–24* (1969), pp. 84–8.
[16] *Leningradskii tekstil'*, 4, 1928, p. 5.   [17] Strumilin, *Naemnyi trud*, table 30 p. 31.

with Leningrad showing the highest levels of remuneration.[18] The net result was predictable. Given the central committee of the union's hesitations after January 1923, attempts to standardize pay met with little success. Tradition re-appeared in the wage packet in the familiar guise of gender and trade. Apart from foremen, overlookers and selfactor spinners, few in 1924 earned more than seventy roubles a month, and few in these trades less than seventy. Though differentials had been reduced somewhat since 1917, the old shop-floor hierarchy, with selfactor spinners at the top, re-asserted itself under NEP (see table 9).[19]

Wage bargaining and conflict

Conflict over wages implied a divergence of interest between the worker and the state. For Bolshevik theoreticians this may have been a difficult matter; for administrators obliged to make their factories pay it was not. Wage rises, for what ever reason, threatened profitability. On one occasion these sentiments manifested themselves in an institution;[20] more frequently executives used the trusts' publications to make their feelings known: 'for the economic year 1923/24', reported Eremin from the Vladimir region, 'the productivity of spinners has risen by 15 per cent, but the percentage of production costs accounted for by wages is 46 per cent. In weaving the figures are 20 per cent and 48 per cent respectively.'[21] Eremin may have had a point for his own trust, but nationally, the picture is less clear. Declining profitability and rising wages only became general in the early autumn of 1924,[22] just as Taylorism was being translated into some kind of reality. Wage policy underwent a sea-change that year (discussed below), but if local tariffs and individual agreements meant that the attempt to rationalize pay in a manner befitting some form of labour

[18] See, for example, *Moskgubotdel VPST 1923–24*, pp. 106–7, 113–14; *Otchet leningradskogo gubernskogo otdela vsesoiuznogo professional'nogo soiuza tekstil'shchikov. Okt, 1924–1925gg* (1926), p. 68 (hereafter *Lengubotdel VPST 1924–25*); *Vladgubotdel VPST 1923–24*, pp. 59–70; *Voprosy truda*, 3, March 1925, p. 157; *TsK VPST 1922–24*, pp. 102–3, 105–6, 118.

[19] V. A. Kungurtsev, *Tekstil'naia promyshlennost' SSSR* (1957), p. 24, also makes the point that selfactor spinners were at the top of the wage hierarchy.

[20] To the unions' alarm a quasi-official 'Bureau of Syndicates' convened in September 1922 to co-ordinate resistance to wage demands; members who broke ranks were to be whipped into line: Carr, *Interregnum*, pp. 51–2.

[21] *Tri goda raboty vladimirsko-aleksandrovskogo tresta khlopchatobumazhnykh fabrik, 1922–24gg* (1925), p. 50.

[22] *Sotsialisticheskii vestnik*, 3(49), 31 January 1923, p. 9; *TsK VPST 1922–24*, p. 113; *TsK VPST 1924–26*, pp. 91, 96.

intensification was made in highly unpropitious circumstances, the other factor determining pay – collective agreements – did little to improve matters.

In March 1922 the union launched a mass campaign to make workers familiar with their collective agreements.[23] Re-introduced in summer 1921, they covered nearly 93 per cent of all industrial workers within twenty-four months. By October 1923 there were 207 operating in textiles alone,[24] but they did nothing to facilitate standardization. When in November 1924 the union's central committee 'categorically' stated that pay rises must be through the medium of collective agreements, it failed to mention that negotiations took place in the localities, fertile ground indeed for all manner of further temporary arrangements, special scales and individual payments.[25] In 1923/24 there were ninety separate agreements in Moscow guberniya's mills for workers and thirty-two for office staff. Vladimir guberniya had sixteen agreements and ninety related tariff contracts. Ivanovo's branch managed to negotiate twenty-two agreements with the nine cotton trusts sprawling across the guberniya in 1925/26, and thirty-eight related tariff agreements, each with a different base for scale point one.[26]

Collective agreements at least provided a legitimate arena for open conflict with enterprise and trust management. Late payment was a major source of contention; 'in our mill they've introduced a new system', commented one worker from Moscow guberniya, 'the workers work and don't get paid'.[27] Another was the friction and tension inherent in the process of negotiation. 'If we look at the movement of pay rates as established by collective agreements', observed Vladimir's union branch in 1923/24, 'and the actual wages received by workers for each month, we see that the second lags

23 *TsK VPST 1922–23*, pp. 129–30.
24 99.5 per cent of all textile workers were covered by collective agreements by the start of 1926: *Professional'nye soiuzy SSSR 1924–1926gg. Otchet VTsSPS k VII s"ezdu profsoiuzov* (1926), p. 118.
25 *Rezoliutsii i postanovleniia 6–go s"ezda professional'nogo soiuza tekstil'shchikov* (1924), p. 33 (hereafter *VI Congress VPST*). Sometime later one worker wrote to say that in his mill people were cautious about a proposal that collective agreements should run for nine months because 'in the course of such a long period of time the standard of living might worsen'. Another correspondent pointed out that since retail prices varied across Russia wage standardization did not necessarily mean wage equalization: *Golos tekstilei*, 27 November 1925; 2 March 1926.
26 *Moskgubotdel VPST 1923–24*, p. 111; *Otchet o rabote ivanovo-voznesenskogo gubernskogo otdela vsesoiuznogo soiuza tekstil'shchikov za vremia s apr. 1925g–mart 1926g. 16-mu s"ezdu soiuza* (1926), pp. 33–4 (hereafter *I–V gubotdel VPST 1925–26*); *Vladgubotdel VPST 1923–24*, p. 67.
27 *Golos tekstilei*, 11 July 1924.

behind the first. This is because after almost every campaign management undertakes an upward review of output norms'.[28] Wrangles
over pay and norms – 905 in total – accounted for three-quarters of all
official disputes in Moscow guberniya's mills in the eleven months
following May 1923. The three largest of these revolved around 857
workers and their transfer to a higher tariff point. For the entire
country forty-three of the sixty-three disagreements referred to the
central committee of the union for a ruling concerned pay, norms and
collective agreements. Next year nearly 60 per cent of disputes settled
by local arbitration courts were about the same issues.[29]

Nevertheless, conflict could not always be contained within official
parameters. *Émigré* Mensheviks put textiles in first place in the league
table of strikes for 1922, with 20,853 participants. Their informants
claimed that most were over pay in some way or other. Much of this is
substantiated by a Soviet author, and these Menshevik figures may be
an underestimation. According to the Soviet source there were sixty-
three disputes involving 62,968 strikers, around a quarter of the total
for all industry and the highest number for any one industry. Ninety-
five per cent of all strikes were about pay. The majority were in
Moscow province: twenty-six textile strikes with over 36,000 participants representing 80 per cent of all strikers in the district. Nationally,
most were short-term. Only one-third of the sixty-three strikes mentioned above lasted longer than five days. Fifty-nine ended with some
formal agreement, two-thirds of them wholly or partly in favour of the
workers.[30]

It is hard to get behind a bare recital of the statistics, but there is
some fragmentary evidence on the way strikes started and how
managers, trusts, workers and the union handled things. An
unknown number of workers from four mills in the Egor'evsk district
struck over late payment in April 1922, and 'seriously interfered with
production ... Some demagogues, people who don't want to work,
exploited the workers' passions.' Ten weavers 'connected with the old
factory owners' were dismissed as an example to the rest.[31] Seven or
eight weeks later trust officials responsible for Orekhovo-Zuevo's
Nikol'skaia complex attempted to lower wages while a collective
agreement was under discussion. The weaving sheds struck on

28 *Vladgubotdel VPST 1923–24*, p. 76.
29 *Moskgubotdel VPST 1923–24*, p. 119; *TsK VPST 1922–23*, p. 224; Strumilin, *Naemnyi
trud*, table 3 p. 174.
30 Strumilin, *Naemnyi trud*, table 2 pp. 158–9, table 3 p. 160, table 4 p. 161, table 5 p. 162,
table 6 p. 163; *Sots.vest*, 22 (44), 21 November 1922, p. 14.
31 *Tekstil'shchik, k stanku*, 25 June 1922.

August 13 and executives responded by threatening to withdraw payment in kind – bread. Thereafter events moved swiftly. Spinners walked out and workers from proximate mills joined them. Within a day or so two mass meetings were held, one outside the trust's offices, the other in a local theatre. Both were apparently restricted to mill hands and, according to the Menshevik journal, workers voiced strong criticisms of Bolshevik economic policy. A local union official received a hostile reception when he turned up to speak to the crowds as did a central committee member who came down from Moscow. Strikers accused the union hierarchy of 'bureaucratism and self-interest' and some factory directors responded by threatening that if the strike was not over by August 21, their mills would 'close indefinitely'. The trust's chairman wanted to dismiss all the strikers; workers retorted that not even the old factory owners took such measures. In spite of union attempts to break the strike, one of the mass meetings delegated a worker to negotiate with the central committee in Moscow. On August 18 the strike was still solid, although, according to the journal's correspondent, likely to collapse soon because of the threat of a lock-out. Two hundred workers had already been sacked, and some 'trouble makers' arrested by the secret police.[32]

Although this was written by a Menshevik sympathizer it does provide a fascinating glimpse of the mood and manners of the times. No corroborating evidence is available in the Bolshevik press, but the account, full of incidental detail, has the ring of truth and first-hand observation. If the Nikol'skaia came out (the biggest mill in the country) along with one or two other mills around Orekhovo-Zuevo, it is quite possible that in excess of 20,000 operatives were involved.

Discontent rumbled on into 1923. Strike committees of some kind were formed around Teikovo and Kokhma in Ivanovo guberniya, and there may have been some organizational continuity, or at least some legacy of bitterness. The Tomna's workers had walked out three years earlier in protest against labour intensification when the mill was classified as 'shock' enterprise.[33] None of the twenty-six strikes listed for that year by a Soviet source took place in Leningrad[34] so the Mensheviks probably got things right by concentrating their reports on the CIR. Their journal reported a 'wave of strikes' there with a strong undercurrent of grumbling and discontent but gave few details. Most were 'disorganized'. In September Moscow city's Tsindel's

[32] *Sots.vest*, 19 (41), 4 October 1922, pp. 14–25.
[33] *Rabochii krai*, 3 November 1920; 4 July 1923.
[34] *Voprosy truda*, 4, April 1924, p. 53.

workers stopped work over pay and conditions. The strike spread to the Trekhgornaia and Malakhovskaia. Kalinin made the short trip from central Moscow to tell workers that there was no more money, and that if the strike continued the factories would shut. Operatives returned to work sometime before the second week in October. Some shops came out in the Serpukhov district, advancing 'groundless demands', according to the only source. Reports of further tension in Orekhovo-Zuevo may be connected with the previous year's events. In spring 1923 twenty-seven trust officials were tried for incompetence and corruption. 'Capitalists' and party members were implicated in a swindle involving pay. Serebriakov, head of the local secret police and nicknamed 'little tsar', was accused of dealing in bread and consumer goods for the preceding three years.[35]

Most of these eruptions were probably a by-product of the regime's response to the sales crises of 1922–24. Strikes in Soviet industry as a whole peaked with scissors and were serious enough to worry the Politburo.[36] It is less clear that they had any overt political motivation or organization, at least in the case of cotton, although the simultaneous attack on the Orthodox Church[37] may have added to the general stock of unrest. Two shadowy opposition groups, however, did emerge in 1923: 'Workers' Truth' and 'Workers' Group'. Both might have been expected to speak to the condition of workers. Both accused the party of being dominated by intellectuals, of losing touch with the working class and of introducing a form of capitalism, and both hoped to penetrate party cells and to organize in mills, factories, soviets and unions. Both were crushed by the secret police within a few months. According to a party report on the Workers' Group there were about 3,000 active members in Moscow city and guberniya in summer 1923. Considering the risks involved this is an impressive number. In cotton districts identified membership was surprisingly high: 471 in Krasnyi Presnesensk district, eighty-two in Bogorodsk, thirty-two in the Naro-Fominsk mill and thirty-one in the Orekhovo-Zuevo region, but a western historian's claim that they might have helped organize strikes cannot easily be substantiated.[38]

This does not detract from the significance of the strikes. What is particularly noticeable is the way in which action in one department quickly engulfed a whole mill complex and then spread outside the

---

[35] *Sots.vest.*, 5–6 (51–52), 16 March 1923, pp. 11–12, 15; 17–18 (63–64), 1 October 1923, p. 18; 19 (65), 18 October 1923, p. 15.

[36] Carr, *Interregnum*, pp. 101–5.   [37] See pp. 120–2.

[38] J. B. Sorenson, *The Life and Death of Soviet Trade Unionism 1917–28* (1969), pp. 176–7; V. G. Sorin, *Rabochaia gruppa (Miasnikovshchina)* (1924), pp. 114–15.

factory gates. So far we have stressed the ways in which operatives were divided – by gender, trade, residence and commitment to factory work – but there is no contradiction here. Workers were clearly capable of perceiving a community of interest and acting in concert when threatened by incompetent, heavy-handed, and even malevolent officials, themselves responding to sharply worded central directives and the novel stimulus of market forces.

The problem of rationalizing wages

Strikes, wage drift caused by local deviations from confused and contradictory official scales and a mass of locally negotiated collective agreements – this was the inchoate, volatile reality with which rationalizers were forced to deal. As with pressure to recast production it took some time for prescriptions to elicit a response. From 1922 onwards the Central Council had been telling its member unions that wages should not rise faster than productivity. The fifth textileworkers' union congress subsequently recommended using piece rates in collective agreements, but none of the forty-three major letters and circulars sent out by the central committee during 1922/23 included a reference to productivity in their title.[39]

Once again alarm over scissors seems to have been the catalyst for action. Early in 1924 Vesenkha and the Central Council wanted to tighten up collective agreements by cutting out branch negotiations, thus making it easier for the centre to hold down wages. The union's central committee replied that this was inappropriate in cotton because mills worked for diverse markets in diverse conditions. For a while longer bureaucratic in-fighting held off change. A compromise emerged. Trusts would negotiate on the basis of Vesenkha guide-lines but with local union branches. Simultaneously a meeting of the union's central committee and some managers led to the creation of a Special Commission on Collective Agreements. It found that wages were lower than in all other branches of Soviet industry. In March directives from the Council, Vesenkha and the party duly recommended that there should be purely nominal reductions in wages.[40] But there was a price to be paid, an unequivocal commitment to individual piece rates, a system much favoured by rationalizers. Flat rates led to the unproductive use of fixed capital, contended one

[39] Carr, *Interregnum*, p. 82; Rashin, *Zarabotnaia plata*, p. 32; *TsK VPST 1922–23*, pp. 17–18.
[40] *TsK VPST 1922–24*, pp. 99–100, 107–8.

rationalizer; workers might be at their machines for only five out of an eight hour shift. On the other hand an operative paid by the piece 'is not late for work, does not spend working time visiting the factory committee or chatting with shop delegates, nor does he leave his work every half-hour or so for a smoke. He will even use the end of the shift to prepare his machine for the following day's work.'[41] To force up productivity individual piece rates were to be introduced from April 1924.[42]

Here Kutuzov and the central committee found themselves in something of a dilemma. Individual piece rates, and productivity deals in particular, caused considerable unease. Even when linking pay to productivity became official policy it was never completely acceptable to the central committee, let alone to provincial branches. The reasons were simple. When discussions arose about labour productivity, observed *Golos tekstilei*, comparisons were made with conditions before 1917, but 'the union considers that in wage negotiations which take place within the framework of the Soviet state, we should not take as the basis the low pay given by the pre-war factory owners'. This was because mill owners relied on cheap labour, women and children, people accustomed to a low return on their work, particularly as they had often migrated from country districts where the land was poor.[43] Vladimir's local union branch advanced the same arguments in negotiations with trust officials in October 1925 – well after the fusion of pay and productivity into a single discourse had temporarily become an anachronism[44] – and they were repeated by a writer on women workers in the industry a year later.[45]

But there was little chance of any immediate fundamental change of policy in 1923–4. In 1923 Moscow's local officials wanted to bring textileworkers' wages up to the level of other industries in the province,[46] but they had no real institutional backing. Low wages had already been grudgingly accepted at the fifth union congress in October 1922. 'Owing to the present state of the industry', observed one resolution, 'there is no sign of any improvement in the immediate future.' Real wages should rise as far as possible in line with produc-

[41] A. Abramov, *Nagliadnyi uchet v tekstil'noi promyshlennosti* (1926), p. 79.
[42] *Otchet gubernskogo otdela soiuza 15-mu gubernskomu s"ezdu tekstil'shchikov ivanovo-voznesenskoi gubernii (apr. 1924g–mart 1925g)* (1925), pp. 68–9 (hereafter *I–V gubotdel VPST 1924–25*).
[43] *Golos tekstilei*, 27 November 1925.   [44] See pp. 185–8.
[45] V. Borodin, *Zhenskii trud v Sovetskoi tekstil'noi promyshlennosti* (1926), pp. 5–6; *Vladimirskii tekstil'shchik*, 11 December 1925.
[46] *Tezisy, priniatye plenumom gubotdela 12 maia 1923g. (Materialy k 5-mu moskovskomu gubs"ezdu tekstil'shchikov)* (1924), pp. 8–9.

tivity, and as the supply crisis and the country's financial resources would permit.[47] The central committee lamented the scissors crisis' immediate effects, the 'tendency in some trusts to cheapen production costs by cutting wages'.[48] Others were not averse to blunt speaking: 'There is no money', workers in Leningrad's Krasnyi Maiak were told next year when they complained about low pay, 'raise the productivity of labour and then you can have everything'.[49]

Attitudes to piece rates were somewhat more complex. They were conditioned by deep-seated traditions in the industry and by the way pay policy mutated in the first few years of NEP. About half the textile workforce was already paid by the piece in September 1923;[50] the irony was that existing methods complicated matters considerably. For a start piece rates had existed before the Revolution. They had evolved as a compromise between capitalism, community and family in Russia. Odell again on Russia's mills just before the Great War:

> Operatives are generally paid by the piece, and in mills working two shifts the production of the spindle or loom is awarded equally to each of the two operatives tending the machine. It would appear that this system would cause complaint amongst the workers, but apparently it does not, and the managers of several mills stated that it actually tended to increase production. The more efficient weaver, for example, 'gets behind' the operative on the same set of looms who is inclined to neglect his work . . . thus increasing the earnings of both weavers. Moreover, wherever possible, two members of the same family operate a set of looms or the same spinning frames, etc. The arrangement is particularly satisfactory in the case of a family with small children; the husband takes one shift and his wife the other, and the children in the home are never left alone.

Although bonus systems and graduated premiums based on the mill's yearly output were just coming into vogue in 1912, piece rates based on collective payment remained firmly entrenched,[51] and persisted into NEP. Here is a description of ring-frame rooms in the 1920s, which draws the opposite conclusion to Odell:

> if work is carried out on two or three shifts, that is, if this or that group of machines is operated at various times by two or three workers, then the output and the corresponding wage is calculated collectively, and . . . divided between [the workers] equally . . . the absence of individual accounting restrains increases in labour intensification, since every additional effort of a shift member adds to the

[47] *TsK VPST 1922–23*, pp. 122–3, 125, 130.   [48] *TsK VPST 1922–24*, p. 187.
[49] *Sots.vest*, 22–23 (93–94), 1 December 1924, p. 20.
[50] Rashin, *Zarabotnaia plata*, p. 33.   [51] Odell, *Cotton Goods*, pp. 24, 37.

general store of wages, and [each worker] does not fully receive his own wage from his own efforts.[52]

This source appears to have missed the crucial point about family ties noticed by Odell.

In addition piece working, whether or not calculated collectively, meant many different things. Pay might be calculated from the value of each unit produced by an operative, the 'direct' piece rate. 'Indirect piece rates', the system described above, applied where individual wages were drawn from the total earnings of a work group. The total wage fund for a *komplekt* might be established by measuring the group's output directly, or on the basis of norms derived from comparisons with other teams.[53] In both cases, in the opinion of one critic, these methods could not create conditions 'for the full intensification of labour'.[54] On the other hand norms might be set by measuring the productivity of a typical skilled worker on a particular frame, the 'removed piece rate'. Under this dispensation no deductions were made for machine stoppages, provided they were not the operative's fault. Accordingly the accusation was made that the removed piece rate was much favoured by those anxious to keep up their earnings with the minimum of effort; workers who stopped their machines 'for some trifling repair',[55] but the system could just as easily work to everyone's disadvantage. Management in one factory increased output norms by between 25 and 50 per cent in July 1924, but old machines could not stand the strain. Attempts to work faster caused breakdowns, small parts could not be replaced quickly enough, so some piece workers were paid at the scale base, and sometimes only at half that level.[56] A third variant was the 'guaranteed piece rate', where wages depended on the value of output but could fall only to a set minimum should something unforeseen alter conditions of work, such as a sharp drop in the quality of raw materials. 'Piece rates with premiums' gave bonuses for exceeding norms. 'Simple or indirect piece rates with premiums for the economic use of materials' added a final complicating touch.

All applied in spinning rooms and weaving sheds in the 1920s, as well as the simple daily rate, sometimes with incentives for productivity. American systems of pay, concluded the author, 'are seldom

[52] Ia. Kvasha, F. Shofman, *Semichasovoi rabochii den' v tekstil'noi promyshlennosti* (1930), pp. 42, 73.
[53] A. F. Ziman, *Tekhnicheskoe normirovanie priadil'nogo proizvodstva. Chast' 1. Otdely: sortiro-vochnyi, trepal'nyi, chesal'nyi* (1928), pp. 51–2.
[54] *Predpriiatie*, 11, November 1925, p. 35.   [55] Ziman, *Chast' 1*, pp. 51–2.
[56] *Golos tekstilei*, 25 July 1924.

to be found'. To add to the general confusion auxiliary workers' pay was often, but not always linked to the productivity of those operatives to whom they were attached;[57] a source of many conflicts, remarked *Golos tekstilei*, and of all kinds of unofficial additional payments.[58] Last of all, each variant had to intermesh somehow or other with the particular wage scale or tariff in use in a given region, and with the type of product under consideration in a given shop.[59] Doubtless machine idiosyncrasy played its part too.

Thus payment by the piece was anything but simple and imposing individual piece rates would be far from easy. Indeed, the following letter, published in *Golos tekstilei* in August 1927, gives the impression that throughout NEP calculating wages involved considerable arithmetical sophistication: 'in his pay book the worker has all kinds of notes and instructions; piece rates, [rates] by the day, overtime rates, workloading rates, working below [standard] *komplekt* rates, pay for machine stoppages, machine cleaning, days off, night work, holidays, explanations of daily and hourly calculations, etc., etc.'[60] Seventeen months earlier a delegate to Leningrad's union congress commented on wall-charts in one of the city's mills displaying the piece-rate valuation system – to the workers 'it's all Chinese'.[61]

These observations tie in with the whole matrix of *komplekt* working, family labour, unofficial hiring, *magarych* and off-mill employment discussed in part II, and they reinforce the point that the world of work was highly complex and intensely localized. Transferring cotton workers to some form of pay system appropriate for *uplotnenie*, therefore, would touch on almost every aspect of workers' lives. Piece work raised no issue of principle, since it could mean almost anything: the problem was one of fracturing an entire culture in order to impose multi-machine working while simultaneously measuring individual output.

Imposing individual piece rates

In 1921 the fourth textileworkers' union congress had accepted the implications of NEP. 'Pay must be based primarily and directly on productivity' through the medium of 'direct piece rates',

---

57 Ziman, *Chast' 1*, pp. 51–2, 159.   58 *Golos tekstilei*, 11 July 1924.
59 This sometimes led to the unwitting perpetuation of gender inequalities. Weavers' pay, for instance, depended on cloth sort, but often women could not gain enough experience of different types of weave to augment their skills because family and domestic work took up too much of their time: Borodin, *Zhenskii trud*, p. 14.
60 *Golos tekstilei*, 20 August 1927.   61 *Leningradskii tekstil'shchik*, 5 February 1926.

but at the same time 'it must give the worker the necessary means to maintain existence'. Moreover, there should be a 'simplification of the tariff . . . a reduction in the number of tariff points'.[62] Sentiments like these came easily when War Communism's egalitarian spirit was only a few months in the past and decisions taken at the tenth party congress might be no more than a passing fashion. Things looked different later on. As we have seen, within a year or two simplified scales were being distorted out of all recognition by local branches, and with central connivance. It seems that all that remained of egalitarianism was a residual commitment to tariff equalization between regions; in 1923 the union's central committee announced that there could be general increases only in the most 'backward' areas.[63] Ivanovo's branch agreed that the principle of equal pay which obtained in 1919/20 could not apply in a period of rapid growth and shortages of skilled labour.[64] The central committee could thus hardly argue against the most theoretically simple form of pay calculation available, particularly after statements like this one from Kutuzov in September 1923: 'in this account you will see all the work we have done for the year, and then you will understand *why you must first of all demand not higher wages, but higher productivity*'.[65] Sixteen months later a curious claim that the system, resisted under capitalism, would in the Soviet Union release what Marx called the 'individual spiritual freedom' of each textile worker,[66] missed the main point. Individual piece rates would either widen differentials and increase inequalities in all directions – and thus create all manner of new tensions – or, if they induced equalization, inflate wages across the board – and thus undermine the centre's desire to hold down wages.

This is because the details of implementation had to be dealt with locally. In Ivanovo guberniya, for instance, substantial changes in wage levels appeared within four weeks of April 1924. On average, the wage fund for flyer-frame operatives rose by 14.1 per cent and for ring-frame and selfactor work teams by 16.4 per cent, with no reductions in manning levels.[67] Moreover, things became ever more complex,[68] probably because there were so many local traditions,

---

62 Cited in *Ocherki istorii Leningrada*, tom 4 (1964), p. 47.
63 *3–go plen TsK VPST 1923*, pp. 10–11.
64 *I–V gubotdel VPST 1925–26*, p. 45.
65 *TsK VPST 1922–23*, p. vi [stress in the original].
66 *Vestnik profsoiuzov*, 1 (28), January 1925, pp. 68–9.
67 *I–V gubotdel VPST 1924–25*, pp. 69–71.
68 By mid-summer rates in the textile industry varied from 13.6 to 8.35 roubles for point one: *Golos tekstilei*, 24 June 1924.

customary practices and machine variations in the region.[69] At the end of June 1924 a special commission with representatives from local government, Ivanovo State Textile Trust, the local economic council, management, the factory committees and the shop floor, met to consider exactly how rates should be worked out for each count and cloth sort. Next month agreed individual piece rates were written into collective agreements covering two trusts. Overlookers took the opportunity to circumvent the fiscal restraints imposed on their wages by operatives. Before April 1924 their pay depended on the average wage of a shop's 'productive' workers; after April calculations were based on the number of working spindles.[70]

Vesenkha and the Central Council quickly stepped in. In July Dzerzhinskii was appointed head of a special commission to review pay and labour productivity. Evidence was taken from three large cotton mills, two in Ivanovo guberniya, one in Tver'. In the Tverskaia there was 'chaos' in the spinning halls on pay day. Spinners often considered that they were being underpaid and much time was wasted checking calculations. After three weeks Dzerzhinskii completed his investigations and ordered the implementation of yet another new tariff scale to reduce sub-categorization without reducing differentials.[71]

Seemingly indifferent to all these high-level instructions, in December 1924 Ivanovo's union branch scratched together a 'revision commission' made up exclusively of factory committee members. A disingenuous gloss appeared on page 28 of its report: 'amongst a mass of various questions ... of particular significance is the question of raising productivity in the mills. Here the [commission] paid special attention to measures directed towards lowering the cost of production, of fixing a norm for the number of auxiliary workers, and of re-organizing the tariff system for some categories of worker.' Immediately below came the recommendations. A mere 421 should be laid off – but spread between six mills. Moreover, each factory should be left to define its own needs in terms of auxiliary workers. Last of all there should be another new tariff sub-division for assistants (based on a thirteen-point scale), and for production workers on piece rates (based on a fifteen-point scale). No thirteen- or fifteen-point scales

---

[69] Norm performance varied considerably. For one example referring to four Ivanovo mills in 1924, see F. E. Dzerzhinskii *et al.*, eds., *K probleme proizvoditel'nosti truda*, vyp. 3 (1925), p. 125.

[70] *I–V gubotdel VPST 1924–25*, pp. 57, 71–2, 79.

[71] *Golos tekstilei*, 11 July 1924. For the second commission, convened in October, see p. 156.

applied anywhere in the textile industry; the factory committees, it seems, simply invented them to suit their own local purposes. All this was supposedly designed to expedite 'tightening up the working day'.[72]

Clearly, some branches took little notice of the union's central committee. Perhaps this is why the union had been excluded from Dzerzhinskii's July commission on pay and labour productivity, though Kutuzov probably had little choice but to go along with the new policy.[73] On August 5 1924 a joint letter from the union's president and Dzerzhinskii appeared in bold type on the front page of *Golos tekstilei*. Pay could now rise only on the basis of rationalization and higher productivity – increases depended 'on the success of our own work'. Four days later 'cheapen cloth to increase pay' was advanced as a new union slogan.[74] Within another two weeks the party's central committee made the first clear announcement that norms must be used to measure productivity and that productivity must rise faster than pay.[75] For union bureaucrats in Moscow the matter was now closed, in public, at least. A lead article from the Central Council reproduced in *Golos tekstilei* drove the point home. Only one official broke ranks, insisting that differentials should be reduced.[76]

Subsequently those union branches which had not acted on the April decision reluctantly fell into line: Leningrad sometime in autumn 1924 (comparisons between mills necessary, a six-month research period required); Moscow in September (a feasibility study on machinery, supply of raw materials, quality of workforce, implementation promised for January 1925); Vladimir the same month (caveats about the quality of raw materials and the condition of machines).[77] Like Ivanovo, Leningrad had its own special commission with managers, trust officials, assessment and conflict commission and factory committee and shop-floor representatives. The local union branch finally

---

[72] *Trud i proizvodstvo*, 1, 31 January 1925, p. 28.
[73] Perhaps as compensation membership of a committee to bring textileworkers' pay into line with Vesenkha's 'unified tariff' seems to have been in the gift of the union: *Golos tekstilei*, 22 August 1924.
[74] *Golos tekstilei*, 5 August 1924; 8 August 1924.
[75] E. H. Carr, *Socialism in One Country*, vol. 1 (1970), pp. 413, 416; *Istoriia rabochikh Leningrada*, tom 2 (1972), p. 159.
[76] *Golos tekstilei*, 23 September 1924.
[77] *Lengubotdel VPST 1924–25*, p. 60; *Rezoliutsii i postanovleniia 7-go gubernskogo s"ezda soiuza tekstil'shchikov, 25–27 okt. 1924g* (1924), pp. 25–6; *TsK VPST 1924–26*, p. 98; *Vladgubotdel VPST 1923–24*, p. 55. Wages in Moscow guberniya drifted away from official tariffs during the summer to stop workers receiving less money for the same work: *Moskgubotdel VPST 1924–25*, p. 76.
[78] *Golos tekstilei*, 2 December 1924; *Vestnik profsoiuzov*, 1 (28), January 1925, p. 68.

ratified individual piece working on December 1 1924.[78] As in Ivanovo, wages rose when mills in Vladimir district eventually got round to implementing piece rates.[79] By November the movement was far too advanced for the union congress to affect matters. Although that month's round of collective agreement negotiations tried to wean the trusts away from making comparisons on the basis of pre-war figures,[80] key resolutions merely echoed the Central Council's clarion call for linking pay to productivity.[81] Circular Number 1 from Kutuzov published on 23 December re-emphasized previous utterances on norms, piece work and productivity,[82] but elsewhere the central committee admitted that its 'basic tasks' for the new year were still to enforce collective agreements for six months and tariff clauses for three, and to 'establish unified principles for the transfer to direct piece rates'.[83]

Though by the end of 1924 wages appear on average to have recovered to something like their 1913 level, the closer one approaches the individual mill the more obscure things become. In view of the fantastic complexities described above, it is doubtful if Vesenkha, the Central Council of Trades Unions, or even the central committee of the textileworkers' union had any clear idea about what had actually happened to pay in any given shop over the previous twelve months, or to what extent the drive to impose individual piece rates had really succeeded. Most probably the only people who did know were local officials and factory committee members, those workers affected by change, and those who effected change. And they only knew about their own mills. None of this augured well for the *uplotnenie* campaign.

[79] *Vladgubotdel VPST 1924–25*, p. 63.   [80] *TsK VPST 1922–24*, pp. 95–6.
[81] *VI Congress VPST*, pp. 4, 32–5. For the Central Council's congress see Carr, *Socialism in One Country*, 1, pp. 415–17. Norms were to be based on average output for seven hours: *Golos tekstilei*, 16 December 1924.
[82] *Golos tekstilei*, 23 December 1924.   [83] *TsK VPST 1924–26*, p. 93.

10   1925

What is the Council of Peoples' Commissars? – capitalism plus a syndicate.

A remark in the Shuiskaia's reading room, early January 1925

The strike movement

Though here and there a start had already been made the *uplotnenie* drive really got underway in January 1925.[1] There were no new surprises; the targets had already been set by Vesenkha six weeks previously.[2] Similarly the early 1925 crop of propaganda was no different from all the other agitation about efficiency and labour intensification described in chapters 8 and 9, but some were uneasy now that the policy was being translated into reality. 'Have we the financial resources', asked Fedotov in February, 'and are the mills technically prepared?'[3], and in an address to the syndicate two months later the union's president followed the by now ritual obeisance to the principle of multi-machine working with a disconcerting observation:

> This is a difficult moment and these are difficult conditions. In the time of the tsar we took strike action against such measures, now we ourselves are carrying them out in order to show the peasants that we mean to increase [supply] and cheapen the cost of manufacture . . . [But] we have already increased the work load of textile workers so much that *a further loading is impossible*.[4]

[1] *Sistema i organizatsiia*, 11, 1925, p. 25.
[2] For details on various rooms see *Biulleten' ivanovo-voznesenskogo gosudarstvennogo tekstil'nogo tresta*, 17/18, April 1926, p. 3; *Izvestiia tekstil'noi promyshlennosti i torgovli*, 1 (141), 7 January 1925, p. 2 (hereafter ITPT); *Sistema i organizatsiia*, 1–2, 1926, p. 67; *Tekstil'nye novosti*, 4, April 1927, p. 143; *Trud i proizvodstvo*, 3, March 1925, pp. 19–22.
[3] *ITPT*, 4 (144–145), 2 February 1925, p. 1.
[4] *Golos tekstilei*, 28 April 1925 [stress in the original].

Kutuzov had every reason to worry. Many cotton workers, perhaps one in five, could remember bitter strikes over this very issue; strikes which went into the making of the 1905 Revolution and the first workers' soviet in Ivanovo-Voznesensk.[5]

There is precious little in Soviet sources about exactly what happened in 1925, but there are plenty of broad hints. Dzerzhinskii and Kutuzov expressed concern about disharmony in the mills in April.[6] Next month the party's central committee spoke of 'mistakes' and 'insufficient preparation'.[7] Kutuzov alluded to 'a series of failures, increases in poor workmanship, etc.', to date 47,000 hours had been lost in Serpukhov's mills due to stoppages. The reasons were not specified.[8] Shortly afterwards Lebedev, the union's secretary, wrote an article discussing tensions between overlookers and operatives. Unions were strong only when they were united: 'why have we forgotten this in relation to our own union? ... amongst our over-lookers at the present time there exists a significant movement in favour of organizational exclusiveness'. This was movement, in fact, to form a distinct association.[9] In July he asked why the Central Council and the party's central committee had turned their attention to the union. 'There's no smoke without fire' – the provinces ignored central policy: 'the directive ... on the transfer to three-loom and three spindle-bank working, thanks to inept implementation, has led to a number of serious conflicts'.[10]

Ivanovo district's party conference of summer 1925 was more forthcoming. There were 'conflicts in a number of enterprises ... which in some shops ... culminated in the form of a strike'. Two mills were mentioned.[11] In October the central committee of the union called its

---

5 In the Balashov and Varentsova, for instance, 16.85 per cent of Rashin's sample for 1929 started work before 1903; it is therefore reasonable to assume 20 per cent for 1925: A. G. Rashin, *Sostav fabrichno-zavodskogo proletariata SSSR* (1930), p. 66; V. M. Sokolov, *Fabrika im. S. I. Balashova* (1961), pp. 26–8; V. M. Sokolov, *Fabrika im. O. A. Varentsovoi* (1955), p. 46.

6 *Golos tekstilei*, 10 April 1925.

7 Cited in N. V. Poliakova, 'Bor'ba rabochikh-tekstil'shchikov za povyshenie proizvo-ditel'nosti truda v 1921–1925gg. (Po materialam Moskvy i moskovskoi gubernii)', *Voprosy istorii*, 6, July 1959, p. 34.

8 *Golos tekstilei*, 22 May 1925.

9 *Golos tekstilei*, 5 June 1925. Lebedev failed to mention the likely cause of their anger. In May the second plenum of the union's central committee insisted that their pay should be linked to the output of the workers they supervised, but as we saw previously (p. 173), they had only just managed to escape from this depend-ency: *Postanovleniia 2-go plenuma TsK vsesoiuznogo soiuza tekstil'shchikov 21–23 maia 1925g v Leningrade* (1925), p. 14 (hereafter *2-go plen TsK VPST 1925*).

10 *Golos tekstilei*, 21 July 1925.

11 *Rezoliutsii 20-i ivanovo-voznesenskoi gubernskoi partiinoi konferentsii (1-4 iiulia 1925g)* (1925), p. 11.

third plenum in association with seventy factory directors to resolve 'serious difficulties',[12] and at the fourteenth party congress in December Tomsky attacked the textileworkers' union openly:

> Conflicts arise chiefly because union organizations are inattentive to the opinions, moods, rights and just demands of the workers . . .trades unions are obliged to defend the economic interests of their workers. The conflicts, arguments and clashes which we had in the spring of 1925 in some textile mills show that the unions often forget this basic task . . . when strikes occur without the knowledge of the union, without the knowledge of party organizations, without the knowledge of management, one must say that here there is no connection between workers and their union.[13]

There are other indications of turmoil. In spring output in the industry dropped coincidently with a sharp rise in wages,[14] and tensions in Vladimir guberniya can be deduced from a fragmentary statistical series for 1925–6; union membership not only failed to keep pace with recruitment, it actually fell, suggesting mass expulsions or a massive loss of confidence. Recovery only became evident a year later.[15]

By turning to the Menshevik press it is possible to get some further idea of what was happening. One early report indicates moods similar to those of 1922 and 1923.[16] Elsewhere there is a suggestion that demobilized soldiers helped to articulate operatives' discontents; in Tver' they could find no work and were obliged to live in poor housing. When jobs turned up in a recently re-opened mill new piece rates forced many to work ten hours a day to make ends meet – 'In a word, life isn't cheerful.' Komsomol agitators kept saying that the workers were the masters now and party cells put all the blame on Trotsky, but no one could speak against prepared resolutions.[17]

More detailed accounts of the impact of *uplotnenie* began to trickle into Berlin in summer. One correspondent confirmed Ivanovo party conference's mention of a stoppage in Teikovo's Bol'shevik mill, a four-day strike starting on May 12. Demands included an end to multi-machine working, reinstatement of those fired for political

[12] *Otchet TsK vsesoiuznogo professional'nogo soiuza tekstil'shchikov k 7-mu vsesoiuznomu s"ezdu tekstil'shchikov. Iiul' 1924g–ianv. 1926g* (1926), p. 7 (hereafter *TsK VPST 1924–26*).
[13] *Golos tekstilei*, 8 January 1926.   [14] *TsK VPST 1924–26*, p. 96.
[15] *Otchet o rabote vladimirskogo gubernskogo pravleniia professional'nogo soiuza tekstil'shchikov okt. 1924g–okt. 1925g. K 8-mu gubernskomu s"ezdu soiuza* (1925), pp. 3, 7 (hereafter *Vladgubotdel VPST 1924–25*); *Otchet o rabote vladimirskogo gubernskogo pravleniia professional'nogo soiuza tekstil'shchikov okt. 1925g–okt. 1926g* (1926), p. 11; *Vladimirskii tekstil'shchik*, 20 April 1926.
[16] See chapter 9. Orekhovo-Zuevo was still simmering. Krasin got a rough reception there at a meeting with workers: *Sotsialisticheskii vestnik*, 20 (90), 22 October 1924, p. 16.
[17] *Sots.vest*, 1 (95), 17 January 1925, p. 15.

reasons – presumably in some earlier conflict – and pay for time lost in dispute. This was too much for the local union branch, and they quickly handed the problem over to the central committee and Vesenkha. After only three days all demands were granted and this sparked off strikes and go-slows in other mills around Sereda. Tomsky took fright. He thought they marked the first step towards politicization – strikers were 'like flies in the ointment' – and blamed union bureaucratism.[18] Sometime in spring or early summer 3,000 operatives in another mill struck and secured a partial victory of some kind or other. Thereafter more workers were encouraged to take action and strikes spread throughout Ivanovo-Voznesensk's mills.

By summer virtually all factories introducing *uplotnenie* were affected; six were mentioned by name, as well as a number of unspecified enterprises in the Bogorodsk and Tver' districts. Executives and managers could do nothing. When party members in one mill refused to work they were expelled by the provincial committee. Elsewhere similar expressions of solidarity met with the same penalty; particularly, it seems, in Bogorodsk.[19] Perhaps the Lenin enrolment played a part in radicalizing some of the party's rank and file: many in Smolensk guberniya joined in the hope of improving factory conditions. 'Absolutely nothing', we learn from the provincial archive, 'can persuade a number of Lenin draft people to agree to plans for the intensification of labour.' This was in the Iartsevo district,[20] home of the Iartsevskaia mill. On the other hand where communists acted as strike-breakers operatives sometimes managed to organize effective defence against them. Exactly how is not made clear. Often communists were in league with administrators and the union who jointly organized lock-outs and mass dismissals, an echo of events in Orekhovo-Zuevo in 1923.[21] Workers thus found themselves in a desperate position but showed incredible determination'.[22]

Correspondents claimed that all regions affected by discontent had strike committees, but named only the Glukhovskaia, Ramenskaia and Bol'shevik, the latter in Ivanovo guberniya, the former two in Moscow guberniya. They were not necessarily *ad hoc* bodies, indeed, organization appears to have centred around factory committees. The

[18] *Sots.vest.*, 11–12 (105–106), 20 June 1925, p. 21; 13 (107), 10 July 1925, p. 15. The Bol'shevik had a reputation for militancy in the last years of the *ancien régime*. Perhaps this was remembered by some workers. See A. Borboff, 'The Bolsheviks and working women 1905–20', *Soviet Studies*, 4, 1974, pp. 552–3.
[19] *Sots.vest.*, 11–12 (105–106), 20 June 1925, p. 19; 13 (107), 10 July 1925, p. 15.
[20] W. G. Rosenberg, 'Smolensk in the 1920s. Party–worker relations and the vanguard problem', *Russian Review*, 36, 2, April 1977, p. 146.
[21] See pp. 164–6.   [22] *Sots.vest.*, 11–12 (105–106), 20 June 1925, p. 19.

union's strongest asset in terms of legitimacy, they were also the weakest link in the transmission belt stretching from Moscow to the most remote mill. In daily contact with operatives and staffed from the shop floor, they were always likely – as became apparent when Vesenkha, the Central Council and the central committee of the union tried to impose unified pay systems – to slip their moorings and break free from central policies.[23] This time workers were more direct. They ignored official regulations and captured factory committees by substituting their own candidates. The same thing happened in shop-delegate elections. Local party organizations were 'close to panic'; there was simply no institutional check, no mechanism of control left. Acting as a 'judicial and legal mask' the committees, with freely elected delegates or co-opted strike leaders, started to negotiate with administrators and left other union organs 'helpless'.[24] The Menshevik press said nothing about exactly how spontaneous election and co-option changed things, but there is a fragment of evidence from Ivanovo. There both shop delegates and factory committees came up for re-election in May 1925. In fifty-two mills the number of successful non-party candidates jumped from just over two-thirds to slightly more than four-fifths of the total. Significantly, 85 per cent of those elected had never before sat on factory committees or represented shops.[25]

As for 1923 there is no propensity for informants to speculate about Menshevik leadership. All agree that multi-machine working, rationalization and wage problems were cause enough, occasionally supplemented by local factors.[26] Although here and there some anti-Bolshevik strikers may well have given the movement an extra fillip, Tomsky's dark hints about politicization reveal less about cotton workers' ambitions and more about the regime's sense of insecurity and heartfelt wish to divert attention away from specific causes. There are, therefore, no real grounds for doubting the general veracity of these accounts. Fragments culled from the Soviet press and cited above complement rather than contradict *émigré* reports; those mills and districts positively identified by both Menshevik and Bolshevik sources were dispersed right across the CIR.

[23] See pp. 172–4.
[24] *Sots.vest.*, 11–12 (105–106), 20 June 1925, p. 19; 13 (107), 10 July 1925, p. 15; 14 (108), 25 July 1925, pp. 9–10.
[25] *Trud i proizvodstvo*, 7, July 1925, p. 23.
[26] *Sots.vest.*, 24 (94), 20 December 1924, p. 15; 11–12 (105–106), 20 June 1925, pp. 19, 21; 14 (108), 25 July 1925, p. 14. Events in Tver', Iartsevo and Bogorodsk have already been mentioned. In Vladimir guberniya's Krasnyi Profintern the administration's decision to raise norms sparked off the strike: *Sots.vest.*, 13 (107), 10 July 1925, p. 15.

It is less easy to say how many people were involved, but if calculations are restricted to known mills and identified regions it is possible to make some tentative estimate. In 1925–6 there were at least nine working factories in Ivanovo-Voznesensk employing 25,754 operatives, two in Bogorodsk with 3,512, two in Tver' with 17,494 and eight in Serpukhov with 18,519 making, with the named mills cited in the sources, a grand total of just over 100,000 cotton workers.[27] About one quarter of the national workforce, therefore, was to be found in districts affected by strikes.

Uplotnenie, shop-floor democracy and wages

It appears that strikers wished to see something done about multi-machine working, but beyond that we do not know exactly what they wanted. For this reason it is difficult to talk about success or failure, gains or losses, but there were changes in several aspects of workers' lives.

For a start several different agencies began to assert that from the very beginning uplotnenie was always intended to be a voluntary affair. It was just possible to interpret matters in this way; Piatakov's telegram of November 1924 was quickly followed by rather more considered instructions,[28] but 'unfortunately', according to ISNOT's Zen'kovich,

> the first 'military command,' with its bald and simple demands, made a deeper impression on the minds of some managers than the subsequent circular . . . because managers tend to work by applying pressure . . . the entire campaign focused on intensifying work on the shop floor and scarcely any attention at all was given to the question of improving, organizing and rationalizing the technical side of production.

What was needed for this 'difficult task', he continued, was 'a little more communication and consultation'.[29] This was hardly enough. Even when workers had been told that uplotnenie was not compulsory there were difficulties. On 12 December 1924 Golos tekstilei carried a report of a 'stormy meeting' in the Krasnyi Perekop. Operatives were afraid that those who subsequently rejected the new regime would be sacked and were thus 'decisively against the planned changes'.[30]

[27] Calculations from Tekstil'nye fabriki SSSR (1927).   [28] See pp. 155–7.
[29] Khoziaistvo i upravlenie, 5, 1925, pp. 51, 54.
[30] 'It should have been explained', wrote the editors, 'that uplotnenie is necessary because the smychka . . . can only be strengthened by increasing output': Golos tekstilei, 1 January 1925.

Perhaps the same notion struck mill hands around Bogorodsk and Shchelkovo. There the trust took space in *Golos tekstilei* to reassure them that *uplotnenie* would not be accompanied by redundancies.[31]

In fact the experience of Krasnyi Perekop's workers was indicative of a general trend. There is little to suggest that advocates of labour intensification took serious account of shop-floor sensibilities at the end of 1924 – had they done so there would have been no strikes – and most probably the Menshevik press was right to claim that agreements generally resulted only because workers were afraid of being sacked.[32] Nol'de, when canvassing for NOT, predicted the difficulties that would arise if trusts and local union branches engaged in the kind of consultations recommended by writers like Zen'kovich: 'the successful introduction of this system depends on establishing output norms, classifying the workforce, introducing premiums and bonuses as a way of rewarding initiative . . . to do all these things at shop-floor level requires such detailed discussions, consultations, meetings, etc., that no real results are achieved'.[33]

By early summer the union seems to have determined to do something about the policy's battered image and its loss of influence amongst workers. In future, wrote one member of the tariff section, increasing the productivity of labour must be predicated on rationalization alone. There must be no more labour intensification. *Golos tekstilei* reminded its readers that *uplotnenie* was permissible 'only on the basis of the voluntary agreement of the workers and with adequate preparation by trusts and local union bodies'.[34] Rationalizers were on the defensive. Things were made clear to them in Moscow's Trekhgornaia mill in July 1925. 'Measures taken to tighten up the working day', resolved the party cell, 'will be introduced only after study by the party and the union, and only after they have been explained to and studied by the shop delegate meetings of those [rooms] concerned with any change'.[35] The guberniya's union branch had already emphasized the need to secure agreement with management over a whole host of factors: cotton quality, spindle speeds, manning levels, ventilation, humidity, lighting, machine layout, count, cloth assort-

---

[31] *Golos tekstilei*, 24 January 1925.   [32] *Sots.vest.*, 14 (132), 26 July 1926, p. 15.

[33] A. A. Nol'de, *NOT v tekstil'noi promyshlennosti* (1924), p. 22.

[34] *Golos tekstilei*, 19 May 1925; 26 May 1925.

[35] Cited in Poliakova, 'Bor'ba rabochikh-tekstil'shchikov', p. 34. It was 'important to study the peculiarities of each factory', said Lebedev at the eighth union congress. Some found the transfer impossible, others were 'so proud' that they pushed ahead with 'extremely unfortunate' results: *Golos tekstilei*, 2 February 1926.

ment and machine cleaning.[36] It was against just these kinds of manoeuvres that engineer Belkin vented his anger and frustration in a speech to a meeting of his union section in August: 'your opponent has a huge arsenal of weapons – the Labour Code, the labour inspectors, the union, the factory committees, labour protection committees, and production conferences – an.armada amassed against the specialist and backed up by all kinds of circulars, instructions, orders, newspaper articles'.[37]

No less important than the issues surrounding *uplotnenie* were those pertaining to factory committees and shop delegates. 'Closer to the masses' and 'broadening the base' of factory committee work had already been incorporated into resolutions adopted at the union's congress in November 1924, but these slogans cut both ways. Before Piatakov's telegram, factory committees were already getting out of control and shop delegates widening their areas of competence. Congress condemned 'spontaneous broadening' in factory commit-tees as a 'negative phenomenon' which hindered union work, and insisted that the resolution of problems in the localities depended upon shop delegates' 'more exact' observance of central rules. The central committee intended to review their position: 'only the most conscious' should be elected and delegates should confine themselves to 'the interests of the shop's workers'; the union would look after the interests of the workers as a whole.[38]

Although *Golos tekstilei* retrospectively complained that these local organizations 'considered themselves independent, and themselves decided the question of three-frame working' when they should have followed central instructions,[39] the second plenum of the central committee, held in Leningrad between 21 and 23 May 1925, signalled a change in policy. The union leadership was now prepared to compro-mise with local aspirations. Conferences at departmental and shift level were now to supplement factory-wide meetings, large enter-prises were encouraged to elect a separate factory committee for each department, and the qualifying number of electors for establishing a committee was halved, from fifty to twenty-five. Moreover, shop delegates were to be given 'real influence' over admission to and

[36] *Otchet o rabote moskovskogo gubernskogo otdela vsesoiuznogo professional'nogo soiuza tekstil'shchikov ianvar.–mart 1925g* (1925), p. 26 (hereafter *Moskgubotdel VPST Jan–Mar 1925*).
[37] *Golos tekstilei*, 11 August 1925.
[38] *Rezoliutsii i postanovleniia 6-go s"ezda professional'nogo soiuza tekstil'shchikov* (1924), p. 22 (hereafter *VI Congress VPST*).
[39] *Golos tekstilei*, 16 February 1926.

expulsion from the union – and over the details of labour intensification. In both instances they were to work closely with factory committees.[40]

It took an instruction from the party's central committee to effect more radical change. Prior to 1925 workers elected their factory committee delegates from lists drawn up in advance by the existing committee plenum, or in the case of Moscow guberniya at least, the local organizational department of the party.[41] In July *Golos tekstilei* announced that the lists were abolished. The decision, taken because 'of the general spread of conflicts in some textile mills switching to three-frame working', especially in Ivanovo guberniya,[42] was manifestly a concession to strikers. The province's fifteenth union congress took up the theme. Mill and shop-level union organizations must give 'personal service' and pay more attention to their members' wishes; previous methods were 'mistaken' – in future all elections must take place in front of general factory meetings after 'broad' campaigns. The central committee of the union clarified the issue at its third plenum in October 1925 by observing that lists interfered with the worker's 'right' to democratic participation in the union. Now, where they still existed, they were 'for guidance' only.[43]

The first elections under the new dispensation were held in autumn, and very little is known about them. But throughout the union the average number of workers per shop delegate fell from 33.8 in 1924 to 18.4 in 1925. Over the same period attendance at delegate meetings in Ivanovo guberniya rose from 30 to 40 per cent to between 50 and 70 per cent of the total cotton workforce. Election meetings were sometimes prolonged, which suggests that candidates did feel themselves to be answerable to their constituency. They often lasted from two to six hours, but in Krasnyi Perekop they appear to have been fought very hard indeed; there the hustings lasted for two days. Perhaps workers

---

[40] *2-go plen TsK VPST 1925*, pp. 4–7; *TsK VPST 1924–26*, pp. 4–5, 8, 33.
[41] *TsK VPST 1924–26*, p. 8; *Otchet o rabote moskovskogo gubernskogo otdela vsesoiuznogo professional'nogo soiuza tekstil'shchikov mai–iiul' 1923g* (1923), p. 24.
[42] *Golos tekstilei*, 21 July 1925.
[43] *Otchet o rabote ivanovo-voznesenskogo gubernskogo otdela vsesoiuznogo soiuza tekstil'shchikov za vremia s apr. 1925g–mart 1926g. 16-mu s"ezdu soiuza* (1926), p. 18 (hereafter *I–V gubotdel VPST 1925–26*); *TsK VPST 1924–26*, pp. 8, 36. Kutuzov tried to convince his audience that the policy of co-operation with management – NEP's 'united front' – was still valid. Zhuk, from Leningrad, brusquely disagreed: 'Industry occupied the central place in comrade Kutuzov's report . . . It is not our business to establish a united front between union and management.' So did Vladimir's Nikitin: 'The united front lowers our influence with the workers.' He went on to say that mill directors regarded the central committee 'as a kindly uncle': *Golos tekstilei*, 14 October 1925; 17 October 1925.

also discriminated between the essential and the inessential. Ivanov's union branch reported that attendance at general meetings 'rarely exceeds 10 per cent of the total number of workers . . . only in the case of meetings called to elect factory committees does it average out at 70 per cent'. It also seems that canvassing took place outside in the wider community. In seventy-four Moscow guberniya mills 64.8 per cent of workers turned up to listen to election meetings but 80.9 per cent of all operatives voted. For twenty-eight Ivanovo guberniya mills the figures are 39 per cent and 68.6 per cent respectively.[44]

At the same time as a renewed emphasis on voluntary *uplotnenie* and a new commitment to shop-floor democracy became evident, so thirty-six months' committee work by Vesenkha, the Central Council of Trades Unions and the central committee of the textileworkers' union on pay policy was thrown to the winds. Five months into 1925 Markov, a member of the union's central committee, wrote a lead article in *Golos tekstilei*: 'until now the pay of textile workers has risen faster than the productivity of labour. We must reverse this relationship.'[45] He was badly out of touch. Though the central committee of the union had discussed the 'painful question' of pay as early as February 1925 – dragged along, perhaps, by the provinces, Moscow's branch wanted a 25 per cent rise for multi-machine workers in January – early summer was once again the key period. The union promised a review which would result in wage rises from July 1.[46] Henceforth auxiliary workers' pay would be calculated not on a daily rate but in proportion to the average earnings of the piece workers they served. This followed discussions in June between the central committee and representatives from local branches. There is no full report of the meeting, but what emerged was an astonishing commitment to a 30 per cent increment across the board plus 25 to 30 per cent again for workers on three looms or spindle banks. Curiously, Leningrad got only 7 per cent. Everything seemed to revolve around Ivanovo district. Increases were to be paid there first. Kutuzov and Lebedev made much of the fact that increments would be higher than elsewhere – 37.5 per cent – and it may be more than coincidental that the announcement was made on the day the guberniya's fifteenth union congress convened.[47] In May the second plenum had already resolved

44 *I–V gubotdel VPST 1925–26*, p. 22; *TsK VPST 1924–26*, pp. 38–9, 44–5.
45 *Golos tekstilei*, 19 May 1925.
46 *Moskgubotdel VPST Jan–Mar 1925*, p. 26; *TsK VPST 1924–26*, pp. 99–100; *Sots.vest.*, 14 (108), 25 July 1925, pp. 9, 14.
47 *Sots.vest.*, 14 (108), 25 July 1925, pp. 9, 14; *Golos tekstilei*, 16 June 1925; 19 June 1925; 6 October 1925; *Otchet leningradskogo gubernskogo otdela vsesoiuznogo professional'nogo*

not to allow any further upward revision of norms in July's collective agreements; although in principle wage increases should still be based on improved productivity, the plenum insisted that pay must rise in districts where rates were below average, and that 'decisive measures' should be taken to bring operatives' pay up to the level for other industrial workers.[48] Indeed, for the last quarter of the year the central committee concentrated on bringing all regions up to the highest levels achieved in summer.[49] Finally, a resolution from the May plenum recognized the strength of the provinces' aspirations: previous instructions on collective agreements were 'temporary' measures characteristic of 'a period of strict regulation of wages and conditions of work', henceforth the plenum accepted the principle of decentralization by transferring full negotiating rights to local branches.[50]

The union's public avowal of devolution stood in opposition to the preference for central control over wage bargaining evident in Vesenkha a year earlier.[51] In fact the Supreme Economic Council was in some disarray on this issue. In September 1925, at a joint congress of Vesenkha and the industry's norm-setters, one resolution attacked wage equalization through wage reduction. Although wage control was essential, reductions should occur only when 'high-earning piece workers form a small minority'; elsewhere equalization must be achieved through levelling up. Another repeated time-honoured phrases about wages outstripping productivity and warned of the threat to future economic growth. A third anachronistically harped on about 'scientific norms' which would guarantee a wage 'commensurate with skill and labour intensity'. Standardization should be enforced everywhere, insisted a fourth. In a magnificent understatement, one other speaker drew his audience's attention to pay systems 'which are not in accordance with the standard tariffs. The

---

soiuza tekstil'shchikov. Okt. 1924–1925gg (1926), p. 60 (hereafter *Lengubotdel VPST 1924–25*); *TsK VPST 1924–26*, pp. 98–100.

[48] *2-go plen TsK VPST 1925*, pp. 3, 13–14. The union's central committee had been hammering away at this issue ever since the sixth congress in November 1924, but with no apparent success. A letter to Vesenkha, made public in *Golos tekstilei*, 4 December 1924, elicited no response – in this newspaper, at least.

[49] *TsK VPST 1924–26*, pp. 94–5. By October most trusts had been affected by July's increases: *Golos tekstilei*, 20 October 1925.

[50] *2-go plen TsK VPST 1925*, p. 14. The central committee went even further in August – 'the tariff system must have a significantly greater number of points': *Golos tekstilei*, 25 August 1925.

[51] See p. 167.

character and degree of complexity of what counts as fulfilled work is often insufficient when measured against the union tariff'.[52]

Vesenkha's confusion may have been the union's opportunity. In November 1925 Iaroslavl's fourth union congress complained bitterly about the old 1922 handbook, now long overtaken by events.[53] Within four weeks, on December 11, a new handbook, planned for over two years but scuttled in 1923,[54] suddenly appeared. 'Experience in the localities' revealed 'mistakes' in the old guide, wrote Lebedev in the introduction, and then went on to explain that the central committee had originally intended to 'correct' the existing handbook in order to bring it into line with the unified tariff. But 1923–5 had changed all that. Now more attention would be paid to the effects of *uplotnenie*. The union opted for a seventeen-point tariff and assigned a scale point for each trade, but there was still ample scope for local deviation. Frequently a given trade was allotted to a range of points; experience, product range and raw material quality were to determine exact placings in the localities.[55]

There are some clues about how wage rises were working themselves through in the provinces before the new handbook was published. In future norms must be set 'in the light of local technical and organizational conditions', resolved the fifteenth Ivanovo union congress mentioned above, and there must be 'no lowering of wages'. Congress anticipated the central committee's huge award and secured a respectable 19 per cent increase on scale point one from the local economic council and Ivanovo State Textile Trust. Average wages for workers in these two trusts rose by almost one-quarter over the year. Increases were even more marked in Ivanovo-Voznesensk. There the average wage for operative families soared by nearly 80 per cent between June and July.[56] Moscow's branch also secured big increases in 1925, on average 44 per cent for point one for the economic year 1924/25, on top of a 2.5 per cent rise awarded in early spring. Norms were re-examined and re-negotiated in July.[57] Overall, taking October

[52] *Rezoliutsii 1–go vsesoiuznogo s"ezda otdelov truda i T.N.B. tekstil'noi promyshlennosti (20–26/IX–1925g)* (1926), pp. 4, 13–14 (hereafter *TNB 1925*).

[53] *Golos tekstilei*, 20 November 1925.   [54] See p. 159.

[55] *Tarifnyi spravochnik tekstil'shchikov* (1926), pp. 3–4. For details of tariff scales by trade see pp. 12–17, 19–22, 30–42.

[56] *Biulleten' ivanovo-voznesenskogo gubernskogo statisticheskogo biuro*, 13, 1927, table 1 p. 31; *I–V gubotdel VPST 1925–26*, pp. 34, 46.

[57] *Itogi raboty moskovskogo gubernskogo otdela profsoiuza tekstil'shchikov s 1 aprelia 1924g po 1 okt. 1925g* (1926), p. 75; *Moskgubotdel VPST Jan–Mar 1925*, pp. 4, 21–3; *Rabota moskovskogo gubernskogo soveta profsoiuzov s oktiabria 1924g po ianvar' 1926g* (1926), p. 85.

1924 as 100, wages for the entire cotton workforce stood at 113.9 in July 1925 and 131.7 next month.[58]

Rashin gives some interesting details on the Moscow area for the entire period of the *uplotnenie* drive and the resultant strikes. Although it is impossible to separate out rises attendant on the kind of 'drift' factors discussed in the previous chapter, and although all official wage lists should be treated with a good deal of scepticism, the figures do indicate real upward movement for the twenty-four months following March 1924, regardless of tariff point. The jump for overlookers was particularly marked; evidence, perhaps, of appeasement after their threat to form a separate association in June 1925. A degree of wage equalization was evident in almost all trades. If negotiation was within the competence of local committees (official or otherwise) and guberniya branches in spring and early summer 1925, and if operatives were really able to make their voice heard, then these tendencies suggest that the majority were opposed to any further widening of differentials. Quite possibly, therefore, the central committee's balancing act evident in the new handbook was a response to just this kind of local pressure – centrifugal tendencies coupled with egalitarian sentiments in the central committee found their formal expression in the tension between devolution and standardization. Conversely, Rashin's tables reveal just how strong shop-floor traditions could be. Equalization affected only the lowest paid. No one disturbed patterns of work on mule frames: what is striking about the selfactor *komplekt* is the way differentials were carefully maintained over the years 1924–6.[59]

The social and technological context

Although voluntary *uplotnenie* democratization on the shop floor and wage increases were important concessions, this is not to say that discontents entirely abated next year. As far as cotton operatives were concerned the Politburo's proclamation of the 'regime of economy' was simply a matter of decanting old wine into new bottles. It is fruitless to try to distinguish between continuing conflicts about piece rates, three-frame working and speed-ups and new ones arising

---

[58] *ITPT*, 2, 15 January 1926, p. 1.
[59] A. G. Rashin, *Zarabotnaia plata za vosstanovitel'nyi period khoziaistva SSSR. 1922/23–1926/27gg* (1927), table 14 pp. 266–7.

from the slogan of the day.[60] Pressure for three-spindle bank and three, and even four-loom working did not cease, and disputes between centre and periphery, between the union, Vesenkha and the Central Council over pay, speed-ups and rationalization continued to trouble the industry in 1926.[61] Some secondary tremors were felt in February: strikes in Moscow guberniya against three-loom working and collective agreements,[62] but it remains the case that by and large the strike movement faded away in summer 1925. Strikers were unable or unwilling to sustain their opposition or to co-ordinate their actions; as one old textile worker put it in conversation with a Menshevik informant, 'we fight one against the other, though each feels that it's necessary to organize'.[63]

There are several reasons why this should be so. To start with there were indeed conflicts of interest between workers, and we can begin to understand them by looking at mule rooms. Many operatives may have wished to avoid the shock of *uplotnenie*, but of all production workers only selfactor spinners as a group had the means to deflect the charge away from themselves.

Spinners' productivity, averred Professor Budanov in 1926, depended on the relationship between the size of the work team and the number of spindles. One would expect this observation to be followed by some trenchant suggestion for labour intensification. Instead, the author slid away into hints and generalities about rationalization improving quality.[64] Others were not even prepared to go this far: 'so that the work of the piecer and doffer will be carried out properly', wrote an expert in the same year, 'so that they can approach the high standards of their English brothers and deal with a greater number of spindles, work on mules must be carried out according to tried and tested methods'.[65] Another, writing in November 1925, came to the conclusion that it was virtually impossible to establish norms because of machine idiosyncrasy and variations in count and cloth sort.[66] Elsewhere there is evidence of the same feeling of

---

[60] 'Sovetskaia kopeika rubl' berezhet': endlessly repeated in Golos tekstilei throughout 1926. For the Politburo decision on the 'regime of economy' see M. Dewar, Labour Policy in the USSR 1917–28 (1956), pp. 119–22.

[61] For nagging conflicts in the industry over the usual themes see Golos tekstilei, ITPT and Tekstil'nye novosti for 1926.

[62] Golos tekstilei, 24 June 1926; Sots.vest., 11 (129), 11 June 1926, p. 13.

[63] Sots.vest., 14 (132), 26 July 1926, p. 14.

[64] D. D. Budanov, Obshchie poniatiia o NOT'e v chastnosti v tekstil'noi promyshlennosti (1926), p. 74.

[65] N. T. Pavlov, Sel'faktor (1926), p. 120.

[66] Sistema i organizatsiia, 11, 1925, pp. 24–25.

helplessness. Gosplan's house journal published an article praising electrification as a technique for rationalization. Because they were developed over a long period of time and because each machine had a different 'character' and construction, the author drew the line at selfactors – it could not be done.[67] Even the norm setters were at a loss. One resolution from their 1925 congress asked Vesenkha 'to give examples of normal manning levels for workers on mule frames'; much depended on 'a subjective opinion of the skill of each spinner', replied the Council.[68] Zen'kovich canvassed for *uplotnenie* on looms, ring-frames, flyer-frames and in sorting departments. He made no mention of selfactors. Nothing seems to have changed over the succeeding five years. Investigating selfactors, concluded a 1930 monograph on rationalization, 'is one of the most difficult tasks facing time-and-motion workers in the textile industry'.[69]

Visions of NOT and labour intensification on selfactors thus boiled down to recommending reductions in *komplekt* numbers and rationalizers fell back on publicizing pre-war manning levels.[70] The net result was that the mule-pair *komplekt* survived 1925 intact, and at the same time spinners received wage increases. Those in the Kambol'nyi Trust got 30 per cent over their normal rate – senior piecers 15 per cent – in exchange for dropping one doffer or creeler.[71] This kind of solution often had quite unintended results. Even when they were obliged to reduce the size of their work teams mule spinners could increase their wages without any commensurate increase in individual effort through 'hard driving', devolving more work on to the backs of their remaining assistants. Some commentators spotted the effects but missed the cause. After pointing out that waste and poor workmanship were on the increase in Krasnyi Perekop's mule rooms, Zen'kovich went on to complain that there had not even been any economy in wage costs: 'on mules spinning thirty-eight count with 1,500 spindles to a pair, for instance, a spinner's wage measured against every ten pounds of thread was 3.66 roubles before *uplotnenie* with a team of five, and 4.34 roubles after *uplotnenie* with four'.[72] There were similar reproaches from Ivanovo and Orekhovo-Zuevo. As trusts in the latter district were obliged to respond to growing demand by

[67] *Planovoe khoziaistvo*, 2, February 1927, p. 201.
[68] *TNB 1925*, p. 17; *Sistema i organizatsiia*, 10, 1925, p. 9.
[69] A. M. Buras, *Osnovy tekhnicheskogo normirovania v tekstil'noi promyshlennosti* (1930), p. 261; *Khoziaistvo i upravlenie*, 5, 1925, p. 59.
[70] For examples see *Khoziaistvo i upravlenie*, 5, 1925, p. 53; F. E. Dzerzhinskii *et al.*, eds., *K probleme proizvoditel'nosti truda*, vyp. 3 (1925), p. 70; *Golos tekstilei*, 22 May 1925; 2 October 1926; *Sistema i organizatsiia*, 10, 1925, p. 6.
[71] *Golos tekstilei*, 2 October 1926.   [72] *Khoziaistvo i upravlenie*, 5, 1925, pp. 53–4.

increasing the number of working mule frames – from 23.5 to 30.3 per cent of total active spindle stock during 1925/26[73] – spinners could afford to take no notice. Leningrad's mule spinners persisted in working one shift while many ring-frame halls worked two.[74] That they understood their position is evident from a remark made two years later: 'for *uplotnenie* a skilled workforce is required, but skilled workers are in short supply ... mule spinners take time off and do as they please because they know that they are in demand'.[75]

Explanations for these expressions of hesitancy, conservatism and spinner insouciance are not hard to find. They reflect the way authority and knowledge were distributed on the shop floor. The spinners' ability to avoid *uplotnenie* rested on the factors discussed in chapter 4. They had little reason to contemplate strike action and, just possibly, they might have had a positive interest in labour intensification – elsewhere. One source provides a clue as to why this might be so. In 1924 the central committee of the union attacked factory committees for referring particular questions to particular individuals on the committees.[76] The evidence discussed in chapters 8 and 9 also shows that policy details of all kinds were thrashed out at local level, with the factory committees. It was no different in 1925.[77] Most decisions about speed-ups, Taylorism or changes in pay policy descended on the mill like a bolt of lightning. There was no real planning and very little consultation. Factory committees were more like the régime's lightning conductors than its transmission belts, and like lightning, decisions found their way to earth by the most expedient route. In chapter 6 a case was made for a strong selfactor-spinner presence on factory committees and in local party cells. In a culture where male spinners, male foremen and male overlookers dominated shop-floor institutions, spinners had the means to protect their own by deflecting the shock of labour intensification to other rooms. Operatives in ring-frame halls, preparatory departments and weaving sheds – shops where women predominated and representation from

[73] *Bol'shaia Kokhomskaia tekstil'naia manufaktura. Proizvodstvennyi al'bom 1925g* (1925), p. 30; *Kratkii otchet pravleniia orekhovo-zuevskogo tresta khlopchatobumazhnykh fabrik o deiatel'nosti v 1925–26gg* (1926), pp. 3–5; *Otchet za 1-e polgodie 1924–1925 operats. goda. Orekhovo-Zuevskii gosudarstvennyi trest khlopchato-bumazhnykh fabrik* (1925), pp. 9–10 (hereafter *O-Z kh.b. trest Oct 1924 – Apr 1925*); *Trud i proizvodstvo*, 1, January 1926, p. 25.

[74] M. Shaginian, *Nevskaia nitka* (1925), p. 40.   [75] *Golos tekstilei*, 21 June 1927.

[76] *VI Congress VPST*, p. 22.

[77] Belkin noted that factory committees asked technicians' advice, but then invariably decided matters from their own point of view. Ivanovo's committees 'took little notice' of central directives or delegate meetings: *Golos tekstilei*, 11 August 1925; *I–V gubotdel VPST 1925–26*, p. 21.

the bench was low – did not, and there the shock was felt most severely. Events in Moscow guberniya's Drezna mill provide what may well be an illustration of this kind of behaviour. There mules were brought back on stream in March 1925. It might reasonably be expected that in such circumstances *uplotnenie* would be on the cards; the sources do not say for how long selfactors had been idle, but old loyalties to work groups could well have weakened. Nevertheless, in fine-spinning halls only ring-frames were touched by *uplotnenie*.[78]

One caveat about selfactor spinning should be mentioned – one which helps to explain another of the strike movement's weaknesses. The Menshevik press made no mention of any discontent in Leningrad,[79] in spite of the fact that the city's mill hands did experience change; indeed *uplotnenie* seems to have been enforced there more vigorously than anywhere else – 60 per cent of all spindles affected by the end of 1925.[80] But change took place in special circumstances. In part this had to do with the industry's technical structure and pre-revolutionary history. Since 1850 cotton mills had been migrating from St Petersburg in order to find labour and to exploit a mass market by manufacturing cheap cloth. Coarse spinning was therefore very much the preserve of the CIR, a feature naturally reinforced by NEP. This had important consequences. Working coarse counts on the selfactor required more effort than spinning high counts, thus Leningrad's mule operatives could probably shrug off *uplotnenie* even more easily than their compatriots to the south. In addition, it is also likely that all rooms in Leningrad were insulated from the threat of periodic redundancy caused by transport bottle-necks and supply shortages, real problems for districts remote from the Baltic ports who did not get raw cotton courtesy of the credits advanced by the Chase National Bank.[81]

But even those provincial hands who did enjoy regular employment suffered a potential disadvantage. Foreign cottons were much easier to deal with than Soviet ones. The best quality cotton came from Egypt

---

78 *Golos tekstilei*, 2 March 1926; *Otchet za 1924–1925 operats god. (Po predvarit. dannym). Orekhovo-Zuevskii gosudarstvennyi trest khlopchatobumazhnykh fabrik* (1926), p. 66; *O-Z kh.b. trest Oct 1924 – Apr 1925*, p. 8. Selfactor spinners may well have been traditional leaders on the shop floor. During a strike in St Petersburg's Sverdlov (Dzhems Bek) in 1911 it was vital for women on ring-frames to win their support: Borboff, 'The Bolsheviks and working women', p. 552.

79 With one dubious exception – the Krasnyi Parus mill: *Sots.vest.*, 24 (94), 20 December 1924, p. 15. The problem is I have found no record of any mill of that name in Leningrad in 1925.

80 *Lengubotdel VPST 1924–25*, p. 63.

81 *ITPT*, 1, January 1928, p. 43; and see above pp. 9–10, 67, 75, 136–7.

via Liverpool and could spin the whole range of counts. 'Sea-island', almost as good, was the staple crop for many of America's plantation states.[82] Bad spinning was therefore likely to be more common in the CIR. Not only did this penalize all CIR operatives in all shops when attempts were made to introduce speed-ups and individual piece rates, but bad spinning divided workers one against the other. To some extent CIR fine spinners, ring-frame and selfactor, could escape from the burden of working up poor cotton by passing shoddy goods on to weavers, and the CIR was Russia's weaving centre. 'Where all the attention of workers is directed to raising output', wrote a weaver from Moscow guberniya in February 1926, discussing mule rooms, 'pre-revolutionary norms have been surpassed', but when thread reached the weavers there were breakages and stoppages, and thus output stayed low.[83] Perhaps this helps to explain why Ivanovo's economic council announced – twice – in autumn 1925 that it was moving away from inferior cotton and low-count spinning.[84]

Several other factors deserve consideration apart from those predicated on technology and technique. Metals and engineering, traditionally high-wage industries, were much more important in Leningrad than in Central Russia. Here depression cut deep into workers' budgets, but in February 1924 Dzerzhinskii pushed for a 55 per cent increase in investment for heavy industry, a decision ratified by the thirteenth party conference in May. This was a harbinger of Gosplan's first steps towards a fully planned economy, weighted towards heavy industry, and a general commitment to industrialization. Both benefited the old capital. In January 1925 Vesenkha and the fourteenth party conference agreed to raise targets for the metal industry and promised the city five years of expansion. Details were published in June,[85] just as strikes were taking place 500 miles to the south.

Taken together, all this adds up to a partial explanation of Leningrad's quiescence and the failure of the city's cotton workers to get pay rises on a par with those in the CIR. Raw materials were easier to work up and families were probably disinclined to reduce income still further by taking strike action, particularly as the régime concurrently announced a series of measures which might promote urban recovery and cut unemployment. Only single immigrants arriving from distant provinces would be free of these considerations; paradoxically this

[82] A. M. Zaikov, *Na khlopchatobumazhnoi fabrike* (1926/27), pp. 9, 22.
[83] *Golos tekstilei*, 23 February 1926.
[84] *Golos tekstilei*, 29 September 1925; 20 November 1925.
[85] R. Day, *Leon Trotsky and the Politics of Economic Isolation* (1973), pp. 108–11, 116; E. H. Carr, *Socialism in One Country*, vol. 1 (1970), pp. 357–63, 369–70.

also made it difficult for them to take action. If there was no hindrance, there was no wider community to give support, and sharp competition for places. One contemporary noted with satisfaction that new operatives recruited to the Krasnyi Maiak and Rabochii mills – 'the less well-off workers, women workers' – settled 'more firmly' into the factories than men. Operatives who left the mills were generally unskilled or temporary workers looking for better conditions. In any case Leningrad had only one trust, and this kept labour turnover down.[86]

This brings us on to a much more obvious difference between Leningrad and the CIR. In 1922 one observer thought that Ivanovo's weavers were not disposed to work hard – 'they are not what they were in the first years of the Revolution'.[87] At the fourteenth party congress Tomsky vaguely remarked that *uplotnenie* was 'not helped' by the massive influx of new workers, peasants interested only in material advantage.[88] Two habitual commentators on the textile industry made the vital connection. Looking back over the 1920s they thought that commuting workers with some interest in agriculture were the 'basic block' to labour intensification: 'this phenomenon is explained firstly, by the more conservative nature of this group, but secondly and more importantly, because the peasant-worker clearly feels that working on three or four machines does not leave him the energy he needs to look after his own farm'.[89] Summaries of factory committee reports explaining the social dimensions of *uplotnenie*'s failure in mid-decade tell the same story. In Sereda there was 'in general, a more willing attitude shown by proletarian-workers. Only the peasant who needs to improve his material circumstances considers labour intensification'. Field work frustrated administrators in Vladimir guberniya, rural workers in one district of Moscow guberniya were 'mainly interested in their own farms'; the 'greatest response' in another district came from those 'cut off from the peasant economy and the peasant family . . . who rarely visit the countryside'. 'I'm not taking on four looms', stated one operative in a weaving shed,

---

[86] *Istoriia rabochikh Leningrada*, tom 2 (1972), p. 160; S. I. Tiul'panov, ed., *Istoriia industrializatsii SSSR. Dokumenty i materialy. Zavershenie vosstanovleniia promyshlennosti i nachalo industrializatsii severo-zapadnogo raiona (1925–1928gg)* (1964), pp. 245–46.

[87] Cited in Iu. F. Glebov, V. M. Sokolov, *Istoriia fabrika Bol'shoi Ivanovskoi manufaktury* (1952), p. 98.

[88] *Golos tekstilei*, 8 January 1926; J. B. Sorenson, *The Life and Death of Soviet Trade Unionism 1917–28* (1969), pp. 204–5.

[89] Ia. Kvasha, F. Shofman, *Semichasovoi rabochii den' v tekstil'noi promyshlennosti* (1930), p. 25.

'I've got a lot of work to do on the land.' Some workers around Shchelkovo – 'kulak-end' operatives who owned horses – simply gave up the factory for good.[90]

The confused manner in which change was effected is also pertinent. Labour intensification could not be imposed by command, as Piatakov imagined, and it was not implemented in the considered way anticipated in the later circular. Faced with conflicting instructions trusts stumbled along as best they could; four took action in January, three more in February, a further four in March and one more in May. Thereafter all cotton districts had some experience of *uplotnenie*. By July some two-thirds of all weavers and ring-frame spinners worked three looms or three banks, but loadings were distributed very unevenly between regions.[91] 'Information on those mills which have already transferred', noted Zen'kovich in May 1925, 'is extremely patchy . . . the remaining trusts have performed badly.'[92]

Beyond this, as Vladimir's local union branch found, not all those affected by change were necessarily hostile: 'because of improvements in conditions of work on three frames, in some cases in some mills there were more operatives applying for *uplotnenie* than available frames . . . in such cases established workers with the highest qualifications were successful'.[93] Variations in count, cloth type and machinery probably account for these differences,[94] but there is also some evidence to suggest that the generational divisions which were to be important in conditioning responses to mobilization later in the decade were already showing through. One *Rabkrin* investigation of two Ivanovo mills mentioned that in general, only younger weavers switched to three looms. Youth participation was particularly marked in another factory.[95]

There is nothing mysterious about this. Although training procedures socialized entrants into well-established shop-floor traditions, adolescents suffered disproportionately from unemployment and when recruited they were, according to one contributor to a booklet on

---

[90] N. Semenov, *Litso fabrichnykh rabochikh, prozhivaiushchikh v derevniakh, i politrosvetrabota sredi nikh. Po materialam obsledovaniia rabochikh tekstil'noi promyshlennosti tsentral'no-promyshlennoi oblasti* (1929), pp. 52–3, 59–60.

[91] *ITPT*, 27–28, 31 July 1926, p. 9; *Sistema i organizatsiia*, 11, 1925, p. 31; *TsK VPST 1924–26*, pp. 99–100.

[92] *Khoziaistvo i upravlenie*, 5, 1925, p. 51.   [93] *Vladgubotdel VPST 1924–25*, p. 67.

[94] See for example *Nashe khoziaistvo* (Vladimir), 4 (45), April 1925, p. 23; *Tekstil'nye novosti*, 10–11, October–November 1927, p. 378; V. V. Isakov, Iu. N. Khalturina, *Izucheniia proizvoditel'nosti i utomliaemosti pri perekhode na tkatskikh fabrikakh s 2-kh na 3-kh stanka* (1928), p. 24.

[95] Isakov, Khalturina, *Izucheniia*, pp. 64–5; *Komsomol'tsy i molodezh' ivanovskoi oblasti v gody stroitel'stva sotsializma (1921–1940gg)* (1967), p. 41.

rationalization edited by Dzerzhinskii, the best multi-machine workers. Many in Vladimir guberniya were on piece rates even while training;[96] youthful dexterity and speed literally paid off. Two sources – a lead article in *Golos tekstilei* anxiously examining the threat to the industry attendant on low adolescent recruitment, and a norm-setters' resolution calling for positive discrimination in favour of youngsters[97] – thus take on connotations beyond altruism. Nevertheless, it would be a mistake to discount the pull of the land in Vladimir, even amongst the young:

> In wintertime, when there's much more talk about productivity and when the work of the Komsomol is at its best, absenteeism is low. But when spring and summer begin, when the spring holiday is held in the countryside and the agricultural work year begins, when the League's work falls off and meetings for the young occur less frequently, absenteeism rises.[98]

The implications of 1925

There is not much need for elaboration. Vesenkha originally wanted things done all at once, but the drive for labour intensification, though by no means entirely unsuccessful, turned out to be a patchy affair, something like a weather front drifting across the CIR after December 1924. As its leading edge touched now one district, now another, and disturbed established patterns of work in particular mills and rooms, so operatives responded with a ragged strike movement. By spring a series of widely dispersed incidents caused enough worry in Moscow to effect change and compromise – voluntary *uplotnenie*, democratization on the shop floor, substantial pay rises. The latter two were doubtless universally popular. The former, a concession to individual circumstances, was important for those placed on the land/residence continuum.[99] Any classification based on urbanization and proletarianization on the one hand and rural setting and tie with the land on the other is, however, too simplistic. A successful peasant with land close to the mill might well welcome *uplotnenie* since it meant more money for investment in the farm, just as a landless mill-hand living far distant might not, as the trade-off might be disadvantageous.

---

96 Dzerzhinskii, *et al.*, *K probleme*, pp. 49, 51; *Golos tekstilei*, 26 May 1925.
97 *Golos tekstilei*, 9 January 1925; *TNB 1925*, p. 26.
98 *Nashe khoziaistvo* (Vladimir), 11–12, November–December 1925, pp. 44–5.
99 The Mensheviks went so far as to claim that opposition to *uplotnenie* took 'elemental' forms similar to peasant risings (*buntarskie nastroeniia*), owing to cotton workers' 'half-peasant social composition': *Sots.vest.*, 14 (132), 26 July 1926, p. 14.

It should be said at once that it is futile to try to classify the strikes as primarily economic or primarily political. Similarly the metaphors of class alliance and class consciousness are quite inappropriate – those of coincidence and conjunction are much more germane. What participants actually wanted – the demise of Bolshevism, independence from or liberalization of the union,[100] voluntary *uplotnenie* or wage rises – is, of course, important; the problem is that there is so little to go on. But discontents, however constituted, did coincide. And they did combine to modify the regime's immediate plans. It is, therefore, possible to say something about the implications of the strikes.

For a start the government was knocked off course. Cloth was already in short supply in the countryside but in August 1925 the syndicate had to shut some of its provincial stores. They had nothing to sell. Next month the union's central committee issued a worried statement about the need to satisfy demand in the country at large, and it is probably no accident that the goods famine, which sparked off another round of grain hoarding and forced the government to inflate the note issue, should come in the autumn.[101] Much of this may have been caused by rising demand but the strikes can only have compounded the régime's difficulties.

More than this, the whole confused development of *uplotnenie* was a response to *razbazarivanie* and scissors, and by now we should find no difficulty in working out the likely course of events for the immediate future. Just as NOT enthusiasts in 1923 and 1924 gradually became aware of the industry's social and technological limitations and diverse pay systems, so 1925 brought policy makers face to face with the problems of effecting even limited mobilization without straining the union or threatening the *smychka*.[102] Here is Kuteishchikov, writing for the syndicate in 1926: 'one must recall that the campaign . . . did not live up to expectations'.[103] And Vorob'ev, a syndicate employee, complaining to the fourth plenum of the union's central committee a year later: 'in textile mills there is no unified system of work. Each

[100] Ivanovo's overlookers walked out again sometime in the first half of 1927, disputing collective agreements. The province's seventeenth union congress attacked their 'narrow-minded shop mentality': *Rabochii krai*, 17 June 1927; 23 June 1927.

[101] Day, *Leon Trotsky*, p. 114; *Golos tekstilei*, 8 September 1925; *Sots.vest.*, 15–16 (109–110), 18 August 1925, p. 39.

[102] 'The localities exist for themselves and the centre for itself', complained Mel'nichanskii in 1926. Next year some Moscow district committees breezily continued to pass resolutions in contravention of central and local policies. A laconic official summed up matters in a nutshell – 'central committee reports are rarely read in the provinces': *Golos tekstilei*, 12 October 1926; 17 March 1927; *Moskovskii tekstil'shchik*, 2 February 1926.

[103] *ITPT*, 16, 30 April 1926, p. 1.

factory operates in its own way. Various mills spin various types of thread from many different varieties of raw cotton. Each factory sets its own machine speeds. Each puts a varying amount of twist into its thread.' And Markov, from Moscow guberniya, at the same meeting: 'in the field of labour intensification we have chaos. In one place they work three looms, in another four, or even six. Here they pay a premium of 25 per cent, there 30 or even 38 per cent. In such circumstances it is impossible to speak of a planned transfer to *uplotnenie*.'[104]

104 *Golos tekstilei*, 21 June 1927.

Part IV

The crisis of 1927 and its consequences

The introduction of the seven-hour day has not lowered wages, but it has given the workers more free time ... and by introducing the three-shift system it has made it possible to increase production, which in turn will quickly satisfy the hunger for cloth.

Kilevits of the textile syndicate, 1928

11   Confusion worse confounded

The Manifesto says there'll be a seven-hour day – it says nothing about *uplotnenie*.

Stepanov, a worker speaking at a general meeting in the
Pavlovo-Pokorovskaia mill early in January 1928

The war scare

In the towns and villages stories spread about poisonous gas, robot soldiers, invisible aircraft, and bombs that could destroy whole cities; 'we're all going to die in a rain of fire', they said, 'America, France, England, Japan, Poland and China are going to attack us.'[1] On 18 June 1927 *Golos tekstilei* started yet another campaign, this time about arson. Cartoons showed foreign agents setting fire to Soviet mills. The union's central committee told workers that they must raise the productivity of labour and rally round the Revolution to counter the military threat posed by the British Empire. A few days later factory clubs were instructed to put more effort into physical training and lay more stress on rifle sport. In line with recent party and union circulars on 'National Defence Week' activists should give war propaganda a high priority.[2]

The possibility of war had been broached late in 1926. In the new year *Pravda* carried speeches and articles by Bukharin, Rykov and Voroshilov predicting hostilities by autumn. Baldwin's government had already expressed sympathy for the notion of territorial adjustments in Eastern Europe and another misfortune came in April 1927 – the violation of the Soviet legation in Peking. In May, following a raid by British security forces on a Soviet office in London, Chamberlain,

[1] V. Kuz'michev, *Organizatsiia obshchestvennogo mneniia. Pechatnaia agitatsiia* (1929), pp. 24–5.
[2] *Ibid.*, p. 24; A. G. Meyer, 'The war scare of 1927', *Soviet Union/Union soviétique*, 5, 1, 1978, p. 1.

egged on by Tory backbenchers, cancelled the 1921 trade agreement and broke off diplomatic relations. Canada followed suit. Next month a bomb exploded in a Leningrad party club and a Soviet official was murdered in Poland. More disconcertingly Franco-German rapprochement was gathering pace by the end of 1926, thus threatening the special relationship with the Weimar Republic, the nearest thing Russia had to an alliance. Alarm increased in September 1927 when the Franco-Russian trade talks collapsed and Paris demanded and secured the return of the Soviet ambassador to Moscow.[3]

Certainly the international situation was unsettled, and one of the Politburo's basic foreign policy aims – keeping the western powers from forming an anti-Soviet bloc – seemed to be failing, but why leaders should have responded in such a dangerous way remains something of a mystery. Unless we are prepared to credit Stalin with cunning and foresight of truly satanic proportions it is hard to believe that the crisis was engineered solely to discredit the opposition. This is not to say that the General Secretary did not seize the moment to accuse his opponents of disloyalty, but the allegation cut both ways; Trotsky and Zinoviev flung the charge back – the ruling clique put the country at risk by failing to industrialize. By August even Bukharin was forced to concede that heavy industries producing for the military should receive more resources.[4]

But the scare had unintended consequences which rebounded on the government. Many Russians had already seen three wars, and outside the Kremlin the issue was inextricably entangled with two other problems; bread and the supply of consumer goods. To complicate matters for the cotton industry, fashions were changing. Throughout the decade the sale of fine-spun cloth increased faster than that of cheap calicos,[5] but coincidental administrative changes in the industry made it difficult for mills to respond sensitively to market forces. Initially, the textile syndicate acted as a sales agent. By 1926/27, however, it had grown powerful enough to absorb all trust stores, warehouses and trading departments,[6] so the individual enterprise was now placed at two removes from the consumer. Moreover, raw materials remained a perennial difficulty, and again the situation was

[3] E. H. Carr, R. W. Davies, *Foundations of a Planned Economy*, vol. 1, part 1 (1969), p. 295; Meyer, 'The war scare', p. 7; J. P. Sontag, 'The Soviet war scare of 1926–27', *Russian Review*, 34, 1, January 1975, pp. 67–74.
[4] Sontag, 'The Soviet war scare', pp. 66–71, 74–5.
[5] Carr, Davies, *Foundations*, 1, 1, p. 273. This may explain why *Ivtekstil'* felt able to announce a switch to higher-count spinning late in 1925: see above p. 193.
[6] See p. 18.

exacerbated by monopoly power. In 1926 the syndicate forced down prices. Some primary producers responded by abandoning cotton cultivation and deliveries fell off.[7] On top of all this the war scare probably disrupted contacts with overseas cotton suppliers, giving planners an added incentive to speed up construction of a railway linking Siberian timber and grain-growing regions to Turkestan's cotton farmers which, it was hoped, would stabilize the situation. But Soviet cotton was far from ideal for fine spinning.[8]

Inexorably, demand kept pressing on supply. Late in 1927 Vesenkha defended investment in textiles, one of the less favoured 'group B' industries, on the grounds that rising purchasing power could not be ignored.[9] The Supreme Economic Council found a supporter at the fifteenth party congress where a delegate from Ivanovo-Voznesensk criticized the 'contempt shown for light industry and especially for the textile industry', which 'was bound in the end to result, and is resulting now in the reduction of grain deliveries and the disturbance of the market'.[10] Perhaps he had been scanning the local press; current letters to the newspapers in Novosibirsk, wrote one investigator, fell into three categories:

> (1) There are rumours in the countryside that the harvest is failing, should we believe them or not? (2) They say there's going to be a war so we'll keep back our bread, should we or not? (3) Why are there no goods from the factories? They say the factories have gone over to war production, is this true or false?[11]

Bukharin's January speech triggered off a rush for consumer goods. A month later cartoons in *Izvestiia* showed people stripping the shops and officials later admitted that panic swept the population in May 1927. There was no let-up as the year progressed. Throughout spring and summer anxious groups roamed the stores buying up textiles and other items.[12] 'Rumours about war began amongst the priests, and then the newspaper readers. After they'd read the papers a dozen or so people would get together and work themselves up into a panic, saying that everything was terrible and that soon it wouldn't be

[7] Carr, Davies, *Foundations*, 1, 1, p. 9; vol. 1, part 2 (1969), pp. 636–7; P. Mathias, M. Postan, eds., *The Cambridge Economic History of Europe*, vol. 7, part 2 (1978), p. 490.
[8] Carr, Davies, *Foundations*, 1, 1, pp. 900–1, 915. See also above pp. 75, 192.
[9] Even then control figures predicted shortages for the period October 1927 to March 1928: Carr, Davies, *Foundations*, 1, 1, p. 299; 1, 2, p. 817.
[10] Cited in Carr, Davies, *Foundations*, 1, 1, p. 305. A month later Smolensk's local party branch complained about a 25 per cent shortfall in cotton fabric supply: O. A. Narkiewicz, *The Making of the Soviet State Apparatus* (1970), p. 165.
[11] Kuz'michev, *Pechatnaia agitatsiia*, pp. 27–8.
[12] Carr, Davies, *Foundations*, 1, 2, p. 699; Meyer, 'The war scare' p. 8.

possible to manage.' Rumour bred rumour – the abolition of free trade, devaluation, famine – ominously, the peasants began to hold back their grain.[13]

The nature of NEP's last fatal grain crisis and the extent to which shortages were a result of hoarding will probably always be a matter of contention. But because marketings never reached pre-war levels, even in the high NEP years of the mid twenties,[14] hoarding cannot be dismissed merely as Stalinist propaganda. After 1921 it was perfectly sensible for any peasant who could manage it to hang on to his produce for a few weeks or months until the price rose. But where the margin between adequate supply and acute shortage was so small, some fortuitous event, in this case the war scare, tended to upset the entire system of exchange between town and country. Russian agriculture could not shoulder the additional burdens resulting from panic buying and panic hoarding.

By now it had become customary for the government to turn to the cotton workforce when the *smychka* was under threat. Looking back, one source thought that the level of grain marketings in late 1927 depended largely on keeping the peasants supplied with cloth. A 'very serious position in the market' forced changes in the mill, wrote another.[15] A third drew attention to 'shortages of factory goods, and in particular those supplying a broad market', which disturbed the *smychka* and encouraged speculation: 'we still have a goods famine because we have insufficient funds to construct new factories, and existing enterprises are not being used to their fullest extent'. A fourth pointed to the need for changes in the cotton industry to underwrite peasant demand and ensure the supply of bread to the towns.[16]

The seven-hour day

One further ingredient added piquancy to this gallimaufry. Ever since 1926 Trotsky, Zinoviev and Kamenev had been demanding a wage review for industrial workers: an inflationary move, according to the leadership. The united opposition called out its supporters in the factories. Their meetings were broken up by the secret police but

[13] Meyer, 'The war scare', p. 8; Kuz'michev, *Pechatnaia agitatsiia*, pp. 22–3, 25.
[14] See H. J. Ellison, 'The decision to collectivize agriculture', *Slavic Review*, April 1961, pp. 189–202. Additionally, town dwellers were demanding more and better food. See A. Wicksteed, *Ten Years in Soviet Moscow* (1933), p. 39.
[15] Ia. Kvasha, F. Shofman, *Semichasovoi rabochii den' v tekstil'noi promyshlennosti* (1930), p. 5; *Sputnik kommunista*, 12 (69), 30 June 1928, p. 14.
[16] *Bol'shevik*, 8, 30 April 1928, p. 42; B. Frumkin, *Semichasovoi rabochii den' i profsoiuzy* (1928), pp. 22–3.

the party's central committee did respond in September of that year by increasing real wages for the unskilled.[17] Meanwhile, with the tenth anniversary of the October Revolution looming, Stalin appears to have felt the need for some flourish which would silence his critics once and for all, something akin to the Lenin enrolment. A bombshell was in the making. In spring 1927 Gosplan published a discussion paper on the possibility of introducing a seven-hour working day in Soviet industry sometime over the next few years. Within a few months, on October 15, the government's Jubilee Manifesto suddenly announced the transfer from the eight to the seven-hour day without any reductions in pay.[18]

Later on less popular aspects of the proposed change dribbled out. Bukharin, who did not have to work in a factory, dreamt of 'a different type of worker, a different tempo of work, a different level of labour intensity'.[19] Indeed, the Manifesto's small print included a commitment to three-shift working;[20] in textiles shortages could not be overcome by new building and machinery was thought to be at full stretch on two shifts. Moreover, although the party promised not to reduce wages the unions were told to prepare themselves for temporary pay falls and to review wage funds and piece rates to take account of the lost hour.[21] Another familiar bone of contention was also back on the agenda: 'the combined plenum of the central committee of the party and the Central Control Commission considers that only the first hesitant steps have been taken in the rationalization of production . . . Rationalization demands the maximum attention of all managers towards technical progress in industry'.[22] 'If we have in mind the organization of production *inside* an enterprise', wrote a high-ranking member of the party, 'then there is no doubt that it must undergo

---

[17] J. B. Sorenson, *The Life and Death of Soviet Trade Unionism 1917–28* (1969), p. 233. Only two sources have been located which refer to oppositionist agitation in cotton, neither of them very useful: *Iz istorii rabochego klassa SSSR* (1972), pp. 5–6; *Vestnik truda*, 11, November 1927, pp. 74–83.

[18] S. Bessonov, *Semichasovoi rabochii den' i ratsionalizatsiia* (1928), p. 25; Frumkin, *Semichasovoi rabochii den'*, p. 5; S. M. Schwarz, *Labor in the Soviet Union* (1953), pp. 259–61. Carr, Davies, *Foundations*, 1, 2, pp. 495–7. *Iz istorii rabochego klassa*, pp. 6–7, claims that the issue was raised by the party in the upper Volga as early as September 1926.

[19] *Ekonomicheskoe obozrenie*, 8, August 1928, p. 42.

[20] Carr, Davies, *Foundations*, 1, 2, pp. 495–7.

[21] I. S. Belinskii, A. I. Kucherov, *Tri mesiatsa raboty semichasovykh fabrik. (Opyt perevoda i raboty semichasovykh fabrik v ivanovo-voznesenskoi gubernii)* (1928), p. 5; Frumkin, *Semichasovoi rabochii den'*, pp. 36–9. According to *Sputnik agitatora*, 23 December 1928, p. 62, 85 per cent of equipment was already on two shifts.

[22] M. Saval'ev, ed., *Direktivy VKP(b) v oblasti khoziaistvennoi politiki za desiat' let (1917–27gg)* (1928), pp. 70–1.

significant changes as a result of reducing the working day'.[23] In textiles this could only mean speed-ups: 'as is well known', remarked someone at an arbitration meeting between the union and management early in January 1928, '*uplotnenie* will occur simultaneously with the transfer to three-shift working'.[24]

No one should have been too startled to find the Manifesto announcement interpreted in this way; warning shots had been firing off throughout 1927. 'Operatives do not work as hard as they could', lectured the union's bureaucrats in June, 'in pre-war times they managed four, or even six looms, now they work only a pair or three'.[25] Two Ivanovo propagandists discovered that some drawing-, flyer- and ring-frame spinners in Iuzha had been working seven hours and three shifts before October,[26] but not everything was going well. In June the director tried to introduce six-loom working 'secretly ... the factory committee knew nothing about it at all'.[27] Shortly afterwards the local union branch discussed 'abnormalities' in another mill where things started 'without the agreement of the workers'. 'Must we', asked Mel'nichanskii, rhetorically, of this particular incident, 'have *uplotnenie* in a factory where machinery is worn out and obselete?'[28] Ivanovo's Krasnaia Vekta became the scene of a fully blown scandal a week or so before the tenth anniversary celebrations; there, under the cover of night, the administration surreptitiously reset ring-frame speeds from 7,800 to 9,400 turns per minute.[29]

Obviously directors and administrators everywhere were under pressure to increase output, and just as understandably, in view of recent events, union officials wished to defend the principle of voluntarism. Perhaps this is why when *Golos tekstilei* trumpeted the news abroad in October it gave no hint that the Manifesto would apply in any special way to its readers. Union leaders also seem to have ignored the issue – in public at least. 'Trust plans for the New Year' published in *Golos tekstilei* on 22 October had nothing to say about any proposed reorganization of the shop floor. Similarly Mel'nichanskii avoided the subject when two days later he toured six Leningrad mills to make speeches celebrating ten years of Soviet power. Only afterwards, in an interview, did he vaguely observe that the seven-hour

23 Bessonov, *Semichasovoi rabochii den'*, pp. 10, 20 [stress in the original].
24 *Golos tekstilei*, 12 January 1928.
25 *Golos tekstilei*, 21 June 1927. On the other hand some claimed that seven-hour/three-shift working was introduced because the industry had made great advances since 1917: Frumkin, *Semichasovoi rabochii den'*, pp. 7–8, 19; V. Shmidt, *Polozhenie rabochego klassa v SSSR* (1928), pp. 67–8.
26 Belinskii, Kucherov, *Tri mesiatsa raboty*, p. 16.   27 *Golos tekstilei*, 21 June 1927.
28 *Rabochii krai*, 9 July 1927; 31 July 1927.   29 *Rabochii krai*, 6 October 1927.

day would be a good thing for workers and admit, giving no further details, that the union was 'actively preparing' for it. Evidence of lack of co-ordination, and perhaps disagreements in the industry, surfaced in the paper on October 29. Inside was a long report on a plenum of the union's central committee. One resolution on the front page discussed the new policy. In view of the industry's previous experience with rationalization, quality control and raising the productivity of labour, the 'question of the switch to the seven-hour day' could be addressed. That was all. But next to it was an article by the syndicate's chairman which failed to mention the subject, and next to that an announcement that the Central Council of Trades Unions – not the textileworker's union – had decided to switch textiles first. The industry had 'some experience' of seven-hour/three-shift working, continued the writer, targeting Vladimir, Ivanovo, Serpukhov and Orekhovo-Zuevo as likely regions. Three days later there were reports of central union resolutions about another new handbook, kindergartens, labour productivity and cotton supply; preparing for seven-hour working came low on the list. Engineers ignored the Central Council's announcement at a plenum of their union section the following week. Only on 7 January 1928 did Mel'nichanskii come clean: seven-hour/ three-shift working signalled implementation of the Jubilee Manifesto. This would increase output, for the sake of grain collection, and make *uplotnenie* possible.[30]

Thus cotton operatives were to experience the change before anyone else. The textile industry was the 'pioneer', enthused two contemporaries; the transfer took place 'almost exactly at the same time as the publication of the Jubilee Manifesto'.[31] At first it seemed that decision makers had learnt from Vesenkha's earlier blunderings over labour intensification. While the newly resurrected *Glavtekstil'* and the union's central committee agreed that the new policy would strengthen the industry and improve workers' lives, they warily decided to try out the idea in just a few mills at first. Both organizations could point to the Manifesto to justify their caution; it stated that the seven-hour day should not strain the economy, reduce output or disturb the exchange of goods between town and country.[32] In November 1927, taking its cue from a Central Council commission set up to oversee implementation, the union agreed to an experiment in

[30] *Golos tekstilei*, 18 October 1927; 22 October 1927; 25 October 1927; 27 October 1927; 29 October 1927; 1 November 1927; 12 November 1927; 7 January 1928.
[31] Kvasha, Shofman, *Semichasovoi rabochii den'*, p. 5.
[32] Frumkin, *Semichasovoi rabochii den'*, pp. 12–14; *Tekstil'nye novosti*, 10–11, October– November 1927, p. 416.

the Abel'man, Krasnyi Profintern, Pavlovo-Pokorovskaia, Vagzhanov and Khalturin mills; the first four in the CIR, the latter in Leningrad. Almost immediately the list began to grow including, within a month, four more CIR mills. By 6 January 1928 the commission, now expanded to include representatives from the Council of People's Commissars and chaired jointly by Mel'nichanskii and Shmidt from the Commissariat of Labour, had picked out another five mills. Two days later the number rose to seventeen, employing in all around 104,000 workers.[33]

Throughout 1927 the government had been plagued by all manner of uncertainties;[34] perhaps the representatives of the national commissariats on the commission transmitted the mood to others. If so, it would help to explain what followed. According to a western historian, reducing hours was always a secondary consideration in the minds of those who drafted the Jubilee Manifesto. The main reason was economic – worries about grain.[35] Whether this was true or not in October there is reason enough to believe that it became so in December. Deliveries to state agencies failed to come up to expectations. Grain collections peaked in September then fell steadily until Christmas, recovering only late in January 1928.[36] All but one of the targeted mills were in the CIR. They were, therefore, not the most efficient, but they were, as pamphleteers pointed out, 'located in the countryside or in industrial villages'.[37] Possibly the commission thought that a mini-*smychka* could be attempted; CIR peasants did not sow much grain but market gardening was probably common enough around Moscow and nearby provincial towns.[38] More likely communications dictated the choice. Moscow, not Leningrad, was at the hub of Russia's railway network so cloth could be distributed quickly to Russia's peasant masses from the CIR.

Whatever the reason, decision makers panicked, this time without the help of Piatakov who was currently in disgrace. They did not wait for a second order from the government, issued on January 17. Alarmed by the grain crisis and anxious to tempt the peasantry into

---

[33] *Biulleten' ivanovo-voznesenskogo gosudarstvennogo tekstil'nogo tresta*, 37/4, February 1928, p. 3; 38/5, March 1928, p. 3 (hereafter *BI–VGTT*); Carr, Davies, *Foundations*, 1, 2, pp. 491, 500; *Golos tekstilei*, 19 November 1927; 10 December 1927; 7 January 1928; *Rabochii krai*, 24 December 1927; 8 January 1928; *Trud*, 7 January 1928. Workforce totals calculated from *Tekstil'nye fabriki SSSR* (1927).

[34] Carr, Davies, *Foundations*, 1, 1, p. 296.   [35] Schwarz, *Labor*, pp. 261–2.

[36] *Statisticheskoe obozrenie*, 3, March 1928, p. 68.

[37] Kvasha, Shofman, *Semichasovoi rabochii den'*, p. 13.

[38] Late in the decade Ivanovo's main newspaper carried advertisements placed by private nurseries (see p. 39).

the marketplace, they suddenly decided to proceed at 'maximum speed'.[39] Directives from the commission were issued on the 6th of January, preparations were to be completed by the 10th, and the change carried out on the 15th.[40]

Finding new operatives

Some were forewarned. The Abel'man's director announced the coming change to the mill's workforce on December 10. On New Year's Day a worker-correspondent wrote that all was ready,[41] but many operatives who read the newspapers must have experienced a sense of *déjà vu*. Equally, not all administrators were happy. Early in December a director from Sereda warned that shortages of skilled labour and insufficient motive power made any change impossible because local power stations could not generate enough current for the night shift.[42] He was ignored. Since November the local trades council had been telling factory committees that they must forestall disorganization and ensure that all difficulties were resolved by mass meetings. Just in case, central and branch officials of the union would be on hand All officials, factory committees and union members must energetically prepare for 15 January, insisted Mel'nichanskii on the 7th.[43]

Prospects for the transition were not good. Almost without exception mills had only a week or so's grace.[44] Later, news of the consequences began to trickle out: 'mechanical' preparation by union activists and the party cell in Sereda; workers were given no clear perspective on the relationship between the *smychka* and *uplotnenie*. There the local union bureau received directives on the 5th. Only 485 workers from two shifts turned up for the first meeting on the 13th, 600 for the second on the 15th. Animated debate marred proceedings at this latter assembly. Mule and ring-frame spinners demanded more auxiliary workers and additional breaks for machine cleaning.[45] Similar discords afflicted Rodniki where one enterprise already had some partial experience of seven-hour/three-shift working. On the 13th – again few came to the meeting, only 600 – all speakers expressed

---

[39] *Sputnik agitatora*, 6, March 1928, p. 25.
[40] *Golos tekstilei*, 7 January 1928; *Rabochii krai*, 8 January 1928.
[41] *Golos tekstilei*, 10 December 1927; 1 January 1928.
[42] *Rabochii krai*, 3 December 1927.
[43] Frumkin, *Semichasovoi rabochii den'*, pp. 33–6; *Golos tekstilei*, 7 January 1928; Belinskii, Kucherov, *Tri mesiatsa raboty*, p. 25.
[44] *Tri mesiatsa raboty*, p. 32; *Puti industrializatsii*, 10, 1928, p. 49.
[45] Belinskii, Kucherov, *Tri mesiatsa raboty*, pp. 25–6, 29–30; *Golos tekstilei*, 19 January 1928; *Sputnik agitatora*, 8, April 1929, p. 45.

disquiet over undue haste. Some were against *uplotnenie*. The local union bureau neglected to comment until early February, almost a month after the transfer began. Because there were so few skilled workers registered at the local labour exchange union officials in Shuia were worried about the possibility of overtime. This was late in December 1927. On January 12 they got round to reading central instructions. Next day, at a meeting attended by half the mill's workforce, the platform pleaded for 'a painless and easy transition to *uplotnenie*', but from the floor many voiced outright opposition to further speed-ups and many more were uneasy about the difficulties presented by obsolete equipment and poor-quality cotton. Oddly, the director was not there. Although he and his engineers had scrutinized ways and means and passed their report to the factory committee on the 3rd, no decisions were taken 'because it was not clear when the switch would begin'. The factory committee did not meet the administration until the 19th. Like their counterparts in Sereda and Rodniki, they attached great importance to the provision of auxiliary workers. In addition, they inquired into the possibility of promotions from the bench to compensate for the paucity of technicians. As implementation gathered pace meeting followed meeting; two in late January where spinners castigated management over poor training and the resultant shortages of experienced workers, and two early the following month restricted to weaving shed overlookers.[46] In the Nikol'skaia, 100 miles to the south-west, the transfer was carried out in three days with no preparation. The nearby Pavlovo-Pokorovskaia's operatives had five days' notice; those in the Riabovskaia had six and those in Tver's Vagzhanov four.[47] In Drezna 'the mood was very unsettled'.[48]

Notwithstanding *Rabochii krai*'s sanguine prognosis concerning the likely diminution of unemployment,[49] of the multifarious problems facing these mills labour supply was the most immediate: how to find workers for the extra shift. The commission sent out instructions to the provinces. First in line for jobs were adolescent trainees, next came operatives 'released' from nearby mills by *uplotnenie* and after them workers' children living in the factory housing with their parents – these would step into jobs vacated by up-graded trainees. It was

[46] Belinskii, Kucherov, *Tri mesiatsa raboty*, pp. 25–32.
[47] Kvasha, Shofman, *Semichasovoi rabochii den'*, pp. 7–9; *Sputnik agitatora*, 6, March 1928, p. 25.
[48] *Kommunistka*, 4, April 1928, p. 46.
[49] 'Thousands of the unemployed will be taken on, millions of meters of cloth will come on to the market, the cost of production will fall': *Rabochii krai*, 8 January 1928.

Table 10. *Registered unemployed textile workers, selected trades, October 1927*

	Leningrad	Moscow	CIR excluding Moscow
Preparatory departments			
Drawing-frame operatives	77	48	325
Flyer-frame operatives	9	74	147
Fine-spinning halls			
Ring-frame spinners	112	60	794
Selfactor *komplekt*			
spinners	0	27	115
senior piecers	0	99	567
Weaving sheds			
Overlookers	0	0	99
Weavers	495	185	1,496
Unskilled workers	565	799	4,050

Source: L. E. Mints, I. F. Engel', eds, *Statisticheskie materialy po trudu i sotsial'nomu strakhovaniiu za 1926–27g* (1927/28), vyp. 4, kn. 4, table 4 pp. 14–15

hoped that somewhere between 10,000 to 13,000 of the estimated 17,000 to 18,000 necessary would be found in this way. The unemployed, to be taken from the labour exchanges, were a house of last resort. In the absence of local bureaux or correspondence points, factory committees were left to arrange things as they saw fit.[50]

These clear-cut orders did not assuage everyone's forebodings. Directors betrayed their anxiety in *Golos tekstilei* on 8 January; while announcing that they were ready many nevertheless took the opportunity to place disguised advertisements, bold-type sentences disclosing vacancies in particular shops.[51] By July 1928 the twenty mills then switched to seven-hour/three-shift working had increased their collective labour force by almost 23,000. Workers' children accounted for 30.4 per cent of new recruits, redundant operatives 12.4 per cent.[52] Labour requirements, however, varied between districts. The Pavlovo-Pokorovskaia scraped by with a mere 13 per cent overall increase, but there was a 20 per cent rise in the Abel'man, 30 per cent in the Seredskaia and 40 per cent in Moscow guberniya's Dedovskaia.

50 *Golos tekstilei*, 7 January 1928; 8 January 1928; *Rabochii krai*, 8 January 1928.
51 *Golos tekstilei*, 8 January 1928.
52 *Planovoe khoziaistvo*, 10, October 1928, p. 305.

The Ramenskaia nearly doubled its workforce.[53] Here less than a third of the pre-existing workforce lived in factory accommodation. Seven hundred were found at once from the barracks but this resource was quickly exhausted; on average, each family had 1.9 members on the shop-floor by the end of the year.[54]

When this factory held a general meeting late in December 1927 the director, after discounting the children of proletarian families and young trainees, asked where the remaining 2,200 night-shift workers would come from, especially as so few registered at the local employment office would be of any use.[55] In fact little comfort could be drawn from a perusal of labour exchange lists anywhere in the CIR. Although in key trades registrations had been rising slowly for the past two years, totals in the Russian Federation were far below requirements,[56] and broken down by region scarcities were more glaring still (see table 10). Nevertheless, some propagandists were not dismayed. Two pointed out that because all targeted mills were located in unemployment black spots there should be no difficulty in finding workers, but this was not true, countered others: one might assume that because the industry was concentrated in Leningrad and the CIR workers made redundant by previous rationalization drives would migrate to thriving mills, but unfortunately, three-quarters of all unemployed mill hands known to the union lived in urban areas while almost all targeted factories were in the countryside where there was no spare housing. If 'mill-end' workers were in short supply and in the wrong places, it was also the case that the preparatory period had been far too brief.[57] A speaker at Moscow guberniya's union congress of April 1928 agreed: Moscow, Serpukhov and Orekhovo-Zuevo had many jobless hands but 90 per cent of the workforce in seven-hour/three-shift zones were actually peasants.[58] 'Even in the Ramenskaia', remarked Shmidt in October, 'only half-an-hour's drive from Moscow, we could not take workers from the city because there was no housing for them'.[59]

But however severe the shortage of qualified workers, in principle the bureaux should have been able to provide directors and factory

[53] Ibid., p. 304; Izvestiia, 17 August 1928; Kvasha, Shofman, Semichasovoi rabochii den', p. 16.
[54] Rabota tkachikh v nochnoi smene (1929), pp. 39, 42; Voprosy truda, 3, March 1928, p. 4.
[55] Golos tekstilei, 20 December 1927.
[56] L. E. Mints, I. F. Engel', eds., Statisticheskie materialy po trudu i sotsial'nomu strakhovaniiu za 1926–27g (1928), vyp. 1, table 4 pp. 15–16; vyp. 2–3, table 2 p. 6, table 4 pp. 9–10; vyp. 4, table 4 pp. 15–16.
[57] Belinskii, Kucherov, Tri mesiatsa raboty, p. 6; Kvasha, Shofman, Semichasovoi rabochii den', p. 13.
[58] Golos tekstilei, 6 April 1928.   [59] Trud, 31 October 1928.

committees with accurate information. Nine months before the commission's hurried announcement of the switch, the Commissariat of Labour, in an effort to curb rural migration, had tightened up its rules. Subsequently workers had to prove their status before registration and the unskilled were obliged to provide evidence of six months' uninterrupted employment.[60] But it was impossible to stem the tide. Peasants took on seasonal work in industry and then found ways of registering at the exchanges.[61] It was not very difficult. Officials took union membership as sufficient proof of past employment,[62] and in December 1928 Tomsky revealed his awareness of the black market in union cards – the relative desirability of each trade finding its reflection in the asking price.[63]

Bureaux officials in targeted zones thus had no clear idea of the skill levels of those on their books, and were 'in no condition at all to meet the demands' placed on them.[64] 'On many occasions', complained one author, 'the exchanges listed as skilled weavers people who, according to social insurance records, had received training a year or two ago. Needless to say, such "qualified" operatives could not work properly.'[65] Only fifteen out of 150 weavers recommended to Serpukhov's Riabovskaia by the labour exchange could manage three looms. The Ramenskaia needed 1,400 skilled workers, the local bureau listed 1,107.[66] Most, however, had not worked for years or were low-grade handloom weavers, and a significant number 'were utterly useless, not even able to clean down a loom'.[67] In such circumstances factories had no option but to cast their nets even wider. In Rodniki and Shuia flyer- and ring-frame spinners were hired 'by other means'. Unskilled recruits were filling skilled vacancies in Ivanovo-Voznesensk, reported the local paper on January 14.[68] Shmidt later admitted that the vast bulk of the new workforce was drawn from the peasantry.[69] How this was done is not made clear. In Ramenskoe people were hired

[60] Schwarz, *Labor*, p. 42.
[61] L. S. Rogachevskaia, *Likvidatsiia bezrabotitsy v SSSR 1917–1930gg* (1973), p. 144.
[62] Schwarz, *Labor*, pp. 42–3.
[63] Sorenson, *Soviet Trade Unionism*, p. 209. Perhaps an offshoot of the black stock exchange around Moscow's Nikol'skii district, where in 1924 great numbers of youngsters worked as runners: M. S. Farbman, *After Lenin. The New Phase in Russia* (1924), p. 87.
[64] *Sputnik agitatora*, 6, March 1928, p. 27.
[65] *Ekonomicheskoe obozrenie*, 8, August 1928, p. 50.
[66] *Ekonomicheskaia zhizn'*, 4 July 1928; *Ekonomicheskoe obozrenie*, 8, August 1928, p. 49.
[67] *Trud*, 11 April 1928. Domestic workers were being forced out of business after 1926 because they could not compete for raw materials: A. Kaufman, *Small-scale Industry in the Soviet Union* (1962), pp. 34–5. Perhaps this drove some of them into the mills.
[68] Belinskii, Kucherov, *Tri mesiatsa raboty*, pp. 35–6; *Rabochii krai*, 14 January 1928.
[69] *Trud*, 31 October 1928.

from the gate, whether or not they belonged to the union, and 1,850 came straight from the villages. Ivanovo, on the other hand, scratched together special commissions to deal with the emergency.[70]

After a few months writers began to review the situation. In 1926/27, compared to other industries, textiles exhibited a high degree of labour stability.[71] Now this was threatened: for a start there were complaints about drunkenness (110 quickly dismissed from the Vagzhanov for this offence) poor time-keeping and low skills.[72] The Ramenskaia's director discovered that 2,424 of his 3,794 new workers were 'completely ignorant', and many of the rest had previously been sacked from the mill 'for various offences'.[73] Others were quick to take up this last theme. One commentator noted that new recruits included people who 'damaged' industry. Another made the same point; those 'earlier dismissed from the mills for this or that offence' frequently found their way back to the shop floor, and he went on to note that 'their discipline is lower than normal'.[74]

Implementing the seven-hour day

While the localities were struggling with Moscow's directives the union's central committee began to quarrel with Vesenkha – exactly how would the new dispensation be put into practice? The Supreme Economic Council tried to foist split shifts on the union; operatives should come onto the shop floor twice every twenty-four hours with a long break in between. Additionally, argued Vesenkha, neither adolescents, pregnant women nor nursing mothers should be exempt from night work.[75] The union did not like these proposals. Mel'nichanskii reminded *Golos tekstilei*'s readers that Russia's capitalists had used a similar split-shift system 'to disguise the existence of the twelve or thirteen-hour working day. It was not profitable to have operatives working twelve or thirteen hours continuously because productivity fell off towards the end of the shift.'[76] Instead, all mills should work seven hours continuously and be left to set breaks as they saw fit. Moreover, exemptions should be maintained, wage

[70] Belinskii, Kucherov, *Tri mesiatsa raboty*, p. 19; *Golos tekstilei*, 19 January 1928; Kvasha, Shofman, *Semichasovoi rabochii den'*, pp. 15–16.
[71] Carr, Davies, *Foundations*, 1, 2, p. 469.
[72] V. A. Buianov, *Tekstil'shchiku, o trudovoi distsipline* (1929), p. 10; *Ekonomicheskoe obozrenie*, 8, August 1928, pp. 48, 50.
[73] Kvasha, Shofman, *Semichasovoi rabochii den'*, p. 16.
[74] *Bol'shevik*, 8, 30 April 1928, p. 43; *Sputnik agitatora*, 6, March 1928, p. 26.
[75] *Golos tekstilei*, 12 January 1928; *Trud*, 12 January 1928.
[76] *Golos tekstilei*, 13 January 1928.

levels for those who had already accepted *uplotnenie* protected, and nurseries, essential for night workers, financed by management.[77]

Mel'nichanskii's brief excursion into labour history probably failed to cut much ice; in view of current imperatives Vesenkha wanted much the same thing as the old mill owners. There was, however, another way for the union to tackle Vesenkha, one likely to appease the productivist ethos: 'it is more expedient to work seven hours without interruption', observed a contributor to a party journal four months later. Experience showed that operatives used the interstices created by split shifts 'not to rest, but to work, either at home or on the land', and that they then came back to the mill tired out.[78] Whether arguments like these were advanced by Mel'nichanskii or not, Vesenkha remained intransigent. To resolve the deadlock the Commissar of Labour agreed to arbitrate. Three days before the first batch of mills transferred, Shmidt patched together a compromise: no split shifts without local agreement, no night work for exempted categories and no pay reductions for existing multi-machine workers.[79]

It was, at best, a partial victory. From the start present conditions weakened the union's case. Even under the eight-hour day, before the Jubilee Manifesto, some 76,000 textile operatives, roughly one-fifth of the total, worked split shifts with a break of four hours or more.[80] By the end of January the Abel'man, Ramenskaia, Riabovskaia, Vagzhanov and one other mill had opted for continuous working, the first two reversing decisions previously obtaining. Moscow's union branch appears to have forced unbroken shifts on the First, Second and Third State Textile Trusts, amongst the biggest in the country,[81] but there were some notable exceptions, most obviously the giant Nikol'skaia. The Drezna and Pavlovo-Pokorovskaia also worked split shifts, and in these three cases shift systems were unique to each mill.[82] *Golos tekstilei* kept up the pressure for three months but resistance was probably never more than half-hearted. The central committee signalled its capitulation in April 1928 when the eighth union congress ordered Tver' to accept split shifts.[83]

But whatever the arrangement, operatives resident in factory

[77] *Golos tekstilei*, 12 January 1928; *Trud*, 12 January 1928.
[78] *Bol'shevik*, 8, 30 April 1928, p. 46.
[79] Carr, Davies, *Foundations*, 1, 2, p. 502; *Trud*, 12 January 1928.
[80] *Golos tekstilei*, 13 January 1928. Examples for particular shops are given in A. F. Ziman, *Tekhnicheskoe normirovanie priadil'nogo proizvodstva. Chast' 1. Otdely: sortirovochnyi, trepal'nyi, chesal'nyi* (1928).
[81] *Golos tekstilei*, 28 January 1928; 2 February 1928; 7 February 1928; *Sputnik agitatora*, 6, March 1928, p. 27.
[82] Kvasha, Shofman, *Semichasovoi rabochii den'*, p. 70.   [83] *Trud*, 13 July 1928.

housing, 'mill-end' workers, suffered considerably. Like many others in the district those in the Sobolevo-Shchelkovskaia's barracks had to put up with 'chaos, noise, hooliganism, drunkenness ... since the switch ... there hasn't been a moment's peace'. In the Ramenskaia they protested about 'uninterrupted din and racket' while those in another mill lived with 'noise for twenty-one out of twenty-four hours'.[84] 'The three-shift schedule', wrote a worker in February,

> has completely upset the accustomed pattern of life in the factory barracks. Day and night the barracks buzz. In the extremely crowded conditions (3.7 people to a room) where about 40 per cent of the families lack rooms separated from others by tight partitions and two and more members of most families go to work, frequently on different shifts, there is no chance for the worker to get normal rest.[85]

For new recruits and established operatives who did not live on the premises, 'village-end' workers, the choice between continuous or broken shifts was a matter of considerable importance. Ivanovo's mass hiring commissions discovered that of all unemployed textile workers listed by the bureaux, 19 per cent had allotments of some kind or other. Amongst those living in rural districts the figure rose to a staggering 61 per cent, and this took no account of peasants taken from the gate or of any other connections with agriculture.[86] Mel'nichanskii pointed out that because many workers lived far away they would perforce find themselves hanging around the mill for twelve or thirteen hours each day,[87] and within a few days of January 15 workers were writing to *Golos tekstilei* grumbling about the time they had to waste in this manner.[88]

It would be a mistake, however, to imagine that all village-end operatives were hurt. The Ramenskaia's story is indicative of the way in which the precise parameters of the land/residence continuum interacted with local choices to penalize some and reward others. As a result of the switch the social characteristics of the workforce underwent significant changes. The guberniya's health department found that subsequently 36 per cent of all non-residents lived within 1.7 miles of the mill, 27 per cent within 3.5 to seven miles and 8 per cent over seven miles distant. *Golos tekstilei* congratulated the factory. Under the old eight-hour/split-shift system which the mill operated

---

[84] *Golos tekstilei*, 15 February 1928; *Komsomol'skaia pravda*, 28 February 1928; *Trud*, 1 August 1928.
[85] Cited in Schwarz, *Labor*, pp. 265–6.
[86] Kvasha, Shofman, *Semichasovoi rabochii den'*, pp. 12–13.
[87] *Golos tekstilei*, 13 January 1928.
[88] *Golos tekstilei*, 17 January 1928; 25 January 1928.

Table 11. *Residence patterns in some CIR mills after the switch to seven-hour/three-shift working*

	% of workforce in mill housing
Moscow guberniya	
Dedovskaia	60.5
Naro-Fominsk	46.8
Drezna	43.2
Ramenskaia	31.7
Pavlovo-Pokorovskaia	24.0
Riabovskaia	17.2
Vpered	6.0
Vladimir guberniya	
Derbenev	45.6
Abel'man	7.6
Tver' guberniya	
Vagzhanov	39.4
Vysokovskaia	27.7
Iaroslval' guberniya	
Krasnyi Perekop	42.9

Source: *Izvestiia tekstil'noi promyshlennosti i torgovli*, 3, March 1930, p. 11

many workers from the countryside took lodgings close to their shops; 'they were unable to return five or eight versts [seven to twelve miles or so] to their homes every day'. Now they could, and this relieved pressure on nearby housing.[89] Throughout the CIR, where the provision of mill barracks was so diverse (see table 11), moods and circumstances were doubtless equally various, but at least some with an interest in agriculture now had more time to spend on their farms and allotments.

Nevertheless, as two writers frequently cited in this chapter pointed out, multi-machine working was 'not a rest from field work'. Workers should choose 'between the land and the mill'; moreover, if choice played a part in the 'first stages' of *uplotnenie* (surely a reference to the compromise of 1925)

> in the succeeding mass transfer ... it should play a less significant role ... In large mills, where workers come from different social groups, it seems to us necessary to move away from a situation where

[89] *Rabota tkachikh*, p. 39; *Golos tekstilei*, 7 February 1928.

the level of labour intensification varies between operatives connected with the land and those who have severed their ties . . . *uplotnenie*
. . . cannot, must not, and will not be based on free choice, on the
voluntary principle.[90]

Sentiments like these do not seem to have been very popular. They
'often meet with opposition from the workers', wrote Shmidt in
January 1928; 'you'll switch us to seven-hours', said operatives, 'but
our working day will become harder and more intensive'.[91] 'From what
I've heard', observed someone from the Derbenev, picking his words
carefully, 'no one has spoken against the seven-hour day, but if you're
talking about *uplotnenie*, about working four spindle banks or four
looms, that's a different matter'.[92] It was just the same across the
border in Ivanovo guberniya, as a worker in the Shuiskaia discovered.
Operatives welcomed the Jubilee Manifesto, 'but they didn't think
there would be any labour intensification. They thought they'd work
for seven hours and get paid for eight.'[93]

Soon the thunderclouds began to pile up across the cotton districts.
During the first four months of 1928 stoppages in the Shuiskaia's
preparatory departments 'assumed a chronic character'.[94] In Leningrad on January 20 the local party committee told the Khalturin's
management to 'pay serious attention to the timely settlement of
disputes arising from questions of pay, norms and piece rates'.[95] That
month, after listing extraneous causes – cold weather and poor quality
raw materials – Ivanovo State Textile Trust's journal mentioned 'other
reasons' for stoppages which should be attended to. Administrators
did not elaborate on these hints, but in March reported failure to
approach normal output in all fifteen of the trust's mills.[96] By July the
outlook was bleaker still:

> of our eight weaving mills only one has worked for the whole month.
> All the others had a two week stoppage. In some big mills where
> productivity has fallen – the Bol'shevik, Tezinskaia and Bonia-
> chenskaia – these unhappy conditions are affecting the production
> plan. Leading technical personnel in these mills must strain every
> nerve to correct these deficiencies in the coming months.[97]

90 Kvasha, Shofman, *Semichasovoi rabochii den'*, p. 26.
91 *Voprosy truda*, 3, March 1928, p. 4.
92 *Izvestiia*, 17 August 1928.   93 *Sputnik agitatora*, 6, March 1928, p. 30.
94 Belinskii, Kucherov, *Tri mesiatsa raboty*, p. 44.
95 S. I. Tiul'panov, ed., *Istoriia industrializatsii SSSR. Dokumenty i materialy. Zavershenie
vosstanovleniia promyshlennosti i nachalo industrializatsii severo-zapadnogo raiona (1925–
1928gg)* (1928), p. 331.
96 *BI–VGTT*, 36/3, January 1928, p. 4; 38/5, March 1928, pp. 3–4.
97 *BI–VGTT*, 43/10, August 1928, p. 4.

This may or may not refer to a strike. Most likely it is a comment on falling labour discipline after workers returned from working on the land during their summer break – but if there was some kind of flurry could operatives have influenced one another? The latter two mills were both located in the same small town, Vichuga. Either way the atmosphere did not clear in the autumn. On 10 October flyer-frame spinners on the Boniachenskaia's night shift stopped work. Seventy-three besieged the manager's office demanding wage rises and shouting that they were being paid less than weavers. Three hours later they were back at the frame, after attending a general meeting where the 'injustice' of their complaints was 'explained' to them.[98] A few days earlier a minor tempest swept through Vladimir guberniya's Karabanovskii Combine. Part of the factory had been transferred to three-shift working in spring. Weavers agreed to make the 'temporary sacrifice' of working extra night shifts until a new power plant came on stream and enabled the administration to reactivate idle looms. When this did not happen trust representatives turned up to explain things to the workers, but 'the meeting assumed a mutinous character'. During the 'tremendous din' which followed weavers demanded that they, and not the assembled workforce, should decide what to do next. Intransigent, but discomforted by weavers' insistent calls that he should leave the hall so they could debate without interference, Glushkov, the mill's director, threatened 645 operatives and a further 147 trainees with dismissal if three-shift working was not accepted at once. Lashkov, the trust representative who started the furore, 'went one step further'. Taking up Glushkov's point that the factory was presently unprofitable he threatened to close the whole enterprise. This was the last straw. 'If that's the case', roared workers, 'why didn't you tell us about it in the production conference? We don't believe you! The looms have been working for twenty-three hours a day without a break!' Intimidated, the meeting eventually voted to accept three shifts, whereupon the weavers stormed out.[99]

Throughout 1928 *Golos tekstilei* betrayed some nervousness, publishing frequent appeals explaining the importance of unity and the necessity of strengthening union work. It is not difficult to see why. A month after the Karabanovo affair and 100 miles or so to the north-east in Teikovo, an old wound re-opened: overlooker Krepikov, party member and factory committee delegate, took the brave step of circulating appeals encouraging his compatriots in other mills to go on strike – 'the factory committee is like the old factory police and the

98 *Rabochii krai*, 20 October 1928.   99 *Trud*, 6 October 1928.

party deceives the workers'. Expelled from the party and the union, Krepikov nevertheless had some following, especially amongst the Bol'shevik's 4,000 new operatives. There was also 'considerable agitation in the factory barracks'.[100] Thereafter attention shifted to Moscow guberniya. In January 1929 *Golos tekstilei* revealed that 'Trotskyists' had been active in the Glukhovskaia's shops and barracks 'for the past two or three weeks'. They spoke out against the party and tried unsuccessfully to persuade workers to go on strike. Apparently this was not an isolated disturbance. A month earlier the same paper launched an attack on 'Trotskyists' in general, defined as operatives who criticized collective agreements which they considered to be unfair.[101]

But we are already running too far ahead. In March 1928 the plenum of Moscow guberniya's union branch lamented the 'forced character' of the switch.[102] Eight months later, in December, Tomsky addressed the eighth Central Council of Trades Unions congress, and, as in 1925, brooded over strikes which occurred without official sanction; the work of the unions in this field was 'hardly commendable'.[103] Nevertheless, the storm never broke. In 1928 the press, Menshevik or Bolshevik, carried no reports of anything like the events in the CIR three years previously.

There is much in this chapter which explains why. Exploitation is a relative concept, and new workers unfamiliar with previous conditions would have no yardstick against which to measure the degree of labour intensification; the socialization process described in chapter 5 had no time to take effect. Moreover, interactions with the land/residence continuum were complex, localized, and particularized. Additionally, one could point to the possibility of gradual habituation to *uplotnenie* amongst established workers after 1925, but in order to explain things more fully it is necessary to turn our attention to the way changes worked their way through on the shop floor.

[100] *Golos tekstilei*, 17 November 1928.
[101] *Golos tekstilei*, 7 December 1928; 29 January 1929.
[102] *Biulleten' moskovskogo gubotdela vsesoiuznogo professional'nogo soiuza tekstil'shchikov*, 3–4 (37), March–April 1928, pp. 7–8.
[103] Cited in Sorenson, *Soviet Trade Unionism*, p. 209.

12 Shop-floor responses

In the textile industry, more than any other, there is a clear system of demarcation and a long promotional ladder ... Usually, if workers do not receive specialist training, they stay on one rung of the ladder for a long time, during which they accumulate a stock of knowledge about all the operations in their shops. When numbers are stable movement to a higher rung occurs only when somebody dies or when there are routine changes in workforce composition.

> Ia. Kvasha and F. Shofman, propagandists for seven-hour
> working in textile mills

A new institution and the new handbook

When, ten years after 1917, Nol'de pointed out that organizing technical control in production immediately raises the question – 'in whose hands should this control be?' and gave his readers the choice between directors, specialists or norm-setters,[1] he failed to mention the hands themselves – a far cry from *The State and Revolution*. Indeed, since Lenin scattered the first seeds abroad NEP had taken root only too well. Many Bolsheviks looked uneasily at this luxuriant growth; to them it seemed that the fruits of October were not being garnered by the workers. In December 1926 the fifteenth party conference, like many other assemblies at many other times, struggled to find a path through the resultant tangle of means and ends which obscured the way forward and threatened to supplant socialism. A few months previously the 'regime of economy' had been promulgated. Now Moscow tried to counter its effects. Amidst accusations that the unions were reviving the old idea of workers' control, 'temporary control commissions' were founded to help wage-earners defend themselves against factory directors stuck with the job of

[1] L. Ia. Shukhgal'ter, ed., *Vnutrizavodskii kontrol' kachestva. Sbornik statei i instruktsii* (1927), pp. 8–9.

enforcing commercial accounting. A joint instruction from the Central Council of Trades Unions and Vesenkha of February 1927 tried to draw their sting; control commissions, with three to seven members attached to each factory committee, should limit themselves to beefing up the work of production conferences.[2]

It was, in the light of past experience with central orders, a hazardous initiative. In September 1927 five mill directors expressed unease; 'confusion' arose because the commissions overlapped with production conferences. *Golos tekstilei* replied ambiguously that the exercise should be regarded as an 'experiment for drawing the workforce into the management and organization of production'. Nevertheless, a later newspaper article reported 'almost universal indifference' on the shop floor[3] – until 1928, that is. In March the union's central committee warned operatives not to use the commissions as a means of interfering with the implementation of seven-hour/ three-shift working. Better still, they should not even be established until after the transfer – it would be 'inexpedient'. Management should execute change and the commissions subsequently monitor effects. It was too late. Twenty-six factories had been chosen for a test run in 1926 and thirteen cotton mills had commissions by autumn next year, including several simultaneously earmarked for the seven-hour day. The number quickly rose to twenty. Of the original group, one was censured by the union for organizing the switch via its commission. To make matters worse the commission had been encouraged by the local union branch.[4]

Beyond this no further evidence of their activities relating to the switch to seven-hour/three-shift working has been found, but temporary control commissions should be added to the list of mill-level institutions discussed elsewhere. Together with factory committees and shop delegate meetings they constituted an unholy trinity which could easily fuse to undo policy or give decisions an unintended twist,

---

[2] M. Dewar, *Labour Policy in the USSR 1917–28* (1956), pp. 127–8; N. B. Lebedev, O. I. Shkaratan, *Ocherki istorii sotsialisticheskogo sorevnovaniia* (1966), pp. 72–3; I. P. Ostapenko, *Uchastie rabochego klassa SSSR v upravlenii proizvodstvom: proizvodstvennye sovershchaniia v promyshlennosti v 1921–1932gg* (1964), p. 45; Z. K. Zvezdin, 'Periodicheskaia pechat' kak istochnik po istorii trudovogo pod"ema rabochego klassa SSSR 1926–1929gg (obzor materialov)', *Problemy istochnikovedeniia*, 8, 1959, p. 17.

[3] *Golos tekstilei*, 27 September 1927; 15 October 1927.

[4] *Golos tekstilei*, 15 October 1927; *Informatsionnaia svodka TsK vsesoiznogo profsoiuza tekstil'shchikov*, 20(32), 10 November 1927, p. 29; 24(36), 10 March 1928, p. 5 (hereafter *IS TsK VPST*); Ostapenko, *Uchastie rabochego klassa*, p. 49; L.S. Rogachevskaia, *Iz istorii rabochego klassa SSSR v pervye gody industrializatsii (1926–1927gg)* (1959), pp. 121–2.

to say nothing of fractious party members or independently minded local union branches.

To add to the industry's problems chance dictated that a new handbook should be published simultaneously with the switch to seven-hour/three-shift working,[5] replacing the 1922 handbook which 'gave no guidance' on multi-machine working and *uplotnenie*, commented Leningrad's local union paper, unaccountably ignoring the 1925 manual.[6] The union's central committee had been mulling over the possibility of changing the handbook ever since March 1927,[7] long before it had any hint of the Jubilee Manifesto. More serious discussions took place in the second week of December. Shortly before the union had announced that the principle of 'no detriment' would apply,[8] but the revamped system, designed to raise pay across the board, push workers up the tariff scale, reduce differentials and take account of labour intensification, was to be financed by lowering the wages of 'excessive earning' workers as well as by the allocation of more funds.[9] Moreover, reflecting renewed concerns in the party and the Central Council over inequalities in Soviet industry at large, wage standardization would be imposed. Henceforth all trusts would pay the same rate for scale point one. The union added that deviation from this rule would be permitted 'only in exceptional cases and with the agreement of the central committee'.[10] Perhaps this was special pleading, but more likely the union was covering itself against the likelihood of local initiatives.

By some mischance the message never seems to have reached the commission overseeing the implementation of seven-hour/three-shift working, which on January 7 1928 merely enunciated the formula that 'the question of pay will be decided by central committee of the union and *Glavtekstil'* in the form of collective agreements'. Next day the union proposed that night workers should receive some kind of bonus, and took a similar line three weeks later at its central committee plenum; there would be supplements to collective agreements – restructuring on the basis of the new handbook was now delayed until February.[11] On the 16th of that month the Moscow branch reported that restructuring was complete in most factories. There was no

[5] *Trud*, 31 October 1928.   [6] *Leningradskii tekstil'*, 4, 1928, p. 5.
[7] *Golos tekstilei*, 29 October 1927.
[8] *Golos tekstilei*, 6 December 1927; *IS TsK VPST*, 21(33), 20 December 1927, p. 20.
[9] Ia. Kvasha, F. Shofman, *Semichasovoi rabochii den' v tekstil'noi promyshlennosti* (1930), pp. 8, 112–13; *Leningradskii tekstil'*, 4, 1928, p. 5.
[10] *IS TsK VPST*, 21(33), 20 December 1927, p. 30.
[11] *Golos tekstilei*, 7 January 1928; 8 January 1928; 29 January 1928.

mention of the differential impact between eight- and seven-hour mills, and a further seven months passed before all factories were drawn into restructuring. Two days before the Moscow branch announcement a long article gave details on changes in major cotton districts; average rises for scale point one of 72 per cent in Leningrad, 57 per cent in the three national trusts, 55 per cent in Tver', 50 per cent in Vladimir and 16 per cent in Ivanovo. This signalled equalization between regions, insisted the writer, and marked a diminution of the importance of piece rates.[12]

These reports should not be taken too seriously. Restructuring 'caused considerable difficulties' commented Kvasha and Shofman.[13] On New Year's Day *Golos tekstilei* gave details of collective agreements just signed with various trusts, but Iaroslavl's union branch was still quarrelling with executives five days later, and the day after this the union's bureaucrats in Moscow urged provincial officials to conclude negotiations as soon as possible. Iaroslavl' signed on the 10th, along with the Moscow and Leningrad branches. Like all others since January 1, however, this report made no mention at all of seven-hour working in any negotiations or agreements. Only the Abel'man's negotiators seem to have tackled these urgent issues but, as of January 7, were still arguing about shift distribution, night and Saturday working, *uplotnenie*, and norms and piece rates.[14] Disputes continued. Ivanovo State Textile Trust and the local economic council could not reach agreement with the union until late February; workers in Vladimir guberniya failed to understand why new tariffs had been introduced at all, and girls put to three or four instead of one or two carding machines in Krasnyi Perekop complained to the press – 'Work began on 12 July, but we still don't know what our wages will be.'[15]

At the eighth union congress in April Mel'nichanskii admitted that there had been much talk about the 'deficiencies of the new handbook ... the central committee has received many letters about short-comings'. Giving no examples and offering no solutions, auditors had to be content with his observation that there were bound to be mistakes and disadvantages for some groups of workers. Two delegates were more forthcoming. Pastukhov, from Leningrad, complained of wage reductions amongst established workers and wage variations between mills. The Iuzhskaia's Ploskareva gave an example

12 *Golos tekstilei*, 14 February 1928; 16 February 1928; 22 September 1928.
13 Kvasha, Shofman, *Semichasovoi rabochii den'*, p. 8.
14 *Golos tekstilei*, 1 January 1928; 5 January 1928; 6 January 1928; 7 January 1928; 11 January 1928.
15 *Golos tekstilei*, 9 February 1928; 20 July 1928; *Rabochii krai*, 21 February 1928.

of how things worked to the detriment of particular shops. The old handbook stipulated that ring-frame operatives spinning low counts were entitled to more help; 'when we worked four banks on twenty count we had assistants, now we work three banks without assistants – the pay's the same, the work's more difficult'.[16] Those in the guberniya who inquired anxiously about the provision of auxiliary workers in their general meetings four months previously obviously sensed which way the wind was blowing.[17] Later on further breaches of the central committee's standardization rule began to show through; a Shuia delegate to a central committee plenum held in July found the new handbook 'unreal' – operatives received various wages in various rooms 'regardless of the kind of work being done'.[18]

Implementation on the shop floor

At first glance the global evidence on wages must have looked encouraging to the centre. Between December 1927 and September 1928, 13,000 workers were sampled, all of whom were at the frame in January, and although the highly paid minority's wages had indeed been reduced somewhat, the overall effect of recent changes was to increase pay.[19] But Shuia was not the only district where practice confounded policy: disparate factors, some deeply embedded in shop-floor culture, others flickering over the mill for no more than a few months, combined to produce a pattern which reinforced wage differentials and, in the end, distorted the entire seven-hour experiment.

The first real distortion arose out of one of the new factors, night work. Shmidt's compromise of early January[20] was not welcomed by all operatives; some feared that if excluded groups remained on day shifts they would be condemned to permanent nights. Nor was it popular with all exempted categories. Fifty-five recently promoted trainees threatened to return to Sereda's factory school if they were barred from night working,[21] but the main opposition came from another direction. On January 24 Ivanovo's union branch reported difficulties in persuading women to obey the Labour Code. Three days later Mel'nichanskii told pregnant women that they should avoid the

[16] *Golos tekstilei*, 5 April 1928; 6 April 1928; 7 April 1928.   [17] See pp. 209–10.
[18] *Golos tekstilei*, 21 July 1928.
[19] Kvasha, Shofman, *Semichasovoi rabochii den'*, pp. 94–5, 113–14.   [20] See p. 215.
[21] Kvasha, Shofman, *Semichasovoi rabochii den'*, pp. 140–1; *Golos tekstilei*, 9 February 1928.

third shift.[22] Management had not gone the right way about implementing *uplotnenie*, he remarked in his opening speech to the eighth union congress, and women should think first of their children and their own health. Warming to the theme at the end of the congress he declared that the central committee was completely opposed to night work for women more than five months pregnant and mothers with infants less than seven months old.[23]

These blandishments were ignored. Pregnant and nursing women in Rodniki voted overwhelmingly against exclusive day working; the local union branch concurred. By June exempted women were back at the frame in four three-shift mills and labour inspectors sanctioned night work in two of these enterprises.[24] Operatives in one of them and in the Naro-Fominsk tried to conceal their pregnancies, and some may have taken more extreme measures: on February 7 *Golos tekstilei* carried an extended review informing its readers of the law, and cautioned women against self-abortion or back-street practitioners.[25] Eight months later Shmidt began to reconsider. Night work in textile mills was unsuitable for women, but reform must be carried out 'so that the introduction of the third shift does not worsen' their position.[26] The war of words continued into the new year; 'Only now', reported the women's section of the party in May 1929, 'have directors in Ivanovo, Moscow, Tver', Iaroslavl' and Vladimir started to ban women from night work.'[27]

Women's discontents should be generalized and put in the context of a whole range of factors; family ties, machine idiosyncrasy, pay systems, traditional patterns of work, social relations at the frame and the disturbing impact of the new workforce. 'They are afraid of losing their own machines', noted one writer in the journal of the women's section, 'or their workmates on their shift, or they consider that it would be more convenient to work nights.'[28] Two others acknowledged that women disliked being separated from their husbands who remained on the old shift, feared that their wages would fall if they were moved to unfamiliar machines and generally exhibited 'a feeling of shift solidarity'. *Golos tekstilei* reported the same sentiments in Moscow guberniya a year later.[29] One operative from the Vladimir guberniya, perhaps a weaver, spoke for herself in August 1928:

[22] *Golos tekstilei*, 24 January 1928; 27 January 1928.
[23] *Golos tekstilei*, 5 April 1928; 7 April 1928.
[24] *Golos tekstilei*, 8 June 1928; S. M. Schwarz, *Labor in the Soviet Union* (1953), p. 264.
[25] *Golos tekstilei*, 7 February 1928; 15 May 1928.   [26] *Trud*, 31 October 1928.
[27] *Kommunistka*, 10, May 1929, p. 31.
[28] *Kommunistka*, 3, March 1928, p. 29.   [29] *Golos tekstilei*, 15 January 1929.

For thirty years I've worked in this mill and I've never had a single complaint to make. Last year I switched from two to three frames and everything was fine. When we went over to the seven-hour day they gave me four frames, but instead of three good ones I had four bad ones. I couldn't cope, so they put me on stand-by. Instead of the sixty I used to earn I now get only thirty roubles a month. I thought I'd stay on stand-by for a month or so, but that was seven months ago. Every day I ask for work, and every time I ask they don't give me any.[30]

She was one of the unlucky ones. On January 12 the Seredskaia's director reported to the factory committee that workers were, to some extent, choosing their own shifts and partners. In fact throughout Ivanovo guberniya experienced women did not want to work with new recruits:[31] 'the insufficiently skilled nature of the new workforce' in the province, wrote two local specialists,

> caused problems over shift placings. Because wages are based on machine output and individual pay is not calculated separately but divided between the shift, operatives were given the right to select their own co-workers. Sometimes misunderstandings arose between shifts. Workers demanded that this or that operative who did not agree or could not work with this loom or that frame . . . should be removed by the administration. There were complaints from old workers that the new workforce, whose productivity was lower than theirs and whose waste rates were higher, lowered their output and pay.[32]

The 'right' to choose is significant. So peremptory were the centre's orders that administrators probably had little option but to clinch hurried deals on the shop floor. It was imperative to get the shifts moving. The Labour Code could wait. But hopes of labour intensification were under threat from the start: 'by introducing *uplotnenie* amongst certain operatives (older workers, recent arrivals in the mills, workers connected with the land)', observed the two specialists mentioned above, 'there arose opposition to these measures (especially in the Seredskaia) because of the dread of not being able to cope and the disinclination to change old habits and conditions'.[33] More will be said about the Seredskaia later. For the moment let us bear in mind that at first the mill's shifts worked independently – the same machines sometimes had four operatives on one shift and two or three on the others.[34]

[30] *Izvestiia*, 17 August 1928.
[31] I. S. Belinskii, A. I. Kucherov, *Tri mesiatsa raboty semichasovykh fabrik. (Opyt perevoda i raboty semichasovykh fabrik v ivanovo-voznesenskoi gubernii)* (1928), pp. 26–7.
[32] *Ibid.*, pp. 19–20.   [33] *Ibid.*, p. 12.   [34] *Ibid.*, p. 20.

Absenteeism amongst new entrants soared alarmingly. In the Ramenskaia, for instance, absences recorded 'for no good reason' were 212 per cent higher for new workers than for established operatives in mid-summer 1928; sickness rates exhibited the same tendency.[35] Much of this probably had to do with the predilection for field work amongst 'kulak-' and 'village-end' operatives fresh from the countryside: a few months earlier Ivanovo's trades council had already started to criticize 'backward' workers drawn from the villages who 'pay great attention to the needs of their farms but have little time for the needs and interests of the mill'. New operatives took time off to work in their fields, avowed Mel'nichanskii in July,[36] and eight months later no less a body than the party's central committee pointed out that one source of the current 'backward mood' infecting textile workers was the influx of landed operatives into seven-hour/three-shift mills.[37]

For the reason mentioned above – fear of having to work alongside the untutored – conflict between workers seems to have been endemic. Established operatives sometimes resorted to go-slows to draw managers' attention to their discontents,[38] and when a worker threatened with the sack in Vladimir guberniya mill produced a letter from his local soviet showing him to be a 'pure proletarian' with no land and two unemployed family members, his shop felt no compunction in letting everyone know that he lived with his father, a handicraft worker, on the family farm. 'We often meet with this kind of document', was the laconic remark of the factory committee before it arranged for his dismissal.[39] Even when they were accepted by their compatriots it was bad tactics for a shop's operatives to advertise their presence: 'when disputes arise involving all the workers in a shop there is usually a general conversation about who will go as their representative to the factory committee or management. Invariably they choose a worker having no connection whatsoever with the peasant economy.'[40]

Additionally, new recruits severely taxed training capacity. In an effort to absorb the thousands now flooding in, the president of Ivanovo State Textile Trust promised substantial overtime pay for workers who agreed to take on apprentices.[41] Nevertheless, training

[35] Tekstil'nye novosti, 7, July 1929, pp. 376–7.
[36] Trud, 21 July 1928; Trud i proizvodstvo, 1, January 1928, p. 6.
[37] Golos tekstilei, 31 March 1929.
[38] Bol'shevik, 8, 30 April 1928, p. 43; Sputnik agitatora, 6, March 1928, p. 26.
[39] Cited in N. Semenov, Litso fabrichnykh rabochikh prozhivaiushchikh v derevniakh, i politrosvetrabota sredi nikh. Po materialam obsledovaniia rabochikh tekstil'noi promyshlennosti tsentral'no-promyshlennoi oblasti (1929), p. 59.
[40] Ibid., p. 45.   [41] Rabochii krai, 19 January 1928.

schedules had to be reduced; subsequently factory schools in Rodniki's mills allowed two weeks for doffers, one month for carders, two
months for flyer-frame operatives and three to three-and-a-half
months for weavers. Even these brief periods were considered generous for the children of established workers. The results were predictable: 'it will be easily understood that such rapid training, such a
rapid passage through the schools, meant that insufficiently trained
workers came onto the shop floor. Output fell, waste rates rose, and
experienced workers criticized the poorly trained.'[42] So alarmed were
some Vladimir weavers that they sent a delegation to the spinning mill
supplying their thread, Leningrad's Ravenstvo. They held that quality
was better in 1925 even though raw cotton was then of a lower
standard, 'but in 1925 old qualified hands were working, and although
they worked in the old ways, they knew what they were doing'.[43]

The shop floor absorbs change

There had been some attempts at *uplotnenie* following the
compromise of 1925 and before the publication of the Jubilee
Manifesto. Since 1926 trusts had been trying to reorganize the labour
process in preparatory departments. 'It is evident', as one investigation into work on flyer-frames pointed out, 'that those operations
requiring the highest skills take up only a small proportion of the
working day (about 10 per cent). For the rest of the time the skilled
worker is occupied directing the work of the less skilled, who are paid
according to the skilled worker's tariff.'[44] And there were some
successes. Numbers in work teams operating flyer-frames declined as
brigades, each with their own hierarchy, took over the jobs of greasing
and cleaning down the machine. The process continued into 1928,
particularly in transferred mills, and was extended to include carriers
and bobbin stackers.[45] As these operatives once belonged to work
teams they suffered a singular disadvantage. Wages might not fall,
they were still paid a percentage of the frame's output,[46] but the
chance of advancement narrowed because brigade members were

42 Belinskii, Kucherov, *Tri mesiatsa raboty*, p. 11.
43 S. Zhukovskii et al., *Pervaia udarnaia* (1931), p. 18.
44 *Tekstil'nye novosti*, 2–3, February–March 1927, p. 93.
45 See *Biulleten' ivanovo-voznesenskogo gosudarstvennogo tekstil'nogo tresta*, 5/38, March
1928, p. 21 (hereafter BI-VGTT); *Bol'shevik*, 8, 30 April 1928, p. 44; *Izvestiia tekstil'noi
promyshlennosti i torgovli*, 3, March 1928, p. 21 (hereafter ITPT); *Predpriiatie*, 7, July
1928, p. 18; *Tekstil'nye novosti*, 4, April 1927, p. 148; 6–7, June–July 1927, pp. 271–2.
46 *Tarifno-spravochnik rabochikh khlopchato-bumazhnogo proizvodstva* (1928), pp. 24–7 (hereafter *1928 spravochnik*).

shut out from the traditional world of training; no longer could they pick up the tricks of the trade from spinners.

Their opportunity came in January 1928. Directors, temporary control commissions or factory committees – whoever made the decisions – had to find competent operatives to man the third shift, and it would be natural for them to prefer workers from these auxiliary groups instead of newcomers to the factory, as in fact they did. Contemporaries noticed rapid advancement up the trade ladder for existing *komplekt* members and the consequent promotion to the frame of auxiliary or stand-by operatives. Moreover, there was an under-current pulling against the brigade system; in the Seredskaia at least, flyer-frame spinners moving from one to two or more sides began to take on assistants.[47] Into the vacancies left by promoted auxiliaries or stand-by operatives stepped raw recruits. One survey of October 1929, admittedly rather late for our purposes, found that 60.6 per cent of a sample of 3,225 stand-by flyer-frame spinners were new entrants, which could only mean that existing stand-by workers had already been promoted.[48] There is a better source based on a close examination of eight CIR mills transferred early in 1928. From this it appears that the wages of all flyer-frame spinners rose in the succeeding nine months, but that, as was to be expected, experienced hands – those in their shops and at their frames before December 1927 – were paid, on average, better than new recruits. Moreover, established workers who remained on one or two spindle banks ran a greater risk of missing out on pay rises than did those workers who opted for *uplotnenie*.[49] Most likely this was because they would be last in line for the newly recruited auxiliary helpers, the fetchers and carriers who kept the spinner supplied with materials and bobbins and thus kept up the piece rate.

The same picture emerges in ring-frame halls. As in preparatory departments the *komplekt* had been under scrutiny for some time. Cleaning brigades – four women to a team, predictably with a male supervisor – cut across established work teams. Fetchers and carriers were similarly reorganized.[50] There is also good evidence to suggest that ring-frame spinners had incentive enough to opt for multi-machine working – pay differentials in nine large Ivanovo mills for

[47] Belinskii, Kucherov, *Tri mesiatsa raboty*, table 3 p. 16; Kvasha, Shofman, *Semichasovoi rabochii den'*, pp. 16–17.
[48] *ITPT*, 3, March 1930, p. 9.
[49] Kvasha, Shofman, *Semichasovoi rabochii den'*, pp. 94–6, 102; *Statistika truda*, 2–3, February–March 1929, p. 7.
[50] *Tekstil'nye novosti*, 2–3, February–March 1927, p. 93; 4, April 1927, p. 150.

1927/28 were considerable[51] – and that the third shift resulted in rapid promotion for existing auxiliary workers. In eight Moscow guberniya mills, for example, only half of all new doffers and one-quarter of all new stand-by spinners came from amongst new arrivals. In a further four mills 45.6 per cent of new spinners on one spindle bank, 39.5 per cent on two, 69.8 per cent on three and 50.1 per cent on four were promotees from auxiliary trades or stand-by operatives. Most of the rest on two, three and four banks were established spinners accepting *uplotnenie*.[52]

But ring-frames were still a nightmare for rationalizers. In the country at large all spinners appear to have worked one, two, three or four spindle banks: 6.7, 46.4, 42.9 and 4.0 per cent respectively in a syndicate sample of 1,803 of December 1927.[53] However, projected reorganizations would, if anything, complicate matters even more. Some hoped that depending on circumstances, ten spinners might work ten groups of three 600-spindle banks without assistants, or two banks of 600 spindles might be served by one spinner, six shared doffers and two stand-by operatives. On the other hand four 800-spindle banks might have eight spinners, six doffers and two on stand-by. Alternatively eight banks totalling 1,600 spindles might be worked by four spinners, six doffers, two creelers and two stand-by operatives.[54] Although after 1928 assistants received three-quarters of their spinner's pay, and tariff points were allocated to any existing greasing brigades, spindle greasers, doffing controllers, doffing brigades, doffing brigade controllers or fetching and carrying teams, much depended on count and cotton type. It is no wonder that the spinner's wage scale was highly fragmented, and that charts in the 1928 union handbook displayed thirty-eight different ways of arriving at any one of the scale points three to thirteen where spinners might eventually come to rest.[55]

'Work in the spinning halls is not going well', reported Ivanovo State Textile Trust in August,

> much of this, of course, is due to the transfer to three-shift working and the influx of many poorly-trained operatives, but (1) there has been no noticeable improvement in the performance of skilled workers, and (2) the fall in ouput ... cannot be blamed on poor

[51] *Srednie godovye zarabotki rabochikh i sluzhashchikh po fabrikam i zavodam ivanovo-voznesenskoi gubernii za vremia s 1/V–1927g po 30/IV–1928g. (K kampanii sel.-khoz. naloga 1928–29g)* (1928), pp. 2–3.

[52] Kvasha, Shofman, *Semichasovoi rabochii den'*, pp. 19, 33, 37.   [53] *Ibid.*, p. 29.

[54] *Tekstil'nye novosti*, 2–3, February–March 1927, p. 93.

[55] *1928 spravochnik*, pp. 18–24, 27–30, 32–4.

quality cotton as it is no worse than for several months back. It is necessary to seek out the reasons for falling productivity and deteriorating labour discipline. Directors and factory committees must pay serious attention to this. It must be remembered that the summer was excellent for spinning; the weather was mild and humid.[56]

The first reason was probably the most important one. Five of the trust's largest mills could not find enough workers for their fine-spinning halls, and in general, throughout the CIR, poor skills led to sharp increases in spindle stoppages in three-shift mills because there were no experienced hands on the bureau lists. Operatives in Drezna and Sepukhov complained about their doffers, and in Tver' there were bottle-necks because of a paucity of auxiliary workers. 153 of the Seredskaia's ring-frame spinners met and resolved to demand that the administration should arrange for machine cleaning every five instead of every six or seven days because of poor-quality assistance, and in one Moscow guberniya mill they wanted their collective agreement re-negotiated over this issue.[57] 'When experienced doffers, upon whom the work of the ring-frame spinner depends, were promoted to the status of spinner', wrote one observer, 'new unskilled workers took their place.' The mills 'suffered conditions of flux', he continued.[58]

It is possible to be a little more specific. As in preparatory departments wages rose overall and differentially, but the pattern was rather more complex. Those remaining on one bank or opting for four banks did noticeably better than spinners who stayed with a pair or three banks.[59] What seems to have been happening is that the latter two groups suffered disproportionately from the influx of new recruits. Spinners on one bank did not need much help, and those opting for *uplotnenie* on four banks would be unfortunate indeed if poor-quality assistance cancelled out all their wage increases. But the rest probably lost auxiliaries. And when auxiliaries left to man the extra shift the inexperienced took their places and so wages started to vary. Machine idiosyncrasy may well have added to their problems. Not all workers remaining on two or three banks would necessarily stay with the same frames; in many instances multi-machine working for some probably

[56] *BI–VGTT*, 10/43, August 1928, p. 3.
[57] Belinskii, Kucherov, *Tri mesiatsa raboty*, pp. 30, 67; *BI-VGTT*, 3/36, January 1928, p. 3; *Golos tekstilei*, 20 July 1928; Kvasha, Shofman, *Semichasovoi rabochii den'*, p. 19; *Puti industrializatsii*, 10, 1928, p. 53; *Sputnik agitatora*, 6, March 1928, p. 25.
[58] *Ekonomicheskoe obozrenie*, 8, August 1928, pp. 48–9.
[59] Kvasha, Shofman, *Semichasovoi rabochii den'*, pp. 94–5; *Statistika truda*, 2–3, February–March 1929, pp. 96, 102.

resulted in re-allocation for others, hence the oft-expressed fear of being moved – 'they know only their own machines', commented someone from the Naro-Fominsk.[60]

That Soviet rationalizers did not share the enthusiasm for group wage calculation in spinning halls and weaving sheds noticed by Odell before the Revolution has already been suggested,[61] and the point was restated once more with reference to the last years of NEP: 'strange as it may seem', mused Kvasha and Shofman, 'there is no method of calculating the individual output of ring-frame spinners and weavers. The necessary devices are absent from the frames and the looms, [and so] calculations take place . . . not on the basis of the work of each shift member, but of all shift members on a given set of machines.' Individual pay should therefore be introduced in shops where currently wages were averaged across work groups, not least because the influx of new operatives had 'created more difficulties' on three shifts than was the case previously.[62]

Early in spring 1927 *Golos tekstilei* examined the two systems and came down heavily in favour of individual pay. Three factories were mentioned: workers in one had the choice and many refused to give up collective payment; 30 per cent in another mill received a wage commensurate with their own output, as did all weavers in Moscow's Danilovskaia. In August 1928 the syndicate announced that all weaving sheds would be switched to individual pay within two weeks and that all spinning rooms would follow suit soon afterwards. Two mills in Moscow guberniya responded quickly,[63] but when the Drezna's factory committee and director put these proposals to weavers and overlookers they 'got a very frosty reception'. Many experienced weavers were doubtful, and 'some completely opposed' to change. Opposition eventually crumbled in the face of higher wages, perhaps because by then the mill's social composition had altered so drastically that there was little point in defending work practices designed for a relatively experienced and stable labour force.[64] New operatives were left behind: 'poor workers came out against individual accounting, backward workers, obliged by this system to equal the average'. Coincidentally another Moscow guberniya mill

---

[60] *Golos tekstilei*, 11 May 1928.   [61] See pp. 169–70.
[62] Kvasha, Shofman, *Semichasovoi rabochii den'*, pp. 41–2, 74.
[63] *Golos tekstilei*, 10 March 1927; 2 August 1928; 12 August 1928.
[64] Kvasha, Shofman, *Semichasovoi rabochii den'*, pp. 76–7. *Golos tekstilei*, 11 November 1928, carried a rash of weavers' letters in favour of individual calculation for just this reason – new, unskilled and inexperienced workers pulled down the wages of the experienced.

reported higher wages for those on individual pay after February 1928 – here weavers had some kind of dial attached to their loom to tell them how their earnings were building up throughout the shift.[65] There is, however, no evidence that any other factories invented Pavlovian devices like this, and the few mills mentioned above do not add up to much. Most weavers stayed on the collective system and rationalizers were once more disappointed. 'A great failure of the introduction of the seven-hour/three-shift system', deplored Kvasha and Shofman, 'is that it did not result in the elimination of this incorrect method of calculating the workers' output and did not lead to the establishment of a pay system based on individual accounting'.[66] In any case the new system was sometimes troublesome. Some weavers in Leningrad took to deprecating the quality of their looms, something they never bothered to do before going over to individual wages.[67]

Nevertheless, some comfort could be taken from the spread of brigades, stripping the weaver, like the flyer- and ring-frame spinner, of auxiliaries. In 1927 Vesenkha's journal for managers thought that further *uplotnenie* would be impossible if mills failed to elaborate the division of labour at the loom.[68] Administrators in Rodniki organized brigades for checking and repair in April 1928, and in Orekhovo-Zuevo, where more than 500 weavers in the Nikol'skaia went over to four looms simultaneously with the switch to three-shift working, greasers, dusters, piecers and warp and weft carriers were all reorganized.[69] Reflecting these developments the new handbook gave details of a vast number of new trades, all on low scale points. Thus weavers too found themselves embroiled in a very complex tariff system – 110 possible ways of arriving at correct pay for those on two looms, 33 for those on three, 53 for those on four, and 46 for automatic loom tenters.[70]

Weaving sheds also demonstrate the familiar pattern of promotion. Established weavers moved up to two, three or four looms along with stand-by operatives and auxiliaries while newcomers took over jobs on single looms. Similarly wage differentials were large enough for weavers to consider *uplotnenie* favourably, and the risk of financial loss was greater for operatives who chose to remain on two or three

65 *Predpriiatie*, 10, October 1928, pp. 64–5; Kvasha, Shofman, *Semichasovoi rabochii den'*, pp. 74–5.
66 Kvasha, Shofman, *Semichasovoi rabochii den'*, p. 80.
67 *Golos tekstilei*, 12 August 1928.
68 *Predpriiatie*, 2, February 1927, p. 44.
69 Belinskii, Kucherov, *Tri mesiatsa raboty*, p. 8; *Predpriiatie*, 4, April 1928, p. 36.
70 *1928 spravochnik*, pp. 83–8.

looms.[71] And there were the same complaints about new workers and poor machinery: 'we're not afraid of working four looms', declared Vorob'eva from the Nikol'skaia's sheds, 'we're afraid of these four looms!'[72] Incompetent bureau recruits came under fire a few miles to the south,[73] and throughout the seven-hour districts 'not only in each mill, not only in each weaving shed, but even on each group of looms' where the new worked alongside the experienced, the latter's wages declined.[74] Some mills responded to these difficulties by increasing the number of auxiliary workers, others did the opposite: in the Abel'man and Derbenev the rate of spoiled work rose by 35 and 46 per cent respectively in the first four months of 1928, consequently the trust was anxious to get rid of 'unskilled ballast'. Two hundred weavers had already been sacked from these two mills within the first twenty-four hours of three-shift working.[75] But there was an extra problem. Because weaving came at the end of the production process everything depended on the quality of semi-finished goods received from fine spinning halls. Soon there were a mass of reproaches about bad spinning: 'serious deficiencies' in Iartsevo (sharp wage falls consequent upon poor thread), 'nothing whatsoever done' to improve yarn quality in Serpukhov (a marked increase in loom stoppages), not enough semi-finished goods coming through to weavers (Shuia), and in the Nikol'skaia concern over raw material quality and spinning off the count[76] – 'give us good warp and weft', added Vorob'eva, 'and then we'll work on four looms.'[77]

All this evidence refers to Lancashire looms, but a minority of weavers operated automatic looms. Though they were very scarce in Russia by 1928 a few were scattered across the CIR.[78] They were much favoured by NOT enthusiasts and rationalizers, especially in view of the imperatives of NEP: 'the lack of a skilled labour force, insufficient housing and the necessity of lowering the cost of production puts the question of their adoption into first place and demands serious consideration', insisted the syndicate[79] – the point being that oper-

---

[71] Kvasha, Shofman, *Semichasovoi rabochii den'*, pp. 18–19, 31–2, 35–6, 40, 94–6, 102; *Srednie godovye zarabotki*, pp. 10–11; *Statistika truda*, 2–3, February–March 1929, p. 7.

[72] *Kommunistka*, 4, April 1928, p. 47.   [73] *Golos tekstilei*, 3 February 1928.

[74] Kvasha, Shofman, *Semichasovoi rabochii den'*, pp. 104–5.

[75] *BI-VGTT*, 3/36, January 1928, p. 4; *Golos tekstilei*, 10 May 1928.

[76] A. Dunaev, Iu. Goriachev, *Iartsevskii khlopchato-bumazhnyi kombinat. (Kratkii istoricheskii otchet)* (1963), p. 68; *Predpriiatie*, 4, April 1928, pp. 35–6; *Sputnik agitatora*, 6, March 1928, p. 25.

[77] *Kommunistka*, 4, April 1928, p. 47.

[78] Belinskii, Kucherov, *Tri mesiatsa raboty*, pp. 7, 53; *Golos tekstilei*, 26 February 1926; *ITPT*, 3, 23 January 1926; *Rabochii krai*, 29 June 1927. See also above pp. 84.

[79] *ITPT*, 3, 23 January 1926, p. 20.

atives generally worked around ten or twelve looms each. There is a nice irony here. Despite the fact that the whole purpose of the machine was to de-skill weaving to the uttermost – all the operative had to do was to replenish a magazine with cops every so often – Ivanovo's union branch ruled in 1927 that only the highly-skilled with not less than five years' experience could work on them. One factory anticipated these local regulations by a year; when 150 frames were purchased from abroad and installed in the mill someone opened a list for prospective operatives. Those selected found themselves working alongside over-lookers who, it had been decided, should operate the machines in order to familiarize themselves with all their technical quirks. Within sixteen months workers rediscovered an old *via media* – promotion from Lancashire looms now involved *magarych*.[80] It is fairly easy to see what was happening. Given the industry's conversion to piece rates after April 1924, working on automatic looms practically guaranteed high wages,[81] and competition for places necessitated selection, which in turn favoured the well-connected and experienced. Social factors were conjuring an ambience of skill around a machine designed for the exploitation of illiterate children. This may have led to attempts to defend conditions and restrict entry to the new 'trade' early in 1928: we do not know why, but for some reason 576 automatic looms in Rodniki stayed on the eight-hour-two-shift system four months longer than the rest of the mill.[82] It is hard to believe that no candidates could be found inside the power-loom sheds, and even more difficult to imagine that management would not want to exploit these machines to the limit.

Intricate changes affected that other eccentric group, the selfactor *komplekt*. A few months before the Jubilee Manifesto the journal of the engineers' section of the union carried an article recommending rationalization; two cleaning teams with eight or nine members, each with a leader, workers and trainees, for every three or four pairs, depending on carriage stretch and cotton count. But nothing was said about spinners, piecers, doffers or creelers *per se*; there was no attempt to discuss the *komplekt* as an institution.[83] These proposals elicited almost no response. It is true that there were alterations in the Seredskaia (discussed below), that in January 1928 administrators in Rodniki succeeded in allocating one duster to every three pairs – a pale

[80] *Golos tekstilei*, 26 February 1926; *Rabochii krai*, 7 January 1927; 29 June 1927.
[81] *Srednie godovye zarabotki*, pp. 10–11.
[82] Belinskii, Kucherov, *Tri mesiatsa raboty*, pp. 7, 53.
[83] *Tekstil'nye novosti*, 4, April 1927, p. 149.

shadow of the brigade – and that in a further mill one spinner and three piecers gave way to one 'adjuster' and two piecers,[84] but elsewhere there was silence. Simultaneously another engineer tried to get to grips with the *komplekt* but could only suggest lopping off creelers and doffers at vectors where warp, weft, count and carriage stretch coincided to make the exercise technically feasible.[85] That the *komplekt* was still flourishing is evident from the relevant sections of the new handbook: first, second and third piecers received 80, 75 and 70 per cent respectively of the spinner's wage, first and second creelers 65 and 60 per cent. Ropers and other fetchers and carriers were paid on a different and lower scale. Spinners received 4 per cent less for working up weft, 4 per cent more for high counts and 10 per cent more for dye-cloths. Their wage scales ran from points thirteen to sixteen, overlapping those for mechanics, foreman and overlookers. Moreover, their control at the frame found its institutional expression in a far more detailed form than the ones obtaining in the 1922 and 1925 handbooks: now a spinner's tariff allocation depended largely on whether or not his work team contracted or expanded in time with count and frame stretch: spinners could choose between less pay and more assitants or more pay and fewer assistants.[86]

Taken together with the influx of new workers into the mills these changes eventually conspired to reduce spinners' pay. Measured against earnings in summer 1927, by August 1928 spinners' wages fell by an average of just over 17 per cent in four sampled mills, although once more established workers did better than new entrants.[87] Selfactor rooms do not appear to have employed stand-by operatives – given the presence of experienced piecers there was no need – so as new work teams were organized for the extra shift they were the constituency from which new spinners were drawn.[88] Similarly doffers could move up to become piecers, and raw recruits find a place on the lowest rung of the trade ladder as doffers. Again, wage differentials were a powerful argument for doffers and piecers contemplating promotion.[89] If this interpretation is correct, it helps to explain why spinners' wages were falling. Established spinners had to take on new

[84] Belinskii, Kucherov, *Tri mesiatsa raboty*, p. 14; *Golos tekstilei*, 3 February 1928.

[85] *ITPT*, 1, January 1928, pp. 44–5.

[86] *1928 spravochnik*, pp. 34–7; *Tarif tekstil'shchikov* (1922), p. 47.

[87] Kvasha, Shofman, *Semichasovoi rabochii den'*, pp. 94–6, 102; *Statistika truda*, 2–3, February–March 1929, pp. 7–9; *Tekstil'nye novosti*, 11, November 1928, p. 527.

[88] No mention of them in Kvasha, Shofman, *Semichasovoi rabochii den'*, a very detailed source. In eight Moscow guberniya mills only 1.2 per cent of new selfactor spinners came from outside the factory: *ibid.*, p. 18.

[89] *Srednie godovye zarabotki*, pp. 4–7.

piecers and – more unsettlingly – raw doffers who slowed down the work process. As a consequence they may have been asking for more doffers to try to lighten the workload, if so they could well slip a rung on the wage scale. Doffers, however, enjoyed substantial pay rises, most probably a combined result of the new policy of levelling up and their likely promotion to senior doffer. But for work teams which were entirely new, wage falls for spinners and piecers were greater and wage rises for doffers smaller; here inexperience affected the whole *komplekt* and not just its lower echelons.[90]

From the beginning Ivanovo State Textile Trust worried about its selfactor halls: 'what is particularly striking', reported the trust in January 1928, referring to mule rooms in the Seredskaia and two other mills, 'is the great number of interruptions arising from systematic stoppages of the main driving belts, indicative of their poor quality . . . It is to be hoped that such stoppages will cease, and that no pay will be allowed for them in forthcoming collective agreements'.[91]

Perhaps this uncompromising statement helped to fan the flames smouldering in the Seredskaia. On January 14 someone wrote to *Rabochii krai* criticizing shop solidarity. Since so few skilled workers were available at the local labour exchange the most simple method of increasing output in selfactor rooms would be to hive off operatives from existing work groups and form new ones. Nothing, however, was ever done, and 'don't ask the foremen about this, they won't say a word'. Three days later mule spinners went into conference to talk about auxiliary workers because management wanted to form brigades. Discussions did not go well. Next day the selfactor rooms stopped work and held impromptu meetings. A compromise emerged, brigades were formed for the lowest trades only, the fetchers and carriers outside the *komplekt*. Encouraged perhaps by the reforming mood, tensions within the *komplekt* began to surface. Piecers complained that although they could do the work, spinners always controlled backing-off and winding-on, and they were reluctant to pass on their experience – they had 'a traditional view of their skills'.[92] After a long pause discontents exploded on the day work resumed after the summer holidays. At two o'clock in the afternoon on August 16, in response to a pre-arranged signal, all selfactor spinners shut down their frames and walked out of the mill. They saw 'only one side' of the

90 Kvasha, Shofman, *Semichasovoi rabochii den'*, pp. 94–6, 102; *Statistika truda*, 2–3, February–March 1929, pp. 7–9.
91 *BI-VGTT*, 4/37, February 1928, p. 3.
92 Belinskii, Kucherov, *Tri mesiatsa raboty*, p. 17; *Rabochii krai*, 14 January 1928; 19 January 1928; 20 January 1928; 22 January 1928.

seven-hour day, hectored *Golos tekstilei*, wages and not productivity; they made 'incorrect and dangerous' demands. In fact their wages had been falling consistently because of poor-quality cotton; on average they were earning about a rouble a day less in July than in February. A special commission waved aside these figures and blamed the strike on 'opponents of the workers' state' who agitated amongst 'backward' operatives. The commission deliberated for five days, the strike was over in two-and-a-half.[93] It found no echo in any other mill, even though selfactor spinners in nearby factories also felt the shock of falling wages.[94] Moreover, there were no reports of further strikes in the Seredskaia.

This incident brings us back to the question posed at the end of chapter 11. Why was there no upheaval analogous to that of 1925? And why was it that even those aristocrats of the cotton trade, the selfactor spinners, caved in without a struggle?

The Sereda strike and the unrest which preceded it encapsulate many of the new factors present on the shop floor. If established mule spinners felt themselves threatened, new spinners – a few months ago piecers anxious about training and promotion – might pause and reflect on recent gains as well as losses. Previously they had little chance of inheriting a pair of wheels until someone died or retired: now the seven-hour/three-shift system, by effectively expanding the number of mule pairs by a third or so, presented them with a new opportunity. And the same is true of operatives in all other shops; in initial processing rooms, preparatory departments, ring-frame halls and weaving sheds. Experienced promotees might look askance at raw recruits if they were not kin, but their new condition blunted discontents. Established workers left in the same jobs were busy keeping strangers away from their frames and out of their work-groups by trying to persuade management to juggle the shifts, and new entrants, more than ever before with some source of off-mill income, reacted to *uplotnenie* by taking time off. Interests had diversi-fied to such an extent that it is difficult to imagine any common bond anywhere in the mill strong enough to unite workers, even in a single shop. The operative from the Derbenev mill cited in the previous chapter who recalled that the seven-hour day enjoyed universal

93 *Golos tekstilei*, 8 September 1928; *Rabochii krai*, 4 September 1928.
94 In Rodniki and Shuia. Like their compatriots in these mills and including those in the Balashov and Bol'shevik, the Seredskaia's spinners also had to put up with adverse count changes: Belinskii, Kucherov, *Tri mesiatsa raboty*, tables 2, 3, pp. 15–16; *BI-VGTT*, 3/36, January 1928, p. 3; 10/43, August 1928, p. 3.

approbation, and carefully indicated that *uplotnenie* was 'a different matter' concluded thus: 'the workers are divided into two camps – those who say we've got more money and those who point out that the work's become harder'.[95]

[95] *Izvestiia*, 17 August 1928. And see above p. 218.

13 The end of rationality

> We still do not know how to work.
>
> *Pravda*, 20 May 1928, commenting on seven-hour/three-shift
> working in textile mills

Taking stock

The syndicate estimated that between December 1927 and September 1928 the number of flyer-frame spinners working one spindle bank had dropped from 71.1 to 1.3 per cent of the total and the number of weavers on two looms from 67.5 to 36.6 per cent. Workers on two spindle banks, on the other hand, now accounted for almost 30 per cent of all flyer-frame operatives as against 19 per cent previously. In weaving sheds, 35 per cent of weavers operated three looms, an increase of 6 per cent, and 25 per cent four looms, an increase of 22 per cent. By October 1928 twenty-one cotton mills employing 117,500 operatives, just under one-quarter of the national total, had been switched to the seven-hour/three-shift day.[1]

Despite these encouraging figures trust and other officials found new opportunities for self-mortification to add to their earlier disappointments. 'For a whole series of reasons', opined a booklet looking back over the first three months of seven-hour working in Ivanovo guberniya, 'the mills considered by the commission were transferred in a forced manner (in three days). This made it impossible for executives and managers to draw up plans for improving the technical state of machinery, the quality of raw materials and the skill of the workforce.'[2] Another regretted that 'the rural market dictated to the industry', and a third deplored the failure of labour intensification;

---

[1] Ia. Kvasha, F. Shofman, *Semichasovoi rabochii den' v tekstil'noi promyshlennosti* (1930), pp. 27–8; *Planovoe khoziaistvo*, 10, October 1928, p. 203.
[2] I. S. Belinskii, A. I. Kucherov, *Tri mesiatsa raboty semichasovykh fabrik. (Opyt perevoda i raboty semichasovykh fabrik v ivanovo-voznesenskoi gubernii)* (1928), p. 5.

'pay has grown *significantly* faster than labour productivity', mainly as the result of the 'mechanical growth of the number of operatives', asserted a fourth.[3] Problems were compounded by the syndicate's inability to supply good quality cotton and the manifest reluctance of mills to standardize count and cloth type.[4]

These quotations confirm the view presented in chapters 11 and 12 that the centre was unable to control the localities, and they can be taken as typical of the many expressions of dismay and recrimination voiced by central authorities throughout 1928 and early 1929.[5] The union did not fail to join in. As early as January 1928 one Moscow official talked about 'mistakes'; Mel'nichanskii lambasted incompetent managers in his opening address to the eighth union congress in April, and on 25 July readers of the Central Council's newspaper were presented with the revelation that the commission which organized the transfer late in 1927 acted 'without the agreement of the union'; lists of targeted mills had already been drawn up before there were any consultations.[6] Two months later, emboldened perhaps by the current mood of disillusionment, the union's central committee turned its attention to the future:

> economic organs wish to increase production chiefly by tightening up the working day, and particularly by introducing three-shift working in all cotton mills. The central committee is strongly against this. It considers that the three-shift system significantly worsens conditions of work. From the point of view of efficiency it has scarcely any justification; equipment will be worn out and consequently . . . will have to be replaced at considerable expense. Moreover, labour protection on night shifts is very poor. On the strength of these observations three-shift working has not, in our opinion, had the expected effect of lowering the cost of production.[7]

Accidents increased, not only because so many operatives were new to the industry, but because administrators neglected safety measures

---

3 *Ekonomicheskoe obozrenie*, 8, August 1928, pp. 51–2; Kvasha, Shofman, *Semichasovoi rabochi den'*, pp. 5–6; *Sputnik kommunista*, 12(69), 30 June 1928, p. 17 [stress in the original].
4 *Sputnik kommunista*, 12(69), 30 June 1928, p. 15; *Izvestiia tekstil'noi promyshlennosti i torgovli*, 8–9, August-September 1930, p. 110 (hereafter *ITPT*); *Predpriiatie*, 2, February 1929, pp. 15–17.
5 See for example: *ITPT*, 3, March 1929, p. 5; V. V. Isakov, Iu. N. Khalturina, *Izucheniia proizvoditel'nosti i utomliaemosti pri perekhode na tkatskikh fabrikakh s 2-kh na 3-kh stanka* (1928); *Sputnik agitatora*, 23, December 1928, pp. 61, 64; *Sputnik kommunista*, 1/2(82/83), 31 January 1929, pp. 57, 62.
6 *Golos tekstilei*, 28 January 1928; 3 April 1928; *Trud*, 25 July 1928.
7 *Trud*, 23 September 1928.

even where funds were available; they regarded labour protection as 'small change', said Mel'nichanskii.[8]

Local branches were no more immune from criticism than anyone else. 'There must not be a single shift without the union present', warned Golos tekstilei in January 1928; because many recruits came from the villages 'shop delegates and factory committees must always be at their posts'.[9] At least two Moscow guberniya mills had done nothing about all this by June, and next month the paper reprimanded Ivanovo's workers for treating factory committee elections as an excuse for drinking bouts: hardly anyone turned up to vote.[10] Temporary control commissions did not know the law, were ignorant of the Labour Code or under the influence of management, lamented the Moscow branch in July; the 3,000 complaints received from the guberniya's mills and passed on to higher bodies over the last five months or so showed that they were not doing their job in resolving conflicts.[11]

In May 1928 the party's central committee turned its gaze towards the cotton industry. After castigating bad management, poor cotton supply, inept training, the failure of the labour exchanges and the chaotic coincidence of uplotnenie, new collective agreements and the new handbook, attention focused on the union: failure to propagandize, failure to 'involve' workers, failure to co-operate with administrators. The seven-hour/three-shift system had led to a 'series of difficulties' in the factories. Henceforth the party, the union and management must make thorough preparations. There must be a commission to draw up a plan with representatives from all relevant local organizations and more attention must be given to raw material supply. Whilst the Council of Peoples' Commissars would attend to the workers' needs – housing, transport, shop opening times in the towns – each mill must take responsibility for a proper dispersal of skilled workers and foremen across shifts. Moreover, the Commissariat of Labour, the Central Council and Vesenkha must increase the number of factory schools and improve training at the frame, and in association with management raise the quality of technicians. Lastly, Vesenkha, the union, the Central Council and managers must encourage more participation by specialists, provide more money for labour protection, prepare more propaganda for the press, and 'before anything else' make clear what norms and pay scale will apply.[12]

8 Golos tekstilei, 3 April 1928.
9 Golos tekstilei, 31 January 1928. The admonition was repeated in Golos tekstilei, 26 May 1929.
10 Golos tekstilei, 8 June 1928; 14 July 1928.   11 Golos tekstilei, 3 July 1928.
12 Golos tekstilei, 20 May 1928; Pravda, 20 May 1928.

No one could object to this admirable summons, but these considered reflections were to have little influence on subsequent events. However fitfully, and however inept the implementation, since 1923–4 the regime had tried to solve the problem of supplying cotton goods to the peasantry by designing policies based on the notion of some more or less objective assessment of means and ends, some simulacrum of NOT. Disenchantment with the seven-hour/three-shift experiment, combined with the general hysteria surrounding the beginning of the First Five Year Plan, signalled a profound change in policy. It is true that late in 1929 the party made yet another hasty lunge at the cotton industry when Larin proposed reorganizing the working week yet again,[13] but now enthusiasm, with the accent on youth, was to substitute for calculation.

Enthusiasm and mobilization

The Komsomol had never been happy with the position of adolescent workers under NEP and the union never seems to have paid much attention to them. 'It is well known' asserted Ivanovo's trades council journal in 1922, 'that when workers are laid off the young are the first to go, and that this feeds the growing army of petty-bourgeois speculators'. The League and the union should work together, continued the writer, but the union regarded itself as dealing with 'adult' affairs.[14] That year the Central Council dismissed the Komsomol's demand that youngsters should be paid for eight when they worked only four or six hours, and while factory cells were welcome to agitate against prostitution, speculation, crime and drink, delegates to the Komsomol's fifth congress, held in 1923, were criticized by Trotsky and Bukharin for unauthorized attempts to improve working conditions and increase wages.[15] Two years later young textile workers in Leningrad resolved to make sure that everyone arrived and left the shop floor on time and to agitate for higher labour productivity,[16] but activists like these do not seem to have been welcome; next year adolescents in the city's Sverdlov mill criticized foremen for reserving the best machines and the best cotton

13 S. M. Schwarz, *Labor in the Soviet Union* (1953), pp. 270–1. And see below p. 257.
14 *Trud* (Ivanovo-Voznesensk), 3–4, April 1922, pp. 4–5.
15 R. T. Fisher, 'The Soviet pattern for youth as revealed in the proceedings of the Congresses of the Komsomol, 1918–1949', Ph.D., Columbia University (1955), pp. 143–6, 206.
16 S. I. Tiul'panov, ed., *Istoriia industrializatsii SSSR. Dokumenty i materialy. Zavershenie vosstanovleniia promyshlennosti i nachalo industrializatsii severo-zapadnogo raiona (1925–1928gg)* (1964), p. 303.

for older workers. There were similar reproaches from Vladimir and at the first national conference of young workers in the textile industry, convened in October 1926. Delegates protested that they were not taken seriously by management, the factory committees or workers.[17]

It was against this background that the Komsomol in Leningrad's Ravenstvo mill initiated the most important of the new enthusiasms, the 'shock brigade'. Responding to CIR weavers' complaints about poor quality thread and to a League resolution of February 1928 encouraging youngsters to rationalize output, Smirnov and Vintsberg decided to fight against absenteeism, indifference, waste and 'backward' workers. In addition they would regulate lunch breaks, edit a wall newspaper and agitate for change in general.[18] This would be done by forming semi-secret groups: 'Do you agree', each aspirant was asked, 'to take part in the work of the shock brigade?' If so, 'together with the whole group you have accepted a huge task and you must expect great difficulties'.[19]

It took some time to get the brigades organized. Not until May had enough adolescents signed up to make the experiment possible and there was immediate and widespread opposition. Managers were 'afraid of failure' and (probably more importantly) did not want to risk damaging machinery by pandering to 'children's pastimes'. Engineers reacted 'coldly'. Operatives were no less hostile: women in drawing-frame rooms 'tried to talk the brigade out of their resolve, pointing out the injustices' that would inevitably follow, ring-frame spinners warned of the resultant 'exploitation, oppression and . . . harsh labour discipline'. Only after the intervention of the local party cell – a direct 'attack' on the factory administration – did the brigaders force their way through.[20]

Their first move was made against the weakest, operatives in rooms where jobs were not regarded as particularly skilled and where workers had less control over their machines; on July 16 forty-nine brigaders started work in preparatory departments and ring-frame halls, sharing out between eight and sixteen frames to each brigade.[21] Selfactor halls were a different matter. When enthusiasts turned up

[17] *Golos tekstilei*, 29 June 1926; 2 October 1926.
[18] I. I. Blinova *et al.*, 'Pervye udarnye komsomol'skie brigady na predpriiatiiakh Leningrada', *Istoricheskii arkhiv*, 6, November–December 1958, p. 38; A. Kapustin, *Udarniki* (1930), p. 15.
[19] S. Zhukovskii *et al.*, *Pervaia udarnaia* (1931), p. 28.
[20] *Leningradskie rabochie v bor'be za sotsializma, 1926–1937gg* (1965), p. 138; Zukhovskii, *Pervaia udarnaia*, pp. 22–3, 27–32, 37, 48.
[21] Zhukovskii, *Pervaia udarnaia*, pp. 27, 31, 37; *Istoriia rabochego klassa Leningrada*, vyp. 1 (1962), p. 67.

they were met by the shop foreman with that untranslatable Russian epithet, an ironic *ladno*! (fine!) – and immediately dispersed around the shop as auxiliaries to existing work teams. Sometime later the brigade made a second attempt, secured a pair of wheels but were supplied with the worst rovings. By now the atmosphere was very tense. Some youngsters may have been the children of established spinners and piecers as there were sharp quarrels at home between fathers and sons. At the third attempt the team decided to accept rovings only from shock brigades in preparatory departments; foremen responded by refusing the *komplekt* permission to adjust their machines, so the brigade began to 'fiddle' with their selfactors in secret to make them draw faster. They also managed to tip the scales in their favour by securing the best quality Egyptian cotton.[22]

Within a month or so shock brigades had spread to four other Leningrad mills and by October 1928 to the CIR,[23] but with them spread discontents. In general 'old workers' spoke against the new methods, reported the Central Council.[24] Operatives in Ivanovo guberniya resented being pushed off the best equipment to make way for youngsters; doubtless this is why the Tomna's brigades were shunted on to ten ancient ring-frames no one else wanted.[25] The Abel'man's team 'sickened' on the first day and was dissolved,[26] and in the Trekhgornaia only a minority took part – 'professional pride' held the rest back.[27] A little pamphlet about the first shock brigade in Vladimir guberniya's Kommunisticheskii Avangard mill confirms the view that CIR operatives and directors were hostile. While 'experience had already shown' that the young were keen to streamline production, increase output and reduce costs, the administration thought that 'rationalization was too serious a matter to be left to "the lads" . . . this was the business of specialists'. Not only were administrators against the brigade 'but also a significant part of the unenlightened workforce. They considered young rationalizers to be "spies" or "production detectives." They gave no help to the brigade, never put forward

22 Kapustin, *Udarniki*, pp. 18, 28–31; Zhukovskii, *Pervaia udarnaia*, pp. 38–9.
23 M. Dosov, *Trekhgorka na sitsevom fronte* (1929), p. 45; A. Dunaev, Iu. Goriachev, *Iartsevskii khlopchato-bumazhnyi kombinat. (Kratkii istoricheskii ocherk)* (1963), p. 69; *Komsomol'tsy i molodezh' ivanovskoi oblasti v gody stroitel'stva sotsializma (1921–1940gg)* (1967), p. 116; *Ocherki istorii leningradskoi organizatsii KPSS. Chast' II, noiabr' 1917g–1945g* (1968), p. 333; P. Tikhonravov, E. Makhov, *V boi za 700 millionov. Kak organizovalis' i rabotali na fabrike 'Kommunisticheskii Avangard' gruppy molodykh ratsionalizatorov* (1929), p. 41; *Trud*, 26 October 1928.
24 *Trud*, 26 October 1928.   25 *Komsomol'tsy i molodezh'*, pp. 116–17.
26 Tikhonravov, Makhov, *V boi za 700 millionov*, p. 41.
27 Dosov, *Trekhgorka*, p. 45.

proposals or suggestions and even refused to speak to us.' Nor did the union offer any support. Nor did the factory committee and nor did technicians; the latter regarded the whole affair as a 'bad joke' and said that 'we were still too young to understand'. As a consequence of all this the brigade worked 'quietly, so that no one knew who we were we concealed our names . . . but this difficult time soon passed'.[28]

Not, it should be stated, with any help from *Golos tekstilei*. In fact the newspaper seems to have been embarrassed by the entire affair, perhaps a reflection of worries in union's central committee about the likely impact of such adventures on workers who had been under continuous pressure for the last five years or so. While in September 1927 the editors had praised the dynamism of young overlookers and skilled operatives and applauded their impatience with conservative work practices, the first mention of the Ravenstvo's brigade was long delayed.[29] Not until 1 December 1928 did Smirnov, Vintsberg and their colleagues merit a feature in their local union paper. Eight days later a restrained article described their initiative, only the second mention in *Golos tekstilei*,[30] but a further report of December 9 does show how shock brigades multiplied. The party took the brigaders under its wing and sent them to other mills to spread the word; the Ravenstvo's youngsters seem to have spent most of the autumn touring Moscow guberniya.[31]

The Ravenstvo's story provides a near-perfect cameo of many of the complex interactions unravelled at greater length in earlier chapters. Previously named the Ekateringorfskaia and owned by Anglo-Russian Cotton Factories Ltd., the mill was one of Ludwig Knoop's foundations, a German entrepreneur who acted as sole agent in Imperial Russia for Platt Brothers of Oldham. It was an English factory *par excellence*; 'an English enterprise on Russian soil', as one of the more nationalistic brigaders put it, 'Russian labour for English profit'. When the building re-opened after the civil war only part of the original labour force returned, but enough to ensure the transmission of a traditional shop-floor culture: youngsters worked 'badly' because they were 'trained by the old in the old methods'; managers were 'old timers', quality and output depended 'exclusively' on experienced operatives and their view of things. In 1927 selfactor spinners had complained about falling labour discipline amongst youngsters, pre-

[28] Tikhonravov, Makhov, *V boi za 700 millionov*, pp. 4, 32–4.
[29] *Golos tekstilei*, 3 September 1927; 8 September 1928.
[30] *Golos tekstilei*, 9 December 1928; *Leningradskii tekstil'*, 23, 1 December 1928, p. 6.
[31] Zhukovskii, *Pervaia udarnaia*, pp. 42–7.

sumably members of their own work teams, much to the chagrin of brigaders who seem to have chafed under paternalism; 'from the spinners to the spool carriers, these workers have still not reconstructed their labour in harmony with socialist principles'. The point here is that notwithstanding all their enthusiasm the shock brigades appear to have remained wedded and glued to tradition – their selfactor teams worked in groups of three, each team to a pair of wheels. It was just the same in Ramenskoe next year. A photograph in *Golos tekstilei* showed a familiar scene; three young male spinners, the first to go over to shock work, posing in front of a mule pair.[32]

Clearly nothing particularly startling was being attempted in either of these mills, but what was under threat was due process. Deference to age and experience and slow rise through the *komplekt* were being challenged, but not the *komplekt* itself. By moving forward to 1930 it is possible to see what happened when there really was a determined attempt to destroy the *komplekt*, once again in the Ravenstvo. Shock brigades had done nothing to improve matters, in fact quality had declined still further; in February 1929 *Golos tekstilei* carried a large photograph displaying the results of bad spinning.[33] Difficulties were compounded by declining numbers of skilled workers and, by the winter of 1929, very poor quality cotton. Spinners constantly stopped their frames to make adjustments. Early in 1930, when the mill had already fallen behind plan, carriage speeds were reduced because the piecing workload had become far too onerous. Agitated by these setbacks three shock brigade spinners decided to 'transfer to a higher form of collective work', the 'production commune'. Henceforth the spinner would be replaced by a commune 'elder' who would lead teams with no attachment to any particular mule pair. Each commune had the right to choose its own members and 'each would help the other during doffings, stacking rovings, etc.' Although mule spinners objected strongly half the mill's selfactors were reorganized under the new dispensation by the end of the month. The new elder, however, was very much like the old spinner, only younger and without so much authority – soon there were complaints that 'lads began to loaf' because 'some elders gave weak leadership'.[34]

Examination of the communes themselves shows that the teams averaged out in much the same way as the old *komplekt* plus auxiliaries; four to fourteen operatives to a pair depending on count, sort and

[32] *Ibid.*, pp. 5, 8, 14, 20, 22, 56–7; *Golos tekstilei*, 3 July 1929.
[33] *Golos tekstilei*, 26 February 1929.
[34] Zhukovskii, *Pervaia udarnaia*, pp. 66–72.

frame stretch.[35] It is not difficult to see that after a while, where, for instance, eighteen youngsters worked six machines, six would naturally gravitate to a pair, especially as there are no reports of any physical re-organization of machinery. As far as is known the mules stayed where they were, a pair with two carriages facing each other. Indeed, it is hard to see how these machines, 100 feet long or so, could be relocated without rebuilding the mill. Roberts' original hopes were as far from realization as ever. Eighteenth-century England still reached out to limit the possible in socialist Russia.[36]

Production communes are but one example of a rash of new attempts at *uplotnenie*, particularly on ring-frames. Seven Leningrad mills started to abolish the trade of spinner in these rooms throughout 1929/30 by re-dividing labour,[37] but the most famous case is that of Vladimir guberniya's Lakin mill, where American functionalism was introduced to try to reduce the amount of time ring- and flyer-frame operatives had spare during the day. In association with the mill's production conference the Central Institute of Labour succeeded in reorganizing work in preparatory departments and fine spinning halls, and they also had some impact in weaving sheds. But the factory was a poor model for the rest of the industry. All machinery had been electrified in mid-decade and the mill corpus substantially rebuilt.[38] More importantly the shop floor was completely untypical. P. Bazhanov, the original owner, unwittingly got the experiment off to a flying start: 'in the Lakin mill there never were any weavers or ring- and flyer-frame spinners, there were only trades like piecers, creelers, dusters and greasers ... this division of labour made it possible for fewer workers to run more machines ... and this significantly reduced the cost of production'. Carding, roving and flyer-frames had all been installed on one floor and carefully placed together, so proximate shock brigades (the real enthusiasts for functionalism, girl piecers, decorated their spindle banks with large banners reading 'Komsomol Shock Brigade') could supply each other and offer support when criticized by older workers. Compare the confident tone of activists here – 'we are all young workers and therefore the change presents no

---

[35] *Ibid.*, p. 74. If anything, numbers were rising above union recommendations. See *Tarifno-spravochnik rabochikh khlopchato-bumazhnogo proizvodstva* (1928), pp. 34–5.

[36] For further evidence of the survival of the selfactor *komplekt* see *ITPT*, 1–2, January–February 1930, pp. 41, 43; *Tekstil'nye novosti*, 1, January 1930, pp. 50–3; 2–3, February–March 1930, pp. 142–3.

[37] *Tekstil'nye novosti*, 1, January 1930, pp. 49–50; 2–3, February–March 1930, pp. 136–9.

[38] I. P. Borisov, L. S. Kheifets, *Chto dala funktsionalka na fabrike imeni Lakina* (1931); Iu. F. Iakovlev, *Vladimirskie rabochie v bor'be i ukreplenie soiuza s krest'ianstvom v 1921–1925 godakh* (1963), p. 33; *Organizatsiia truda*, 4, October–December 1929, pp. 45, 60.

difficulties for us'[39] – with the sense of isolation evident in the Ravenstvo, Kommunisticheskii Avangard and other mills.

In the final analysis, as one syndicate writer acknowledged in March 1929, all these initiatives depended on workers' attitudes: 'in enterprises with poor equipment . . . where the class consciousness and discipline of the workers is as high as that of technicians, we often have much more success than in those mills with good equipment . . . where backward elements amongst the workers have greater influence and where labour discipline is at a low level'. Labour discipline was the greatest single threat to the industry, he continued, and absenteeism the most important single manifestation of poor discipline.[40] One book devoted exclusively to the problem went on to speak of rising machine stoppages, indifference to managerial authority and the 'theft of goods, materials and equipment in almost all mills'. Elsewhere the same author advised directors to keep a reserve of skilled workers on their pay-roll so that machinery would not stand idle when workers were absent, but neglected to tell administrators where these operatives might be found.[41] Nol'de took a broader view. For the past three or four years much attention had been lavished on rationalization, but to very little effect. While failure was partly due to external constraints, transport and supply problems, 'haphazard use of the forces of production' was equally to blame.[42] Others chipped in around the same time: all local party and union organizations have failed to cope adequately with problems attendant on the development of the industry, protested a party central committee resolution in March; 'rationalization in the textile industry has still not given the necessary results', admitted Vesenkha in April, the 'broad mass of workers' still awaited mobilization. In Moscow's mills, contended the engineers' section of the union in May, absenteeism, carelessness, drunkenness and the failure of the factory committees 'to utilize fully the consciousness of established workers' were responsible for shortfalls in production.[43]

Consciousness, it was hoped, might be raised by utilizing the 'inter-mill visit'. Tver' claimed to have invented the idea in 1927 when production conferences in the district organized inter-factory inspec-

[39] Borisov, Kheifets, *Chto dala funktsionalka*, pp. 10–14, 22, 29. The Komsomol banner is shown on p. 11.
[40] V. A. Buianov, *Tekstil'shchiku, o trudovoi distsipline* (1929), pp. 8–9.
[41] I. G. Eremin, *Trudovaia distsiplina v tekstil'noi promyshlennosti* (1929), pp. 12–13; ITPT, 3, March 1929, p. 4.
[42] *Sistema i organizatsiia*, 1, 1929, p. 9.
[43] *Golos tekstilei*, 31 March 1929; *Sistema i organizatsiia*, 4, April 1929, p. 1; *Tekstil'nye novosti*, 5, May 1929, p. 268.

tions and reviews by groups of workers,[44] but the movement expired almost at the moment of birth. *Golos tekstilei* never mentioned it and *Rabochii krai* made only a passing reference to the campaign in January 1929; one letter from a worker complaining that his factory committee did nothing, that there was no propaganda, and that almost no money was collected for excursions. The other from Shuia; hardly any workers had ever heard of the visit and no general meetings were ever called to discuss the initiative because 'there was no time'.[45]

Socialist competition had a much better pedigree and was to be mythologized in Soviet historiography in much the same way as were shock brigades, though there was scant reason for celebration in cotton mills in 1929. On April 10 *Rabochii krai* reported that 58,000 Ivanovo operatives had taken a 'revolutionary vow', an agreement signed between the province's workers and those in Moscow and Tver'. Appropriate slogans were adopted: 'Forward to new victories! For the general line of the Party! For reducing the cost of production!'[46] In December the local union branch revealed that 16 per cent of Moscow guberniya's textile workers were competing against each other; nevertheless a series of letters carried by *Golos tekstilei* five months previously accused the branch of failing to give leadership on the shop floor.[47] But workers were equally to blame, 'formalism' and indifference amongst women in Iartsevo, for instance.[48] In the Tverskaia the thirty-six agitators dispersed round the shops in March succeeded in persuading 200 or so operatives to keep an eye on their neighbours' performance, but many new workers from rural districts 'did not like the general enthusiasm of the proletariat'. They 'circulated propaganda amongst themselves . . . we don't need competition, we work hard enough already'.[49] By the following year as failure became still more glaring criticism became ever more hysterical: poor attendance at production conferences in Ivanovo guberniya was now 'a crime against the proletariat' warned *Golos tekstilei* early in January, the union's central committee regarded the slogan 'face to production' as 'mere paper' insisted some local activists. Next month the paper reported that all Leningrad's cotton mills were failing to reach their

---

[44] N. B. Lebedev, O. I. Shkaratan, *Ocherki istorii sotsialisticheskogo sorevnovaniia* (1966), p. 78.

[45] *Rabochii krai*, 5 January 1929.

[46] 'We vow to lower the cost of production, strengthen discipline, eliminate waste and poor workmanship and raise productivity': *Rabochii krai*, 10 April 1929.

[47] *Golos tekstilei*, 18 July 1929; 31 December 1929.

[48] Dunaev, Gorachev, *Iartsevskii khlopchato-bumazhnyi kombinat*, p. 72.

[49] M. Amshinskii, *Vyzov priniat! Opyt organizatsiia sotsialisticheskogo sorevnovaniia na 'Proletarskoi manufakture' v gorode Tveri* (1929), pp. 7–12.

production quotas, accused management and factory committees of indifference, and found that workers in at least one mill were ignorant of their own individual targets.[50] The syndicate dispatched an extraordinary commission to Vladimir guberniya in February where in three mills waste rates were running at between 28 and 75 per cent.[51]

It would be easy to misinterpret these phenomena. Disquiet over falling labour discipline and poor workmanship coupled with the urge to mobilize were by no means specific to the cotton industry. They should be put in the context of the First Five Year Plan. Revised several times and finally adopted in spring 1929,[52] it was, by the time Vladimir's extraordinary commission met, beginning to change the face of Russian industry and the character of the Soviet workforce at large. Labour turnover in Soviet factories in general had become 'colossal' by autumn 1930, admitted the Commissariat of Labour. Prerevolutionary workers long inured to time-work discipline and new entrants who came in as the industry recovered from War Communism and were subsequently put to the frames by their elders were thus, in cotton as elsewhere, being swamped by rural immigration on an unprecedented scale.[53]

The end of NEP in the mills

NEP is sometimes characterized as the golden age of the technical intelligentsia. To the extent that its destruction signalled the beginning of the end for the old specialists this interpretation is obviously correct, but engineers, in spite of their ability to sell their expertise dear, were always in an insecure position. They were obliged to try to implement policies which were often not of their own making in conditions not of their own choosing;[54] success invited the hostility of the workforce, failure the condemnation of the party. Moreover, 1921 to 1928 was only seven years, and afterwards there was little for them to look forward to. Fedotov had been considered as a defendant in the March 1928 'Shakhty Affair' trial and then

---

[50] *Golos tekstilei*, 3 January 1930; 4 January 1930; 5 January 1930; 4 February 1930.
[51] *Rabochii krai*, 14 February 1930.
[52] For a detailed account see E. H. Carr, R. W. Davies, *Foundations of a Planned Economy*, vol. 1, part 2 (1969), pp. 837–97.
[53] Unskilled operatives in Leningrad's Khalturin were 'leaving by floors' for seasonal work or jobs in metal factories because the pay was better. Spinners and weavers registered as unskilled workers at the labour exchanges in order to avoid being sent back to the shop floor: *Voprosy truda*, 9, September 1930, pp. 15, 20.
[54] Only seven textile engineers belonged to the party in autumn 1928: Carr, Davies, *Foundations of a Planned Economy*, 1, 2, p. 580.

unaccountably dropped at the last minute.[55] The news surely spread through the profession.

In autumn 1928 Shmidt suggested that specialists had become thoroughly fed up with the antics surrounding seven-hour/three-shift working: 'engineers and technical personnel reacted thus – "this reduction of the working day was introduced without consulting us. As far as we're concerned, therefore, all the problems that arise have nothing to do with us".'[56] Tensions were indeed there right from the start. On February 3 1928 the Shuiskaia's factory committee informed the mill's engineers that they must adopt 'a more responsible attitude' and be 'more sympathetic to the workers' demands' in the coming transfer.[57] Technicians experienced 'great difficulties' in Ivanovo guberniya. They became the focus of all the discontents engendered by clashes over *uplotnenie*, the failure to sort out the pay system, and quarrels between skilled and unskilled workers.[58] In May engineer Shmelev told the national congress of his union section that there was much conflict and bad feeling in the Trekhgornaia when workers were required by specialists to change their places on the shop floor. Later there were threats of physical violence.[59] Mel'nichanskii's address to the congress ignored these problems. Instead he attacked delegates and the technical intelligentsia in general for manipulating the old-boy network, which apparently embraced members of the old régime and former factory owners, to their own advantage. The section must strive for 'greater Soviet patriotism' and 'full unity'. The role of unions in the Soviet Union, delegates were reminded, 'is different from the role of trade unions abroad ... our unions actively support the new socialist economy', and this was the task for engineers.[60] A month or so later 'former people', old landowners and factory owners, were discovered working in one Moscow guberniya trust, and falling wages in the Ramenskaia were blamed on a book-keeper kept over from tsarist times who, hand-in-glove with the mill's deputy director, supposedly cheated workers out of their pay.[61] In October a foreman was murdered in the Nikol'skaia. Workers' letters indicate that violent assaults were not uncommon.[62]

55 A. Solzhenitsyn, *The Gulag Archipelago*, vol. 1 (1974), p. 375.
56 *Trud*, 31 October 1928.
57 Belinskii, Kucherov, *Tri mesiatsa raboty*, p. 28.   58 *Izvestiia*, 17 August 1928.
59 Dosov, *Trekhgorka*, pp. 5–6; *Golos tekstilei*, 11 May 1928.
60 *Golos tekstilei*, 13 May 1928.
61 *Golos tekstilei*, 10 June 1928; 8 July 1928.
62 *Golos tekstilei*, 4 October 1928. The situation deteriorated sharply next year. For specific incidents see Eremin, *Trudovaia distsiplina*, p. 27; *Predpriiatie*, 3(67), March

In April 1928 the party lumped together the old specialists, kulaks, the *nepmeny* and representatives of international capitalism; they were all wreckers who were determined to destroy the Soviet Union. Next year Gosplan's journal explained that problems in the textile industry were caused by wrecking.[63] Fedotov and two other senior textile engineers were duly included in the 'Industrial Party' trial. Agents of French imperialism, they had created disproportions between supply and demand, hindered the development of machine production and confused workers by ordering them to produce unstandardized cloth from a variety of cotton sorts. They had also arranged for the construction of two new cotton mills in excess of capacity. Situated in White Russia, these were to have served as barracks for the invading French army. All received ten-year sentences. Fedotov may have been executed in 1937.[64]

As for ordinary Russians, they had almost no time to recover from the war scare of 1926–7. In spring 1928 rumours of a new tax on the peasants spread across the country.[65] In July Mel'nichanskii addressed the second plenum of the union's central committee. *Golos tekstilei* reported his speech: 'some part of the workforce . . . is saying that we are returning to War Communism, to forcible grain collections'. And so did the Central Council's newspaper: because of 'difficulties' in collecting grain the 'mood' of the cotton workforce, particularly of those connected with the land, was 'very unsettled'. To them 'it seems that the emergency measures taken by Soviet power mark a return to previous methods of work'.[66] They turned out to be right. The fabric of NEP was coming apart at the seams. Bread rationing was introduced in Odessa and some other Ukrainian cities early in 1928, spread to Leningrad in January 1929 and to Moscow three months later. Ivanovo's engineers travelled there in search of food for their mills' workers.[67] By early 1930, when the murders and

1929, pp. 24–5; *Sputnik agitatora*, 8, April 1929, p. 46; *Tekstil'nye novosti*, 5, May 1929, pp. 268–9.

[63] K. E. Bailes, *Technology and Society under Lenin and Stalin: Origins of the Soviet Technical Intelligentsia, 1917–41* (1978), p. 98; N. Lampert, *The Technical Intelligentsia and the Soviet State: a Study of Managers and Technicians, 1928–35* (1979), pp. 40–1.

[64] Bailes, *Technology and Society*, pp. 96–7; *ITPT*, 12, December 1930, pp. 1–2; Lampert, *The Technical Intelligentsia*, p. 42; Solzhenitsyn, *Gulag Archipelago*, 1, pp. 378, 381, 384; N. Valentinov, 'Non-Party specialists and the coming of NEP', *Russian Review*, 30, April 1971, pp. 161–2; N. Valentinov, *Novaia ekonomicheskaia politika i krizis partii posle smerti Lenina* (1971), p. 25.

[65] V. Kuz'michev, *Organizatsiia obshchestvennogo mneniia. Pechatnaia agitatsiia* (1929), p. 30.

[66] *Golos tekstilei*, 21 July 1928; *Trud*, 21 July 1928.

[67] V. A. Kungurtsev, *Tekstil'naia promyshlennost' SSSR* (1957), p. 84.

deportations were well under way, most basic foodstuffs and many consumer goods, including textiles, were on ration in urban areas.[68]

As for the problems of labour discipline and poor workmanship, for these reasons it would be wrong to over-specify discontents in the cotton industry. Cotton workers' sufferings were now subsumed in a national tragedy, collectivization, the history of which is too well known to be rehearsed here, but the union president's remarks do highlight one specific point; Mel'nichanskii's opening words at the plenum linked the bread crisis to poor performance on the shop floor, and while the plenum was in session the Council of Peoples' Commissars published a resolution on the emergency which included an instruction to the industry to produce more goods for the peasant market. Workers, continued *Golos tekstilei* in September, must be more disciplined and produce more so that grain shortfalls could be overcome.[69]

Admonitions like these are no different from many others cited in previous chapters, but there was another version of the relationship between cotton workers and peasants, a *smychka* in a minor key which was never really heard throughout the 1920s. In 1925 the union's central committee recommended that precisely because so many were close to the village, operatives should become the link between town and countryside, the agency for spreading literacy and encouraging co-operation amongst the peasants. They should also organize excursions to the factory from nearby villages to make the peasants familiar with working-class culture.[70] Understandably, these interesting ideas were never developed: factory committees and mill directors had other, more pressing problems to attend to. Only with the collectivization drive were they resurrected, and then in a quite different guise. An open letter from the central committee of the union appeared in *Golos tekstilei* on 19 July 1929; because many mills were in the countryside and many workers close to the land they had the opportunity to help with grain deliveries. They should organize joint peasant-worker committees, send brigades to the villages and agitate amongst the peasants when they went home from the shop floor. In October a more urgent instruction appeared – all local mill organizations must take measures to assist with grain col-

[68] S. M. Schwarz, *Labor*, pp. 135–6.
[69] *Golos tekstilei*, 21 July 1928; 8 September 1928.
[70] *Postanovleniia 2-go plenuma TsK vsesoiuznogo soiuza tekstil'shchikov 21–23 maia 1925g v Leningrade* (1925), p. 11. For a brief description of such activities (the *shefstvo* system) see W. E. Chase, *Workers, Society, and the Soviet State. Labor and Life in Moscow, 1918–1929* (1987), pp. 301–20.

lection[71] – and next month the Central Council ordered the union to send textile workers out to the Central Asian cotton fields. Moreover, operatives connected with the land should be prepared for 'active' work in the 'socialist transformation of the countryside'.[72]

Some brigades had already been formed, 242 with 1,660 members in Moscow guberniya, mostly for servicing and repairing agricultural machinery, and 4,000 more from the CIR left their mills in January and February 1930.[73] But it was expecting rather a lot for workers with land to go out into the villages and collectivize themselves: in January *Golos tekstilei* reported that while Leningrad and Nizhegorod had supplied their quotas of workers, Moscow guberniya was lagging behind. A correspondent for Orekhovo-Zuevo pointed out that the union had undertaken no preparatory work and that factory committees in the district expressed no interest, and went on to draw the obvious conclusion that this was because many cotton workers there held land. In Ivanovo-Voznesensk only thirty engineers and sixty 'politically developed' workers who were willing to take part could be found.[74]

Worse was to come. Secret police agents close to the Iartsevskaia's spinning shops reported discontent about the lack of food and remarks against dekulakization. Sometime before June 1929 cotton workers in Orekhovo-Zuevo went on strike and one communist from Ivanovo-Voznesensk told a Menshevik informer that operatives were 'extremely restive'. Like those in Ivanovo, the Iartsevskaia's workers expressed opposition to *uplotnenie* and harsh labour discipline, and they also disliked the party's drive against religion.[75] Late in October *Golos tekstilei* came out with a lead article on 'agents' and 'class enemies'. Some local union organizations were guilty of 'petty-bourgeois deviation'. 'Backward' workers in a mill in Ivanovo guberniya led by the factory committee's chairman opposed socialist competition; the same thing happened in Tver'. The Drezna's factory committee 'hindered' *uplotnenie* and in Ramenskoe workers on the afternoon shift refused to endorse the party line against the kulaks. Spinners and weavers in Bogorodsk deliberately slowed their work rate as a protest against *uplotnenie* and wage falls.[76]

71 *Golos tekstilei*, 19 July 1929; 20 October 1929.
72 Cited E. A. Kuznetsov, 'Rol' profsoiuza tekstil'shchikov v sotsialisticheskom preobrazovanii sel'skogo khoziaistva (1927–1934gg)', Avtoreferat (1974), pp. 22–3.
73 *Ibid.*, p. 18; *Golos tekstilei*, 2 January 1930; 4 January 1930; 14 January 1930. The paper listed departures almost every day.
74 *Golos tekstilei*, 4 January 1930; 5 January 1930; 7 January 1930.
75 M. Fainsod, *Smolensk under Soviet Rule* (1958), pp. 307, 311, 317; *Sotsialisticheskii vestnik*, 12(202), 14 June 1929, p. 14.
76 *Golos tekstilei*, 26 October 1929; *Sputnik kommunista*, 8(89), April 1929, p. 51.

Despite these clues there is no evidence that factory committees were captured or utilized by operatives in the same way as in 1925. The cotton workforce had undergone a considerable transformation, and the events associated with the introduction of seven-hour/three-shift working drives refracted through the shop floor in a manner which tended to deflect and diffuse rather than concentrate opposition. Moreover, the entire political mood had changed; political debates were much coarser, political responses much more brutal. If there was any organized opposition it may have been inflected through religion, through the kind of dissenting communities discussed at the end of chapter 6. The possibility of this happening is not so surprising. Church groups were the only organizations enjoying some measure of autonomy from the party and the state to which workers could belong. Moreover, the late 1920s marked the beginning of a powerful new campaign against religion, and thus for some operatives secular concerns could no longer be separated from spiritual ones. Though the evidence is very slim and the sources hostile, they do merit consideration.

Larin's 1929 proposal for reorganizing shifts, mentioned above, rested on the notion of the 'uninterrupted working week' as a means of avoiding night work.[77] Instead of three shifts spread over five-and-a-half days factories would be open for seven days. As work time would now be out of synchronization with the calendar week time off would fall on different days for all workers throughout the month, not just Saturday afternoons and Sundays. The party central committee directed all local bodies to prepare for the new system in September 1929, and in November a central committee plenum insisted that two-thirds of all industry should be on the continuous week by October 1930. The syndicate and the central committee of the union agreed. The system would be better for workers' health and would raise productivity. Subsequently all mills which had so far escaped seven-hour/three-shift working were instructed by the syndicate to opt for the new alternative instead. Some enterprises already on the even-hour day reconverted, and by February 1930 one-quarter of all cotton operatives worked under the new arrangement. A further 122,000 were to be switched before October.[78]

On 30 November 1929 *Golos tekstilei* claimed to discover 'not less

[77] *ITPT*, 1–2, January–February 1930, p. 6; *Okhrana truda*, 9(50), September 1929, p. 5.
[78] *ITPT*, 1–2, January–February 1930, pp. 5–10; *Voprosy truda*, 4 April 1930, p. 5. Elaborate compromises were worked out for mills already on seven-hours, see *Okhrana truda*, 9(50), September 1929, p. 5.

than 10,000 evangelists' in the Kostroma district who were accused of taking the lead in agitation against uninterrupted working, socialist competition and *uplotnenie*. The author strongly suggested that this was a women's movement. Next month someone wrote from another CIR mill where sectarians were active. As there was much overlap with party membership a compromise had quietly been arranged, one which had been functioning smoothly for some time past; leading sect members were tacitly allowed time off work for church duties, but the proposed switch to uninterrupted working, warned the writer, coming as it did so close to Christmas, was bound to lead to trouble.[79]

Because it meant Sunday working the new system may have been the catalyst which galvanized some into action, but there are hints which suggest that sectarians were already reacting against the regime. In March the party's central committee specifically criticized union and party organizations in the Kommunisticheskii Avangard – a mill, as we have seen, in which the workforce had strong religious commitments.[80] Three months later *Rabochii krai* picked up a story from Ivanovo guberniya's Navol'skaia mill, a strike in ring-frame rooms over *uplotnenie*. Much was made of the fact that the two women leaders were married to successful peasants. One 'had some experience' of what was happening in Moscow guberniya's mills, the other had been excluded from the party last year for observing religious holidays. In July the paper turned its attention to another of the guberniya's mills. There unspecified discontents were blamed on 'anti-Soviet' elements, but the report made out that leaders were Christians who, somewhat absurdly, sympathized with the Union of Russian People. A further article discussing Ivanovo guberniya emerged in *Golos tekstilei* in August. The editors said that they had received many letters about sectarians calling each other brother and sister on the shop floor. Operatives in yet another mill expressed anti-Soviet sentiments, continued the writer, and when women ring-frame spinners struck as a protest against *uplotnenie* in the factory, participants were said to be sectarians. They were also in written communication with other sect members – from the Navol'skaia.[81]

These fragments are all we have, but whatever the role of sectarian communities, Christians, like all other cotton operatives, were now obliged to live and work under a new and ferocious dispensation; one

[79] *Golos tekstilei*, 30 November 1929; 3 December 1929.
[80] *Golos tekstilei*, 31 March 1929, and see above p. 119.
[81] *Golos tekstilei*, 25 August 1929; *Rabochii krai*, 25 June 1929; 9 July 1929.

where any form of overt collective action taken by workers was – to say the least – extremely hazardous, and most unlikely to succeed. The cotton industry was no longer in the forefront of a peaceful struggle to build an economic bridge between town and countryside. Stalin had stumbled into a bloody conflict with the peasantry, and since the *smychka* was now just an empty word, our story ends here.

Conclusion

Theory is grey, my friend, but green is the eternal tree of life.

A favourite quotation of Lenin's

Following the tenth party congress the government came to believe that the maintenance of the *smychka* and the pursuit of commercial viability in the cotton industry were inseparably bound up one with the other, thus inside the mill NEP hinged on the never-ending struggle to keep production within the financial reach of the peasantry and to supply them with finished goods at an ever-faster rate. It was considered essential, therefore, for mills to reduce their costs. It was also thought that they could do this only via a massive programme of capital investment, by some form of Taylorist experimentation, or by a more intensive use of the labour force. But as hopes of economic integration with the west faded, and as the paucity of all manner of domestic resources became evident, the last course – labour intensification – seemed to be the only available option. It does not matter whether all this was true or not, the point is that élites believed it to be true and acted as if it were true.

Once labour intensification was seen as the key to improving productivity, the first problem facing the régime was that the expropriation of the means of production after 1917 had not left it with a *tabula rasa* upon which new social relations of production could be inscribed at will. Cotton factories were far from uniform. The means of production were not 'value free'. In many rooms a choice of technique had already been made over half a century previously. Equally cotton operatives were not much like the Bolshevik vision of a working class. They exhibited all the social and regional variations that could be seen in a day's train ride from Moscow's Iaroslavl' station to Kostroma. Operatives' lives were to a very large extent bound by local, familial and shop loyalties, to say nothing of those features transmitted from

Lancashire from as far back as the 1790s. And these permeated every aspect of factory culture; hiring practices, training techniques, pay systems – even the details of work on a single machine.[1]

Only when the regime felt itself obliged to try to change things inside the mill, however, did the strength of this traditional world become apparent. This happened twice during the 1920s. Once during and after the scissors crisis in 1923 and again after the war scare of 1926–7. In both cases politicians tried to raise productivity via labour intensification to head off what they believed to be serious grain crises. But the implementation of policy in the factory was a highly sensitized point of engagement between the régime and the constituency in whose name it acted. Here the party-state encountered workers *in situ*, and where discontents arose operatives could make their presence felt in Moscow – most obviously in 1925 – precisely because of the imperatives of NEP: cotton was too important for the régime to take a hard line, even if it wished to. Later on, with the switch to seven-hour/ three-shift working, customary practice proved strong enough to give the policy an unintended twist. In both cases *uplotnenie* did have some effect, but was inflected through existing arrangements which emasculated the drive towards higher productivity.

Moreover, as the 1920s drew to a close, there was a move away from compromise and towards something resembling mobilization on the part of the government. Whilst after 1923 Moscow was willing to accommodate itself to the workforce – voluntary *uplotnenie*, factory committee democratization and concessions over pay – in 1927–8 the centre tried to promote fundamental change, most obviously through shock brigades. Notwithstanding Bolshevik protestations shock brigades owed less to socialist theory and more to the urgently felt need to increase output, but in many ways they were virtually indistinguishable from the *komplekt*; team working, shared responsibility and a feeling of loyalty lay at the heart of both institutions. The difference was that while *komplekt* loyalties ran laterally, between team members, those in shock brigades were supposed to run vertically. Rationalizers wanted to break up these old work communities and replace them with new ones – new social forms which would be responsive to the productivist ethos emanating from above.

The *komplekt*, however, was not necessarily an anachronism in the

---

[1] In fact this study invites us to reconsider Soviet workers in general. If the usual dichotomies of 'new' and 'old' or 'proletarian' and 'peasant' workers do not tell the whole story as far as the ways in which cotton operatives responded to change are concerned, the same may well be true of workers in other industries.

1920s and we can start to appreciate this by quoting Solzhenitsyn's posthumous defence of Fedotov's position at the Industrial Party trial:

> From the profound economic consideration that in America capital is cheap and labor dear, and that the situation here is just the opposite, and that we therefore ought not to borrow things with monkey-like imitativeness, Fedotov concluded that it was useless for us to purchase expensive American assembly-line machinery. For the next ten years it would be more profitable for us to buy less sophisticated English machinery and put more workers on it, since it was inevitable that in ten years' time whatever we had produced would be replaced anyway, no matter what. And we could then buy more expensive machinery.[2]

Melnichanskii and the union's central committee also believed that given the way changes were imposed on the mill late in the decade, machinery, old or new, would be worn out at an unnecessarily rapid rate.[3]

Nobody writes about the 1920s without an awareness of what went before and what came after. The whole debate about the viability of NEP, therefore, cannot be separated from the historian's attitude to the Revolution, or to the desirability or inevitability of Stalinism. But while it is possible to appreciate their panic, their profound sense of weakness and isolation, the lurch into forced industrialization and collectivization only becomes inevitable if we take on board certain Bolshevik aspirations and fears – their determination to break with Russia's 'backward' past, their longing to catch up with the west, and their deep suspicion of the peasantry. But this view of things does not have to be accepted. It must be kept in mind that the government chose to abandon NEP. The contention that forced collectivization and industrialization were Russia's destiny cannot now be advanced with much confidence, and to date the consensus seems to be that NEP was flawed but workable.[4]

Whether or not trying to improve cotton's productivity in harmony with existing patterns of work inside the mill would have made NEP more successful and therefore more attractive to political élites, and

---

[2] A. Solzhenitsyn, *The Gulag Archipelago*, vol. 1 (1974), p. 380.   [3] See p. 242.

[4] To be sure, growth rates would probably have been far less spectacular than those obtaining under the First Five Year Plan, but the rationality of the Plan itself is also in doubt – simply in economic terms, setting aside the more important question of human costs. For this debate see M. Harrison, 'Why did NEP fail?', *Economics of Planning*, 2, 1980; H. Hunter, 'The over-ambitious first Soviet Five Year Plan', *Slavic Review*, June 1973; J. B. Millar, 'Mass collectivization and the contribution of Soviet agriculture to the First Five Year Plan', *Slavic Review*, 4, December 1974.

perhaps made them pause before effectively destroying the *smychka* at the end of the 1920s, is a matter of conjecture; but Fedotov for one thought that for the time being old methods had much to commend themselves, and the régime had turned to the industry each time the *smychka* was threatened, and at first had been willing to search for a compromise with the cotton workforce in order to protect the social and political order.

Given the direction in which these events seemed to point, it is not hard to imagine that throughout the decade shop-floor culture could have been utilized – in the defence of NEP, in a context of growth, and within the ambience of a socialist ethos – to a far greater extent than was actually the case. Lenin left a few brief notes on co-operation. Bukharin began to move towards a less ambitious vision of socialism. Trotsky suggested a method whereby the Soviet economy could measure its performance against others. These men were coming to terms with Russia. Others might have noticed that, however flawed, something like co-operative working could be seen in the *komplekt*, some scaled-down version of socialism appropriate to current realities, as well as a pay system which, though far from egalitarian, did offer an alternative to the worst features of individual piece rates, particularly as so many work groups were based on the primary social unit of the family, a feature which allowed significant numbers to arrange time-sharing schemes amongst themselves so that they could attend to any other business they might have outside the mill and thus keep up their standard of living. The *komplekt* could also have been used as one element in some scheme of international co-efficients. Even the 25 per cent or so of workers holding land might have been incorporated into some vision of the future – they were, after all, overcoming the division of labour between town and country which haunted the socialist conscience for more than a century. And with a little imagination an attempt could have been made to organize at least some reforms in the industry in harmony with tradition and customary practice through those shop-floor institutions with which operatives were familiar: established work teams, factory committees, shop delegate meetings, production conferences and temporary control commissions.

The second problem was that the changes imposed on the mill after 1923 and 1927 started life as policies advanced by people in Moscow who knew very little about the historical background to the industry or the daily routines of factory life, and who were unwilling or unable to put aside their preconceptions about the nature of large-scale production and the social structure of the cotton workforce. As a consequence they often fragmented when refracted through a particular shop, giving quite unexpected results, or simply faded away when they struck the opacities of a specific form of production. This is because they were inflected through a living culture, a kaleidoscopic arrangement of shop-floor traditions which allowed some workers some choices in their responses, within the limits imposed by technology and working technique. To impatient polemicists this was 'backwardness'; and indeed, there was no idealized proletariat of revolutionary mythology to be found in Russia's mills.

Once things had been formulated in these terms, once workers themselves were seen as a problem which had to be overcome, operatives began to defend themselves as best they could, and mill culture proved strong enough to deflect much of the pressure emanating from the centre. The ability of the cotton workforce to frustrate the dictates of Moscow could thus be added to that bundle of dilemmas which resulted in the abandonment of the *smychka* and the lurch into forced collectivization.

Appendix

GLOSSARY OF TRUSTS AND MILLS

The glossary lists all the trusts and mills researched for this book.

1 Trusts

(a) Cotton trusts and other textile trusts which controlled cotton mills, with
   abbreviations subsequently used:

1-i gosudarstvennyi khlopchatobumazhnyi trest	1KhT
2-i gosudarstvennyi khlopchatobumazhnyi trest	2KhT
3-i gosudarstvennyi khlopchatobumazhnyi trest	3KhT
Gusevskii kombinarovannyi trest (Gus'-Kristalnyi kombinat)	G-KK
Iaroslavskii gosudarstvennyi khlopchatobumazhnyi trest	IKhT
Iaroslavskii GSNKh trest	IGSNKh
Ivanovo-voznesenskii gosudarstvennyi tekstil'nyi trest	I–VTT
Ivanovo-voznesenskii GSNKh trest	I–VGSNKh
Ivanovo-voznesenskoe ob"edinenie ('Ivtekstil'')	Ivtekst
Kambol'nyi trest	KT
Klintsovskii tekstil'nyi trest	KTT
Krasavinskaia gosudarstvennaia fabrika	KF
Leningradskii gosudarstvennyi tekstil'nyi trest	LTT
Moskovskii pestrotkannyi khlopchatobumazhnyi trest	Pest
Moskovskii trest viazal'no-trikoatazhnoi promyshlennosti	Trik
Mossukno	M
Penzenskii sukonnyi trest	PST
Riazanskii GSNKh trest	RGSNKh
Saratovskaia manufaktura	SM
Smolenskii GSNKh	SGSNKh
Tambovskii sukonnyi trest	TST
Turkmenskii SSR trest	Turk
Tverskii gosudarstvennyi khlopchatobumazhnyi trest	TKhT
Tverskii GSNKh trest	TGSNKh
Ul'ianovskii sukonnyi trest	UST
Vladimirskii gosudarstvennyi khlopchatobumazhnyi trest	VKhT
Vladimirskii GSNKh trest	VGSNKh

(b) Trusts were frequently re-organized throughout NEP. Listed below are the main changes for 1922–27:

Bogorodsko-shchelkovskii khlopchatobumazhnyi trest, divided between: 3KhT; Pest; Turk.

Egor'evsko-ramenskii khlopchatobumazhnyi trest, almost all to: 2KhT.

Kovrovskii trest, all to: VGSNKh.

Moskovskii khlopchatobumazhnyi trest, all to: 1KhT.

Moskovsko-klintsovkii khlopchatobumazhnyi trest, divided between: 1KhT; I–VGSNKh; Pest; VGSNKh.

Orekhovo-zuevskii khlopchatobumazhnyi trest, almost all to: 3KhT.

Orzerskii trest, all to: Pest.

Krasno-Presneskii khlopchatobumazhnyi trest, all to: 2KhT.

Serpukhovskii khlopchatobumazhnyi trest, divided between: 1KhT; M.

Spass-klepinskovskii khlopchatobumazhnyi trest, almost all to: 1KhT.

Vladimirsko-aleksandrovskii khlopchatobumazhnyi trest, divided between: VKhT; VGSNKh.

2 Mills

Cotton factories and textile mills which produced cotton goods often changed their names, and frequently two unconnected enterprises shared the same name. To keep things clear only one name has been used for each mill. On the left is the name used if it is referred to in the text, where known other pre- and post-revolutionary names appear next, then the mill's location and trust.

Abel'man	A. Treumov	Kovrov, Vladimir guberniya	VKhT
Anisimov	Novaia bumago-priadil'naia	Leningrad	LTT
Annenskaia	Konovalovskaia/ Krasnyi Oktiabr'	Vichuga, Ivanovo guberniya	I–VTT
Afanas'ev	Petrishchevskaia/ Vitovskaia	Ivanovo-Voznesensk	Ivtekst
Aseev	Krasnyi Oktiabr'	Fab. poselok, Saratov guberniya	PST
Avangard	T-vo Osiannikova i Ganshina	Iur'ev-Pol'skii, Vladimir guberniya	VGSNKh
Balashov	Bol'shaia Dmitrovskaia/ Bol'shaia I–V Tkatskaia Manufaktura	Ivanovo-Voznesensk	I–VTT

Bol'shaia Kokhomskaia	Kokhomskaia Ob"edinenaia/ Shcherbakov/Br. Iasiuninsk	Kokhma, Ivanovo guberniya	I–VTT
Bol'shaia Shuiskaia	Shuisko-Novinskaia/A. T. Shorygin	Novinki, Ivanovo guberniya	Ivtekst
Bol'shevik	Teikovskaia/A. Karetniko i S-ni	Teikovo, Ivanovo guberniya	I–VTT
Boniachenskaia	Konovalovskaia/ Nogin	Vichuga, Ivanovo guberniya	I–VTT
Chernitskaia	Kolmazin/Priakhin i Rysin	Shuia, Ivanovo guberniya	I–VGSNKh
Danilovskaia	Frunze	Moscow	1KhT
Dedovskaia	O-va Anonimonogo	Guchkovo, Moscow guberniya	2KhT
Derbenev	Sverdlov	Kameshkovo, Vladimir guberniya	VKhT
Dmitrovskaia	Nemkov/1-e Maia	Dmitriev, Moscow guberniya	Pest
Drezna	Ziman	Drezna, Moscow guberniya	3KhT
Dzerzhinskaia	[new 1929]	Ivanovo-Voznesensk	I–VTT
Giubner	Sverdlov	Moscow	2KhT
Glukhovskaia	Bogorodkso-Glukhovskaia/ Lenin	Bogorodsk, Moscow guberniya	3KhT
Golutvinskaia	?	?	?
Gorod-ishchenskaia	S. Morozov	Fab.poselok Moscow guberniya	3KhT
Gorko-Pavlovskaia	V. M. Skorynin	Gorki, Ivanovo guberniya	I–VGSNKh
Iakhromskaia	Pokhrovskaia	Iakhroma, Ivanovo guberniya	2KhT
Iakovlevskaia	Svet	Pivovarovo, Vladimir guberniya	VGSNKh
Iartsevskaia	Khludov	Iartsevo, Smolensk guberniya	2KhT
Istomkinskaia	Shibaev/Trotsky	Drezna, Moscow guberniya	3KhT
Iuzhskaia	A. Ia. Balin	Iuzha, Ivanovo guberniya	I–VTT

Ivanteevskaia	Lyzhin	Pushkino, Moscow guberniya	M
Kalinin	Aleksandrovskaia Tkatskaia	Aleksandrov, Vladimir guberniya	VKhT
Kamenskaia	?	Novo-Troitskoe, Ivanovo guberniya	I–VGSNKh
Karabanovksii Combine	III Internatsional/ Br. Baranov	Karabanovo, Vladimir guberniya	VKhT
Karl Libnekht	Zalogin i Shevetsov	Sergeikha, Vladimir guberniya	VKhT
Karl Marks	S. V. Borisov	Bryzdanovo, Vladimir guberniya	VKhT
Khalturin	Nevskaia Nitochnaia	Leningrad	LTT
Kineshemskaia	I. K. Konovalov	Kineshma, Ivanovo guberniya	I–VTT
Kolobovskaia	Br. Gorbunov	Kolobovo, Ivanovo guberniya	Ivtekst
Kommunist- icheskii Avangard	Sobinskaia/Losev	Sobinka, Vladimir guberniya	VKhT
Komsomolets	Diev	Kholshchevo, Vladimir guberniya	VGSNKh
Krasavinskaia	Ia. Gribanov	Krasavino, Dvinsk guberniya	?
Krasnaia Nit'	Nevskaia Nitochnaia	Leningrad	LTT
Krasnaia Roza	K. O. Zhiro	Moscow	?
Krasnaia Talka	[new 1927]	Ivanovo- Voznesensk	I–VTT
Krasnaia Vekta	Volzhskaia/Br. F. i A. Razorenov	Kineshma, Ivanovo guberniya	Ivtekst
Krasnoe Ekho	Pereiaslavl'skaia	Pereiaslavl', Vladimir guberniya	VKhT
Krasnoe Znamia	Kersten	Leningrad	LTT
Krasno- kholmskaia	A. Shrader	Moscow	KT

Krasnyi Luch	Muromskaia	Murom, Vladimir guberniya	VGSNKh
Krasnyi Maiak	Petrogradskaia Nitochnaia/ Rossiiskaia Bumago- priadil'naia/ Voronin/Liutsh i Chesher	Leningrad	LTT
Krasnyi Oktiabr'	?	? Penza guberniya	?
Krasnyi Perekop	Bol'shaia Iaroslavskaia	Iaroslavl'	IKhT
Krasnyi Profintern	Iu. S. Nechaev- Maltsev	Gus'Kristal'nyi, Vladimir guberniya	G–KK
Krasnyi Tekstil'shchik	N. N. Konshin	Serpukhov, Moscow guberniya	1KhT
Krasnyi Tkach	Tornton	Leningrad	LTT
Krasnyi Vostok	Sel'faktor	Sasovo, Riazan guberniya	RGSNKh
Krizhachskaia	Nedykhliaev/ Rabochii	Krizhach, Vladimir guberniya	VKhT
Krupskaia	Malo- Dmitrovskaia/ Polushin	Ivanovo- Voznesensk	Ivtekst
Kuntsevskaia	Shersto-tkatskaia	Kuntsevo, Moscow guberniya	KT
Kutuzov	Krasnyi Pereval/Norskaia	Fab. poselok, Iaroslavl' guberniya	IGSNKh
Lakin	Undol'skaia/P. Bazhanov	Undol', Vladimir guberniya	VKhT
Lenin	Rumiantsevskaia/ Protopopov	Zhadovka, Ul'ianovsk guberniya	UST
Lezhnevskaia	Karl Libnekht i Roza Liuksemburg	Lezhnevo, Ivanovo guberniya	Ivtekst
Likino	A. V. Smirnov	Likino, Moscow guberniya	3KhT
Livers	Moskovskaia Kruzhevnaia	Moscow	Trik
Malo- Kokhomskaia	?	Kokhma, Ivanovo guberniya	?

Naro-Fominsk	Voskresenskaia	Nara, Moscow guberniya	1KhT
Navol'skaia	Navol'skaia Privolshskaia/ Kommuna/ Mindovskii i Bakanin	Kineshma, Ivanovo guberniya	I–VTT
Nerl'skaia	Aronov/ Blagoveshchens- kaia	Nerl', Ivanovo guberniya	I–VGSNKh
Nikol'skaia	S. i V. Morozov/ Proletarskaia Diktatura	Orekhovo-Zuevo, Moscow guberniya	3KhT
Nogin	Aleksandrovskaia Nevskaia/K. M. Pal'	Leningrad	LTT
Novo- Gorkinskaia	Gorkinskaia	Gorkino, Ivanovo guberniya	2KhT
Novo-Ivanovo- Voznesenskaia	Z. Kokushkin i K. Marakushev	Ivanovo- Voznesensk	Ivtekst
Novo-Uvodskaia	?	? Ivanovo guberniya	?
Novyi Mir	A. A. Gol'mberg	Pereiaslavl', Vladimir guberniya	VGSNKh
Oktiabr'skaia	Popov	Manikhino, Moscow guberniya	M
Oktiabr'skaia Revoliutsiia	Staro-Gorkinskaia/ Malakovskaia	Malakova, Moscow guberniya	2KhT
Organizovannyi Trud	Lemeshenskaia/A. Nikitin	Bogoliubovo, Vladimir guberniya	VKhT
Osvobozh- dennyi Trud	Petr Alekseev	Moscow	M
Pavlovo- Pokorovskaia	Russko- Frantsutskaia/ Chicherin	Pavlovo-Posad, Moscow guberniya	3KhT
Perevolotskaia	?	Tver'	TKhT
Pistovskaia	I. I. Skvortsov	Pistovo, Ivanovo guberniya	Ivtekst
Pobeda Proletariata	Bardygin	Egor'evsk, Moscow guberniya	2KhT

Proletarii	Khutarev	Marapova-Okhta, Moscow guberniya	M
Proletarskaia Otrada	I. I. Baskakov	Klebinkovo, Moscow guberniya	KT
Rabochii	Petrovskaia	Leningrad	LTT
Rabotnitsa	Lebedeva	Leningrad	LTT
Ramenskaia	Krasnoe Znamia/Maliutin	Ramenskoe, Moscow guberniya	2KhT
Rassvet	Krizhachaskaia	Krizhach, Vladimir guberniya	VGSNKh
Ravenstvo	Ekateringofskaia	Leningrad	LTT
Reutovskaia	Turkmanufaktura/ L. Rabnek	Reutovo, Moscow guberniya	Turk
Revoliutsiia	Iur'evskaia/ Prokhorov	Iur'ev-Pol'skii, Vladimir guberniya	VKhT
Riabovskaia	Nogin	Serpukhov, Moscow guberniya	1KhT
Riazanovskaia	I. I. Baskanov	Riazanovo, Moscow guberniya	KT
Rodnikovskaia	A. Krasil'shchikov	Rodniki, Ivanovo guberniya	I–VTT
Samoilovskaia	T-vo Tiuleva	Leningrad	LTT
Samosonev'skaia	Oktiabr'skaia	Leningrad	LTT
Saratovskaia	Samoilovskaia	Khmelevki, Saratov guberniya	SM
Savinskaia	V. Morzov	Obiralovka, Moscow guberniya	3KhT
Seredskaia	Skvortsov i Gorbunov	Sereda, Ivanovo guberniya	I–VTT
Shagov	Nikol'sko-Bogoiavlenskaia/ Morokin i Tikhomirov/ Nikol'skaia	Kineshma, Ivanovo guberniya	Ivtekst
Shakomskaia	?	? Ivanovo guberniya	?
Shcherbakov	Rabochii	Ozero, Moscow guberniya	Pest

Shuiskaia	Pavlov/Br. Rubachev i A. A. Balin/Shuiskai I i II	Shuia, Ivanovo guberniya	I–VTT
Shuisko-Sukonnaia	Ts. Novik	Shuia, Ivanovo guberniya	I–VTT
Smirnov	Oktiabr'skaia	Borovkovo, Vladimir guberniya	VGSNKh
Sobolevo-Shchelkovskaia	Liudvik Rabenek	Shchelkovo, Moscow guberniya	Pest
Sokolovskaia	5-i Oktiabr'/A. Baranov	Strunino, Vladimir guberniya	VGSNKh
Sosnevskaia	Sosnevskaia Ob"edinenaia/ Pokrovskaia/ P. N. Griaznov/ N. Garelin	Ivanovo-Voznesensk	Ivtekst
Sovetskaia Zvezda	Nevskaia Nitochnaia	Leningrad	LTT
Stalin	Rabenek	Bol'shevo, Moscow guberniya	Pest
Staro-Posadskaia	D. G. Burylin	Ivanovo-Voznesensk	I–VGSNKh
Staro-Vichugskaia	F. i I. Razorenov	Vichuga, Ivanovo guberniya	I–VGSNKh
Stavrovskaia	Belov/Kutuzov	Koloksha, Vladimir guberniya	VKhT
Svoboda	Ganshin	Bel'kovo, Vladimir guberniya	VGSNKh
Sverdlov	Dzhems Bek	Leningrad	LTT
Tabolka	Prokhorovskaia	Vyshnii-Volochek, Tver' guberniya	TKhT
Tezinskaia	Krasnyi Profintern/ Kovorev i Razorenov	Vichuga, Ivanovo guberniya	I–VTT
Tomna	Krasno-Volzhskaia/ Tomenskaia/ Bol'shaia Kineshemskaia	Tomna, Ivanovo guberniya	I–VTT

Trekhgornaia	Prokhorovskaia Trekhgornaia/ Krasno-Presnenskaia	Moscow	2KhT
Trud	?	? Kaluga guberniya	?
Trudiashchiisia Rabochii	Vanilovskaia/ Gusev	Vanilovo, Moscow guberniya	2KhT
Tsindel'	Pervaia Sitsenabivanaia	Moscow	1KhT
Tverskaia	Tverskaia Proletarskaia/ Kalininskaia/ Proletarka	Tver'	TKhT
Vagzhanov	Rozhdestvenskaia	Tver'	TKhT
Varentsova	Bol'shaia Ivanovo-Voznesenskaia/ Kuvaevskaia	Ivanovo-Voznesensk	I–VTT
Vasil'evskaia	Boltushkinskaia	Vasil'evsko, Ivanovo guberniya	I–VGSNKh
Vera Slutskaia	Voronin/Liutsh i Chesher	Leningrad	LTT
Volodsarskaia	Staro-Nikol'skaia/ Kochetkov i S-ni	Vakhromsevo, Vladimir guberniya	VGSNKh
Volochek	Parizhskaia Kommuna/ Prokhorovskaia	Vyshnii-Volochek, Tver' guberniya	TKhT
Voronov	Ravenstvo	Pozniakovo, Vladimir guberniya	VGSNKh
Vos'moi Marta	Ikonikovskaia/ A. M. Gandurin i S-ni	Ivanovo-Voznesensk	I–VTT
Vozhd' Proletariata	Br. Khludov	Egor'evsk, Moscow guberniya	2KhT
Voznesenskaia	Lepeshkinskaia	Sofrino, Moscow guberniya	1KhT
Vozrozh-denskaia	Surnov	Aleksandrov, Vladimir guberniya	VGSNKh
Vpered	Katsepov	Kanabeevo, Moscow guberniya	2KhT

Vyshne-volotskaia	Riabushinskaia	Vyshnii-Volochek, Tver' guberniya	TKhT
Vysokovskaia	?	Klinskii uezd, Moscow guberniya	TKhT
Zariad'e Voznesenskaia	I. Gorelin/N. F. Zubkov	Ivanovo-Voznesensk	I–VTT
Zheliabov	Rossiiskaia	Leningrad	LTT
Zvonkov	Shchapov/O. Zvonkov	Moscow	Pest

Bibliography

ARCHIVES

Records of John Hubbard & Co. (1847–1948), Russian merchants, and of its companies: Anglo-Russian Cotton Factories Ltd (St Petersburg); Petroffsky Spinning & Weaving Co. (St Petersburg); Spassky Spinning & Weaving Co. (St Petersburg); Schlusselburg Calico Printing Co., Guildhall Library, London, L69.55 MS11, 759–62.

NEWSPAPERS

Ekonomicheskaia zhizn'
Golos tekstilei
Izvestiia
Komsomol'skaia pravda
Leningradskii tekstil'shchik
Moskovskii tekstil'shchik
Pravda
Rabochii krai
Tekstil'shchik, k stanku
Trud
Veselyi tkach
Vladimirskii tekstil'shchik

JOURNALS

Biulleten' ivanovo-voznesenskogo gosudarstvennogo tekstil'nogo tresta
Biulleten' ivanovo-voznesenskogo gubernskogo statisticheskogo biuro
Biulleten' moskovskogo gubotdela vsesoiuznogo professional'nogo soiuza tekstil'shchikov
Biulleten' otdela TsK RKP(b) po rabote sredi zhenshchin
Biulleten' podotdela statistiki TsK vsesoiuznogo professional'nogo soiuza tekstil'shchikov
Biulleten' TsK vsesoiuznogo profsoiuza tekstil'shchikov
Biulleten' vserossiiskogo tekstil'nogo sindikata
Bol'shevik

Ekonomicheskoe obozrenie
Iaroslavskii statisticheskii vestnik
Informatsionnaia svodka TsK vsesoiuznogo profsoiuza tekstil'shchikov
Izvestiia tekstil'noi promyshlennosti i torgovli
Khar'kovskii tekstil'shchik
Khoziaistvo i upravlenie
Kommunistka
Leningradskii tekstil'
Nashe khoziaistvo (Tver' guberniya economic council)
Nashe khoziaistvo (Executive of Vladimir guberniya's planning committee)
Okhrana truda
Organizatsiia truda
Planovoe khoziaistvo
Pod znamenem kommunizma
Predpriiatie
Puti industrializatsii
Rabochaia zhizn'
Sistema i organizatsiia
Sotsialisticheskii vestnik
Sputnik agitatora
Sputnik kommunista
Statisticheskoe obozrenie
Statistika truda
Tekstil'nye novosti
Tekstil'shchik
Textile Recorder
Trud (Ivanovo guberniya's textileworkers' union and trades council)
Trud i proizvodstvo
Vestnik manufakturnoi promyshlennosti
Vestnik profsoiuzov
Vestnik truda
Voprosy truda

TEXTILEWORKERS' UNION REPORTS

Congresses and conferences

Rezoliutsii 4-oi vserossiiskoi konferentsii soiuza tekstil'shchikov, 23–27 oktiabria 1923g, Moscow (1923)
Rezoliutsii i postanovleniia 6-go s"ezda professional'nogo soiuza tekstil'shchikov, Moscow (1924)

Central committee

Otchet TsK vserossiiskogo professional'nogo soiuza tekstil'shch kov sent. 1922g–sent. 1923g. K IV vseross. konferentsii soiuza 1923g, Moscow (1923)
Otchet TsK vsesoiuznogo professional'nogo soiuza tekstil'shchikov k VI vsesoiuznomu s"ezdu tekstil'shchikov. Okt. 1922g–okt. 1924g, Moscow (1924)
Otchet TsK vsesoiuznogo professional'nogo soiuza tekstil'shchikov k 7-mu vsesoiuz-nomu s"ezdu tekstil'shchikov. Iiul' 1924g–ianv. 1926g, Moscow (1926)

Postanovleniia 2-go plenuma TsK vsesoiuznogo soiuza tekstil'shchikov 21–23 maia 1925g v Leningrade, Moscow (1925)

Rezoliutsii 3-go plenuma TsK soiuza tekstil'shchikov (12–15 aprelia 1923g), Moscow (1923)

Ivanovo branch

Otchet gubernskogo otdela soiuza 15-mu gubernskomu s"ezdu tekstil'shchikov ivanovo-voznesenskoi gubernii (apr. 1924g–mart 1925g), Ivanovo-Voznesensk (1925)

Otchet o rabote ivanovo-voznesenskogo gubernskogo otdela vserossiiskogo professional'-nogo soiuza tekstil'shchikov za vremia s 1 iiunia 1923g po 1 apr. 1924g. XIII–XIV s"ezd, Kineshma (1924)

Otchet o rabote ivanovo-voznesenskogo gubernskogo otdela vsesoiuznogo soiuza tekstil'shchikov za vremia s apr. 1925g–mart 1926g. 16-mu s"ezdu soiuza, Ivanovo-Voznesensk (1926)

Leningrad branch

Otchet leningradskogo gubernskogo otdela vsesoiuznogo professional'nogo soiuza tekstil'shchikov. Okt. 1924–1925gg, Leningrad (1926)

Moscow branch

Itogi raboty moskovskogo gubernskogo otdela profsoiuza tekstil'shchikov s 1 aprelia 1924g po 1 okt. 1925g, Moscow (1926)

Otchet o rabote bogorodskogo uezdnogo otdeleniia tekstil'shchikov za period s okt. 1925g po 1 ianv. 1927g, Bogorodsk (1927)

Otchet o rabote moskovskogo gubernskogo otdela vsesoiuznogo professional'nogo soiuza tekstil'shchikov mart 1922g–mart 1923g, Moscow (1923)

Otchet o rabote moskovskogo gubernskogo otdela vsesoiuznogo professional'nogo soiuza tekstil'shchikov mai–iiul' 1923, Moscow (1923)

Otchet o rabote moskovskogo gubernskogo otdela vsesoiuznogo professional'nogo soiuza tekstil'shchikov avg.–okt. 1923g, Moscow (1923)

Otchet o rabote moskovskogo gubernskogo otdela vsesoiuznogo professional'nogo soiuza tekstil'shchikov okt.–dek. 1923g, Moscow (1923)

Otchet o rabote moskovskogo gubernskogo otdela vsesoiuznogo professional'nogo soiuza tekstil'shchikov mai 1923g–mart 1924g, Moscow (1924)

Otchet o rabote moskovskogo gubernskogo otdela vsesoiuznogo professional'nogo soiuza tekstil'shchikov okt.–dek. 1924g, Moscow (1925)

Otchet o rabote moskovskogo gubernskogo otdela vsesoiuznogo professional'nogo soiuza tekstil'shchikov ianv.–mart 1925g, Moscow (1925)

Rezoliutsii moskovskogo gubotdela soiuza tekstil'shchikov za period oktiabr' 1924g–fevral' 1925g, Moscow (1925)

Tezisy, priniatye plenumom gubotdela 12 maia 1923g. (Materialy k 5-mu moskovskomu gubs"ezdu tekstil'shchikov), Moscow (1924)

Vladimir branch

Otchet o rabote vladimirskogo gubernskogo pravleniia professional'nogo soiuza tekstil'shchikov s 1 sent. 1922g po 1 avg. 1923g, Vladimir (1923)

Otchet o rabote vladimirskogo gubernskogo pravleniia professional'nogo soiuza tekstil'shchikov s sent. 1923g po sent. 1924g. K 7-mu gubernskomu s"ezdu soiuza, Vladimir (1924)

Otchet o rabote vladimirskogo gubernskogo pravleniia professional'nogo soiuza tekstil'shchikov okt. 1924g–okt. 1925g. K 8-mu gubernskomu s"ezdu soiuza, Vladimir (1925)

Otchet o rabote vladimirskogo gubernskogo pravleniia professional'nogo soiuza tekstil'shchikov okt. 1925g–okt. 1926g, Vladimir (1926)

Rezoliutsii i postanovleniia 7-go gubernskogo s"ezda soiuza tekstil'shchikov 25–27 okt. 1924g, Vladimir (1924)

Rezoliutsii i postanovleniia (8-go) vladimirskogo gubernskogo s"ezda soiuza tekstil'shchikov 13–18 dek. 1925g, Vladimir (1925)

Sbornik postanovlenii pravleniia soiuza, prezidiuma i soveshchanii pri prezidiume gubotdela (za mart–aprelai 1925g), Vladimir (1925)

TRUST REPORTS

Leningrad
Otchet za 1924–25g. Leningradskii gosudarstvennyi tekstil'nyi trest 'Leningradtekstil'', Leningrad (1925)

Moscow region
Kratkii otchet pravleniia orekhovo-zuevskogo tresta khlopchatobumazhnykh·fabrik o deiatel'nosti v 1925–26gg (za 11 mesiatev; okt. 1925g–avg. 1926 po predvarit. dannym) pered shirokoi rabochii proizvodstvennoi konferentsei v Orekhove 16 oktiabria 1926g, Orekhovo-Zuevo (1926)

Obzor deiatel'nosti krasno-presnenskogo tresta za 1924–1925 operats. goda, Moscow (1925)

Otchet za 1-e polgodie 1924–1925 operats. god. Orekhovo-Zuevskii gosudarstvennyi trest khlopchato-bumazhnykh fabrik, Moscow (1925)

Otchet za 1924–1925 operats. god. (Po predvarit. dannym). Orekhovo-Zuevskii gosudarstvennyi trest khlopchatobumazhnykh fabrik, Moscow (1926)

Ivanovo region
Otchet ivanovo-voznesenskogo gosudarstvennogo tekstil'nogo tresta za 1923–24gg, Ivanovo-Voznesensk (1925)

Vladimir region
Tri goda raboty vladimirsko-aleksandrovskogo tresta khlopchatobumazhnykh fabrik, 1922–1924gg, Moscow (1925)

DOCUMENT COLLECTIONS

Komsomol'tsy i molodezh' ivanovskoi oblasti v gody stroitel'stva sotsializma (1917–1940gg), Ivanovo (1967)

Nauchnaia organizatsiia truda, proizvodstva i upravleniia, (1918–1930gg), Moscow (1969)

Resheniia partii i pravitel'stva po khoziaistvennom voprosam (1917–1967gg), tom 2, Moscow (1967)

Saval'ev, M., ed., *Direktivy VKP(b) v oblasti khoziaistvennoi politiki za desiat' let (1917–1927gg)*, Moscow-Leningrad (1928)

Tiul'panov, S. I. ed., *Istoriia industrializatsii SSSR. Dokumenty i materialy. Zavershenie vosstanovleniia promyshlennosti i nachalo industrializatsii severozapadnogo raiona (1925–1928gg)*, Leningrad (1964)

Vek truda i bor'by. Dokumenty i materialy po istorii kalinskogo khlopchatobumazhnogo kombinata 1858–1958gg, Kalinin (1961).

Vosstanovlenie promyshlennosti Leningrada, (1921–1924gg), tom 1, Leningrad (1963)

Vosstanovlenie tekstil'noi promyshlennosti ivanovo-voznesenskoi gubernii, 1920–1925gg, Ivanovo (1966)

OTHER PUBLISHED MATERIALS

Bibliographies and reference works

Atlas Souiza Sovetskikh Sotsialisticheskikh Respublik, Moscow (1928)

Bibliograficheskii ukazatel' knig i broshiur po istorii fabrik i zavodov, Moscow (1932)

Cherepnin, V. A., *Knizhnaia literatura po tekstil'nomu delu za 1927g. (Ukazatel')*, Moscow (1929)

Genkina, E. B., ed., *Sovetskaia strana v period vosstanovleniia narodnogo khoziaistva (1921–1925gg): bibliograficheskii ukazetel' dokumental'nykh publikatsii*, Moscow (1975)

Hetherington and Sons Ltd., *Illustrated Catalogue of Textile Machinery and Views of Mills Equipped*, Manchester (1906 and 1931)

Howard and Bullough Ltd., *Illustrated Catalogue of Cotton Preparing, Spinning, Doubling and Manufacturing Machinery*, Accrington (1906)

Combined Illustrated Catalogue, Machine Calculations and Useful Memoranda, Accrington (1925)

Kaplun, S., *Ukazatel' literatury na russkom iazyke po NOT i smeshnym voprosam*, Moscow-Leningrad (1924)

Karta zheleznykh, vodnykh i shosseinykh putei soobeshchaniia evropeiskii chasti SSSR, Moscow (1925)

Kogan, M. I., *Kratkii tekhnicheskii russko-nemetsko-frantsuzko-angliiskii tekstil'nyi slovar'* Ivanovo-Voznesensk (1928)

Mikhailov, A. S., Rumianshchev, I. N., *Russko-angliiskii tekstil'nyi slovar'* tom I–V, Ivanovo-Voznesensk (1928)

Narodnoe khoziaistvo SSSR v 1921–1925gg: ukazetel' sovetskoi literatury 1921–1924gg, Moscow (1980/81)

Periodicheskaia pechat' SSSR 1917–1949gg, bibliograficheskii ukazetel', Moscow (1978)

Poleshaev, V. I., *Istoriia predpriiatiia SSSR. Ukazatel' sovetskoi literatury, izdannoi v 1917–1978gg*, vyp. I–III, Moscow (1979)

Rogachevskaia, L. S., 'Obzor literatury po istorii fabrik i zavodov izdannoi v 1956–1960gg', in *Voprosy istoriografii i istochnikovedeniia istorii rabochego klassa SSSR*, Leningrad (1962)

Schlomann, A., *Illustrierte Technische Worterbucher. Band XV. Spinnerei und Gespinde*, Oldenburg, Munich (1925)

Shevtsova, A. F., 'Massovye profsoiuznye zhurnaly 1917–1937gg kak istochnik po istorii rabochego klassa. (Po materialam zhurnal'nogo fonda GPB im. M E Saltykova-Shchedrina)', in *Istoriia rabochego klassa Leningrada*, vyp. 1, Leningrad (1962)

Tekstil'naia promyshlennost'. Bibliograficheskii ukazatel' 1917–1965gg, tom 1–3, Moscow (1982)

Tekstil'nye fabriki SSSR, Moscow (1927)

Zemskov, V. N., ed., *Rabochii klass SSSR 1917–1977gg. Ukazatel' sovetskoi literatury izdannoi v 1971–1977gg*, Moscow (1978)

Zvezdin, Z. K., 'Periodicheskaia pechat' kak istochnik po istorii trudovogo pod"ema rabochego klassa SSSR 1926—1929gg (Obzor materialov)', *Problemy istochnikovedeniia*, 8, 1959

Books and articles

Abramov, A., *Nagliadnyi uchet v tekstil'noi promyshlennosti*, Moscow-Leningrad (1926)

Aleshchenko, I. M., 'Iz istorii rabochego klassa Moskvy v vosstanovlennyi period (1921–1925gg)', *Istoriia SSSR*, 1, January–February 1959

Amshinskii, M., *Vyzov priniat! Opyt organizatsiia sotsialisticheskogo sorevnovaniia na 'Proletarskoi manufakture' v gorode Tveri*, Moscow (1929)

Andreev, I. G., *Nevskie priadil'shchiki. Kratkii ocherk istorii priadil'no-nitochnogo kombinata im. S. M. Kirova*, Leningrad (1959)

Andrle, V., *Workers in Stalin's Russia: Industrialization and Social Change in a Planned Economy*, Harvester Wheatsheaf, Brighton (1988)

Ankydinov, L. E. 'Podgotovka kadrov molodykh rabochikh (po materialam Leningrada)', in *Istoriia rabochego klassa Leningrada*, vyp. 1, Leningrad (1962)

Avdakov, Y. Borodin, V., *USSR State Industry During the Transition Period*, Progress, Moscow (1977)

Bailes, K. E., *Technology and Society under Lenin and Stalin: Origins of the Soviet Technical Intelligentsia, 1917–41*, Princeton University Press, Princeton (1978)

Baines, E., *History of the Cotton Manufacture in Great Britain*, Fisher, Fisher and Jackson, London (1835)

Bandera, V. N., 'Market orientation of state enterprises during NEP', *Soviet Studies*, 1, 1970

Belinskii, I. S. Kucherov, A. I., *Tri mesiatsa raboty semichasovykh fabrik. (Opyt perevoda i raboty semichasovykh fabrik v ivanovo-voznesenskoi gubernii)*, Ivanovo-Voznesensk (1928)

Bessonov, S., *Semichasovoi rabochii den' i ratsionalizatsiia*, Moscow (1928)

Bineman, Ia. M., ed., *Trud v SSSR 1926–30gg*, Moscow (1930)

Blackwell, W. L., *The Beginnings of Russian Industrialization 1800–1860*, Princeton University Press, Princeton (1968)

Blinova, I. I. *et al.*, 'Pervye udarnye komsomol'skie brigady na predpriiatiiakh Leningrada', *Istoricheskii arkhiv*, 6, November–December 1958

Bol'shaia Kokhomskaia tekstil'naia manufaktura. Proizvodstvennyi al'bom 1925g, Ivanovo-Voznesenesk (1925)

Bol'shakov, A. M., 'The Soviet countryside 1917–1924; its economics and life', [Leningrad, 1924], *Journal of Peasant Studies*, 4, 1, October 1976

Borboff, A., 'The Bolsheviks and working women 1905–20', *Soviet Studies*, 4, 1974

Borders, K., *Village Life under the Soviets*, Vanguard, New York (1927)

Borisov, I. P., Kheifets, L. S., *Chto dala funktsionalka na fabrike imeni Lakina*, Moscow/Ivanovo-Voznesensk (1931)

Borisov, Y. S., *et al.*, *Outline History of the Soviet Working Class*, Progress, Moscow (1973)

Borodin, V., *Zhenskii trud v Sovetskoi tekstil'noi promyshlennosti*, Moscow (1926)

Braginskii, M. O., *Zhilishchnyi vopros v tekstil'noi promyshlennosti*, Moscow (1927)

Brailsford, H. N., *The Russian Workers' Republic*, George Allen & Unwin, London (1921)

Braverman, H., *Labor and Monopoly Capitalism. The Degradation of Work in the Twentieth Century*, Monthly Review Press, New York (1974)

Brodskii, N. L. *et al.*, *Tekstil'shchik (istoria, byt, bor'ba)*, Moscow (1925)

Budaev, D. I., *Estafeta pokolenii. Ocherki istorii k 100 letiiu iartsevskogo kh. b. kombinata*, Moscow (1973)

Budanov, D. D., *Obshchie poniatiia o NOT'e v chastnosti v tekstil'noi promyshlennosti*, Ivanovo-Voznesensk (1926)

Buianov, V. A., *Tekstil'shchiku, o trudovoi distsipline*, Moscow (1929)

Buras, A. M., *Osnovy tekhnicheskogo normirovaniia v tekstil'noi promyshlennosti*, Ivanovo-Voznesensk (1930)

Carr, E. H., *The Bolshevik Revolution 1917–23*, vol. 2, Penguin, Harmondsworth (1966)

The Interregnum 1923–24, Penguin, Harmondsworth (1969)

Socialism in One Country, vol. 1, Penguin, Harmondsworth (1970)

Carr, E. H., Davies, R. W., *Foundations of a Planned Economy 1926–1929*, vol. 1, part 1, Macmillan, London (1969)

Foundations of a Planned Economy 1926–1929, vol. 1, part 2, Macmillan, London (1969)

Catling, H., *The Spinning Mule*, David & Charles, Newton Abbot (1970)

Chase, W. J., *Workers, Society, and the Soviet State. Labor and Life in Moscow, 1918–1929*, University of Illinois Press, Urbana and Chicago (1987)

Cohen, S. F., *Bukharin and the Bolshevik Revolution: a Political Biography 1888–1938*, Vintage Books, New York (1975)

Conyngham, W. J., *Industrial Management in the Soviet Union: the Role of the CPSU in Industrial Decision-making, 1917–1970*, Hoover Institution Press, Stanford (1973)

Crisp, O., 'Labour and industrialization in Russia', in P. Mathias, M. M.

Postan, eds., *The Cambridge Economic History of Europe*, vol. 7, part 2, Cambridge University Press, Cambridge (1978)

Studies in the Russian Economy Before 1914, Macmillan, London (1976)

Day, R., *Leon Trotsky and the Politics of Economic Isolation*, Cambridge University Press, Cambridge (1973)

Derevnina, L. I., 'Material'noe polozhenie rabochikh. Povyshenie trudovoi aktivnosti truzhenikov promyshlennosti, in *Istoriia rabochikh Leningrada*, tom 2, 1917–1965gg, Leningrad (1972)

Rabochie Leningrada v period vosstanovleniia narodnogo khoziaistva: chislennost', sostav i material'noe polozhenie, Leningrad (1981)

'Vosstanovlenie petrogradskoi promyshlennosti. Izmeneniia v chislennosti i sostave rabochikh', in *Istoriia rabochikh Leningrada*, tom 2, 1917–1965gg, Leningrad (1972)

Deutscher, I., *The Prophet Unarmed. Trotsky: 1921–1929*, Oxford University Press, Oxford (1970)

Soviet Trade Unions: Their Place in Soviet Labour Policy, Royal Institute of International Affairs, London (1950)

Dewar, M., *Labour Policy in the USSR 1917–28*, Royal Institute of International Affairs, London (1956)

Dobb., M., *Soviet Economic Development Since 1917*, 6th ed., Routledge & Kegan Paul, London (1966)

Dosov, M., *Trekhgorka na sitsevom fronte*, Moscow-Leningrad (1929)

Dostizheniia i nedochety tekstil'noi promyshlennosti SSSR. (Po materialam tekstil'noi sektsii NK RKI SSSR), Moscow (1926)

Dunaev, A., Goriachev, Iu., *Iartsevskii khlopchato-bumazhnyi kombinat. (Kratkii istoricheskii ocherk)*, Smolensk (1963)

Dunn, R., *Soviet Trade Unions*, Vanguard Press, New York (1928)

Dzerzhinskii, F. *et al.*, eds., *K probleme proizvoditel'nosti truda*, Moscow-Leningrad (1925)

Ekzempliarskii, P. M., *Istoriia goroda Ivanova. Chast' 1. Dooktiabr'skii period*, Ivanovo (1958)

Ellison, H. J., 'The decision to collectivize agriculture', *Slavic Review*, April 1961

Emel'ianova, E. D., *Rabota kommunisticheskoi partii sredi trudiashchikhsia zhenshchin v vosstanovitel'nyi period*, Smolensk (1961)

English, W., *The Textile Industry*, Longmans, London (1969)

Eremin, I. G., *Trudovaia distsiplina v tekstil'noi promyshlennosti*, Moscow, Leningrad (1929)

Fabrichno-zavodskaia promyshlennost' g. Moskvy i moskovskoi gubernii. 1917–1927gg, Moscow (1928)

Fainsod, M., *Smolensk Under Soviet Rule*, Macmillan, London (1958)

Farbman, M. S., *After Lenin. The New Phase in Russia*, Parsons, London (1924)

Farnie, D. A., 'Platt Bros & Co. Ltd. of Oldham, machine makers to Lancashire and the world: an index of production of cotton spinning spindles 1880–1914' *Business History*, 23, March 1981

'The textile industry: woven fabrics', in C. Singer, *et al.*, eds., *A History of*

Technology: The Late Nineteenth Century c1850 to c1900, vol. 5, Clarendon Press, Oxford (1958)

Farson, N., *Seeing Red Today in Russia*, Eyre & Spottiswoode, London (1930)

Feoktistov, V. I., *Ekskursiia na bumagopriadil'nuiu fabriku*, Leningrad (1924)

Filtzer, D., *Soviet Workers and Stalinist Industrialization: The Formation of Modern Soviet Production Relations, 1921–1924*, Pluto Press, London (1986)

Fraser, J. F., *Russia of To-day*, Cassell, London (1915)

Frumkin, B., *Semichasovoi rabochii den' i profsoiuzy*, Moscow (1928)

Genkina, E. B., 'Ob osobennostiakh vosstanovleniia promyshlennosti v SSSR (1921–1925gg)', *Istoriia SSSR*, 5, 1962

Glebov, Iu. F., Letukov, T. N., *Ivanovo*, Iaroslavl' (1981)

Glebov, Iu. F., Sokolov, V. M., *Istoriia fabrika Bol'shoi Ivanovskoi manufaktury*, Ivanovo (1952)

Gordon, M., *Workers Before and After Lenin*, Dutton & Co., New York (1941)

Griffith, H., *Seeing Soviet Russia*, John Lane & The Bodley Head, London (1932)

Gutarov, A. N., 'Proizvodstvennye soveshchaniia na leningradskikh pred-priiatiiakh (1926–1929gg)', in *Istoriia rabochego klassa Leningrada*, vyp. 1, Leningrad (1962)

Harris, C. D., *Cities of the Soviet Union. Studies in their functions, Size, Density, and Growth*, Rand McNally, Chicago (1970)

Harrison, M., 'Why did NEP fail?', *Economics of Planning*, 2, 1980

Hills, R. L., *Power in the Industrial Revolution*, Manchester University Press, Manchester (1970)

Hunter, H., 'The over-ambitious first Soviet Five Year Plan', *Slavic Review*, June 1973

Iakobson, Iu. A., 'Proizvodstvennye soveshchaniia na ivanovo-voznesenskikh tekstil'nykh fabrikakh (1924–1925gg)', in *Iz istorii rabochego klassa SSSR*, Ivanovo (1967)

'Uchastie ivanovo-voznesenskikh rabochikh v formirovanii komandnykh kadrov tekstil'noi promyshlennosti (1921–1925gg)', in *Iz istorii rabochego klassa SSSR*, Ivanovo (1967)

Iakovlev, Iu. F., *Vladimirskie rabochie v bor'be i ukreplenie soiuza s krest'ianstvom v 1921–1925 godakh*, Vladimir (1963)

Il'ina, G. I., 'Chislennost', sostav i material'noe polozhenie rabochikh Petrograda v 1918–1920gg', in *Istoriia rabochikh Leningrada*, tom 2, 1917–1965gg, Leningrad (1962)

Il'inskii, V. V., *Ivanovskii tekstil'shchik. Sostav i sotsial'naia kharakteristika rabochikh-tekstil'shchikov ivanovskoi promyshlennoi oblasti*, Ivanovo-Voznesensk (1930)

Initsiativnyi sovet po nauchnoi organizatsii truda pri tsentral'nom komitete soiuza tekstil'shchikov. Kratkii otchet, Moscow (1924)

Isakov, V. V., Khalturina, Iu. N., *Izucheniia proizvoditel'nosti i utomliaemosti pri perekhode na tkatskikh fabrikakh s 2-kh na 3-kh stanka*, Ivanovo-Voznesensk (1928)

Itsikson, M. B., *Reutovskaia priadil'naia fabrika. Ocherk*, Moscow (1928)

Ivanova, N. A., 'Sotsial'no-ekonomicheskoe razvitie Rossii v 1907–14gg.

Izmeneniia v riadiakh rabochego klassa', in *Istoriia rabochego klassa SSSR. Rabochii klass Rossii. 1907–fevral' 1917g*, Moscow (1982)

Ivanovo-Voznesenskaia guberniia za desiat' let oktiabr'skoi revoliutsii (1917–1927gg), Ivanovo-Voznesensk (1927)

Jenkins, D. T., 'The textile industries; general survey', in T. Williams, ed., *A History of Technology: The Twentieth Century c1900 to c1950*, vol. 6, part I, Clarendon Press, Oxford (1978)

Johnson, R. E., *Peasant and Proletarian. The Working Class of Moscow in the Late Nineteenth Century*, Leicester University Press, Leicester (1979)

Joyce, P., *Work, Society and Politics: The Culture of the Factory in Later Victorian England*, Rutgers University Press, New Brunswick NJ (1980)

Kaiser, M. C., 'Russian entrepreneurship', in P. Mathias, M. M. Postan, eds., *The Cambridge Economic History of Europe*, vol. 7, part 2, Cambridge University Press, Cambridge (1978)

Kanatchikova, B., *Rabotnitsa v leningradskoi promyshlennosti*, Leningrad (1925)

Kapustin, A., *Udarniki*, Moscow-Leningrad (1930)

Kaufman, A., *Small-scale Industry in the Soviet Union*, National Bureau of Economic Research, occasional paper 80, New York (1962)

Khromov, P. A., *Ocherki ekonomiki tekstil'noi promyshlennosti SSSR*, Moscow-Leningrad (1946)

Kilevits, F. F., *Tekstil'naia promyshlennost' i rabochie tekstil'shchiki*, Moscow-Leningrad (1928)

Kir'ianov, Iu. I., *Zhiznennyi uroven' rabochikh Rossii (konets XIX – nachalo XXv)*, Moscow (1979)

Komsostav krupnoi promyshlennosti. (Po materialam orgraspred, otdela TsK RKP), Moscow (1924)

Korneev, A. M., *Tekstil'naia promyshlennost' SSSR i puti ee razvitiia*, Moscow-Leningrad (1957)

'Krasnyi Perekop.' Priadil'no-tkatskaia fabrika v Iaroslavle. Proizvodstvennyi al'bom Iaroslavl' (1926)

'Krasny Profintern' bumago-priadil'naia, tkatskaia i otdelochnaia fabrika v s.Tezino, ivanovo-voznesenskoi gubernii. Proizvodstvennyi al'bom, s.Tezino (1926)

Krichevskii, S. I., *Sbornik lektsii chitannykh na proizvodstvenno-ekonomicheskikh kursakh pri TsK soiuza tekstil'shchikov*, vyp. 3, Moscow (1926)

Kruze, E. E., 'Leningrad v period vosstanovleniia narodnogo khoziaistva (1921–1925gg)', in *Ocherki istorii Leningrada*, tom 4, Moscow-Leningrad (1964)

Kungurtsev, V. A., *Tekstil'naia promyshlennost' SSSR. Issledovanie i materialy*, serii II (rotatornye izdaniia), no. 61, Institut po izucheniiu SSSR, Munich (1957)

Kuromiya, H., *Stalin's Industrial Revolution: Politics and Workers 1928–1932*, Cambridge University Press, Cambridge (1988)

Kuz'michev, V., *Organizatsiia obshchestvennogo mneniia. Pechatnaia agitatsiia*, Moscow-Leningrad (1929)

Kuznetsov, V. A., 'Predvestniki massovogo sotsialisticheskogo sorevnovaniia', in *Leningradskie rabochie v bor'be za sotsializma, 1926–1937gg*, Leningrad (1965)

Kvasha, Ia., Shofman, F., *Semichasovoi rabochii den' v tekstil'noi promyshlennosti*, Moscow (1930)

Lampert, N., *The Technical Intelligentsia and the Soviet State: a Study of Managers and Technicians, 1928–35*, Macmillan, London (1979)

Laverychev, V. Ia., 'Protsess monopolizatsii khlopchato-bumazhnoi promyshlennosti Rossi (1900–1914gg)', *Voprosy istorii*, 2, February, 1960

Lavrikov, Iu. A. *et al.*, *Ocherk ekonomicheskogo razvitiia leningradskoi industrii za 1917–1967gg*, Leningrad (1968)

Lavrova, A., *Kak zhivut i trudiatsia rabochie-tekstil'shchiki*, Moscow (1926)

Lawton, L., *The Russian Revolution 1917–26*, Macmillan, London (1927)

Lazonick, W. H., 'Competition, specialization and industrial decline', *Journal of Economic History*, 41, 1, March 1981

'Factor costs and the diffusion of ring-spinning in Britain prior to World War One', *The Quarterly Journal of Economics*, 46, 1, February 1981

'Industrial relations and technical change; the case of the self-acting mule', *Cambridge Journal of Economics*, 3, 1979

'Production relations, labor productivity, and choice of technique: British and U.S. cotton spinning', *Journal of Economic History*, 41, 3, September 1981

Lebedev, N. B., Shkaratan, O. I., *Ocherki istorii sotsialisticheskogo sorevnovaniia*, Leningrad (1966)

Lediaev, G. F., 'Bor'ba partiinykh organizatsii verkhnei Volgi za nakoplenie sredstv dlia sotsialisticheskoi industrializatsii (1925–1929gg)', in *Iz istorii rabochego klassa SSSR*, Ivanovo (1972)

Lenin, V. I., *Selected Works*, vols. 2–3, Progress, Moscow (1976)

Leninskii prizyv RKP(b), Moscow-Leningrad (1925)

Lewin, M., *Lenin's Last Struggle* (trans. A. M. Sheridan-Smith), Pluto Press, London (1975)

Russian Peasants and Soviet Power, George Allen & Unwin, London (1968)

Magaziner, L., *Chislennost' i sostav professional'nykh soiuzov SSSR*, Moscow (1926)

Makarov, V. M. Fedotov, A. A., eds., *Trudy soveshchaniia proizvodstvennikov v tekstil'noi promyshlennosti. Moskva, 2–4 iiunia 1924g*, Moscow (1925)

Malysheva, A. A., Chugunova, K. F., 'Na fabrike "Ravenstvo"', in *Zhenshchiny goroda Lenina*, Leningrad (1963)

Mann, J. de L., 'The textile industry: machinery for cotton, flax, wool, 1760–1850', in C. Singer *et al.*, eds., *A History of Technology: The Industrial Revolution c1750 to c1850*, vol. 4, Clarendon Press, Oxford (1958)

Marx, K., *Capital*, vol 1, (trans. S. More & E. Aveling), The Modern Library, New York (1906)

Matiugin, A. A., 'Izmeneniia v sostave promyshlennykh rabochikh SSSR v vosstanovlennyi period (1921–1925gg)', in *Izmeneniia v chislennosti i sostave sovetskogo rabochego klassa*, Moscow (1961)

Rabochii klass SSSR v gody vosstanovleniia narodnogo khoziaistva (1921–1925gg), Moscow (1962)

Meyer, A. G., 'The war scare of 1927', *Soviet Union/Union soviétique*, 5, 1, 1978

Mikhailov, A. K., *et al.*, 'Tekstil'naia, trikotazhnaia i shveinaia promyshlennost', in *Leningradskaia promyshlennost' za 50 let*, Leningrad (1967)

Millar, J. B., 'Mass collectivization and the contribution of Soviet agriculture to the First Five Year Plan', *Slavic Review*, 4, December 1974

Miller, M. S., *The Economic Development of Russia, 1905–1914*, P. S. King & Son Ltd., London (1926)

Mints, L. E., Engel', I. F., eds., *Statisticheskie materialy po trudu i sotsial'nomu strakhovaniiu za 1925–26g*, vyp. 1, Moscow (1927)

Statisticheskie materialy po trudu i sotsial'nomu strakhovaniiu za 1926–27g, vyp. 1, kn. 2, 3; vyp. 4, kn. 4, Moscow (1927–28).

Mironov, B. P., Stepanov, Z. V., 'Stroiteli sotsializm', in *Rabochie Leningrada. Kratkii istoricheskii ocherk 1703–1975gg*, Leningrad (1975)

Na novykh putiakh. Itogi novoi ekonomicheskoi politiki 1921–1922gg, vyp. 3, Moscow (1923)

Narkiewicz, O. A., *The Making of the Soviet State Apparatus*, Manchester University Press, Manchester (1970)

Nol'de, A. A., *NOT v tekstil'noi promyshlennosti*, Moscow (1924)

'Obzor arkhivnykh materialov po istorii fabriki "Krasnyi Perekop" (1722–1929gg)', *Krasnyi arkhiv*, 63, 1934

Ocherki istorii leningradskoi organizatsii KPSS. Chast' II, noiabr' 1917g–1945g, Leningrad (1968)

Odell, R. M., *Cotton Goods in Russia*, Department of Commerce and Labor, special agents series 51, Washington (1912)

Okhrana truda v tekstil'noi promyshlennosti, Moscow (1927)

Ostapenko, I. P., *Uchastie rabochego klassa SSSR v upravlenii proizvodstvom: proizvodstvennye sovershchaniia v promyshlennosti v 1921–1932gg*, Moscow (1964)

Ozdorovlenie truda i revoliutsiia byta, vyp. 4, chast' 1, Moscow (1924)

Partiia v period stroitel'stva sotsializma i kommunizma, Moscow (1977)

Pashkevich, E. F. Shkaratan, O. I., 'Na kul'turom pod"eme', in *Leningradskie rabochie v bor'be za sotsializma 1926–1937gg*, Leningrad (1965)

Pavlov, N. T., *Sel'faktor*, Moscow (1926)

Pazhitnov, K. A., *Ocherki istorii tekstil'noi promyshlennosti dorevoliutsionnoi Rossii: khlopchato-bumazhnaia, l'no-pen'kovaia i shelkovaia promyshlennost'*, Moscow (1958)

Pikhalo, V. T., 'Trestovanie promyshlennosti SSSR v 20-e gody', *Istoriia SSSR*, 4, July–August 1971

Pis'mennyi, A., *Na Glukhovke za 20 let. Glukhovskii khlopchatobumazhnyi kombinat im. V. I. Lenina*, Moscow (1937)

Poliakova, N. V., 'Bor'ba rabochikh-tekstil'shchikov za povyshenie proizvoditel'nosti truda v 1921–1925gg. (Po materialam Moskvy i moskovskoi gubernii)', *Voprosy istorii*, 6, July 1959

Polozheniia i instruktsii fabkomam i komissiiam, Moscow (1923)

Portal, R., 'The Industrialization of Russia', in H. J. Habakkuk, M. Postan, eds., *The Cambridge Economic History of Europe*, vol. 6, part 2, Cambridge University Press, Cambridge (1965)

'Muscovite industrialists: the cotton sector (1861–1914)', in W. L. Blackwell, ed., *Russian Economic Development from Peter the Great to Stalin*, New Viewpoints, New York (1974)

Postoiannaia promyshlennaia pokazatel'naia vystavka VSNKh. Vystavka tekstil'nykh trestov. 16 oktiabria 1922g, Moscow (1923)

Professional'nye soiuzy SSSR 1922–1924gg. Otchet VTsSPS k VI s"ezdu profsoiuzov, Moscow (1924)

Professional'nye soiuzy SSSR 1924–1926gg. Otchet VTsSPS k VII s"ezdu profsoiuzov, Moscow (1926)

Profsoiuz tekstil'shchikov (kratkii istoricheskii ocherk), Moscow (1963).

Rabota moskovskogo gubernskogo soveta profsoiuzov s oktiabria 1924g po ianvar' 1926g, Moscow (1926)

Rabota tkachikh v nochnoi smene, Moscow (1929)

Rashin, A. G., *Sostav fabrichno-zavodskogo proletariata SSSR*, Moscow (1930)

ed., *Trud v SSSR. (Statistiko-ekonomicheskii obzor, oktiabr' 1922g–mart 1924g)*, Moscow (1924)

Zarabotnaia plata za vosstanovitel'nyi period khoziaistva SSSR. 1922/23–1926/27gg, Moscow (1927)

Zhenskii trud v SSSR, vyp. 1, Moscow (1928)

Rezoliutsii 1-go vsesoiuznogo s"ezda otdelov truda i T.N.B. tekstil'noi promyshlennosti (20–26/IX–1925g), Moscow–Leningrad (1926)

Rezoliutsii 20-i ivanovo-voznesenskoi gubernskoi partiinoi konferentsii (1–4 iiulia 1925g), Ivanovo-Voznesensk (1925)

Rigby, T. H., *Communist Party Membership in the USSR, 1917–1967*, Princeton University Press, Princeton (1968)

Rogachevskaia, L. S., *Iz istorii rabochego klassa SSSR v pervye gody industrializatsii (1926–1927gg)*, Moscow (1959)

Likvidatsiia bezrabotitsy v SSSR 1917–1930gg, Moscow (1973)

Sotsialisticheskoe sorevnovanie v SSSR. Istoricheskie ocherki 1917–70gg, Moscow (1977)

Rosenberg, W. G., 'Smolensk in the 1920s. Party–worker relations and the vanguard problem', *Russian Review*, 36, 2, April 1977

Rozenbaum, N. A., *Gigiena truda v bumagopriadil'nom i bumagotkatskom priozvodstvakh*, Moscow (1928)

Russia: the Official Report of the British Trades Union Delegation to Russia and Caucasia, November and December 1924, Trades Union Congress, London (1925)

Santalov, A. A., Segal, L., eds., *Soviet Union Yearbook 1928*, George Allen & Unwin, London (1928)

Soviet Union Yearbook 1929, George Allen & Unwin, London (1929)

Soviet Union Yearbook 1930, George Allen & Unwin, London (1930)

Schwarz, S. M., *Labor in the Soviet Union*, Cresset Press, London (1953)

Selunskaia, V. M. *et al.*, eds., *Izmeneniia sotsial'noi struktury sovetskogo obshchestva 1921–seredina 30–kh godov*, Moscow (1929)

Semenov, N., *Litso fabrichnykh rabochikh, prozhivaiushchikh v derevniakh, i politrosvetrabota sredi nikh. Po materialam obsledovaniia rabochikh tekstil'noi promyshlennosti tsentral'no-promyshlennoi oblasti*, Moscow (1929)

Sereda, S. P., ed., *Kustarnaia promyshlennost' SSSR*, vyp. 1, Moscow (1925)

Shaginian, M., *Nevskaia nitka*, Moscow-Leningrad (1925)

Shipulin, A. V., 'Uchastie ivanovo-voznesenskikh rabochikh v stroitel'stve sovetskogo gosudarstvennogo apparat (1917–1919gg)', in *Iz istorii rabochego klassa SSSR*, Ivanovo (1967)

Shkaratan, O. I., 'Izmeneniia v sotsial'nom sostave fabrichno-zavodskikh rabochikh Leningrada 1917–1928gg', *Istoriia SSSR*, 5, 1959

'Nachalo rekonstruktsii leningradskoi promyshlennosti', in *Leningradskie rabochie v bor'be za sotsializma 1926–1937gg*, Leningrad (1965)

Problemy sotsial'noi struktury rabochego klassa SSSR. (Istorichesko-sotsialogicheskoe issledovanie), Moscow (1970)

'Rost riadov i sotsial'noe spolchenie leningradskikh rabochikh', in *Leningradskie rabochie v bor'be za sotsializma 1926–1937gg*, Leningrad (1965)

Shmidt, V., *Polozhenie rabochego klassa v SSSR*, Moscow–Leningrad (1928)

Shneider, S. I., *Trud i zdorov'e rabochikh bumagopriadil'nogo proizvodstva*, Moscow–Leningrad (1925)

Shostak, Ia. E., *Zabolevaemost' tekstil'shchikov g.Ivanovo-Voznesenska v 1927 godu*, Ivanovo-Voznesensk (1931)

Shukhgal'ter, L. Ia., ed., *Vnutrizavodskii kontrol' kachestva. Sbornik statei i instruktsii*, Moscow–Leningrad (1927)

Shvarabovich, A. F., *Kak uberech' sebia ot neschastnykh sluchaev v khlopchatobumazhnom proizvodstve*, Moscow (1926)

Simchenko-Sosnovkin, *Tekstil'naia molodozh na profrabote i v proizvodstve. Rabota soiuza tekstilei sredi molodezhi*, Moscow (1926)

Smith, S. A., 'Bolshevism, Taylorism and the technical intelligentsia: the Soviet Union, 1917–41', *Radical Science Journal*, 13, 1983

Sokolov, V. M., *Fabrika im O. A. Varentsovoi*, Ivanovo (1955)

Fabrika im S. I. Balashova, Ivanovo (1961)

Solzhenitsyn, A., *The Gulag Archipelago*, vol. 1, (trans. T. P. Whitney), Collins/ Fontana (1974)

The Gulag Archipelago, vol. 2 (trans. T. P. Whitney), Collins/Fontana, (1976)

The Gulag Archipelago, vol. 3 (trans. H. T. Williams), Collins/Fontana (1978)

Sontag, J. P., 'The Soviet war scare of 1926–27', *Russian Review*, 34, 1, January 1975

Sorenson, J. B., *The Life and Death of Soviet Trade Unionism 1917–28*, Atherton Press, New York (1969)

Sorin, V. G., *Rabochaia gruppa (Miasnikovshchina)*, Moscow (1924)

Sotsialisticheskoe stroitel'stvo SSSR, Moscow (1934)

Spisok fabrik, zavodov i drugikh promyshlennykh predpriiatii ivanovo-voznesenskoi gubernii. Po dannym vserossiiskoi promyshlennoi i professional'noi perepis' 1918 goda, Moscow (1919)

Spravochnik po voprosam okhrany truda v tekstil'noi promyshlennosti, Moscow (1924)

Srednie godovye zarabotki rabochikh i sluzhashchikh po fabrikam i zavodam ivanovo-voznesenskoi gubernii za vremia s 1/V–1927g po 30/IV-1928g. (K kampanii sel.-khoz. naloga 1928–29g), Ivanovo-Voznesensk (1928)

Stenograficheskii otchet 1-go vserossiiskogo s"ezda rabotnikov tekstil'noi promyshlennosti v Moskve 12–16 okt. 1922g, Moscow (1923)

Stepanov, Z. V., 'Chislennost', razmeshchenie i sostav rabochikh', in *Istoriia rabochikh Leningrada*, tom 2, 1917–1965gg, Leningrad (1962)

'Voznikovenie i deiatel'nost' massovykh proletarskikh organizatsii', in *Istoriia rabochikh Leningrada*, tom 2, 1917–1965gg, Leningrad (1962)

Strumilin, S. G., ed., *Naemnyi trud v Rossii i na zapade 1913–1925gg*, chast' 1, Moscow (1927)

Zarabotnaia plata i proizvoditel'nost' truda v russkoi promyshlennosti za 1913–1922gg, Moscow (1923)

Sutton, A. C., *Western Technology and Soviet Economic Development* vol. 1 1917–1930, Hoover Institution Press, Stanford (1968)

Suvorov, K. I., *Istoricheskii opyt KPSS po likvidatsii bezrabotitsy, 1917–1930gg*, Moscow (1968)

Tarif tekstil'shchikov, Moscow (1922)

Tarifno-spravochnik rabochikh khlopchato-bumazhnogo proizvodstva, Moscow (1928)

Tarifnyi spravochnik tekstil'shchikov, Moscow, 1926 (11/XII–1925)

Ten Years of Soviet Power in Figures, 1917–1927, Moscow (n.d.)

Tikhomirov, A. A., *Odin den' na priadil'noi fabrike*, Moscow-Leningrad (1927)

Tikhonravov, P., Makhov., E., *V boi za 700 millionov. Kak organizovalis' i rabotali na fabrike 'Kommunisticheskii Avangard' gruppy molodykh ratsionalizatorov*, Vladimir (1929)

Tippett, L. H. C., *A Portrait of the Lancashire Textile Industry*, Oxford University Press, London (1969)

Tokarev, Iu. S., Rost politicheskoi aktivnosti petrogradskikh rabochikh', in *Istoriia rabochikh Leningrada*, tom 2, 1917–1965gg, Leningrad (1972)

Trifonov, I. Ia., 'Rabochii klass SSSR v period vosstanovleniia narodnogo khoziaistva (1921–1925gg)', in *Iz istorii rabochego klassa SSSR*, Leningrad (1962)

Trudy pervogo vsesoiuznogo s"ezda po ratsionalizatsii v tekstil'noi promyshlennosti. 19–24 maia 1926 goda, Moscow–Leningrad (1926)

Trudy tsentral'nogo statisticheskogo upravleniia, tom XVII, vyp. 1. Vserossiiskaia gorodskaia perepis' 1923 goda; tom XVIII, sbornik statisticheskikh svedenii po Soiuzy SSR 1918–1923gg, Moscow (1924)

Ure, A., *Philosophy of Manufactures*, Charles Knight, London (1835)

Valentinov, N., 'Non-Party specialists and the coming of NEP', *Russian Review*, 30, April 1971

Novaia ekonomicheskaia politika i krizis partii posle smerti Lenina, Hoover Institution Press, Stanford (1971)

Vasil'ev, N. A., ed., *Sel'faktor (dlia gladkoi i pushistoi priazhi)*, Moscow (1922)

Vas'kina, L. I., *Rabochii klass SSSR nakanune sotsialisticheskoi industrializatsii. (Chislennost', sostav, razmeshchenie)*, Moscow (1981)

von Laue, T., 'Russian labor between field and factory, 1892–1903', *California Slavic Studies*, 3, 1964

'Russian peasants in the factory, 1892–1904', *Journal of Economic History*, 20, 1, 1961

Vsesoiuznaia perepis' naseleniia 1926 goda, tom XVIII, severnyi raion, leningradsko-karel'skii raion; tom XIX, zapadnyi raion, tsentral'nopromyshlennyi raion, Moscow (1929); tom XXXIV, SSSR, otdel II: zania-tiia, Moscow (1930)

Vybory i predlozhenie po dokladu o sostoianie partraboty na sukonnoi fabrike im. tkacha Petra Alekseeva (vysh. Iokish.), Moscow (1925)

Vydro, M. Ia., *Naselenie Moskvy (po materialam perepisei naseleniia 1871–1970gg)*, Moscow (1976)

Whewell, C. S., 'Textile manufacture', in T. Williams, ed., *A History of Technology: The Twentieth Century c1900 to c1950*, vol. 6, part I, Clarendon Press, Oxford (1978)

Wicksteed, A., *Ten Years in Soviet Moscow*, John Lane & The Bodley Head, London (1933)

Yaney, G., *The Urge to Mobilize. Agrarian Reform in Russia, 1861–1930*, University of Illinois Press, Illinois (1982)

Zaikov, A. M., *Na khlopchatobumazhnoi fabrike*, Moscow-Leningrad (1926/27)

Zhukov, I. G., *Stakhanovskoe dvizhenie ivanovskikh tekstil'shchikov. (Istoriko-ekonomicheskii ocherk)*, Ivanovo (1951)

Zhukovskii, S. *et al.*, *Pervaia udarnaia*, Moscow–Leningrad (1931)

Ziman, A. F., *Normirovanie tkatskogo stanka. (Kratkoe prakticheskoe rukovodstvo)*, Moscow–Leningrad, 1926

Tekhnicheskoe normirovanie priadil'nogo proizvodstva. Chast' 1. Otdely: sortirovochnyi, trepal'nyi, chesal'nyi, Ivanovo-Voznesensk (1928)

Tekhnicheskoe normirovanie praidil'nogo proizvodstva. Chast' 2. Lentochno-bankabroshnyi i vaternyi otdely, Ivanovo-Voznesensk (1931)

Zvezdin, Z. K., 'Vsesoiuznyi tekstil'nyi sindikat v 1922–1929gg', *Istoricheskie zapiski*, 88, 1971

UNPUBLISHED SOURCES

Fisher, R. T., 'The Soviet pattern for youth as revealed in the proceedings of the Congresses of the Komsomol, 1918–1949', Ph.D., Columbia University, New York (1955)

Kuznetsov, E. A., 'Rol' profsoiuza tekstil'shchikov v sotsialisticheskom preobrazovanii sel'skogo khoziaistva (1927–1934gg)', Avtoreferat, kand. ist. nauk, Moscow University (1974)

Poliakova, N. V., 'Rabochie-tekstil'shchiki Moskvy i moskovskoi gubernii v bor'be za vosstanovlenie promyshlennosti v periode perekhoda na mirnuiu rabotu, (1912–1925gg)', Avtoreferat, kand. ist. nauk, Moscow University (1952)

Index

Vesenkha *cont.*
  147; and *uplotnenie*, 153–4, 156; and
  piece rates, 167–8, 173; and wages,
  167, 186–7, 186n48; on metal
  industries, 193; and investment, 203;
  on marketings, 203n9; on shift work,
  214; on temporary control
  commissions, 222; on
  rationalization, 250
Vladimir: population in, 43n52. *See also*
  CIR
Vladimir guberniya: location of mills in,
  23, 33; employment in, 25;
  population in, 42; housing in, 43, 44,
  45–6, 46n70, 49; trades in, 59; wage
  scales in, 160, 160n12; and piece
  rates, 174–5; wages in, 224;
  productivity in, 252. *See also* CIR
Voroshilov, K. E., and 'war scare', 201
Vysokovskaia mill, workforce in, 35

War Communism, and housing, 42. *See
  also* Cloth sorts
Weaving. *See* Automatic loom;
  Handloom weaving; Jacquard loom;
  Lancashire loom
Witte, S. Iu., 2
Women: employment of, 24–5; and
  Textileworkers' union, 26–7, 114;
  and 'tie with the land', 41; and
  factory schools, 96; and *magarych*,

100; and shift work, 100, 225–26;
  literacy of, 104n77; and party
  membership, 110, 112–13, 117; and
  delegate conferences, 114–15,
  115n30; and factory committees,
  116–17; and religion, 118–19, 258;
  and unemployment, 133–4, 138–9,
  140; and ISNOT, 145; and piece
  rates, 171n59; and *uplotnenie*, 191–2;
  in Leningrad, 194; and night work,
  225–6; and abortion, 226; and
  'machine loyalty', 226; and shock
  brigades, 245, 249; and
  functionalism, 249; and socialist
  competition, 251
Workers' and Peasants' Inspectorate. *See
  Rabkrin*

Young Communist League. *See*
  Komsomol
Young workers: and wages, 100–1; party
  membership of, 111–12; and
  uplotnenie, 195–6; and shift work,
  210

Zamyatin, E., 142n3
Zinoviev, G. E.: and 'scissors crisis',
  129–30; and 'war scare', 202; and
  wages, 204–5; mentioned, 130n14
Zvonkov mill, and job inheritance, 101

Soviet and East European Studies

The following series titles are now out of print: